Challenges
of
Retrenchment ❧

Strategies for Consolidating Programs,
Cutting Costs, and Reallocating Resources

James R. Mingle
and Associates

Challenges
of
Retrenchment

Jossey-Bass Publishers

San Francisco • Washington • London • 1981

Library of Congress Cataloging in Publication Data

Main entry under title:

Challenges of retrenchment.
  Bibliography: p. 354
  Includes index.
  1. College attendance—United States.
2. Universities and colleges—United States—
Finance. I. Mingle, James R.
LC148.C46   379.1'224'0973   81-47770
ISBN 0-87589-507-7   AACR2

Manufactured in the United States of America

JACKET DESIGN BY WILLI BAUM

FIRST EDITION

Code 8121

The Jossey-Bass
Series in Higher Education

✑ Foreword ✑

The great expansion of higher education over the past generation has been a nationwide phenomenon. Sharp state and regional
contrasts in the scope and quality of postsecondary education have
been replaced by striking similarities. Individual institutions may
face widely different futures, but state and campus policy makers
everywhere are responding to a parallel set of conditions: declines
in traditional college-age populations, fiscal uncertainty or even
abrupt cutbacks, overexpansion of some programs and the neglect
of others, and a greatly heightened atmosphere of competition and
conflict. Colleges and universities that have experienced retrenchment in the past have often had little time for careful consideration
of the right way or the wrong way to adjust. Events overtook them,
leaving little opportunity to control the impact of contraction.

The Southern Regional Education Board (SREB) in recent
years has intensified its concern for a planned approach to contraction—an approach that finds institutional leaders and public officials considering options for rational consolidation of higher
education's strengths in the face of enrollment decline and financial stringency. Many of these concerns were enunciated by the
board in a set of priorities adopted in 1976 to stimulate planning
efforts in the fourteen states of the southern region. SREB also
published enrollment projections and a likely profile of educational
characteristics in the 1980s.

In 1979 SREB initiated the project that has culminated in
publication of this volume. Our first objective was to study and
analyze the institutional impact of retrenchment and the management strategies developed for responding to decline. The second
major objective was to study specific public policies that had
emerged as the result of no-growth and retrenchment. In October
1980, with help from the Ford Foundation, we were able to bring

ix

together a group of state legislators, state governing and coordinating board members, and institutional leaders for a national symposium to discuss these issues and the preliminary findings of some of the studies under way. Following that symposium, additional papers were commissioned, and the work of scholars examining related areas was combined to provide the comprehensive coverage of the management of decline found in this book. Throughout this project SREB has benefited from the wise counsel of its advisory committee, whose names are listed elsewhere. Under the project's aegis, many case studies were conducted of states and institutions that had already been buffeted by budget shortfalls and enrollment slumps. We found much to be disturbed about in the practices of some institutions; at the same time, we found encouraging instances of faculty and administrators willing to set priorities and take difficult actions. A number of public and private institutions were successfully doing more with less by cutting back in ways that protected quality and provided funds for new growth from internal resources.

Mindful that political and educational leaders have an important role in higher education policy today, the Southern Regional Education Board has long provided a forum at which these two groups can meet. Our premise has been that complete and open discussion conducted outside the immediate press of circumstances in a particular institution or state capital can contribute toward resolution of common problems. The 1980 symposium reminded us in higher education that well-intentioned, honorable elected officials were struggling to weigh the competing claims from a wide variety of state agencies, each of which viewed its needs as first in priority. At the same time, they were seeking ways to upgrade public services that had suffered from neglect in the past. We were also reminded that higher education policy must by necessity be concerned less with the survival of individual institutions than with meeting the needs of students—which above all requires upholding the integrity and quality of needed higher education programs, wherever they may be offered.

George Bonham of the Council on Learning began the 1980 symposium with enunciation of a growing doubt "about the inherent and fundamental ability of the academic structure to reform itself, to shift to new grounds, or to carry on its business in anything but a slightly amended and cosmetically changed form." He called for "a very special combination of national courage, of imagination, and of compassion mixed with utility" to address and solve higher education's problems. It is our hope that this volume will contribute to productive discussion and effective solution of the problems ahead.

On behalf of SREB, I would like to thank the Ford Foundation for partial support of this study, and Jossey-Bass Publishers for giving the authors' findings national distribution.

Atlanta, Georgia   WINFRED L. GODWIN
September 1981   *President*
                              Southern Regional Education Board

❧ Acknowledgments ❧

This study has benefited from the contributions of many people and organizations. Most important have been the support and encouragement provided by the Southern Regional Education Board (SREB) and its president, Winfred L. Godwin. In addition, the Ford Foundation provided a grant which allowed the project to broaden its scope to national dimensions and to hold a symposium at which preliminary versions of some of these chapters were presented and discussed. The Ford grant also underwrote the expenses of the SREB advisory committee to the project. Providing valuable assistance and guidance, the committee included Robert O. Berdahl, professor of higher education, University of Maryland–College Park; Larry J. Blake, state president, Department of Community Colleges, North Carolina; Patrick Callan, director, California Postsecondary Education Commission; Gordon K. Davies, director, State Council of Higher Education for Virginia; Emmett B. Fields, president, Vanderbilt University; Arthur M. Gignilliat, former state representative, Georgia; Howard Jordan, Jr., vice chancellor for services, Board of Regents of the University System of Georgia; David K. Karem, state senator, Kentucky; Marvin W. Peterson, director, Center for the Study of Higher Education, University of Michigan; John F. Porter, Jr., former executive director, Commission on Higher Education, Alabama; and Max Sherman, president, West Texas State University.

I want to express my appreciation to the numerous institutional administrators, faculty, and state officials who gave so willingly of their time and expertise during the conducting of the research by the authors involved in this study. In particular, Laura Clausen, of the Massachusetts Board of Regents, and Nan Robinson, formerly of the Connecticut Board of Higher Education, provided careful reviews of some of the case studies. And the Information Exchange Center of the Georgia Institute of Technology Library provided expert assistance in bibliographical searching and reference checking.

I would also like to acknowledge the contributions and efforts of the other authors of this volume, especially those of Donald Norris of the University of Houston, whose ideas and encouragement were in large part the genesis of the SREB project.

Several of my colleagues at SREB made important contributions: E. F. Schietinger, director of research; Mark Musick, state services officer; and Bruce Schultz and Margaret Sullivan, of the publications department. I am especially indebted to Jacqueline Smythe, who served as the principal editorial assistant for the book.

Atlanta, Georgia   JAMES R. MINGLE
September 1981

✌ Contents ✌

PART FIVE: STATE POLICY CHOICES: PRIVATE INSTITUTIONS

PART SIX: CONCLUSION

✍ The Authors ✎

James R. Mingle is research associate at the Southern Regional Education Board in Atlanta, Georgia. Since 1979 he has been project director of the study presented in this volume. Dr. Mingle has served as consultant to policy studies in several southern states and is the author of publications in such areas as state planning, institutional management and program evaluation, tuition policy, and minority access. He was a contributing author to *Black Students on White Campuses: The Impacts of Increased Black Enrollment* (1978), a study conducted by the Institute for Social Research at the University of Michigan. Dr. Mingle received his bachelor's and master's degrees in history from the University of Akron and his doctorate of philosophy from the Center for the Study of Higher Education at the University of Michigan. He is married to Pamela Tenney Mingle and has two daughters, Dana and Katharine.

ROBERT J. BARAK, *Director of Research and Academic Affairs, Iowa State Board of Regents*

ROBERT O. BERDAHL, *Professor of Higher Education, University of Maryland at College Park*

E. GRADY BOGUE, *Chancellor, Louisiana State University at Shreveport, and former Associate Director for Academic Affairs, Tennessee Higher Education Commission*

FRANK M. BOWEN, *Consultant, Sausalito, California*

DAVID W. BRENEMAN, *Senior Fellow, The Brookings Institution*

GAIL S. CHAMBERS, *Ph.D. Cand., University of Rochester*

EUGENE C. CRAVEN, *Assistant Vice President, The University of Wisconsin System*

EDWARD A. DOUGHERTY, *Assistant to the Vice President for Academic Affairs, The University of Michigan*

JAMES M. FURMAN, *Executive Vice President, John D. and Catherine T. MacArthur Foundation, and former Executive Director, Illinois Board of Higher Education*

LYMAN A. GLENNY, *Professor of Higher Education, University of California at Berkeley*

JOHN A. GRAY, *Associate Professor of Business Law, Loyola College, Baltimore, Maryland*

RICHARD W. JONSEN, *Deputy Director, Western Interstate Commission for Higher Education*

KENNETH P. MORTIMER, *Professor and Research Associate, Center for the Study of Higher Education, The Pennsylvania State University*

DONALD M. NORRIS, *Director, Institutional Studies, University of Houston*

JOSEPH P. O'NEILL, *Executive Director, Conference of Small Private Colleges, Princeton, New Jersey*

MARVIN W. PETERSON, *Director and Professor, Center for the Study of Higher Education, University of Michigan*

DONALD K. SMITH, *Senior Vice President Emeritus, University of Wisconsin System, and Professor of Communication Arts, University of Wisconsin at Madison*

DAVID S. SPENCE, *Executive Director, Florida Postsecondary Education Planning Commission*

PAUL STROHM, *Professor and Chairperson, Department of English, Indiana University*

GEORGE B. WEATHERSBY, *Commissioner, Indiana Commission for Higher Education*

Challenges
of
Retrenchment ❧

Strategies for Consolidating Programs,
Cutting Costs, and Reallocating Resources

1

Challenges of Retrenchment

James R. Mingle

Challenges of Retrenchment concerns the difficult management and policy issues facing higher education and government because of expected declines in enrollment and in financial support. It seeks answers to two questions: First, how can institutions confronting such prospects plan for and respond to decline in ways that will be consonant with their basic educational goals? The chapters in Parts Two and Three review the full range of options open to institutions—including personnel and program cutbacks, institutional reorganization, merger, and even closure. Second, what are the public policy issues facing the states during a period of contraction? The important decisions affecting higher education in the coming decade will be made by the states, not the federal government. For state government and the coordinating and governing agencies with planning responsibilities, the central questions may be "What degree of regulation should be applied under these circumstances?" and "What should be the relationship between the states and private colleges and universities under conditions of distress?" The chapters in Parts Four and Five speak to these issues. Rather than consensus, my colleagues and I seek to offer a compre-

1

hensive range of tools, strategies, and solutions for consideration by faculty groups, institutional administrators, system executives, lay board members, and state officials as they wrestle with the intertwined problems of declining enrollment, declining financial resources, and declining quality.

Growth of Today's Problems

For most of the nearly 1,700 private colleges and universities in the United States, the ability to maintain a constant enrollment is closely linked to financial health and stability. For many public colleges and universities, the problems of the 1970s were more the result of sudden and irregular cutbacks in public subsidies, and the less apparent effects of inflation, than the result of enrollment decline. Nevertheless, while some public colleges undergoing enrollment drops have enjoyed stable financial support, enrollment levels for most public institutions remain an important factor in funding. Now, with widespread expectations that total enrollments nationally will soon decline, state governments are asking whether they should not expect a lessening of the burden of higher education expenditures, especially in light of excess capacity in some locales and of other pressing social needs beyond education.

As early as 1965, Allan Cartter warned about the overexpansion of higher education—especially graduate education. Challenging the long-held belief that there was a shortage of qualified faculty, he maintained that a downturn in the academic labor market could soon be expected (it became evident in some fields as early as 1969). Further ahead, Cartter saw the possibility of significant declines in total enrollment if the trends in fertility, also first noted by the U.S. Bureau of the Census in 1965, continued. "Looking backward," he said in 1976, "it seems evident that this emerging problem could (and should) have been recognized by public policy makers a decade ago" (p. 23). It was not, however. The annual production of doctoral degrees increased 87 percent from 1965–66 to 1975–76 before beginning a gradual decline (National Center for Education Statistics, 1980a).

As the decade progressed, the demographic configuration of the remainder of the twentieth century became firm. The
college-age population would begin to decline early in the 1980s,
show a small increase later in the decade, and then drop again
precipitously in the 1990s. Despite this knowledge, enrollment
projections done in the 1970s were widely inconsistent. Based on
different assumptions about participation rates, economic factors,
and public policy changes, analysts presented a range of estimates.
(Centra, 1978a, and Glenny, 1980, review the various projections
done in the past ten years.)

Although analysts of enrollment and enrollment behavior
have disagreed, there has been little disagreement among those
who, regardless of demographic or economic factors, have wished
to sustain the growth of the higher education enterprise. A series of
reports by the Carnegie Commission on Higher Education (1971a,
1971b, 1973) outlined the details of what the commission hoped
would be a revolution in adult continuing education. This goal has
in part been realized. In 1979 the U.S. Bureau of the Census observed that students over twenty-five years old accounted for 51
percent of the 2.4 million increase in college enrollment between
1970 and 1978—an increase resulting from the growth in numbers
of this age group and from increasing rates of participation. How
long higher education's growth can be sustained by older populations is questionable, however. The number of twenty-five- to
thirty-four-year-olds, like their younger "college-age" cohorts, will
decline in the coming decade, and some suspect that a plateau may
shortly be reached in participation rates among this group of older
students (Glenny, 1980). Still the debate goes on. In an effort to
mobilize state and institutional leaders to action, Crossland (1980)
has widely publicized the extent of the declining high school population in the Northeast and the Midwest. Frances (1980b) has
responded by reminding institutions that they are in large part
masters of their own destiny and that declines can be countered by
the recruitment of underenrolled populations and by positive support from public policy makers.

In recent years enrollment analysts have pinpointed more
exactly the regional and institutional impact of decline (their find-

ings are reviewed by David Breneman in Chapter Two). Clearly, the institutions of higher education face widely different futures in the next twenty years—a prospect that greatly complicates planning in the fifty divergent states of the nation. This volume sheds no new light on the magnitude of national enrollment declines. Rather, it sets aside that question, assuming that the increased competition already evident in every state will have important implications for both institutions and state policy makers and that some institutions in every state—as was the case in the 1970s—will face severe adjustments.

Institutional Choices: To Plan or React? To Resist or Adapt?

Nearly one third of all institutions underwent enrollment decline in the decade of the 1970s (Carnegie Council on Policy Studies in Higher Education, 1980), but many of these institutions did not anticipate the changes that overtook them. Signs of stress had begun to appear in the early 1970s for the private sector (Cheit, 1971), but it was the economic recession of 1974–75 that caused the first significant retrenchment in the public sector. In a Carnegie Council survey of college presidents in the mid-1970s (Glenny and others, 1976), the presidents described a variety of negative impacts on programs and faculty. As we shall see in the chapters that follow, the first brush with retrenchment stimulated a number of planning efforts and strategies for coping with cutbacks. One of the objectives of this volume is to present examples of responses—successful and unsuccessful—to enrollment decline and financial cutbacks.

Planning for the future has never been easy, especially for organizations such as colleges, with loosely defined and diverse and sometimes conflicting goals. In a period of decline, the difficulty is heightened. Kaufman (1971) believes that successful adaptation is the exception, not the rule, in organizations: "So formidable is the collection of forces holding organizations in their familiar paths that it is surprising that any changes ever manage to run the gauntlet successfully" (p. 40). But colleges and universities do overcome the constraints that hold them, or they adapt themselves to the circumstances they face. Leadership is an important element that shapes this response. In a speech to the regents of the University of the State of New York, Boulding (1975) called for a new kind of manager in higher education—one who can carry out the "management of decline" with "empathy and . . . an all too rare mixture of compassion and realism" and develop a "creative widening of agendas" (p. 64). Various chapters in this volume clearly indicate that such a breed of managers is developing in higher education.

Faced with actual decline or with the prospects of decline, institutions must make a series of decisions that will affect their ability to respond. The first one is basic—whether to act now or to wait. This is a most difficult question to answer in many institutions. Few presidents and board members remain ignorant of the general circumstances; but the impact of those general trends on their particular institutions is far more relevant. Will this institution continue to grow in spite of a general decline in college-age population? Is last year's decline an aberration, or is it part of a long-term trend? Should new programs be implemented and new clienteles sought in order to sustain growth, or should the institution seek a smaller, more compact mission and size by carrying out consolidation and retrenchment? Must the institution wait for a crisis, or can plans be developed to carry out change before events overwhelm the college?

Levine (1978) notes that organizations will respond to decline either by attempting to *resist* it or by attempting to *adapt* to it. The first response is usually resistance, but this approach has its risks, and "no responsible manager wants to be faced with the prospect of being unable to control where cuts will take place or confront quantum cuts with unpredictable consequences" (p. 320). In practice, colleges faced with declines in enrollment and traditional revenue sources often seek to find new sources of revenue *and* to cut expenditures. Usually, however, one can discern an overall climate that sets the tone of the institutional approach. The chapters in this volume deal more extensively with accommodations to decline—through consolidation and retrenchment—than with revenue-producing strategies. The emphasis in the 1970s was on resistance, and this was reflected in the literature. Kotler (1975) transferred the concepts of marketing as applied in the profit sector to nonprofit institutions; others (Ihlanfeldt, 1980; Carter and

Garigan, 1979; College Entrance Examination Board, 1976) demonstrated the specific applicability of these concepts to the higher education setting. Stadtman (1980), using a Carnegie Council survey of institutions conducted in 1978, shows how pervasive the consumer-related policies of the colleges and universities became during the past decade. More than two thirds of all institutions had "stopout policies" allowing easy reentry (recommended by the Carnegie Commission on Higher Education, 1971b). Almost three quarters of all public institutions in the sample were offering evening programs, and 50 percent of the few remaining ones without such programs were considering starting them. Riesman (1981) describes in detail the decline in faculty hegemony and the rise of student consumerism during the 1970s.

In addition to employing the marketing activities of business, higher education planners have turned to another concept long popular in the business world—strategic planning. Strategic planners try to orchestrate the future for their organizations—instead of projecting that future and then responding to it. They ask, "What is our business?" and "How can we gain a competitive advantage in this field?" Cyert (1978) suggests that the process of strategic planning in colleges is similar to the process of diversification in business. Collier (1981), in a review of the strategic-planning concept, warns colleges, however, to think carefully about the future they may be creating. Not all "opportunities" (new professional programs, for example, in a liberal arts college) will necessarily create "desirable" futures if implemented. In contrast to the conceptual models of the strategic planners, others have taken a more pragmatic approach in analyzing decline. Minter and Bowen (1978, 1980) have followed closely the financial status of independent colleges and universities and have developed financial indicators of health and distress. In *Surviving the Eighties,* Mayhew (1979) provides vignettes, drawn primarily from the private sector, of strategies for "maintaining enrollment" or "controlling program and faculty costs" (including a lengthy checklist of ways of increasing revenue and cutting costs, developed by the Academy for Educational Development).

In a perceptive analysis of management in universities of constant or decreasing size, Cyert (1978) outlines the problems created in this climate. As organizational slack disappears, so do opportunities for promotion; as a result, the university has difficulty in recruiting new members with fresh ideas for the organization and, as organizational conflict increases, in retaining high-quality managers and faculty. Cyert simultaneously calls on organizations to conduct strategic planning and to find an "equilibrium position" at some smaller size. The greatest danger in a period of decline is that individuals lose the drive for excellence, according to Cyert. Excellence in higher education has usually been bought through surplus funds, not from priority setting and reallocation.

In recent years the discussions about higher education and its future have been dominated by concerns about *quality*. These concerns include:

- Fears that increased competition for students results in "body counting" and "survival of the slickest" (Ashworth, 1979).
- A need for a code of "fair practices" and for a strengthening of the accreditation process (Carnegie Council on Policy Studies in Higher Education, 1979).
- The weakening of academic standards and of rigor in such programs as teacher education (Weaver, 1979; Stoltz, 1981) and the decline in general of meritocratic values in higher education (Riesman, 1981).
- The decline in faculty compensation relative to that of other professionals (Bowen, 1981).

The impact of decline on the quality of higher education is a central concern of several chapters in this volume. Lyman Glenny and Frank Bowen, in Chapter Three, provide institutions with a list of thirty "warning signals"—indicating the often unapparent impact on quality that accompanies traditional budgeting and staffing practices during a period of cutback. In Chapter Four, James Mingle and Donald Norris discuss the institutional strategies developed by a wide variety of public and private institutions in response to enrollment decline and financial cutbacks. Their case studies present strategies of resistance (increasing retention, improving student life, tightening standards, and attracting new sources of revenue) and adaptation (adjusting staffing practices, consolidating administration, eliminating or limiting courses and programs). The authors outline a process of reassessment, involving faculty and administration, which institutions have successfully used to establish priorities and reallocate the funds needed to carry out these changes.

Central to the priority-setting process in institutions—which is the essence of qualitative improvement in a period of no growth—are methods of evaluating programs. Edward Dougherty, in Chapter Five, presents examples of institutions that have discontinued programs through systematic program review. He discusses the various program review procedures being established and the criteria by which decisions are being made.

For institutions faced with major adjustments to enrollment decline, Gail Chambers (Chapter Six) suggests ways in which merger opportunities can be successfully explored and consummated and discusses financial, legal, and academic factors that "buyers" and "sellers" need to consider when negotiating mergers.

The chapters in Part Three deal specifically with the effects of contraction on faculty. In labor-intensive higher education, adjustment to a smaller scale of operations inevitably leads to personnel actions. Eugene Craven, in Chapter Seven, describes policies and practices that will help colleges effectively manage faculty resources in a period of decline. He notes the three tasks central to that management: to maintain institutional flexibility, so that layoffs of tenured faculty can be avoided; to sustain the faculty's intellectual vitality and morale; and to increase productivity. He also suggests planning tools and programs to be applied at different organizational levels. Paul Strohm, in Chapter Eight, presents his view of faculty rights and responsibilities in a period of retrenchment. Noting the erosion of faculty power and the arbitrariness of many administrators during periods of retrenchment, Strohm suggests several ways in which faculty can become involved in institutional planning before states of financial exigency overtake an institution. In Chapter Nine Kenneth Mortimer discusses the experience of the Pennsylvania State University System with retrenchment and offers a set of guidelines to be used in establishing policy for terminating tenured faculty. John Gray (Chapter

Ten) analyzes the rulings of the courts in cases where financial exigency has led to the dismissal of faculty, presenting examples of both "good faith" and "bad faith" efforts. In his conclusion Gray speculates on the future issues that will be brought to the courts.

State Policy Choices: Free Competition or Managed Contraction?

The search for a coherent state policy toward higher education is an elusive one. Not only are policy decisions made differently in each of the states, but within states policy is the product of negotiation and compromise among multiple groups: the governor's office and other state agencies and departments, the legislature and its increasingly well-staffed committees, the independent lay coordinating boards and commissions with responsibilities for planning, and the multicampus governing boards who seek to bring their separate campuses into a cohesive "system." The authors of this volume, who are concerned primarily with the *statewide perspective,* may discuss any or all of the above groups.

The term *statewide boards* has become shorthand to describe the diverse organizations for higher education coordination in the fifty states. In 1946, only seventeen states had what might be called central higher education agencies—the overwhelming majority of these in less populated states, which had established single boards to govern their public institutions. By 1980 all but three of the fifty states had established either coordinating boards—with advisory or regulatory powers—or consolidated governing boards for major sectors of public higher education. Millard (1976) and the Carnegie Foundation for the Advancement of Teaching (1976) have described in detail the diverse coordinating and regulating activities that exist at the state level. Lee and Bowen (1975) analyze the planning and policy-setting activities of large public multicampus systems; and Berdahl (1977) has reviewed the growing legislative oversight of public higher education.

As for state policy toward the private sector, Breneman and Finn (1978, pp. 44–45) note that it has been "inherently awkward, often ambivalent, and frequently unclear. . . . The states must simultaneously assume the roles of regulator, licensing agent, and central planner for their respective postsecondary systems that embody both public and private elements. At the same time, they are a source of funds besieged with requests from their private colleges and universities." One of the major criticisms of state planning for higher education has been the failure to consider a full *system perspective*. Such a perspective would enable planners to consider the contributions of private institutions to statewide goals and the impact of public-sector decisions on private colleges and universities. As we shall see, some of the authors of this volume call for a significant broadening of the agenda of the states in this regard.

Many in higher education, however, believe that the agenda of the states is already too broad. In 1959 the Committee on Government and Higher Education (financed by the Ford Foundation and chaired by Milton Eisenhower) argued forcefully and unequivocally for exemption of the higher education enterprise from the growing oversight of state government (Moos and Rourke, 1959). That year, however, Lyman Glenny, in *Autonomy of Public Colleges,* suggested that the way to protect the freedom, initiative, and autonomy of colleges and universities was through the development of statewide coordinating bodies, which would stand between the institutions and the states and look both ways. In *More Than Survival,* the Carnegie Foundation for the Advancement of Teaching (1975) noted the pervasive shift of decision making to higher levels as enrollment growth slowed. The statewide boards have been in large part the beneficiaries of that upward shift (see Berdahl, 1971; Millard, 1976). In many states, however, their increased authority has not significantly stemmed the growth of executive and legislative oversight in higher education. The effectiveness of the state boards has also been limited by the attitudes of the higher education community itself, which has suffered from acute ambivalence over the issue of statewide coordination. Opposed to the regulatory power imposed on them by their own multicampus system managers or by the more alien "bureaucrats" of the state coordinating boards, the institutions have at the same time—when it served their self-interest—welcomed the security of a regulated marketplace (not unlike the attitude of American business toward federal regulation). The Carnegie Foundation for the Advancement of Teaching (1976) was so pessimistic about the regulatory role of the coordinating boards that it advised states to choose either the advisory form of coordination or the single consolidated board, in order to avoid regulatory abuses. While the consolidated governing boards are generally viewed as stronger advocates of higher education than are coordinating boards, "Nobody really loves a state board of higher education or its staff, because it is inevitably seen by the institutions it governs as a delimiting agency and by those who fund higher education as one remiss in its control of the idiosyncrasies, excesses, and financial demands of the institutions it governs" (Dressel, 1980, p. 81).

Although the long-range goals of the state boards were not always clear (critics have consistently noted the state boards' neglect of their planning functions—see Palola, Lehmann, and Blischke, 1970; Berdahl, 1975b; Southern Regional Education Board, 1976), their role as gatekeeper of the size, scope, distribution, and quality of their respective systems became increasingly explicit in the 1970s. (For a widely accepted model of statewide coordination and "guidelines for practice" in state boards, see Glenny and others, 1971.) By the end of the decade, the primary regulatory functions of the state boards, subject to the limits of formal authority and informal influence, fell into three broad categories:

1. *Determination of funding adequacy and equity.* This activity is best embodied in the development and negotiation of funding formulas, which exist in many states, and in the budget analysis conducted by the state boards. Although the determination of "need" remains as perplexing as ever, the formulas have at least contributed to a sense of equity in public funding and a reduction of conflict.

2. *Regulation of the "supply" of higher education programs delivered in the marketplace.* This function, among the coordinating bodies' most controversial, can be found in their role—sometimes advisory, sometimes regulatory—in approving new programs and, increasingly, in reviewing existing ones. Advocates of program expansion call on the agencies to serve the goal of access by authorizing new or duplicative programs. Those seeking efficiency demand that the agencies not only avoid additional proliferation but rectify the mistakes of the past by eliminating the redundancy that presently exists.

3. *Establishment of minimum standards of educational practice as a way of protecting a vulnerable and usually uninformed consumer.* Believing that major loopholes have been left by the voluntary accrediting agencies, some state boards have sought to eliminate or control abuses in off-campus operations and in nontraditional programs operating across state lines, and the more obvious abuses of bogus "degree mills."

These activities embody the primary, and sometimes conflicting, goals of state higher education policy—of access, efficiency, and quality. Implicit in these objectives is the idea that state policy must be as broad in perspective as possible. While the states, with few exceptions, have failed to account for the regional and even national dimensions of planning and policy making, at least there has been growing recognition of the private sector within the state. Evidence of this recognition can be seen in the formulation of what might be called a fourth goal of policy in some states—that is, the protection of the private sector from undue harm because of high subsidies and excessive expansion of public higher education. Fearing that the burden of contraction in the future would fall disproportionately on the private sector, the Sloan Commission on Government and Higher Education (1980) has called on the states to conduct mandatory qualitative reviews of all programs in public institutions. Despite the threat of such reviews to institutional autonomy, the commission believes that "the impending enrollment decline justifies so radical a step" (p. 16). Reviews would be used to redefine the mission of an institution, change its role, or even close it. William Friday, president of the University of North Carolina and a member of the Sloan Commission, dissented in this recommendation because of its failure to include the private sector, which, he noted, in the past decade has become one of the "major claimants on state funds" (p. 40).

All these activities of the state have been controversial enough during higher education's growth period but have become doubly so in states undergoing financial stringency and retrenchment. As have institutions, some states have used the recent past to test a variety of strategies to deal with the problem of contraction. Several authors in this volume confront directly the implications of decline for state policy, discussing the wisdom and efficacy of the full range of policy options that could be taken, including how to respond to college closings.

David Breneman, in Chapter Two, establishes a framework whereby the state policy changes proposed in Parts Four and Five of this volume can be judged. He contrasts the elements of pure market and planning strategies and suggests that states will continue to use a "mixed" approach. Frank Bowen and Lyman Glenny, in Chapter Eleven, discuss the controversial application of "enrollment management" at the state level through use of enrollment quotas and funding caps. Using examples from four states, they evaluate the effectiveness of enrollment ceilings in protecting quality and in redirecting students to underutilized campuses. In Chapter Twelve Robert Barak considers the applicability of state-level program evaluation in a period of decline—a process which, despite its limited use, he concludes is essential for rational retrenchment.

Two chapters discuss state funding. David Spence and George Weathersby, in Chapter Thirteen, describe several new rationales being developed for funding in a period of decline, including formulas that recognize the fixed nature of many costs. They also review the issue of "minimum size" and the explicit funding of quality and suggest ways to improve productivity in higher education. James Furman, in Chapter Fourteen, analyzes the problem of state budget reduction as the result of revenue shortfalls. He reviews the appropriate roles of the governor, the legislature, and the institutional and statewide boards, recommending changes that he believes will substantially reduce the crisis aspect of state budgeting.

The next chapter deals with planning for cutbacks in a multi-campus public system. In 1975 Governor Patrick Lucey asked the University of Wisconsin System to present a plan for "reducing the scope" of its operations. That initiative encouraged a process of "contingency planning" that was already under way. Donald Smith, in Chapter Fifteen, presents an overview of the management and planning tools developed by the university system, including the establishment of criteria and a process for considering major changes in mission and closure. Smith comments on the difficulty of planning for orderly enrollment decline in the face of far more severe and unpredictable fiscal contraction in Wisconsin.

In Chapter Sixteen James Mingle, Robert Berdahl, and Marvin Peterson examine the pressure that the climate of decline has placed on the governance structures of public higher education. In excerpts from three case studies of states that have considered the volatile issues of system consolidation, merger, and closure, the authors outline the central themes of both the proponents and opponents of these changes and the reasons for political success or failure. Contraction in the public sector, they conclude, will be accompanied by significant governance changes, including reorganization of the central coordinating mechanisms in the states.

In Part Five the state policies being developed to respond to private college distress are discussed. Richard Jonsen, Grady Bogue, and Gail Chambers (Chapter Seventeen) recommend needed changes for including the independent sector in state master planning. They also discuss ways in which states can monitor the health of private colleges and evaluate requests for public assistance. In an excerpt from a lengthier case study, Chambers describes the involvement of the state of New York in approving mergers between private institutions. Joseph O'Neill, in Chapter Eighteen, outlines state issues involved in private college closings (which, he suggests, may occur increasingly in the coming years). O'Neill suggests a role for the state in effecting the appropriate timing of closings, transfer of students, maintenance of records, and transfer and distribution of assets.

In the concluding chapter, the editor of the volume reviews the major themes discussed and offers his own conclusions.

For Further Reading

There is a growing body of literature on the "management of decline" in higher education, which is reviewed by the authors of this volume. Readers may find it valuable to refer also to the experience of the elementary and secondary school systems with enrollment decline (see especially Minnesota State Planning Agency, 1976; Rideout and others, 1977; Keough, 1975). For a comprehensive review of this literature, readers are referred to Berman and McLaughlin (1977). The experience of public agencies with cutback management and decline also has applicability to higher education. In addition to Levine (1978), previously mentioned, see Behn for a discussion of "closing a government facility" (1978a) and for "hints for the would-be terminators" (1978b). Mitnick (1978) discusses deregulation as a process of organizational reduction in the federal government, while Glassberg (1978) reviews the impact of budget reductions on municipalities in recent years. For a comprehensive review of *Fiscal Stress and Public Policy*, readers are referred to Levine and Rubin (1980).

✌ 2 ✌

Strategies
for the 1980s

David W. Breneman

A decade ago, in his report on *The New Depression in Higher Education*, Cheit (1971) announced the theme that would preoccupy college and university administrators and state education officials throughout the 1970s, as higher education suddenly confronted a slowdown of growth in enrollments and revenues. The fears of impending disaster, of soaring operating deficits, and of wholesale college bankruptcies slowly gave way during the 1970s to a more tough-minded and realistic assessment of the changing economic circumstances of higher education, and to the need to make "more effective use of resources" (Carnegie Commission on Higher Education, 1972).

By mid-decade the perennial optimism of the higher education community began to reassert itself, and the Carnegie Foundation for the Advancement of Teaching (1975) issued a call for "more than survival." Total college enrollments had not, in fact, fallen but had increased by 30 percent between 1970 and 1975. The number of small private colleges that had closed was insignificant, and improved management on campus was bringing operating deficits under control. The federal government's new student aid

16

programs, particularly Basic Educational Opportunity Grants (now called Pell Grants), were making college attendance possible for large numbers of low-income students; and successes in attracting older, part-time, adult students to campus suggested the potential for developing new markets.

Nonetheless, with the 1980s came the realization that what was originally feared for the 1970s—the culling out of institutions—was likely to occur in the new decade. The eighteen- to twenty-one-year-old population, still the bulwark of full-time enrollments, will decline sharply in this decade, and the demographic problem is further complicated by a sluggish, inflationary economy, seemingly incapable of improvement. Ushering in the new decade, the Carnegie Council on Policy Studies in Higher Education (1980), in the title of its final report, *Three Thousand Futures,* seemed to suggest—perhaps unintentionally—that in the 1980s it would be each institution for itself, in a struggle for survival.

Outlook for the Economy

The annual report of the Council of Economic Advisers, submitted to President Carter in January 1981, opened with this sobering observation: "In the 1980s the United States will confront a variety of stubborn problems that have developed during the past fifteen years. Chief among these problems is one that is shared by most other industrial countries—the persistence of large wage and price increases, even in the face of high unemployment and slack production. This problem poses the single most important challenge to United States economic policy—reducing inflation while maintaining a reasonably prosperous and growing economy" (p. 29). The council also pointed out related economic problems, including the standstill in productivity growth, the end of an era of cheap energy, and the country's increased vulnerability to supply disruptions. To deal with these problems, the council advocated three essential goals for macroeconomic policy: "maintaining a persistent and prudent course of demand restraint; putting in place an improved incomes policy, using tax incentives to induce wage moderation; and increasing the share of the nation's output going

to investment" (p. 84). According to the council's projections, the
unemployment rate will decline slowly, from 7.7 percent in 1981 to
5.9 percent by 1986; the consumer price index will move from a
12.6 percent annual increase in 1981 to 6.0 percent in 1986; and the
gross national product (GNP) will grow by 1.7 percent in 1981 and
by 3.7 percent annually through 1986 (p. 178).

The early months of the Reagan administration have sig-
naled a dramatic change in economic policy, as "supply-side" economic theorists are being given the opportunity to ply their wares.
President Reagan's new economic program, announced in February 1981, includes proposals for sharp business and personal
income tax cuts, as well as sizable cuts in federal spending for most
domestic programs (*Economic Report of the President*, 1981). By reducing government's share of the economy and shifting resources
from public to private sectors, the new plan is designed to increase
saving and investment, unleash productive energies previously
stifled by high marginal tax rates, and alter expectations—and
hence behavior—that contribute to continuing high rates of inflation. How much of this program Congress will accept is unclear at
this writing, as is its efficacy, if adopted, to work the miracles
claimed for it. What is clear is that the economy is being launched
on a new and uncertain course, rendering economic forecasts subject to greater than usual error. For the immediate future, the most
pronounced effects of the Reagan economic program on colleges
and universities will be at the microeconomic level, through
changes in federal policy toward higher education. Whether college administrators and state officials should accept President
Reagan's proposals reducing support for higher education, in the
hope that budget cuts will aid the economy, is one of the tougher
questions facing the education community. It would be easier to
answer in the affirmative if the new economic program were based
on more than simple faith and assertion. Details of the changes
proposed for federal higher education programs are discussed
later in this chapter.

Prospects for Sectors of Higher Education

If forecasts of the economy are subject to greater than usual
uncertainty, then so must be one's view of how the various sectors

of higher education will fare in this decade and the next. In addition to the vagaries of the economy are the uncertainties surrounding enrollment projections and levels of financial support. Equally hard to predict are the responses of policy makers to institutions in financial and educational distress: will the market's verdict on the fate of individual colleges be accepted, or will exceptional efforts be made to keep all institutions afloat, even in markedly different form? Although one of the aims of this book is to assist thinking about the management of decline, it is not possible to predict with certainty the outcome of events in this decade. We begin, however, with a brief look at enrollment projections.

The range of forecasts available is so wide as to make them almost useless, as the comparison published in *More Than Survival* makes clear (Carnegie Foundation for the Advancement of Teaching, 1975, p. 41). In relation to 1974 enrollment levels, forecasts (or scenarios) range from a nearly 50 percent drop in the mid-1980s to a 200 percent increase by the year 2000. These extremes highlight the importance of behavioral assumptions and also remind us that enrollment levels are not mechanistically determined but can be influenced by policy decisions.

More recently the Carnegie Council reviewed the literature and data on enrollment trends and concluded that undergraduate enrollments nationally will drop by 5 to 15 percent from the early 1980s to the late 1990s (Carnegie Council on Policy Studies in Higher Education, 1980, p. 34). The council also noted that widespread regional differences are likely, with the Northeast and upper Midwest experiencing greater than average decline, while the Southwest and several southeastern states fare better than average, possibly even experiencing modest increases in enrollments (p. 71). Although extreme scenarios of growth or decline can still be concocted, the Carnegie Council's view seems realistic and is accepted for the discussion in this chapter.

Given the Carnegie Council's projections and assuming no sharp breaks in current public policy, what are the prospects for the various sectors of higher education? Two groups of institutions are likely to absorb the bulk of enrollment decline: (1) nonselective private liberal arts colleges and (2) public state colleges, many of them former teachers colleges, now often labeled universities. Some analysts predict that as many as 200 small (enrollment under

1,000) tuition-dependent private colleges will close during the 1980s (Behn, 1979). The fate of public colleges and universities that suffer large enrollment loss is less clear, since state institutions can be kept afloat indefinitely by political choice. Even in the private sector, no institution will succumb without a battle, and some faltering colleges may merge with—or be absorbed by—stronger private or public institutions. Less dramatic than closure, but perhaps more damaging to the vitality of higher education, would be the lingering death of colleges that manage to hang on, while eroding steadily in quality, in faculty morale, and in institutional purpose. Decline short of death can be expected in both public and private institutions, posing difficult problems for accrediting agencies, public officials, and trustees charged with responsibility for evaluating and maintaining institutional health. Concern over the prospect of declining educational quality prompted the controversial recommendation of the Sloan Commission for periodic quality reviews by the states (Sloan Commission on Government and Higher Education, 1980, pp. 102-105).

While the major research universities, public and private, should have little difficulty in maintaining undergraduate enrollments, their greatest problems in the 1980s will occur in graduate education and research, their distinctive activities. The academic labor market for new Ph.D.s in most fields will remain depressed for another decade (Cartter, 1976); and programs designed to assist young scholars in the interim—whether by a Junior Scholars Program (Radner and Kuh, 1978) or through Research Excellence Awards (National Research Council, 1979)—have not yet generated much support. Thus, research universities face the difficult task of maintaining high-quality graduate programs at a time when financial resources will be scarce and the attractions of doctoral study limited. Similarly, the costs of engaging in high-quality research and scholarship continue to outpace the capacity of most universities to keep up, as the price of everything from scientific research equipment to scholarly books and journals continues to soar (National Science Foundation and Department of Education, 1980, pp. 38-39; National Enquiry into Scholarly Communication, 1979).

Community colleges are generally thought to be in a good position to weather the next decade, for they have successfully broadened their "open-door" philosophy to include the entire community. The original junior college mission, emphasizing academic transfer programs, was extended to include vocational/technical programs and then noncredit community service activities—resulting in the comprehensive community college. If "lifelong learning" proves to be the way of the future, community colleges will be the main beneficiaries. Warning signals for these institutions do abound, however: a steady decline in the share of revenues provided from local taxes, threatening local control and program flexibility; the continued restriction of most student aid programs to those enrolled at least half time in credit courses; and the failure thus far to convert the rhetoric of lifelong learning into specific policies for its financial support. In addition, community colleges face heightened competition with high schools for adult basic education; with area vocational centers, industry, and proprietary schools for vocational/technical instruction; and with four-year colleges and universities for both traditional and nontraditional students (Breneman and Nelson, 1981).

It seems accurate to conclude, therefore, that no sector of higher education will be spared the challenges posed by the 1980s.

Federal Policy in the 1980s

The legislative framework that was to have governed the principal federal programs for higher education through 1985 was signed into law by President Carter on October 3, 1980. Known as the Education Amendments of 1980 (94 Stat. 167), this legislation reauthorized and modified the Higher Education Act of 1965, as previously amended. Specific provisions of the legislation, particularly the all-important Title IV student aid programs, were debated intensely during 1979 and 1980, and the bill that emerged was warmly received by the higher education community (Gladieux, 1980). If these were normal times, one might assume that most of the issues surrounding Washington's role in supporting higher education for the next few years were settled, but these are far from normal times. Less than three months after signing the bill, President Carter submitted a fiscal 1982 budget that proposed substantial changes in the Guaranteed Student Loan (GSL) program, in an attempt to curb its soaring costs (U.S. Office of Management and Budget, 1981). The Reagan administration accepted most of these GSL modifications and proposed further cuts in student aid, including changes in eligibility requirements for Pell Grants serving low- and middle-income students. In considering these proposed changes, we need to take into account the principles guiding the new administration as it fashions an approach to domestic programs.

First, and most obviously, the new administration is embarked on a crusade to stem the growth of federal spending and regulation in most domestic sectors of the economy, including education. Second, heavy emphasis is placed on returning control over programs to state, local, and institutional levels, reducing federal intervention wherever possible. Third, the federal government's role in redistributing income from rich to poor is being deemphasized. Fourth, tax cuts are a central feature of the new supply-side program, since the administration is convinced that such cuts will unleash productive forces in the private sector of the economy.

What are the implications for higher education of this approach to government? They can be summed up simply as "reduced intrusion and reduced support." Education is one of the principal activities that the Reagan administration plans to return as fully as possible to state, local, and private control, a move evident in the proposal for block grants at the elementary/secondary level and in plans to demote the Department of Education from cabinet status. For higher education no new programs are likely, with the possible exception of tax initiatives such as a tuition tax credit and extension of the charitable deduction to those who do not itemize. An attempt is being made to undo much of the Middle Income Student Assistance Act of 1978, as eligibility for Pell Grants is scaled back and GSL interest subsidies are ended for upper-income families.

In short, if Congress adopts President Reagan's proposals, the federal government will be less actively involved in supporting higher education and students; instead, responsibility for shaping the future of this service industry will be placed squarely on the backs of state officials, administrators, trustees, and private citizens. The most significant financing change, if implemented, would be the restrictive provisions governing access to subsidized student loans. Student borrowing would be limited to verifiable need remaining after parents' expected contribution and all other forms of financial assistance; the in-school interest subsidy would be ended; and the new parents' loan program would carry a market interest rate, with no federal subsidy. Should these changes reduce the willingness of banks to lend under the program, as some observers predict, many students would be hard pressed to finance an education in high-priced private colleges or in graduate and professional schools. In that event, financial pressures on these institutions and programs would increase dramatically, and state officials (among others) would be forced to grapple with near-crisis situations on many campuses. It is clearly in the interest of all parties to find a way to curb the excessive costs of the GSL program, while still ensuring a supply of credit for students who truly require it (Rivlin, 1981; Pechman, 1981).

The one new initiative that the Reagan administration is pledged to support is a tuition tax credit. The type of tax credit commonly proposed for higher education ($250 to $500 against tuition) has few, if any, redeeming features: it would be regressive, in that benefits would flow disproportionately to high-income families; inefficient, in that student decisions regarding whether to enroll—or where—would be largely unaffected; and expensive, with a drain on Treasury revenues of $2 billion or more annually, depending on the configuration of the credit (Breneman, 1978). For higher education, therefore, a tuition tax credit would simply amount to a wasteful tax expenditure (no one would design a grant program with such features), and it would be doubly unfortunate if some or all of its costs were levied against the grant programs for truly needy students.

Changes proposed for two other programs outside the Department of Education are worth noting in this brief review. First, student benefits under Social Security are to be phased out within four years. If this proposal is adopted, annual outlays of more than $2 billion linked to attendance in higher education would be eliminated (U.S. Congressional Budget Office, 1981, p. 134). Second, several bills proposing to reinstate a GI Bill for education are currently before Congress, and such legislation may be enacted in some form in the near future. Community colleges would probably benefit most from this program, although specific provisions of the legislation cannot be predicted with much accuracy. It would be ironic, but not unusual, if one of the most significant pieces of federal legislation affecting higher education in this decade were adopted to "solve" a problem elsewhere, in this case one of military recruitment and retention.

State Strategies for the 1980s

The preceding discussion suggests that the federal government will not play an active role in shaping the development of higher education during the difficult years ahead. Instead, providing financial aid for low- and middle-income students will continue to be the main federal activity, with funds delivered—through a combination of programs that roughly meet the test of fairness—to the institutions and students involved. While federal aid will continue to be crucial to the survival of many institutions, it will not be distributed with that end in mind; the fate of particular institutions will not (and probably should not) be a fundamental concern of the federal government. The key public policy decisions governing higher education in the years ahead, therefore, will fall to state governments. The balance of this chapter discusses the approaches that state governments can follow in fashioning policies responsive to the unique demands of a time of retrenchment.

Broadly speaking, state policies can follow one of two approaches: reliance on the market or reliance on central planning. Because most states are unlikely to adopt either course in the extreme, mixed strategies involving elements of each approach will be most common. The merits of a mixed strategy become clear when we consider what it would mean to implement either the market or the planning approach in its pure form.

The Market Approach. As the competition for students and for resources heats up, it is natural to ask whether a state policy of simply letting institutions compete would not lead to the best outcome. Presumably, the better colleges and universities would win out, and if some schools must close, what better method than to let students make those decisions through their choices of where to enroll? Few elected officials want to be placed in the position of having to decide explicitly which schools will thrive and which fail; how much simpler—and less divisive—to let impersonal market forces determine the outcome.

Before we succumb to the economist's siren song, however, we need to examine more closely how the market for higher education actually works. Does this market meet the tests of equity and efficiency in the allocation of resources? One way to address that question is to list some of the salient features of the market for higher education as it currently exists in most states:

1. The "firms" in this industry are not seeking to maximize profits or to minimize costs for a given level of activity (Bowen, 1980). It is not clear what objectives guide the behavior of colleges and universities, although some observers suggest that prestige, status, and quality are the central goals animating most academic behavior (Garvin, 1980).
2. The educational services produced by colleges and universities are not priced to the student at marginal cost, average cost, or even full cost. Instead, a wide range of net prices exists in this industry, reflecting more than cost or quality differences. The crazy-quilt pattern of subsidies to institutions and to students must give pause to anyone who would argue that prices do perform the task of allocating resources efficiently within or among institutions in this industry.
3. The information available to students about colleges can hardly be considered complete (or even adequate) in many cases; and, because each student usually buys only one college education in a lifetime, he cannot easily correct initial errors by switching brands until he finds the best product.
4. Some firms in this industry (the state institutions) receive substantial public subsidies, whereas comparable firms (the independent institutions) do not. As a result, the prices charged for comparable services differ. They may also vary depending on the student's place of residence (in state or out of state).

These features of the higher education market deviate in important ways from the conditions required to achieve optimal resource allocation through that means. Although a state may still choose to "rely on the market" to cope with the 1980s, the rationale for that decision cannot include any assurance that the outcomes will reflect economic rationality or carry any moral weight. The market in most states is tilted against independent institutions that receive lesser state subsidies than public colleges and universities. One result of a pure market approach in the 1980s will be the demise of many small, nonselective, tuition-dependent private colleges, unable to attract sufficient tuition-paying students to keep the doors open. Perhaps that would be the "best" outcome, but there would be no reason to accord it any of the legitimacy granted to outcomes of properly functioning markets. In states with a sizable number of small private colleges, therefore, a decision to rely on the market is a political choice—not a neutral decision—favoring the public over the private sector.

For those state officials who would like to rely on the market while overcoming its main imperfections, the obstacles are severe. A meaningful marketplace would be national, or at least regional, in scope, not limited to institutions within a state's boundaries. The tendency in state decision making, however, is to erect de facto tariff barriers at the state line, with out-of-state tuition differentials for the public institutions and eligibility for state scholarships limited to residents attending public or private colleges within the state. Rather than a national market, the result is fifty minimarkets. This pattern of rational, but suboptimal, state behavior might be overcome by an active federal policy of matching grants for student aid, with the requirement that these grants be portable across state lines (Hartman, 1978). As was noted earlier, however, this type of active federal policy, although intended to improve the market for higher education, is not likely to be supported by the current administration. Higher education will be treated primarily as a state responsibility, and the states will foster pricing policies that discourage interstate mobility of students. During the 1970s, however, many states did develop scholarship programs that help private colleges compete for in-state students with public colleges, a gain for the market approach.

Various additional features of the competitive market can be noted. First, only up to a point can colleges influence the level of enrollment; after that, increased competition becomes a zero-sum game, with one college's gain being another's loss. In such circumstances each college is forced to match its competitor's increased outlays for advertising and recruitment, draining resources away from the educational program, simply to remain in place. The problem is analogous to what occurs when all spectators leap to their feet at a football game—no one sees any better, and everyone is less well off.

Second, increased competition tends to erode the division of labor among institutions, as each college or university seeks to increase its potential markets. Thus, universities expand into the community college market for adult and remedial education, while liberal arts colleges introduce vocational/technical programs and noncredit courses. If total resources do not increase proportionately with these expanded efforts, educational quality is likely to suffer, and the educational comparative advantage of particular institutions will slowly be lost.

Finally, the 1980s may witness an outbreak of price warfare among institutions, as tuition discounts not based on financial need become a more common form of competition (Deitch, 1981). Shrinking enrollments will drive home the economist's logic of decision making at the margin. When a college must choose between enrolling a student whose partial tuition more than covers incremental costs and losing that student and his tuition contribution entirely, the incentive for price cutting will be strong. To the extent that tuition discounting does not appreciably increase total enrollments nationally, becoming instead another zero-sum game, then the benefits to students of lower prices will be offset by declining educational quality.

The Planning Approach. If the higher education marketplace has its limitations, either as a pure form or in practice, what can be said for increased central planning? Over the past ten to fifteen years, most states have created some form of coordinating or governing board for higher education, and the authority of these statewide agencies could be increased to cope with the problems of retrenchment. When the resources available to a complex organization are declining, control over those resources usually becomes increasingly concentrated at the top. Similarly, it could be argued that the decision-making power of statewide boards of higher education should be increased in order to achieve a balanced and planned approach to retrenchment, rather than leave the outcome to the chaotic and unpredictable forces of competition. A planning agency could make detailed enrollment projections for all institutions in the state and use these projections to determine the number and location of academic programs needed to accommodate demand. Wasteful duplication of programs would be uncovered, and objective peer evaluations could be made to decide which redundant programs to close. New programs could not be started without the approval of the planning agency, and each institution would have a clear set of functions within the state system of higher education. Private colleges and universities would be required to participate in the plan as a condition of receiving state aid. Ensuring an efficient use of resources during a period of retrenchment would be the driving force behind such plans.

Although this brief description of central planning may sound like a caricature, it is not far from reality in some states. The review of doctoral programs in public and private universities undertaken by the regents of the University of the State of New York, for example, is consistent with this model, and most readers will recognize elements of this approach in their own states. Certainly, the trend toward more active statewide planning and control has been apparent during the past decade, and the problems of retrenchment in the 1980s could easily accelerate the shift of power from campus to state capital. Are there any sound reasons for public policy to resist this seemingly inexorable drift toward increased state control?

The problems with centralized control of an economy are well known, and some of the principles are surely applicable to systems of higher education as well. Local initiative and creativity—what economist Harvey Leibenstein (1966) has referred to as "X-efficiency"—are blunted, and the system takes on a rigidity and inflexibility often found in complex bureaucratic organizations. (Of course, institutional leaders may display a good deal of initiative as they try to circumvent rules and regulations imposed by the state governing board.) Campus autonomy and the freedom of faculty to develop distinctive educational programs are deeply held values, and institutions will not casually relinquish control over these areas to statewide governing boards.

Similarly, enrollment patterns of students are not easily controlled or manipulated to meet a central plan. Nor are these patterns easy to forecast with accuracy for specific institutions or fields of study. As long as students are permitted the considerable freedom of choice that they currently enjoy in selecting colleges and fields of study, state planners are certain to experience frustration in trying to fit students into a prearranged plan.

Mixed Strategies. Few states are likely to adopt either pure market or pure planning approaches to management of higher education in the 1980s. Instead, common sense, the demands of practical politics, and respect for the autonomy of institutions will dictate some form of mixed strategy in most states, involving elements of both the market and planning approaches. This chapter does not advocate a particular strategy as ideal for all states, for needs will clearly vary among them. However, it is possible to indicate in a general way the factors that should be considered in striking a balance between the two approaches.

Most states are closer in current practice to reliance on the market than to strong and effective central planning, and it seems likely that most will remain that way. The decade or more of retrenchment that lies ahead, however, will expose the limitations of the market as a mechanism for organization, control, and resource allocation. We noted earlier several of the imperfections in this market that will create strong pressures not to accept its outcomes as just or socially desirable. Increased statewide planning is certain to be an alternative that policy makers will consider, although it seems unlikely that any state will go to the extremes sketched earlier. The marketplace has its problems, but they are relatively minor when compared with the difficulties of implementing a full-blown planning and control system. Nonetheless, a view that encompasses the state "system" of higher education in its entirety provides an important and legitimate perspective on the issues of retrenchment, and it is the recognition of that legitimacy that prompts the move toward statewide planning.

Perhaps the market can be improved as the central control mechanism if some of the concerns noted above are incorporated into the rules and procedures that govern market competition. For example, in order to make public-private competition more fair, some states have established aid programs for students attending private colleges. States could also examine financing formulas currently in use, to be certain that the incentives built into the formulas are consistent with intended state policies. For example, enrollment-driven formulas provide strong incentives for public colleges to maintain or expand enrollments, putting further pressure on private colleges. Designing financing formulas that do not put a premium on enrollment growth may be one of the best—and most equitable—ways to improve the market.

While the market's performance can no doubt be improved, state officials will not wish to leave certain areas to the market, even if it were technically possible to do so. The state may wish to regulate the addition of new degree programs, for example, reserving the right to veto programs that fall outside an institution's mission. The state may not wish to accept the distribution of enrollments among public institutions and fields of study that an unregulated market would produce, opting instead for policies that ration access to oversubscribed areas (see Chapter Eleven of this volume). While it is easy to multiply examples of areas where state control could be extended, such extensions will be highly controversial and seen as an unwarranted intrusion into the management of colleges and universities. No other set of issues in higher education today generates such intensity of feeling as government regulation, and a prolonged era of retrenchment is virtually certain to make things worse. Free and open discussion of the policies that will govern each state's approach to enrollment decline is doubly important, therefore, at a time when university-government relationships are already strained. The chapters in this volume should make a valuable contribution to that discussion.

For Further Reading

Readers who wish to contrast coordination and governance of higher education in the United States with practices in other countries are referred to Clark's (1978) excellent multinational study. For additional discussion of the relationship between the federal government and higher education, readers should review the essays found in *Government Regulation of Higher Education,* edited by Hobbs (1978). For further discussion of the growing state role, see Southern Regional Education Board (1980), with essays by George Weathersby, Clark Kerr, and Harold Geiogue (see also "Coordinating Higher Education," 1980). For a comprehensive review of *Public Policy and Private Higher Education,* see Breneman and Finn (1978).

ॐ 3 ॐ

Warning Signals
of Distress

Lyman A. Glenny
Frank M. Bowen

Early in 1979 we presented two related reports to the California Postsecondary Education Commission. One was a description of how ten California public institutions were responding to enrollment and financial stress (Bowen and Glenny, 1980). The other— summarized here—was a checklist consisting of a number of indicators, signals, or early-warning signs of such stress (Glenny and Bowen, 1980). Both reports were based on responses to a preliminary questionnaire, field interviews at the ten institutions, and two meetings with the chief executive officers of the ten institutions or their representatives.

Neither report was founded on any theoretical or conceptual framework. Our intent was to describe conditions as we found them and to relate these conditions to the three very different public segments of higher education in California. With regard to the indicators, our questions were generally open-ended ones: "When did you decide your campus was in trouble?" "What particular factors first called your attention to enrollment difficulties?"

The indicators in the report and in this chapter were provided by responses to questions such as these.

Our attempt to list indicators of enrollment and financial stress grew out of the assumption that almost all colleges and universities will have to adjust to substantial financial, enrollment, and programmatic stress over the next dozen years. The indicators could alert an institution to an impending need for changes in policies and activities under certain circumstances. The caveat on the use of most indicators is the phrase "under certain circumstances." An indicator may presage nothing at all, or it may be fairly accurate in predicting an outcome. An example is the relationship between the number of applications for admission and the number of students actually enrolling from the applicant group. If institutional history shows a high, steady relationship, then this indicator may be an excellent predictor. But if the historical relationship between the numbers has fluctuated widely, the most recent numbers would indicate little. In other words, an indicator becomes such only if the conditions that it describes apply directly to either the internal or the external operations and environment of a specific institution. One institution will find a particular indicator of value while another may find it useless. A cluster of indicators all pointing in the same direction (without different sets giving countervailing signals) will be more reliable than a single indicator.

The number of ways in which the indicators might be classified is almost endless. The thirty indicators discussed in this chapter are divided into ten over which the institutions have little or no control and twenty over which institutional control exists to some degree.

Our checklist of indicators does not purport to have the breadth of earlier attempts to develop social indicators (U.S. Department of Health, Education and Welfare, 1969) or the narrow specificity of more recent efforts to detail economic indicators for higher education (Minter, 1979). It is a checklist only, and not one that pretends to be exhaustive. Although these indicators are not solely or even primarily relevant to the coming years of almost inevitably declining enrollments, the uncertainties of enrollment and funding trends give the current need for such information an urgency that it did not have in the past.

Finally, many volumes would be required to present even the major ramifications of all thirty indicators, and no claim is made that such a presentation has been attempted. The discussion that immediately follows the statement of each indicator is merely intended as clarification. Similarly, the suggestions for response or action—usually in the final paragraph for each section—are illustrative only.

Indicators That the Institution Cannot Control

Indicators over which the institution has little or no control usually arise out of broad trends and social forces. Although the institution is part of that environment, it does not have the capacity to change the trends or forces. Those most likely to affect higher education in the immediate future include (1) low birthrates, resulting in fewer applicants from historical enrollment pools; (2) public pressures to reduce or stabilize governmental expenditures; and (3) increasing student interest in vocational, occupational, and professional programs and declining interest in the liberal arts. Although the institution cannot control such trends or forces, it can respond to them so as to mitigate their impact on its mission. Only indicators that appear to be most pertinent to higher education are mentioned.

1. *Shifts in the Ethnic Mix of the Institution's Service Area.* Given the differences in college attendance rates of different racial and ethnic groups, an institution needs to be aware of shifts in its area. Blacks have a much lower high school participation rate than whites, and, proportionately, far fewer of them graduate from high school (U.S. Bureau of the Census, 1979). This is characteristic of the Hispanic population as well. An increasing presence of either minority group will, in the short run, mean lower enrollment and usually the necessity for more remedial work.

An individual college can obtain data for shifts in ethnic composition by surveys of elementary and high schools in its service area or from special populations studies conducted by the U.S. Bureau of the Census.

2. *Shifts in the Socioeconomic Mix of the Institution's Service Area.*
Shifts in socioeconomic composition can have the same impact as
shifts in ethnic composition. Historically, the lower the socioeconomic level of a group, the lower the college attendance rate (U.S.
Bureau of the Census, 1979); the higher the level, the higher the
attendance rate. Hence, shifts (whether up or down) in the socioeconomic mix of the service area will require college adaptations.

3. *Federal Subsidies.* The federal government (and sometimes
state governments as well) subsidizes training and research to reach
policy objectives. Federal space, environment, and energy objectives are identified at least a year or two before subsidies are appropriated. Most of these programs require specialized manpower.
Often, the array of specializations requires the government to
provide financial aid to students and categorical incentive grants to
institutions to strengthen existing programs or to create new ones.

Institutional administrators can keep alert to these shifts in
federal policy. Institutions with early proposals for subsidized education and training will have a decided advantage over less energetic and imaginative ones. Continuous review of policy shifts may
also warn institutional administrators of when to adjust to cutbacks
in existing federally subsidized programs.

4. *Changes in Labor Demand in the College Service Area.* The
market for college graduates is largely shown in local data. Surveys
of business, industry, and government help in making such assessments; so do data on trends of students entering the various
programs of a college.

An institution should have a planning group that reviews local
surveys and regional predictions of occupational trends. The lead
time for planning from such data is not great—probably no more
than five years; but that is sufficient time for a college to respond to
projected changes. Longer-term, tentative planning can build in
contingencies, so that plans can be revised as new data appear.

5. *Live Births and the Demand for Teachers.* Since 1974 the
number of live births has risen about 8 percent, rather than continuing to decline sharply. In the fall of 1979, the number of five-
year-olds began to increase, and there will soon be a need for newly
trained teachers. The Bureau of the Census projects a gradual rise
in the birthrate, which should lead to a substantial increase in the

number of live births by the year 2000 (U.S. Bureau of the Census, 1977). Teachers will be needed for the early elementary grades and then for upper grade levels. Migration trends within the service area as well as local live birth trends must be considered in projections for each school area.

Caution must be used in relation to all projections. The Bureau of the Census has been greatly in error in its national projections of live births for the past ten years, so institutions should examine birth data in their own service area rather than accepting national or even state trends as applicable locally. Institutional planners should be familiar with *Current Population Reports* and related special reports of the Bureau of the Census and with vital statistics of the U.S. Public Health Service.

6. *Source of Students by Geographical Area.* Some colleges and universities draw students from certain geographical areas not immediately contiguous to the institution, especially from the largest city in the state. For example, several California institutions draw heavily from the Los Angeles area. The population shifts indicate that the great majority of the people in Los Angeles will soon be minority, black and Hispanic. These shifts will affect enrollment not only in the Los Angeles colleges but in others, such as those in San Diego, which draw a substantial portion of their students from Los Angeles.

Institutions should know the geographical source of their students and, if they draw from distant localities, examine the demographic data for those localities to determine whether major changes in ethnic composition or socioeconomic level are taking place. Shifts conceivably could result in either increases or decreases in enrollment.

7. *Changing Student Profiles.* Student age, sex, ethnicity, and level of ability all have an impact on program choice, full-time or part-time status, and other aspects of an institution's mission. These characteristics, if shown quantitatively and by trend lines, will give an institution strong indications of the changing nature of its environment, thus preparing it for program changes, for modifications in student services, and for faculty staffing needs.

Most of the information needed is already available, but the institutional planning staff must array it over time to ascertain the trends that are indicators of change. Much, for example, is often made of the trend of increasing average age of students, but this trend must be reviewed by trends in median age of all students and by dimensions of full-time and part-time status.

8. *Student Flow from High Schools.* The relationship between college attendance and a student's program of study in high school is sometimes overlooked. A review of local high school records can reveal the numbers and proportions of students from each school with particular academic interests who attend the college. Increasingly, colleges are using the declarations of program interest made by students on college entrance examinations to pinpoint potential applicants and to monitor trends.

Few colleges have necessary data available on high school areas of emphasis and later college programs. If some majors are not attracted, institutional planners will need to find out why they are not and try to correct the problem—perhaps by building closer professional relationships between the faculty and the high school instructors.

9. *Average Student Loads.* If the average credit-hour load of students is decreasing, a greater number of students is required to justify the budget formerly generated on a full-time-equivalent basis. In recent years the average number of students has increased among institutions, but the full-time-equivalent numbers have decreased (National Center for Education Statistics, 1980a, p. 88). That reduction adversely affects institutions even though they publicly announce enrollment increases. The trend of decreasing work loads seems to arise from societal forces over which the institution has little control. In the long run, such reduced work loads may be of much benefit to the nation; in the short term, however, they can also mean weaknesses in program, faculty, or services. Sometimes the weaknesses can be corrected.

Careful monitoring of students in various majors and programs may lead to indications of why they are reducing loads—for example, hard courses may require excessive study time. Whatever the cause of the trend, the institution must be aware of its implications for program support, class size, and number of classes, as well as the probable financial losses that will result from reduced loads.

10. *Uncertainty in Obtaining the Next Budget.* When funding sources themselves become unreliable and unpredictable, the resulting ad hoc and stop-gap measures weaken the quality of pro-

grams, create poor morale, and prevent the efficient use of resources. The more distinguished faculty and administrators will
search for other jobs, and potential applicants will do the same.

The only current escape from the impact of uncertainty is
through use of reserve funds, budget slack, or large endowments.
Most institutions are rapidly losing these options, if for no other
reason than soaring inflation. Public policy can be directed to relieving budgetary uncertainty by encouraging multiyear budgeting procedures that, at least in principle, guarantee support levels.

Indicators That the Institution Can Control

Internal management problems will surely limit the capacity
of most institutions to adjust to changing conditions in the 1980s.
Because of restrictions imposed by law and collective bargaining
agreements, management is faced with an increasing proportion
of faculty with tenure, greatly diminished fiscal flexibility, and reduced program and personal flexibility. The following twenty indicators have often grown out of these overarching trends. They
remain, however, indicators over which the campus has some or
total control.

11. *Physical Environment of the Campus.* The campus environment in all its aspects can be an important attraction for students.
An indicator of financial stress is the delay of maintenance of campus buildings and grounds. If the delay continues because maintenance budgets are cut in order to protect jobs or to support
low-priority programs, the institution is in trouble.

Institutional leaders are the only ones who can ensure that
budget priorities in times of stress do not neglect the ambience of
the campus, for neglect will probably lead to further enrollment
and resource losses and will almost certainly increase the ultimate
costs of repair and reconstruction.

12. *Proportion of Total Budget Composed of Soft Money.* If a
major fraction of essential operations and any proportion of the
tenured faculty are supported on soft money, an institution can be
in almost instant trouble. Dependence by many predominantly
black colleges on federal Title III support illustrates the danger to
institutions that have relatively few other sources of support. But

for all institutions, shifting regular faculty members' pay from grant or contract funds to the regular budget can cause havoc. Programs started originally with soft money may have become an integral part of the curriculum.

The campus financial plan should take soft-money operations into consideration and should contain contingency provisions that will assure continuation of those soft-money operations that are most vital to the institutional mission.

13. *Decrease in Transfer Students at Two-Year Colleges.* As the two-year colleges have responded to student demand by establishing additional technical and occupational programs for job entry, the proportion of students preparing for transfer to four-year institutions has diminished. As transfers decrease, the four-year campuses recruit more freshmen to compensate for the lost transfer enrollments. As a result, fewer freshmen enter the two-year colleges. Such practices are self-defeating, since they further reduce the pool of transfer students—which was the original source of the problem. Furthermore, because of this reduction in transfer students, administrators of two-year colleges fear that their institutions will become technical institutes or ones known primarily for adult and continuing education.

Planners at four-year campuses and the two-year colleges from which transfers have historically come should jointly examine local trends. Changes in articulation agreements or program sequence, for example, might enable them to maintain historical missions and differentiation of function.

14. *Lower Admissions Standards.* The lowering of admissions standards by higher-prestige institutions adversely affects institutions that are lower in the prestige scale. Even without a formal change in standards, the most prestigious campuses will be able to increase enrollments at the expense of others by reaching deeper into the pool of qualified applicants. Any substantial change in the average qualifications of the student body may well mean an unexamined change in the mission of the campus. Faculty trained for one mission may find that they are expected to pursue a drastically different one.

Institutional leaders should be alert to changes in the scholastic qualifications of admitted applicants. They should be aware of the implications of a less scholastically qualified student body for academic programs established for a more qualified group.

15. *Hiring from Within.* When a campus hires from within or hires its own graduates, that is usually a sign of financial stress or of conservatism, or perhaps both. Nationwide or regional searches for the best persons possible for both faculty and administrative positions were common in the 1960s. Now, even with affirmative action regulations, institutions tend to cut costs by limiting the search and to cut risks by considering local people whose capabilities are already known—even if their talents are modest.

Solutions are not easy. Money may not be available to pay the competitive salaries necessary to attract outsiders—or even to pay their moving expenses. But, at a minimum, administrators and faculty should protect and enhance their most critical programs by filling vacancies from a regional or national pool of applicants— even if, as a result, programs judged not as essential cannot be funded.

16. *Increasing Unit Costs.* A college is probably in growing trouble if the costs of many programs are increasing faster than inflation indicators. If, as enrollment drops, an institution maintains its programs and faculty much as it did with higher enrollments, unit costs will rise in some proportion to the enrollment drop. Most colleges wish to release faculty by attrition (motivated by humanitarian concerns); however, attrition does not necessarily occur in the subject areas where cutbacks need to be made. Consequently, reliance on attrition usually means general program deterioration—and certain detriment to the students enrolled.

If the weakest programs *and* the *faculty* in them are discontinued, resources become available for strengthening better programs or starting new programs with greater relevance to campus objectives than those terminated; at the same time, overall costs will be reduced. Discontinuance of courses and subprograms reduces costs very little unless related faculty and staff are also released.

17. *Increasing or Decreasing Percentages of Part-Time Faculty.* Full-time, tenured faculty are institutional hostages to fortune, and part-time faculty are a form of insurance against adversity. As signs of financial trouble deepen, the part-time people are let go, and the

courses or programs that they staffed are dropped or are picked up by the regular faculty. But—in two-year colleges particularly—the part-time instructors may be highly qualified specialists, so their loss may mean the loss of a critical course or program.

The strategy of having a reserve of part-time faculty can be successful, but the strategy must be implemented under very controlled conditions, with the *quality of programs* as the chief goal. Those who implement this strategy should recognize the problems and possible inequities in the creation of a large, permanent, part-time staff of instructors who may be personally and professionally alienated from the institution—and perhaps from their profession and from society.

18. *Percentage of Faculty Teaching Outside Primary Specialization.* Even if the proportions of full-time and part-time faculty remain constant, a sure sign of stress is an increase in the number of the tenured faculty who are teaching in their secondary or tertiary fields of interest. The quality of a program is in peril when a full-time instructor is teaching outside his known specialty. Assigning faculty to tasks that they are not capable of performing with excellence leads only to the diminishment of program quality and institutional reputation and, ultimately, to further enrollment losses.

Reassignment of faculty must be carefully monitored. Certainly, judicious transfers of qualified faculty will benefit both the individual and the program. But program improvement, not job protection, ought to be the purpose of all transfers of teaching assignments.

19. *Regular Faculty Assigned to Unusual Teaching Hours.* Increasing assignment of faculty to evening and weekend courses when this has not been the custom usually indicates that part-time faculty have been released because of financial stress or dropping enrollments. Where part-time or adjunct faculty formerly were hired to teach in these "undesirable" time periods, the regular faculty are now assigned. The fact that these tenured faculty take the odd hours indicates that they too realize the deteriorating financial condition of the institution.

Monitoring of teaching assignments to odd hours is required. In specific situations such assignments may not indicate stress. The institution may be starting new programs at unusual hours to cater to a new clientele and may be using regular, full-time faculty to ensure maintenance of quality.

20. *Decreasing Rates of Funding for Additional Students.* If the college or university does not continue to receive in constant dollars the same amount for incremental increases in students as it has in the past, one can be sure that some source of revenue is drying up. The source could be a major one, such as the state appropriation for public institutions or the income fund from tuition or from sales of products or services by the institution. Whatever the source or cause, the institution is in financial trouble and under stress.

Administrative and faculty leaders should have a reasonably accurate idea of the marginal costs of additional students. If funding has been on an average-cost basis, fewer incremental dollars for additional students may not require reduction of existing programs. But seeking additional students when not even marginal costs can be expected to be covered is inviting difficulty; for the greater the success of the search, the greater the financial loss.

21. *Encouragement of Unselective Early Retirement.* Encouraging faculty to retire early may or may not be a sign of financial trouble, but it does indicate stress. If encouragement is not selective, it means that an attempt is being made to save dollars from the retirement of expensive full professors to hire less costly assistant professors or lecturers. Such an attempt places budgetary considerations above program priorities.

Administrators who encourage early retirement must be sure that they are doing so for the sake of program quality. For example, early retirement of professors who are past their prime may make room for younger and more energetic instructors; or it may enable an institution to bring in a "star" to lead a critical program. The uses of early retirement will vary among the departments within a campus.

22. *Proportion of Faculty with Overloads or Underloads.* If faculty members are gradually but surely acquiring larger classes or heavier teaching loads, either the campus is in budget stress or else money is being diverted into new enterprises within the institution. Evidence that larger teaching loads diminish program quality is not conclusive, but there is obviously a limit to each person's capacity to perform effectively as numbers increase. Currently popular

programs—for example, business administration and engineering—may be dangerously understaffed. At the same time, less popular ones—foreign languages, philosophy—may be overstaffed.

Trend data on faculty work loads by discipline or program are necessary internal guides for campus management. Essential service programs must be identified and a core of faculty kept employed regardless of demand. But staff reductions in less essential programs to avoid overload in more essential ones may be the only solution to maintaining the quality of all programs.

23. *Period Between Closing of Applications and Registration.* As the closing date for applications moves closer and closer to the registration date, it is a sure sign that the institution is in enrollment difficulty. Almost without thinking seriously about it, administrators may move the date for closing applications nearer to the actual time of registration in order to attract more students— particularly if enrollment has already shown some drop. An almost certain warning is the moving of the closing date toward the first day of classes.

Institutional leaders should monitor the closing dates for application that are set by schools and departments. Reasons for changes should be identified as possible indicators of changes in student demand for particular programs.

24. *Drop in Application Rates for Admission.* If declines in application rates have resulted historically in enrollment declines, the monitoring of these rates can provide a valuable indicator. These trends are difficult to analyze, since students often apply to more than one college or university.

Monitoring of these rates by institutional leaders can provide advance notice of changes that may be required to accommodate the projected registrations, whether that number be up or down. Planning must account, however, for the differential rates found among programs and disciplines.

25. *Increasing or Decreasing Dropout Rates.* Dropout rates of students fully enrolled in a program give some indication of the appropriateness of the program for students and the general worth of it in serving its particular clientele. Under normal conditions an increasingly high dropout rate means that a program is not properly serving the students it attracts to the institution. Gradually

declining dropout rates usually indicate an improving program and teaching situation—provided the decline is not taking place during an economic recession. An economic downturn usually leads to greater retention and to a tendency for increases in enrollment.

Monitoring of dropout rates is essential, and the results of such monitoring can point out need for changes—for example, better screening of entering students, curricular modifications, or changes in particular faculty teaching assignments.

26. *Overload of Career Counselors.* Counselors can be overloaded with student demands for service if the students cannot easily find career programs that fit their occupational goals. If programs are limited in scope or if unemployment occurs in fields for which the institution prepares workers, the students turn to more counseling.

Counseling loads should be monitored; if demands increase, the chances are that the institution needs to examine its programs, class schedules, and the quality and appropriateness of existing services. An obvious caveat is that counseling loads may increase because counseling positions have been earlier victims of financial stress. They often are.

27. *Placement of Graduates.* Data analyzed over time on the number of graduates, their placement by type and location of job, initial salary, and other elements can reveal whether current graduates are doing as well as or better than those of previous years. Major shifts in any of these elements may tell the program leaders about outside environmental conditions that they would otherwise be unaware of. Shifts may also warn them that the program and its graduates are no longer viewed with the former degree of esteem.

Every department needs placement data, although the data are rarely easy to obtain or to keep current. If available centrally to an institutional research office, these data aid in setting internal program and personnel priorities.

28. *Reduction in Supply, Equipment, and Travel Budgets.* If supplies, travel, and equipment budgets in instructional units are cut or more carefully examined or if the time line for purchases is extended, the faculty should be alerted that trouble is really beset-

ting the institution—or that it is imminent. These items are highly vulnerable to early cuts at the inception of budget stress, usually following cuts in nonacademic areas and preceding cuts in courses, programs, and faculty.

Institutional leaders are the only people with both the perspective and the power to ensure that academically critical supplies, equipment, travel, and other instructional support are not reduced without careful consideration of their programmatic impact. Some reductions in instructional support may be unavoidable, but the reductions should be informed and selective.

29. *Faculty Salaries Increasing Disproportionate to Total Budget.* If the salary budget for academic personnel gradually increases in proportion to the total budget, then it is very likely that the institution is already in financial trouble and that cuts are being made in classified personnel and other nonacademic areas. Supporting services and related activities can be wiped out almost entirely if their budgets are used to offset inflationary impacts or to keep tenured faculty completely intact. Initial reductions should be carefully selected, and an immediate review—on an institution-wide basis—of all academic programs and support services should be made to determine priorities. If reductions are made hastily and without careful consideration, permanent damage to the quality of instruction can result.

30. *Increased Fees for Support of Selected Services.* If the state government dictates the initiation of a fee or a fee increase, the institution may not be in financial trouble; but if the institution does the initiating, it is a sign of internal money problems and of changing priorities. An early method of recovering lost resources when an institution is in financial stress is to charge fees for services that were formerly free to the student or faculty client. As funds become more difficult to obtain, the fees gradually creep upward; and the effects of these increases on the programs themselves are not taken into account.

Institutional leaders should have data available that relate fee trends to program objectives and constituencies. Traditional college-age students may or may not be adversely affected by fee increases, depending on the socioeconomic class from which they are drawn. Students from older age groups normally are employed and come from higher-income brackets, but this may not be true at a particular campus or for a particular program.

The art of supplying indicators dates back at least to the oracles of Delphi, and even today the selection of indicators remains mostly an art—an art informed by data and trends but still a matter of preference, not of science. Our thirty indicators are an attempt to cut the shapeless demographic and economic trends and threats down to a size where their institutional impacts can be recognized. The impacts will vary among the states and among campuses within a state, and institutional leaders must be alert to the implications of each of the many facets of stress on their individual campuses. Although not all planned objectives can be achieved in the coming decade, some, particularly the maintenance of program quality, can be—but only if senior administrators and faculty leaders are aware of the debilitating forces at work and if they do much more than simply cope on a day-to-day basis with the unexamined effects of an unknown environment.

For Further Reading

Over the past several years, John Minter Associates has been extensively involved in analyzing the financial condition of colleges and universities. Peat, Marwick, Mitchell & Co. (1980), in collaboration with Minter, has published a guide to assessing an institution's financial condition. Institutional administrators would particularly benefit from familiarity with Dickmeyer and Hughes' (1980) *Financial Self-Assessment: A Workbook for Colleges*. See also Ryland's (1981) brief summary of current state studies and a report on trends in financial indicators by Gomberg and Atelsek (1981).

❦ 4 ❧

Institutional Strategies for Responding to Decline

James R. Mingle
Donald M. Norris

Higher education's familiarity with retrenchment was heightened greatly during the 1970s. Despite continued growth in total enrollment, the Carnegie Council on Policy Studies in Higher Education reported in 1980 that 29 percent of all postsecondary institutions experienced enrollment declines from 1970 to 1978. An even larger number of colleges and universities experienced the imbalances that accompany enrollment shifts among programs, as students sought out occupational fields and shunned the liberal arts. As for financial support, it was a decade of ups and downs, as state revenues fluctuated with the economy, and tuition increases failed to keep pace with inflation. Highly dependent on the flow of state revenues, many public institutions had their first encounters with retrenchment when revenue shortfalls and midyear cutbacks followed the recession of 1974–75, the less severe downturn of 1979–80, and the recent tax-cutting initiatives in some states.

The experiences of the 1970s and the prospects for the 1980s led the Southern Regional Education Board (SREB) to sponsor a series of case studies to examine more closely the responses of colleges that had already undergone enrollment decline and/or financial cutbacks. We visited twenty institutions—public and private, large and small—in eleven states in the Northeast, Midwest, and South: states such as New York and Wisconsin, where past experience with decline was fairly widespread, and states such as Texas, North Carolina, and Georgia, where decline had been more selective. In the public sector, we were led more often than not to medium-sized regional state colleges outside metropolitan areas—colleges that had been especially affected by the increased competition for students and by changes in program interest in the 1970s. These case studies illustrate a number of substantial and creative approaches to the management of decline, refuting the folk wisdom that threatened institutions universally have been unwilling or unable to deal with adverse conditions. Combining our observations from these case studies with the literature on the management of decline, this chapter suggests practical and proven combinations of strategies for the coming years.

Causes of Decline

In few institutions is decline caused by a single, clearly identifiable factor. Declines in traditional college-age populations and changes in migration patterns are expected to strongly influence the prospects of higher education in general in the 1980s, but the future of individual colleges depends on a much more complex set of internal and external factors. Competition between institutions, changes in state and federal policy, and internal decisions that create the mix of academic programs available and the public's perception of an institution can all affect institutional enrollments—either countering downward demographic forces or exacerbating them.

Demographic Shifts. While the national projections of traditional college-age populations and enrollments show declines, demographic patterns vary substantially from state to state (Centra, 1978a; Carnegie Council on Policy Studies in Higher Education,

1980). Regional data also can be misleading. There may be, for example, a halo effect to sun belt growth, which obscures large areas where population growth is modest. In the South, for instance, Florida and Texas alone accounted for half of the region's growth in the 1970s (Smartt, 1980). Within a state, shifts in population from rural to urban centers and from central city to suburban locations, as well as changes in the racial and economic mix of a population, can have an important effect on college participation rates and on a specific institution's ability to attract students.

Public Policy Changes. One objection to demographically driven enrollment projections is their deterministic cast (Frances, 1980a). The level of enrollment, critics note, depends on the support and often inadvertent incentives provided by local, state, and federal governments. This was clearly the case in the 1950s and 1960s, when, as the result of federal financial aid initiatives, the participation rates of blacks and other minorities increased (Gamson and Arce, 1978). While not an explicit goal, participation rates of males increased because of education deferments to the military draft. In state systems, funding formulas, devised to minimize political conflict through an equitable distribution of funds, also served as an incentive to maximize enrollment. These enrollment-driven funding formulas continue to operate in many states (Southern Regional Education Board, 1978).

But public policy can just as easily have a negative impact on enrollment. Draft-induced enrollments declined after the Vietnam War. Public institutions in Wisconsin, when they no longer received full funding for additional students, began to revise their enrollment strategies and to limit growth (see Chapter Fifteen). And when states changed their policies as subsidizers of various types of students, some institutions saw an immediate and devastating impact on enrollment levels. For example, reacting in part to student unrest, many states dramatically increased nonresident tuition in the late 1960s and early 1970s, causing declines in institutions located near state borders or with traditionally national student bodies. When Texas reduced its support and increased its regulation of off-campus operations in the late 1970s, several public institutions suffered substantial declines in both enrollment and revenue.

Public policy can have a redistribution effect as well. Federally mandated plans for desegregation of formerly *de jure* segregated state systems in the South and Midwest have called for increases of "other-race" enrollment in predominantly black and in predominantly white institutions. The impact of these plans on black colleges has been the subject of great debate and controversy (Thomas, 1981; Godard, 1980b). In the South enrollment in the black colleges in the 1970s began to slow as enrollment in white colleges accelerated (Arce, 1976). In the latter part of the decade, public black colleges in the South began to experience enrollment decline (Mingle, 1980), although it is unclear what the specific impact of desegregation plans has been (Brazziel and Brazziel, 1980). Some black colleges, however, clearly have suffered short-term enrollment declines as the result of court orders that merged institutions or redistributed programs (Godard, 1980a).

The redistribution effect can also be seen in state policy. Private higher education has long protested that much of the growth of public higher education has come at its expense, but the expansion of public higher education has been justified on the basis of the expanded access it could provide for students from low-income families. Now, however, there is competition within the public sector—in urban areas such as Baltimore, where suburban and urban campuses compete against one another, and in rural areas such as South Texas, where a regional state university competes against new campuses and centers located in medium-sized metropolitan areas. Furthermore, enrollments at some public institutions, which once had exclusive rights to a popular program area, have declined as state agencies authorized duplicative programs.

Internal Factors. Despite frequent claims from institutions that their problems are not of their own making, we found that in most cases internal factors—specifically, the management decisions that shaped an institution's academic, physical, and social climate— contributed materially to the institution's success or failure in attracting students and in responding to external conditions.

In the regional state colleges and universities we visited, the academic program mix was critical. Institutions that had diversified their offerings beyond teacher education and the liberal arts had often recovered from the decline in interest in these two areas.

Institutions without programs in business, accounting, computer science, and nursing and other health-related fields struggled to gain the necessary state approval to initiate them; institutions with these programs sought ways to channel additional resources to these areas and to cover their flanks by opposing any additional proliferation of such programs by the state coordinating agencies. Some institutions, however, were suffering from negative reactions to curriculum innovations: interdisciplinary programs that failed to appeal to students; academic schedules that broke up the traditional semester or quarter term and caused confusion among prospective students; new programs, such as law enforcement, which provided a sudden increase of enrollment from a target group of students and then just as rapid a reduction when the market was saturated.

One institution caught in the 1970s with a troublesome program mix was the State University of New York at New Paltz. Located in a small town in the Hudson River Valley, an hour and a half's drive north of New York City, New Paltz suffered a loss of nearly 25 percent of its total enrollment in three short years. Much of this decline came in graduate teacher education programs. The market for such programs had dried up suddenly as the region's employed teachers completed master's degrees and new enrollments virtually ceased, since the school systems of the region were no longer hiring new teachers. Furthermore, with its programs in business and nursing only on the drawing boards, New Paltz was losing ground at the undergraduate level as well.

Beyond academic program mix, the public perception of an institution's reputation plays an important role. In several of our cases, administrators reported that changes in this perception, whether accurate or not, had caused enrollment declines. Reputation was viewed as a fragile commodity, highly volatile and subject to quick deterioration. At some institutions negative reaction to reports of drug activity or campus violence lingered on long after the initial coverage in the media had been forgotten.

Some institutional leaders also expressed fears that they were seeing a backlash against their open-admissions policies. They thought their institutions might be approaching "tipping points," where further increases in minority enrollment would result in declines in the numbers of white students. The manner in which administrators reacted to these racial attitudes differed. Most continued to pursue racially neutral policies, but some were making subtle adjustments in their policies—for instance, a lessening of recruitment efforts in metropolitan areas or careful assignment of dormitory students to avoid objections about roommates of another race.

While many of these factors probably had some impact on enrollments of new students, the social and academic climate on campus affected the retention rates of students already enrolled. A "spiral of decline" could be observed in some cases. A state revenue crisis or a drop in freshman enrollments could lead to expenditure cuts, resulting in physical deterioration of a campus, cuts in counseling and in student services, personnel cuts, and sagging morale among faculty who remained. The attitudes of students also were affected as they witnessed the conflict and deterioration of services. (In some institutions faculty and staff had directly enlisted students as political allies in fighting staff reductions.) The results were declines in retention rates and thus another round of retrenchment.

Resisting Decline

Institutions clearly prefer to resist decline, by seeking new students and new sources of revenue, before they try to adapt to a smaller scale of operations, by cutting programs and faculty. While the satisfactions for institutional leaders are greater in strategies that seek further growth, so are the risks. (See Levine, 1978, for a discussion of cutback strategies in public agencies.) Each institution must decide on the amount of emphasis to be placed on the strategies of resistance and adaptation—goals often pursued simultaneously. In shifting the balance from one to the other, timing is important. Because of the collegial nature of academic decision making, colleges generally require a long lead time to develop consensus over the need to retrench. Presidents may wait too long or feel that only a crisis will allow them to cut expenditures. Even when the inevitability of retrenchment is accepted, institutions may continue to employ strategies to increase their enrollments within reasonable limits. At some point in size, institutions have no choice: they must either seek to resist further decline or find some dignity in orderly closing.

The art of resistance to decline in higher education was perfected during the 1970s and has been amply discussed by others (Mayhew, 1979; Ihlanfeldt, 1980). Marketing techniques have been widely adopted and directed at traditional students as well as at new groups of older women, minorities, and employed workers. The institutions that we visited were at various stages of professionalizing their admissions and marketing approaches through the search services provided by the College Entrance Examination Board and the American College Testing Program. As did the Carnegie Council surveys of 1978 (Stadtman, 1980), we found many an institution combating decline through additional off-campus offerings, evening programs, flexible admissions deadlines, and new forms of conditional or provisional admissions. While we were more interested in creative adaptations to decline, we offer below some examples of strategies to resist and overcome decline which have the potential for success in a wide range of institutions. Unlike approaches that call for extensive new program development, these offer the advantage of generally being low in cost and easily implemented.

Retention. Retention and attrition have emerged as major considerations in institutions experiencing enrollment decline (Astin, 1975; Tinto, 1975; Lenning, Beal, and Sauer, 1980; Terenzini and Pascarella, 1980). Indeed, retention may be the *key* issue in enrollment planning, not just as a way of increasing enrollment but as a necessary means of dealing with the greater numbers of low-ability students on many campuses. Many of the institutions were making at least modest efforts to retain marginal students through special counseling and remedial programs. Not finding the necessary teaching skills among its own faculty, one institution had turned to the employment of local high school teachers. Despite pressing needs in many of the four-year public institutions, remedial programs have suffered from poor support from the state. As Glenny (1980) notes, states have failed to designate remediation as a major role of specific institutions and to provide the commensurate support. The result is a dilution of effort and "failure an almost foregone conclusion in the vast majority of cases" (p. 367).

When retention programs deal with students who may be dropping out for other than academic reasons, they are more successful. Western Carolina University, for example, has a comprehensive retention program aimed at such students. Faced with high attrition of freshmen who were eligible to return, Western Carolina undertook a detailed analysis of retention and used the findings to make several changes in institutional practices. Emphasizing that retention efforts would be aimed at academically able students greatly increased the legitimacy of the effort with faculty. (At the same time that retention was being studied, academic policies and regulations for continuation were being tightened.) Once dropouts were identified, the analysis compared characteristics of this group of students with the characteristics of continuing students: academic performance, student major, geographical origin, race, sex, and other characteristics. This information was supplemented by questionnaires to dropouts, which asked them about their current activities, the reasons they dropped out, and their perceptions of the institution. Findings were submitted to the university-wide retention committee, which made recommendations for changes in institutional practices. The institution found, for example, that attrition was highest among freshmen who were undecided about their academic programs; so it devised a career-planning program with substantial faculty involvement. Other changes were aimed at involving students in the life of the campus in order to increase their commitment to the institution. The admissions office began more aggressively to recruit prospective students from the western part of the state, since such students tended to adapt better to the relatively isolated mountain location of the campus, and deemphasized recruitment from areas where attrition in the freshman year was high. What distinguished the Western Carolina program from other efforts was its comprehensive involvement of the entire institution—admissions and academic support staff, senior academic officers, department heads, and individual faculty.

Improving Student Life and Campus Climate. It takes no special insight to know that the best recruiters (and the cheapest) are students who are already enrolled. As with a good movie, word-of-mouth news spreads rapidly as students return to their hometowns to praise or damn the food service, the social life, or the faculty. Yet student services are often the first casualties in a retrenchment climate. Some institutions, therefore, sought to counter the deterioration of these services by placing renewed emphasis on the quality of student life. For instance, West Texas State University responded to complaints about its food service and its dormitory life by involving students in setting policies and by turning over the management of the food service to a private firm. Winthrop College in South Carolina placed great emphasis on a strong campus-wide intramural sports program and on a general strengthening of its student affairs activities. Developing a sense of community among students and faculty also pays dividends.

Tightening Standards and Attracting Bright Students. While the regional state colleges we visited were not retreating from their open-door admissions policies, some believed that they were suffering from poor reputations among high school guidance counselors and prospective students because of low admissions standards and lax retention policies. West Georgia College in 1979 undertook a gradual policy of raising the grade point requirements for continuation at the junior and senior levels. Regional state colleges were also especially interested in creating scholarship programs to attract bright students to their campuses. Honors programs, while expensive to implement and difficult to sustain, were being considered at some public colleges we visited. The College of Charleston (South Carolina), formerly a private institution, has initiated an honors program, with rigorous curriculum requirements and special seminars. Riesman (1981) supports such programs in public colleges as havens for students and faculty in sometimes intellectually hostile environments. Programs to attract bright students are not a quick fix for enrollment problems, however, and, if overemphasized, can often conflict with an institution's goal to attract a broader constituency. Once attracted, bright students must be challenged; otherwise, they will depart dissatisfied, and the word will reach back to the high school guidance counselors.

Attracting New Sources of Revenue. College presidents have always been on the lookout for new sources of revenue, but with decline their vision has sharpened. It was surprising to find the degree of interest among the smaller public colleges and universities in raising private support from local areas. Many of these efforts were hampered, however, by a lack of organization and effective strategy for approaching potential benefactors. One successful effort took place at West Texas State, which had undertaken an aggressive campaign for private support to be used for student scholarships and to provide tuition waivers for faculty dependents. The most effective example of fund raising in independent colleges was at Queens College in Charlotte, North Carolina. This small women's college had experienced significant enrollment decline and faculty retrenchment in the 1970s. In 1978 a new president implemented major academic changes, which were directly linked to a financial campaign to raise support from the Charlotte business community and from graduates. The institution had long suffered financially from its image as an elite "girls' school," which did not warrant the support of the growing corporate community of Charlotte. Without abandoning its primary mission as a liberal arts college for women, the institution developed a small, selective, coeducational graduate program in business (which enlisted some of the community's captains of industry as adjunct professors) and an aggressive continuing education program. The results have been an enrollment resurgence in the liberal arts college, popularity of its new programs beyond expectation, and significant broadening of its financial base, through increased alumni and corporate giving.

Adapting to Decline

As we have seen, institutional leaders generally resisted enrollment decline in the 1970s. In contrast, as Mortimer and Tierney (1979) have predicted, the 1980s probably will be a decade of "reduction, reallocation, and retrenchment"—in short, a period of adaptation to decline. Adaptation implies reconciliation of institutional goals to new circumstances; it does not mean resignation. Adapting successfully calls for more than mere cutting of expenditures in the face of revenue shortfall; it calls also for careful planning in anticipation of decline, so that both the timing and the nature of the contraction can be controlled.

Use of Planning Tools. Although widely developed in higher education, planning tools still have only a marginal influence on contraction at many institutions. The most common way of dealing with decline remains a reactionary one. Contraction takes place only when revenue shortfall creates a crisis—and then first in the areas with the weakest political clout in the organization (such as maintenance and clerical and support staff, student services, and the library).

The SREB study set out to find cases where adaptation to decline was taking place in a planned and rational manner and where the institutions were reordering priorities and carrying out an orderly contraction. The most successful responses to decline were those that anticipated the changes in student characteristics, program interests, and nature and size of enrollment through the development of extensive enrollment-planning information. At several institutions enrollment planning was linked directly to contraction strategies. For instance, the State University of New York College at Plattsburgh, using models for projecting enrollment by program area, established a long-term reallocation schedule and enrollment caps for some programs. At Goucher College in Maryland, state-by-state projections of high school graduates and careful analysis of future market shares were the starting point of a comprehensive strategy for dealing with decline. (For a summary of the enrollment data requirements of planning see Chapter Seven.)

At the state level, the system offices and coordinating boards with the most well-developed enrollment projections also were those with the most advanced contingency plans for contraction. Analytical packages developed by state agencies provided comprehensive, detailed information and analysis on *all* institutions in the state—information that could not possibly have been assembled or analyzed by an individual institution, except perhaps by the state's major research university. The joint institutional-state process of developing projections also was a significant consciousness-raising activity for both parties as they discussed trends and ways of helping institutions cope with the likely future.

Enrollment planning, however, offers few clues to how an institution should respond to a projected decline. For this, institutions must turn to a closer analysis of their own institutional goals and priorities. Unfortunately, the all-embracing, gauzy missions statements of the past have offered little assistance to institutions grappling with a diminished future. Thus, a sincere and direct assessment of the university's mission is a key ingredient in planning for decline. It is unimportant whether this assessment is translated into a written document or is communicated in some other way.

Southern Methodist University (SMU) used the opportunity provided by its ten-year reaccreditation study to launch a comprehensive planning activity dealing with resource adequacy, quality, and mission of its programs. As a result of this activity, administrators had a sound basis for the program discontinuance decisions that had to be made at SMU. The University of Houston also used its reaccreditation in 1975 to launch a mission self-study, out of which came evaluations of academic program quality and centrality and subsequent reallocation activities.

One way in which institutions have "discovered" their missions is through a systematic evaluation of the quality, costs, and importance of their programs. Program review is not a new activity in higher education—just a more rational and analytical process than the one that served the institutions in the growth years. It can be conducted in any number of ways, with either external or internal evaluators (see Chapter Five), and it is sometimes an expensive, lengthy process with few tangible returns. Poulton (1978) found in his case studies that the process was not highly regarded by central administration but was considered valuable by administrators at the department and college levels because it provided them with information that could be used to improve their programs. One problem with external program evaluation is that it often focuses on issues of quality rather than on the "centrality" of the program to the institution's mission—a determination that often can be made only by faculty and administrators from the institution itself. Even given the limitations to the effective application of program review as a planning tool, we encountered a number of successful examples, which are discussed later.

Cost studies are key planning tools. Measures of student-faculty ratios, support dollars per credit hour produced, and other similar indicators are being widely used by institutions to identify programs that seem to be overfunded. Comparisons are made in two ways: between different academic programs at the same institution and between programs in a particular discipline at different institutions. At the State University of New York College at

Plattsburgh, these cost studies, combined with enrollment projections, were used to formulate a long-range reallocation plan.

We found that cost data or interinstitutional comparisons were being shared in formal data exchange arrangements among groups of institutions which had defined themselves as "peers" or through state and regional analyses, where individuals outside the institutions had grouped institutions for comparison. While problems of compatibility are continually argued, these analyses can at least alert decision makers to possible problem areas. Closer program comparisons, using qualitative factors, can then be made.

Because personnel costs consume such a large proportion of institutional budgets, effective management in a period of decline requires detailed information on the composition and characteristics of the college work force. Older faculty are more expensive than younger ones; and tenure is a constraint on an institution's ability to respond, regardless of its other benefits. Thus, the monitoring of tenure density has become a key ingredient in institutional planning during a period of retrenchment, so that managers may know the degree of flexibility that exists and can make appropriate changes.

The Reassessment Process. Institutions of higher education need more than a sophisticated array of planning tools in order to adapt successfully to decline. They must apply those planning tools to a process that can fund new growth through an internal reallocation of resources and/or provide a way of contraction in absolute size and scope. Reallocation has long been used, implicitly or explicitly, by institutions to maintain a balance between resources and demands on academic programs. In reallocation a faculty position is normally the unit of exchange, and the annual budget process is the vehicle. Some institutions focus on the need to earmark funds for new program development and have set up pools of funds for which departments compete with new program ideas. Examples of these are the Priority Fund used at the University of Michigan, the Program Development Fund at Western Michigan University, and the Excellence Fund at Oklahoma State University, where funds are made available to individual programs on the basis of priority (Karman, Mims, and Poulton, 1980).

While reallocation procedures controlled by central administrations have worked well in institutions experiencing moderate cost-revenue pressures, more severe declines have called for more comprehensive approaches with wider participation. For some of the colleges that we visited, the signals that "something drastic had to be done" were unmistakable: in private colleges cash-flow crises following years of deficit spending; in public colleges mandated cuts from state budget offices. But what about institutions where the impact of decline was less apparent, where leaders sought to mobilize their institutions before the crisis overtook them? In general, these reassessment efforts were aided by external stimuli. Campuses of the University of Wisconsin had been stimulated by the careful planning accomplished at the system level; the system, by pressure from the governor and legislature. Presidents of private colleges often received valuable support and prodding from active board members. Other institutions were inspired to action by the arrival of a new president—an outsider who brought fresh perspectives and a sense of urgency.

One stumbling block in initiating major reallocations or cutbacks has been failure to develop commitment and consensus from faculty (see Chapter Eight). In many public institutions that we visited, especially where state agencies (whether system offices or executive branch budget offices) held tight fiduciary control over the campuses, administrators were not even attempting such efforts. In more decentralized public systems and in private colleges with a tradition of faculty governance, "educating" the faculty was an important role of the president and the dean. At the University of Wisconsin's Platteville campus, for instance, when the faculty reacted with skepticism and surprise to discussions of impending layoffs in the mid-1970s, administrators concluded that in the future the analysis leading to retrenchment decisions should be done in the open and that the circumstances facing the college in the years ahead should be widely known. The result was the "Platt Map," a public display in the institution's "war room," of information on characteristics, performance, and costs of each of the institution's eighteen departments and five colleges. Faculty committees hold their meetings in this room, and departmental comparisons are readily apparent. So too are graphs of enrollment projections, whose downward slope faces committee members as they discuss budget priorities, tenure, and program changes.

Reassessment efforts involving significant cutbacks and reallocations should have a structure that allows faculty input. At Platteville it was an academic planning council charged with the responsibility of an annual review of each department. At Vanderbilt University two parallel reassessment panels were formed in 1979—one composed of faculty, the other of administrators. Both panels were asked to recommend ways to fund new programs and make quality improvements from the existing budget.

At Goucher College the administration and faculty have worked closely together to handle the problem of personnel cutbacks and program redirection. After years of deficit spending, this small, selective women's college in suburban Baltimore underwent a significant retrenchment in the mid-1970s, resulting in the dismissal of tenured faculty. These cuts—coupled with energy-related savings, a new investment policy, and a reorganized admissions operation—had eliminated the annual deficit of the college by 1980. Yet the administration remained pessimistic about the institution's ability to maintain its market share in the face of projections of significant declines in the numbers of high school graduates from Goucher's traditional drawing areas. In a report to the board and the faculty, the president noted that major academic changes would have to be made within the next five years; otherwise, Goucher would face the depletion of its expendable endowment—a circumstance that would probably result in the closing of the college. The administration offered a set of alternatives and appointed an academic planning committee to make an independent assessment. The faculty committee concurred with the administration and advised it to proceed with faculty retrenchment without regard to tenure—but only to the degree necessary to fund new programs that would increase enrollments. Rather than designating faculty to be terminated, the committee devised a productivity formula to be used as a guideline in retrenchment. Although there was bitter faculty opposition from some quarters, the faculty governing body as a whole approved the new programs proposed (in computer science and management) and declined to take a stand on the question of rehiring the terminated faculty. The

Goucher case is unusual, since these actions (dismissal of tenured faculty being the most serious) were taken not in response to an immediate crisis but to projections of what the future of the college would be without significant change. (John Gray, in Chapter Ten, comments on the likely view of the courts in this and similar cases where dismissal of tenured faculty is not a response to immediate crises but to longer-term projections.)

Reassessment efforts eventually must deal with the criteria by which cuts will be made. This, of course, is the great stumbling block for faculty, who are unaccustomed to having to make choices that will mean continued employment and prosperity for some of their colleagues and possible job loss for others. Even when faculty terminations are not involved, it is difficult for faculty to accept the idea that, without outside sources of funding, *new* programs and qualitative improvements must come at other programs' expense. Furthermore, at many institutions it is not a matter of cutting low-quality, marginal programs but programs viewed as laudable and needed but too expensive to maintain.

The reassessment panel at Vanderbilt developed seven criteria as a general guideline in evaluating their academic programs:

1. *Essentiality of the Program to a University* (required/not required). How central is this program to the "generic" ideal of a university? How essential is it to this particular institution?
2. *Quality of the Program* (excellent/strong/adequate/weak). The program's "potential quality over the next several years" is judged in reference to national standards. An excellent program is one with a potential quality matched by few institutions.
3. *Need for the Program* (high/medium/low). Intended to be normative, this criterion calls for the university's "own view of society's educational needs without regard for whether the members of society see them in exactly the same way."
4. *Demand for the Program* (high/medium/low). Demand for the program is measured in three ways: by enrollment of majors in the program, by enrollment of other students, and by demand for the program's majors in the employment market.
5. *Locational Advantage* (yes/no). Are there clearly demonstrable

advantages of the program's specific location at Vanderbilt? Geographical advantages? Demographic? Cultural? Other?

6. *Cost–Revenue Relationships* (favorable/unfavorable). Data on student-faculty ratios, cost per credit hour, prospects for external funding, and other measures are used to assess the program's status as a financial asset or liability.

7. *Cost Implications of Maintaining or Changing Program Role* (high/ medium/low). How much are the increases (or decreases) in cost required to bring the program to a desired level of fulfillment? [Vanderbilt University, n.d.]

With this approach, program judgments do not depend on a single factor; rather, a composite picture emerges, which allows the establishment of priorities. At Vanderbilt the first round of reassessment reallocated $1.5 million from administrative services and from athletic tuition subsidies to improvements, primarily in faculty salaries and in the library. At the same time, the reassessment committee, which had had difficulty in making precise qualitative judgments about the institution's many academic programs, suggested that several of the programs should be studied in the next round of reassessment for possible expansion or contraction. In a similar round of reassessment activities, Southern Methodist University used the same generic types of measures as used at Vanderbilt. Generally, the reassessment processes at private institutions were more comprehensive, embraced program discontinuance more quickly, and were bolder in thrust. The public institutions tended more toward incrementalism. A key difference was that, while many of the public institutions had experienced some enrollment decline, they had often been protected from precipitous revenue declines.

Cutback Strategies. Institutions attempting to adapt to a smaller scale of operations must somehow adjust personnel costs to match revenue. As a first solution to this central problem, institutions usually attempt to adjust staffing practices. Although the courts have upheld the right of colleges to terminate contracts on the basis of financial exigency (see Chapter Ten), colleges understandably wish to avoid both the trauma and the costs of such

action. Many institutions have increased their use of part-time lecturers and similar faculty appointments, as a means of reducing
costs and of increasing institutional flexibility in the face of possible
retrenchment (Leslie, 1978). For instance, at public institutions in
Wisconsin, some full-time faculty—those considered expendable
in case of a decline—are given fixed-term appointments. Since
these people perform all the functions of tenure-track faculty, it is
questionable, however, whether terminating these faculty would be
less traumatic than terminating tenure-track faculty.

Another way of increasing flexibility is by assigning faculty
to teach courses outside their own departments. At the University
of Wisconsin-Oshkosh, for example, the faculty selected for reassignment were senior members of departments, not junior faculty
who were still struggling with tenure and problems of departmental affiliation. Moreover, the faculty were reassigned for a maximum of only 50 percent of their appointment. Whether this approach could be as effective in other institutional settings, or in
institutions with heavy graduate programs, remains to be seen.
Glenny and Bowen (Chapter Three) note that such practices are a
clear signal of stress and can result in a decline in quality as faculty
move into areas outside their own areas of expertise. (For further
discussion of staffing practices and of faculty retraining, see Chapter Seven.)

Another solution to the problem of excessive personnel
costs—one chosen by several public institutions—is to consolidate
the administrative structure. (Generally, the private colleges we
visited were already operating with lean administrative support.)
Since administrators hold short-term contracts, such cutbacks can
be made quickly, especially by a new president, who can consolidate
upon arriving. A new president at West Texas State University,
where retrenchment had led to low faculty morale, eliminated
three vice-presidencies and required each academic dean to teach
one course per term (the latter type of move will receive opposition
in a union environment). Within two years of arrival at SUNY-
Plattsburgh, a new president had consolidated the central administration and reorganized the faculties of the college, decreasing
them from five to two, which eliminated several senior adminis-

trative positions. Interestingly, at both of these institutions, we did not find overworked, haggard administrators but, instead, a tightly integrated management team whose members welcomed the added responsibility.

A third solution, elimination of academic programs and departments, is the most difficult one for colleges to carry out. It is a method, however, of concentrating faculty cutbacks where they will do the least harm to the mission of the institution. Program review activities in the past have concentrated on elimination of "paper" programs, with no resulting impact on personnel; but in a period of retrenchment, these program cutbacks will involve faculty reductions. At Southern Methodist University in 1979, the institution discontinued academic programs involving five tenured and fifteen nontenured faculty. Some of these programs were viewed as high quality but peripheral to SMU's core mission. (See Chapters Five and Twelve for further discussion.)

Finally, liberal arts colleges and small universities that have difficulty in cutting back their limited program offerings extensively or repeatedly can adopt a fourth solution: limiting course offerings of existing programs. The first round of retrenchment at Goucher College eliminated the classics department and some foreign language programs; but by the second round, the faculty believed that the institution's current programs, which they viewed as the essential liberal arts core curriculum, should be protected. The college then chose instead to eliminate elective courses (and the faculty who taught them), leaving existing majors intact.

Whether institutions choose to eliminate courses or programs, the faculty work force will be reduced. The extent to which attrition is a viable tool for cutback in the long term or the short term depends on the campus setting and on certain characteristics of the faculty. Many of the faculties studied, especially at the regional state universities, were relatively middle-aged and were highly tenured, which did not promise much attrition through retirement. And since the academic market for faculty may decline even more dramatically in the coming years than in the recent decade, the possibility of attrition through turnover may also diminish. The extent to which attrition can be used depends largely on the success of the various reallocation and reassignment measures discussed earlier, which enable an institution to trim its operation while still meeting its academic commitments.

Conclusion

Higher education stands in various stages of readiness for the impending enrollment decline of the 1980s. The experience of the past ten years has given some institutions the motivation to prepare contingency plans, which include some reduction in size and scope. Others, sincerely believing that any retreat from growth is a sign of weakness, seek to exempt their institutions from the general decline through a strategy of aggressive expansion.

Unfortunately, many institutions continue to take these stands on the basis of poor information. An absolutely essential element in planning in the context of a general decline is substantial information about the size and composition of future enrollment populations. This information can provide a road map for an institution to identify its major resource difficulties and a way of mobilizing the necessary internal support for making significant changes of direction. Institutions where such data were available and appropriately distilled and communicated had better-developed contingency plans than institutions where the data were unavailable, poorly presented, or tightly held by administration. Institutions in a growth mode tend to speak of this type of planning as "marketing," while those cutting back call it "enrollment planning," but both consist of the same family of activities: an analysis of the characteristics, orientation, and geographical location of the students the college has attracted in the past and can expect to attract in the future and a realistic assessment of the susceptibility of enrollment to institutional policies. When that analysis is extended to students already enrolled and when student characteristics are related to measures of "success and failure," the institution has a comprehensive retention program on which to base changes in institutional practices.

In addition to enrollment planning, institutions must carefully evaluate their programs and activities in light of carefully defined institutional goals. Add a process of reassessment which involves faculty, and the institution has a mechanism for setting priorities and reaching retrenchment decisions. Faculty involvement in this reassessment process is of critical importance. While termination decisions on specific personnel are the responsibility of administration, faculty governance and advisory bodies must give academic direction to these decisions.

The range of cutback strategies developed by institutions that have undergone decline in the 1970s is impressive, as is the degree of reduction possible without apparent impacts on quality and access. None of the institutions we visited, however, had found solutions to the problem of low faculty turnover and the inability to grow through the infusion of new teachers and scholars. On the other hand, action rather than inaction in many cases had instilled new vigor—at least among the survivors. But our generalizations are limited to institutions that are not threatened with immediate disaster. Based on these case studies, we offer the following advice:

- No single strategy should be relied on for the whole savings needed. A combination of course-offering cutbacks, program termination, staffing adjustments, and administrative consolidation should be considered. The cumulative effect of the marginal savings from each strategy can be substantial.
- Precious time can be lost debating the likelihood of decline. Our advice is to plan for the worst and hope for the best. Early action is needed to mobilize support. Institutions that waste away the last gasp of growth will be worse off than those that use the time of growth to prepare for decline.
- Once embarking on reassessment and cutback strategies, an institution should be bold. Incrementalism is fine under conditions of growth but may not suffice under decline. In our cases the most successful retrenchments cut deeply enough to meet immediate shortfalls and to mount new programs or enhance existing ones. This second order of cuts will be the positive side of retrenchment.
- Finally, strong leadership is undoubtedly an element in a successful response to decline. The most effective examples of leadership in our case studies were presidents who were internally oriented—individuals willing to educate, cajole, and in-

spire their faculties and staffs to face up to the task of making choices. Striking a balance between the unacceptable poles of unilateral decision making and indecision by committee, these presidents and their academic deans carefully laid out the prospects of their college to faculty and worked cooperatively to formulate plans to meet the challenges of decline. As a result, these leaders often captured a wellspring of creative energy in their faculty and staffs, even those threatened by decline. As it turns out, uncertainty and inaction are probably even more disheartening than retrenchment.

For Further Reading

One of the case studies discussed in this chapter has been published in detail by the Southern Regional Education Board (see Burke, 1980). In this study the president of the State University of New York College at Plattsburgh describes the planning tools and processes developed at his institution to cope with financial cutbacks and decline. In another study Lee (1981) describes the experience of four Pennsylvania institutions with decline and draws conclusions about the different responses in the public and private sectors. For a description of the experience of the City University of New York with retrenchment, see Volpe (1977). The most comprehensive volume on institutional efforts to cope with decline is Mayhew's (1979) *Surviving the Eighties*. Discussing primarily the experience of private colleges and universities with decline, he provides strategies and procedures for upgrading recruitment and admissions efforts, increasing faculty performance, and controlling costs. Stadtman (1980), using a survey of institutions conducted by the Carnegie Council, describes the responses made in the 1970s to increasing enrollments and suggests strategies for the 1980s.

❧ 5 ❧

Evaluating and Discontinuing Programs

Edward A. Dougherty

Faculty and administrators in higher education have grown increasingly aware of the threats to quality and flexibility in their institutions—for example, the threat of shrinking state support for higher education. They are also aware of a certain "chilling effect" on quality and flexibility resulting from an anticipated decline in enrollment; with such a decline, they envision fewer new programs, fewer new faculty positions, and less revenue available from student fees and enrollment-sensitive funding patterns from public and private sources. Increases in programs for older learners and minorities may offset the overall population trend, and a higher proportion of the population may attend and be retained by institutions of higher learning; but, at best, these offsetting factors will only ease the decline, not reverse it.

Another apparent threat to the quality and flexibility of higher education is the low level of faculty turnover. Because the faculty hired at a rapid rate in the 1950s and 1960s are largely middle-aged, few retirements can be expected during the next five to ten years. Coupled with a tightening of enrollment, the overall result is a decrease in positions for young faculty members, who have traditionally been a source of new ideas that enhance the quality of our institutions.

Inflation also robs higher education in a pervasive and devastating way. Faculty salaries are declining in real-dollar buying power, and more money has to go to pay the electric and telephone bills instead of going into teaching and research. High inflation rates affect all areas of operation, but they affect some areas more severely than others, and the teaching and research support seem to be the most likely areas to come up short when the bottom line is totaled.

All these factors—shrinking support, anticipated enrollment decline, low levels of faculty turnover, and inflation—force faculty and administrators to look for new mechanisms that can help maintain or improve quality and flexibility. They know that an institution of higher education cannot stand still. New areas of intellectual interest will arise that ought to be incorporated into the teaching and research programs of the colleges and universities. Students will want to be taught new subjects and develop new skills. Government and industry will place new demands on the institutions of higher learning for research and service. Furthermore, faculty and administrators want to take a more aggressive stand in shaping the future and not just wait to react to a crisis as it may arise.

Assuming that everything possible is being done to stimulate external support for higher education, the only alternative for maintaining or increasing quality and flexibility in higher education is to look at the internal operation of the institutions. Bowen and Douglass (1971) and the Carnegie Commission on Higher Education (1972), among others, have suggested a number of changes that can be made to increase the overall efficiency of institutions; and in the last two recessions (1974–75 and 1979–80), a number of these suggestions were implemented. But the problems facing higher education in the 1980s require more than simply increasing efficiency. If quality and flexibility are to be maintained or increased in the face of declining resources, then institutions must begin to think about how to reduce the scope of their offerings.

Colleges and universities in the future are likely to be smaller and leaner. The challenge to faculty and administrators will be one of maintaining or increasing quality and flexibility as the overall scope of programs is reduced.

Two basic alternatives exist for reducing the scope of institutions of higher education: cuts can be made across the board, or they can be made programmatically. This chapter focuses on the strategies available to reduce resources programmatically, rather than across the board, because, in my view, only academic program discontinuance can help institutions deal with long-term financial difficulty.

Those who favor across-the-board cuts argue that such cuts are more equitable solutions to financial difficulties. The problems they create in the long run, however, are immense. First, such a solution assumes that the institution began with an equitable distribution of funds to programs, so that all cuts should affect programs equally. Even if such a perfect distribution did exist, the demand for teaching, research, and service is constantly changing, and across-the-board cuts do not give the institution the flexibility to meet these changing needs. Second, some programs are better able to absorb cuts than others. For example, programs with more endowment and programs with a high volume of research allow for the transfer of some faculty salary lines to research programs. Third, this kind of contraction will discourage the best and the brightest faculty from pursuing their work at a declining institution, and those who remain will begin to settle for mediocrity out of frustration (Cyert, 1978). Finally, at the program level, cutting across the board results in a decline in initiative because program leaders know that there is no hope of starting anything new, and, even if there were, the new programs are more likely to get cut than the established ones in the next round of cuts.

Another form of cutting programs across the board is to reduce them by attrition. Proponents of this position argue that this process operates as a form of natural selection. The problem with this argument is that the reduction of programs by attrition in no way corresponds to the demand for a program from students or those in need of research or service. Cuts by attrition are completely dependent on the randomness of retirements and the mobility of faculty. In fact, if one assumes that the higher-quality faculty are the most likely to leave, then reduction by attrition will affect the best programs most negatively. In addition to its uneven effect, the process of reducing programs by attrition is not usually rapid enough to produce significant relief from financial distress, even in the long run, because program directors will simply wait for more prosperous times to make the case for replacing those faculty who were lost in leaner years.

The argument for academic program discontinuance cannot be made on the grounds that it will help in the short run. There is a curious paradoxical relationship between program discontinuance and short-term financial crisis—paradoxical because program discontinuance would probably never receive serious consideration by faculty or administrators without some short-term crisis to stimulate thinking about it. Some sense of urgency, usually financial, is needed to get program discontinuance moving; yet program discontinuance itself is not likely to help an institution through its immediate, short-term crisis (Dougherty, 1979). Often, a financial crisis becomes apparent in the middle of an academic year, and the shortfall needs to be made up by the end of the year. In 1980–81 public institutions in Michigan found that they had to operate on 95 percent of *last* year's budget—after they had budgeted salary increases and set tuition levels based on an anticipated 10 to 12 percent increase. Because the governor has to end each year with a balanced budget, further midyear cuts can come—all of which have to be made up by the end of the fiscal year. Numerous short-term procedures have been set in motion to make up that deficit, but no one believes that the discontinuance of academic programs can be implemented quickly enough to help. At the same time, program discontinuance is discussed widely, and specific proposals have been made to eliminate some academic programs. But such discontinuance will be a response to longer-term problems, not short-term problems—a distinction not always recognized by faculty.

Academic discontinuance is a helpful mechanism for achieving long-term goals and should be viewed as part of a process of setting institutional priorities. It is a tool of long-range planning and priority setting. In order to set institutional priorities, several things are needed: (1) a mechanism for reviewing programs,

(2) agreed-upon criteria for evaluation and priority setting, (3) an organizational structure that will allow for program discontinuance and priority setting, (4) an understanding of the mission of the institution, and (5) adequate leadership that is willing to make decisions about what will go and what will stay. Before we turn to a discussion of the variety of procedures available under each of these headings, let us look at some of the barriers to discontinuance and some definitional problems.

Barriers to Program Discontinuance

Why do faculty and administrators find it so hard to discontinue an academic program? They often recognize the need to close programs in order to maintain or improve the quality of remaining programs and increase the flexibility of the institution to respond to new demands, but they find it very difficult to make the cuts. They are willing to tell junior colleagues that they cannot get tenure, but they are unwilling to close entire programs, even if doing so does *not* involve the release of tenured faculty. There are both psychological and practical reasons for this unwillingness.

First, as Michael (1968) points out, society is not prepared for decline. American society in general and academic society in particular find it very difficult to deal with issues of decline. After centuries of expansion, Americans have been socialized to expect growth. Contraction is equivalent to defeat and death.

Second, institutions are built to survive and to outlast the coming and going of individual bureaucrats (Deleon, 1978); they survive by adapting to new problems through addition rather than subtraction.

Third, organizations develop a certain "ideological inertia" (Cameron, 1978) that tends to support the status quo, existing policies, and programs already in place.

Fourth, significant political groups—including participants in the threatened program and those who have benefited from the teaching, research, or service of the program—will oppose the termination of academic programs (Deleon, 1978).

Fifth, there are legal and moral obstacles to discontinuance. Rood (1977) has outlined some of the legal problems, especially when programs are closed for reasons of "financial exigency." He points out that the courts have not clarified the meaning of the term and urges institutions to develop their own understanding of how and when programs must be closed, rather than allowing the courts to do it for them. Furniss (1977) and Brown (1976) have discussed the American Association of University Professors' regulations relating to program discontinuance. Although these regulations do not have legally binding authority, they do represent important moral principles of academic freedom and tenure that cannot be ignored. There are two problems, however, with the AAUP regulations. First, they try to separate financial and educational considerations in an unrealistic way. No educational decision can be made today without financial consideration. Second, the AAUP guidelines place the burden of initiation for program discontinuance on faculty. While faculty must be involved in every phase of the discontinuance process, they do not generally discontinue programs. The legal and moral aspects of discontinuance are important to take into account but should not prevent institutions from implementing priority decisions. (See Chapters Nine and Ten for further discussion.)

Finally, as Deleon (1978) points out, no one wants to admit being wrong in starting and continuing a program; therefore, policy makers will look for alternatives to deal with the problem. Policy makers also fear that discontinuing an academic program will do serious damage to the prestige and morale of an institution. These costs must be weighed against the long-term benefit that can come to an institution through enhancing the quality of remaining programs and increasing institutional flexibility to respond to new demands.

Definitional Problems

There are two major problems of definition: What do we mean by "discontinuance" and what do we mean by "program"?

Defining "Discontinuance." For the most part, discontinuance is a process that takes a time frame of nine to twelve months, or longer. A typical pattern is illustrated by the University of Michigan's discontinuance of its population-planning program. In the summer of 1976, an external review of the program was conducted.

The results of the review were considered by the dean and the executive committee of the School of Public Health, in which the program resided. They recommended discontinuance in the winter of 1976–77 and began a lengthy process of consultations with program faculty and others in the School of Public Health. The vice-president for academic affairs also held open forums and met with both internal and external groups during the winter term. The regents of the university finally took action in April of 1977, agreeing to begin the actual process of closing the program. During the next academic year, the nontenured faculty were given notice and arrangements were made for tenured faculty to locate in other units. Safeguards were built in to allow students to finish their work, and some teaching and research were continued on a much reduced basis. Several of the tenured faculty in the program left the university, and, combined with the savings from release of nontenured faculty, the school saved about $200,000 annually, or approximately 5 percent of its general-fund salary budget. This savings was realized only three or four years after the time the program was originally reviewed.

Discontinuance can also be defined as the "normal" process of shifting academic resources over a more extended period of time. Many faculty and administrators would not consider this process "discontinuance" at all, and at a place like Michigan, which has formal discontinuance guidelines, such shifting would not normally fall within the guidelines. This process simply involves the decision of a dean or department head not to replace a faculty member in a given area and to reduce the course offerings accordingly. Over a period of five to ten years, the faculty are reduced to the point that the program fades from view. This process is mentioned here because it may be important not to interfere with this ongoing process of change as an institution develops more formal guidelines for program discontinuance.

The normal process of shifting resources may not be rapid enough or self-conscious enough to meet the needs of institutions of higher education in the 1980s. In using program discontinuance as a mechanism for implementing long-range plans and priorities, policy makers may wish to narrow the time frame, so that both internal and external constituencies become aware of the institutional priorities and see the visible effects of the implementation of those priorities. An ideal case might be written that includes identification of a well-defined sense of mission, the development of operational objectives, and identification of program priorities. Program cuts would then be made to implement these priority decisions. Ideally, the process should be ongoing, and program discontinuance should be viewed as an investment in the future rather than as a one-time penalty for an overdrawn account. Just as industry is constantly eliminating unprofitable lines so that it can more fully develop profitable ones, so higher education should continuously consider discontinuance of low-priority areas in order to strengthen high-priority areas (Cyert, 1978).

Defining "Program." To protect against arbitrary decisions during the painful process of discontinuance, one needs to specify mechanisms for review, criteria for evaluation, and safeguards for faculty and students. The problem with developing such formal procedural guidelines is that they may be interpreted to protect vested interests, so that no change ever takes place. A clear definition of what programs fall under a formal set of discontinuance guidelines is needed to make them usable.

The University of Michigan guidelines on program discontinuance have an intentional vagueness about what should fall under the university's purview, leaving the question of program definition up to the individual schools and colleges. If the dean or the executive committee feels that formal discontinuance guidelines should be followed in the phasing out of a program, such a recommendation will be brought to the vice-president and the governing board for consideration. The advantage of this system is its flexibility, but the problem is that no one is sure when the guidelines apply and when they do not. Consequently, few programs have been brought forward for consideration.

One alternative to this intentional vagueness is to define programs by exclusion rather than inclusion. One can maintain the desired flexibility and yet clear up some of the uncertainty of what should fall under a set of discontinuance guidelines. In this process of definition by exclusion, only programs that cannot be handled under a normal process of curricular revision come under the formal discontinuance guidelines.

Program Review Procedures

The details of program review have been written about extensively in the last several years—for example, in the *New Directions for Program Evaluation* series (Jossey-Bass) and the *Evaluation Studies Review Annual* (Sage, 1976–1980). Some of the issues discussed in these volumes are particularly relevant to program discontinuance. Choices made about the review process are especially important because the review document will be the primary point of reference when decisions are made about the continuation or discontinuation of a program. On the basis of the review document, faculty and administrators will make priority decisions that will shape the future of the college or university. If that document has been carefully assembled through a fair and equitable process that allows all interested parties to be heard, then the decision to close a program can be justified and completed even in the face of strong antitermination opposition. Without an adequate review process and document, the whole prospect of discontinuance will be jeopardized. Following are a number of questions that need to be addressed by policy makers as they begin to think about reviewing programs for possible discontinuance.

1. What type of evaluation should be done? Dressel (1976) identifies four major types of program evaluation: (1) evaluation of needs in the broader society, for the purpose of developing new programs; (2) evaluation of resources used to attain program goals; (3) evaluation of the results of past decisions; and (4) evaluation of a program's attainment of specific goals. In evaluating programs for possible discontinuance, one should include elements of all four types of evaluations. For example, when the School of Criminology was eliminated at the University of California at Berkeley, it was reviewed from the point of view of (1) the broader social context and the need for people trained in criminology; (2) the use of financial and human resources; (3) the instructional, research, and service decisions made by the school; and (4) the number of graduates, research reports, and service activities of the school.

2. Where does the initiative for program review rest? Virtually everyone claims authority for program review: the faculty, the department, the college, the governing board, the coor-

dinating agency, the accreditation agency, and sometimes even the state legislature. In any event, the responsibility for initiating a review should be clearly understood at the outset. Only then can rational planning take place. At many institutions the graduate dean is responsible for conducting reviews. This was the case at Berkeley in the review of the School of Criminology; after the graduate school committee began its review, it was asked to look at the undergraduate programs in criminology as well. However, such cooperation between those with responsibility for reviewing graduate and undergraduate programs may not always prevail. For example, two separate review procedures were set up at the Riverside campus of the University of California. At the University of Michigan, the responsibility for review rests with the deans of the various schools and colleges and with the academic vice-president. Reviews done at Michigan are usually timed to correspond with the ending of a term appointment of a department head or dean, providing the administration with the opportunity to make personnel changes if warranted by the outcome of the review. Such personnel changes may be viewed as an alternative to discontinuance.

The question of authority becomes more complex if agencies outside the institution claim authority for program review. For example, the Regents of the University of the State of New York claimed authority to review and "deregister" doctoral programs. The Albany campus took the regents to court when they recommended deregistration of doctoral programs in history and English at Albany. The campus representatives felt that these programs were essential to the core of the university; the courts, however, decided that the regents did have authority to register and deregister programs, and the graduate components of history and English were discontinued. The Albany situation points out the importance of clarifying the question of responsibility for program review. Most campuses and state agencies have informal understandings about who will review programs, but as questions of discontinuance become more central to the life of higher education, these informal agreements may be challenged and more formal procedures may have to be adopted.

3. What programs should be reviewed? Policy makers considering program discontinuance can find themselves caught be-

tween a desire to review a few programs comprehensively and a desire to compare the quality of all programs at once. Berdahl (1975a) points out the value of selecting a few programs that can be evaluated in depth, so that faculty will not criticize the reviews as superficial. On the other hand, policy makers who feel the need to make priority decisions on the basis of comparable data will argue for a review of all programs. The state of Washington's Council for Postsecondary Education, for example, reviewed all Ph.D. programs in the state to identify duplicate programs and programs with low degree productivity. Once these programs were identified, they were further evaluated on the basis of largely quantitative criteria. This procedure allowed for comparable information to be gathered about this subset of Ph.D. programs, and some programs were eliminated as a result. Other state agencies, such as those in Florida, Louisiana, and New York, have reviewed all programs in a given field, such as nursing, at the same time, allowing for a somewhat more in-depth evaluation without sacrificing comparability.

State coordinating and governing boards are particularly anxious to make priority decisions and, hence, to compare programs on some equitable basis. Faculty and institutional administrators are more concerned with assessing the quality of individual programs and making judgments on the merits of each case. Such considerations may determine what programs should be reviewed. A combination of both approaches is possible. For example, indicators—such as student credit hours produced or the number of degrees granted—may be used to select programs for more thorough reviews, or all programs in similar areas can be reviewed on a regular schedule. In order for a college or university to make priority decisions, it must have some baseline for comparing program quality. Even if decisions about program discontinuance are to be made on a program-by-program basis, there must be some basis for making judgments about quality, and each institution will have to develop its own standards for deciding what programs will be reviewed.

4. What methods of evaluation are most appropriate? Gardner (1977) discusses five evaluation frameworks for higher education: (1) evaluation as professional judgment, rendering expert judgment about the quality, effectiveness, or efficiency of a

program; (2) evaluation as measurement, using some formalized instrument for measuring the results, effects, or performance of a program; (3) evaluation as congruence between performance and objectives, comparing specified goals or objectives with data about the program performance; (4) evaluation oriented toward decision making, providing feedback about the effects of previously made decisions; and (5) goal-free evaluation, judging effect without considering previously stated goals. Each of these methods has strengths and weaknesses. For example, the first and last may be too subjective, while the middle three may be too rigid and too narrowly focused for use in program discontinuance; yet elements of all methods may be helpful to decision makers.

Faculty and administrators in institutions of higher education have by and large looked for experts in the field to render peer judgment about the quality of a program. The experts will, presumably, look at measurable factors and trends in the program, such as student credit-hour production or faculty research activity, but the most important thing that the experts bring to the evaluation task is their judgment about what is important and what is trivial in the field under question. They are able to ask whether the faculty in the program are teaching the right subjects and pursuing the right research questions. The responses to such questions undoubtedly will be subjective, but many believe that the pooled wisdom of those in the field is the best source of information about the quality of a program.

The further removed the review is from the experts in the field, the more one must depend on factual, measurable data, and the more one will be subject to criticism from faculty. The Washington Council for Postsecondary Education was criticized by faculty at the University of Washington, for example, for its dependence on strictly measurable factors in making judgments about programs. Barak and Berdahl (1978), dealing with state-level reviews, point out that state coordinating and governing agencies may depend on internal staff studies and accreditation self-studies but also will use outside consultants in making decisions about programs.

Need for Timeliness. The Council for Postsecondary Education in Washington was criticized not only for its dependence on quantitative methods of evaluation but also for taking nearly three years to complete its review of Ph.D. programs. By the time the staff made recommendations to the council, either the institutions had already made significant changes or circumstances had changed substantially. There are, undoubtedly, examples from individual institutions of equally protracted reviews. The State University of New York at Albany was able to do timely reviews and determine what programs to cut in a very short time (two to three months) because it already had in place a series of individual program evaluations that had been prepared over the previous seven years. Without those more thorough reviews in place, Albany could not have done the job so quickly.

Need for Adequate Financial Analysis. In addition to timeliness, policy makers thinking about program discontinuance should also consider the importance of adequate financial analysis. They need to look not only at gross savings realized by closing a program but also at costs incurred by such things as possible retraining of faculty, "buying out" faculty with early-retirement options, unemployment compensation, law suits, and lost income from research grants and student fees. For example, the University of Pennsylvania did a significant amount of financial analysis in considering the discontinuance of its School of Allied Medical Professions. Analysts concluded that the closure would save money for the university only if the tuition revenue lost by closing the school was made up for in other schools or colleges. A similar conclusion was reached at the University of Michigan when it decided to discontinue its population-planning program. Analysts found that savings could be realized only if the lost enrollments in the discontinued program were made up by other programs in the School of Public Health without increases in their faculties. Thus, the savings did not come immediately but only as the process of discontinuance was completed three to four years later.

Degree of Faculty Participation. One of the most difficult problems facing policy makers considering discontinuance is the degree of faculty participation in the process. On the one hand, the administration does not want to imply that faculty input should be sidestepped; on the other hand, there is a danger of being "due processed" to death. As Behn (1980) points out, one of the differences between business and public agencies is that the businessman can make a decision and then bring everyone in on it, whereas the government bureaucrat finds that everyone has an opinion and wants to have an input before the decision is made. Higher education is on the same side of this dilemma as government; in fact, it may be even more prone to bringing everyone in on the act, because it is largely staffed by faculty who view themselves as experts and as highly independent entrepreneurs.

The problem of faculty participation is especially difficult in larger schools and colleges, where it is not possible to include everyone in the evaluation process. While faculty may be given the authority to shape the curriculum, they cannot exercise that authority except as departmental units, and departmental units are not likely to vote themselves out of existence. One possible solution to this problem is to have the governing faculty elect a smaller body to represent them in matters of discontinuance. Either an existing body, such as a college executive committee or curriculum committee, or a newly created body could act for the faculty.

Criteria for Evaluation

Just as there are numerous review methodologies to choose from when one is considering program discontinuance, so there are a great many criteria for evaluating programs and making priority decisions. Policy makers must decide on the combination of methods and criteria most appropriate for their situation.

Clark (1979) and the Educational Testing Service have devised a system for evaluating graduate programs that combines numerical rankings and quality criteria. According to Clark, graduate students and faculty can use this system to make reliable judgments concerning program quality. Measures of faculty quality are based on quality of teaching, as rated by students; average number of articles and book reviews published by faculty over the last three years; and amount of research being conducted by faculty members. Other measures used to determine the overall quality of a graduate program include the quality of students in the program, the "humaneness" of the environment within the department, the resources available to students and faculty, and the performance of program alumni. In addition, the review system looks at the clarity of program objectives, course and program offerings, admissions policies, and a variety of other operational procedures. While the system depends largely on peer rating of these factors, it does have the advantage of giving a comprehensive, multidimensional analysis of program quality.

Colleges and universities often evaluate many of the factors mentioned above in a less formal way. Typically, an evaluation will begin with a self-study (initiated as a part of reaccreditation) or a study by an internal review committee that will look at the historical background of the program, the demonstrated need it is serving, curriculum, students, faculty, finances, facilities, and support services. These internal reports can become a source of acrimony if decision makers decide to use them as a basis for discontinuance. The only way to avoid this result is to agree at the outset what criteria will be used and how they will be evaluated. Faculty and administrators, for example, could agree that a program will be judged on the basis of (1) centrality of the program to the mission of the university; (2) overall quality of faculty and curriculum; and (3) extent of future demand for students, research, and service in the area (see Chapter Four). They could also agree that available factual data will be collected and that a team of outside evaluators made up of peers in the field will make judgments about these three concerns. If these agreements can be reached, then an effective review can be conducted.

For several reasons, a college may decide to use a small number of overarching criteria rather than an infinite number of specific criteria. First, the three major issues that seem to recur in discussions of discontinuance are centrality, quality, and social demands. Second, these more general criteria can be elaborated on by the review committee to fit the circumstances of the individual program. Third, many faculty react negatively to long lists of criteria, especially if they have not had a hand in developing them. In any event, a clear statement of the criteria to be used in making discontinuance decisions will greatly facilitate the process of actually closing a program.

Institutional Missions

In times of retrenchment, institutional mission becomes increasingly important because it can provide the basis on which decisions are made about what stays and what goes. Alfred (1978, p. vii) asks, "Should [the institution] attempt to become 'all things to all people,' as in the growth years of the 1960s, or should it concentrate on doing well things that it does best and avoid getting into areas not central to its mission?" An institution that does not know what is central to its mission will eventually find itself stretched in too many directions, which can result in financial problems. When policy makers decide that it is time to cut programs to help the financial situation, they will not know what to cut without a clear understanding of institutional mission.

Defining mission can be a difficult task and can result in generalized statements that are open to various interpretations. In order for a mission statement to have meaning, it needs a certain degree of operational specificity. This specificity can take a number of forms. For example, an institution can specify the program areas or program levels it will include. One institution may emphasize vocational preparation, another may stress the liberal arts, and yet another may focus on professional education or graduate training and research. Some institutions may focus on lower-level education; others may focus on upper-level education; others may decide to eliminate undergraduate education altogether and focus on graduate and professional education and research. Specificity in institutional mission can also come in the form of qualitative definitions. An institution can define itself as offering programs to specific levels of students—some appealing to the very bright, others to the average student, and still others to the educationally disadvantaged. At Berkeley, for example, the professional schools defined their mission in terms of quality, while the School of Criminology was interested primarily in expanded access for minorities and women. The disparity in mission between the school and the campus was one of the factors that led to the school's discontinuance.

Specificity of mission can be quantitative as well as qualitative. For example, the University of California at Riverside has set minimum standards for the number of faculty in each of its graduate programs. If the number of faculty falls below the minimum, then a decision is made either to replace the faculty or to discontinue the program. This decision is based not only on numbers but on other institutional priorities as well. The quantitative factors do serve, however, as important indicators of the need for further study. Similarly, an institution could use enrollment to trigger further review. For instance, Florida State University discontinued its Engineering Division when student numbers declined in the mid-1970s.

A clear mission with specified objectives enables a college or university to develop priorities for decision-making purposes. On the basis of previous work (Dougherty, 1979), it seems clear that the programs most likely to be discontinued are somehow outside the acceptable range of institutional objectives. When a program no longer contributes to the mission of the institution, it becomes vulnerable. The mission may, in fact, lack clear articulation or may be arbitrarily redefined by administrators to achieve their purpose, but it gains the force of a well-thought-out statement in times of hardship. An institution is much more likely to control its own destiny and decide what it will keep and what it will cast away if it has a clear mission statement with specified objectives. The alternative may be to have an outside agency or the courts decide what that mission should be in order to preserve the financial well-being of the institution.

Leadership Styles

Program discontinuance is seldom initiated by faculty groups; rather, in examples to date program cutbacks have been the result of strong leadership from institutional administrators. These people are usually high-level administrators who are willing to make the hard decisions and convince others that the institution will be better off, in the long run, without the program under question. At SUNY-Albany, for example, cuts were initiated under two different presidents. The first began the process of program review and set up the mechanisms for arranging programs in priority order; as a result, nine programs were eliminated. The next president was the prime mover in speeding up the process of review and decision making necessitated by state budget reductions— a process that led to the closure of twenty more programs. He played a significant role in the process, sharpening the institutional mission and implementing the planning processes to support that mission. At the University of Washington, a home economics program was closed under the leadership of the dean in the College of Arts and Sciences. After deciding not to continue the program because it was not of high enough priority, he was able to persuade the provost and the president that the college and the institution as a whole were better served by reallocating available funds elsewhere.

Cyert (1978) points out that one of the major leadership tasks under conditions of contraction or of constant size is to maintain the morale of faculty while at the same time providing for the effective utilization of resources. Strong leadership is necessary to assure faculty that discontinuance does not mean decline in quality but may be the only means of assuring quality and flexibility in the face of declining resources. Real leadership will move the institution and its faculty beyond mere survival to a focus on the enhancement of quality among programs that remain.

Conclusion

Program discontinuance may be viewed as nothing more than a solution looking for a problem, but it also may be viewed more positively—as one of several mechanisms that can help maintain or improve the quality and flexibility of an institution in the face of declining resources. Discontinuance should be among the tools available for the implementation of long-range plans developed by faculty and administrators. It allows for the speeding up of the normal process of resource reallocation. Sometimes that process is simply too slow to keep up with the shifting priorities of the institution or the broader society. Sometimes the normal processes of program change are too costly to keep the institution alive and healthy.

Program discontinuance involves significant effort on the part of faculty and administrators, and it will not produce immediate savings in most cases; over the long run, however, the savings can be substantial. The closing of Michigan's population-planning program has produced an annual savings of over $200,000 for the School of Public Health. SUNY-Albany was able to realize more immediate financial savings to meet the demands of the state budget cuts, but its methods probably represent an exception to normal practice. In any case, long-term savings can be realized through discontinuance.

The advantages of discontinuance are substantial: the increased resources that become available to the remaining programs and faculty, the clarification of institutional priorities, and the increased flexibility gained to respond to new demands from the academic disciplines and the broader society. The alternative to discontinuance may be prolonged across-the-board cuts, which can result only in the dissipation of quality because scarce resources have gone to programs that are of marginal importance to the institution. Discontinuance is not a panacea for every difficulty. Although some may view it as an easy way out of difficulty, it is never easy and will consume the time and energy of many faculty and administrators, but the long-run gains can produce greater quality and flexibility for the institution.

For Further Reading

Further reading on academic program review, a subject that has gained considerable attention in recent years, should begin with Dressel's (1976) comprehensive *Handbook of Academic Evaluation*. For qualitative review of graduate programs, see Clark, Hartnett, and Baird (1976). The experience of the State University of New York with terminating academic programs is discussed by Fields (1976). For similar essays on academic program review, see Hample (1981) and Craven (1980).

6

Negotiating Mergers Between Institutions

Gail S. Chambers

During the 1970s Pace University, a comprehensive urban institution in New York, discussed merger with three different financially troubled schools—the College of White Plains, Bennett College, and Briarcliff College—with three strikingly different results. In 1975 the College of White Plains became a branch of Pace, with its students continued, its salaries increased, and its academic programs augmented by a law school and other graduate programs. Two-year Bennett College raised the question of merger with Pace, but distances and the nature of Bennett made it an unlikely match for Pace. However, Pace accepted some of Bennett's students and staff after Bennett closed and now services its records and alumni. As for Briarcliff, Pace had leased dormitories from Briarcliff and privately had urged merger for a number of years while Briarcliff still had financial solvency. When Briarcliff's bankruptcy became imminent, Pace offered to absorb students, some faculty and programs, and the campus. Strong opposition from the Briarcliff campus and a passing interest expressed by New York University delayed negotiations until Briarcliff ran out of both credit and cash. Pace underwrote the rest of the year's program and then agreed to pay off all creditors in exchange for the plant and equipment.

The different ways in which Pace negotiated in these three merger attempts, what it acquired, and the outcome for the different colleges illustrate sets of questions that policy makers and institutional leaders now raise about the merger of financially troubled colleges. Perhaps certain factors lead one merger negotiation to success and another to closure. Perhaps some particular form of college merger is more likely to be negotiable during the next decade than other forms will be. And perhaps there are ways in which successful mergers can be encouraged. To examine such questions, this chapter draws on case studies of mergers that have and have *not* taken place during the past decade to suggest what institutions need to know in order to locate and evaluate merger possibilities. Because of the conditions anticipated by this book and because college mergers usually have a dominant party, much of the analysis concerns a stronger institution "buying" one that foresees a future of financial exigency—a pure case approximated by all but a few college mergers. Also, because merger is usually a mixed blessing to the successor institution, this chapter looks for ways that institutions and others can help make merger a more workable option. Cases are drawn from a full range of institutional types, from seminaries to universities.

Types of College Mergers

Merger is a generic term used to describe a range of unique legal arrangements whereby separate colleges are forged into a single unit. Because these arrangements can be very different from one another, it is misleading to speak of "merger" or "consolidation" without reference to the actual legal structure established. In the merger of Western College with Miami University of Ohio, for instance, administrators on one campus discussed the arrangements in terms of affiliation; those on the other campus spoke in terms of acquisition and were excited about the uses they might make of their new campus. Both institutions were discussing merger, but their differing interpretations led to painful misunderstandings. And in the merger of Hamilton and Kirkland Colleges in New York, differences between the legal and the common meaning of "consolidation" brought the institutions within one vote of a court battle.

Institutions have designed mergers according to four basic patterns: consolidation, dissolution/acquisition, interlocking corporations, and a form resembling a holding company. In the past the most common form was consolidation, in which all assets and liabilities of two or more institutions pass to a new successor corporation and the previous corporations cease to exist. So typical is this form that commentary about college mergers often assumes this legal relationship. In an increasing number of cases, however, institutions are arranging dissolution/acquisition mergers, in which one institution dissolves while its assets and liabilities pass selectively to the other institution. Consolidation is the least flexible of the structures, since it perpetuates the interests of the separate institutions and at the same time sacrifices their original corporate identities. Dissolution/acquisition, on the other hand, allows selective perpetuation of the interests of one institution and retains the full corporate identity of the other, but it is more complex in execution.

While the dissolution/acquisition merger offers the clear advantage of selectivity to the surviving institution, it may not be the appropriate legal instrument if the use of highly regarded assets is conditional to the continuation of the original corporate entity and its purposes (for example, endowment restricted to a specific educational goal). In these circumstances institutions may choose one of the two remaining forms of merger, which are used to perpetuate the corporate identity of both institutions while still creating a merged unit. Two schools can "interlock" by electing the trustees of one to the board of the other. In the merger of the Parsons School of Design with the New School of Social Research in New York City, the trustees of Parsons resigned and those of the New School were appointed as their replacements (Haines, 1980). The holding company structure is even more flexible. When seminaries in Pennsylvania and Ohio merged their academic programs with New York's Colgate Rochester Divinity School, for example, each retained a corporate identity, the Ohio school to meet requirements of canon law and the Pennsylvania school to retain assets that its state courts might otherwise have directed to other purposes.

Merger Combinations in the 1980s

In his study of ten mergers from the 1960s and early 1970s, Millett (1976) found that either immediate or anticipated financial distress was the determining force behind college mergers. Both buyer and seller institutions showed the same concern, an institution electing merger only if it could save or strengthen its operation. The question is whether vulnerable institutions will be able to use merger to help resolve their difficulties. Their ability to do so will depend on the readiness with which weakened institutions can find willing partners. A forecast of industry strategy for the next decade may suggest where to look for such partners and what they will require. Forecasting for dramatically new conditions is, of course, chancy at best, but drawing an analogy to other industries that have undergone similar changes may be helpful. For private colleges the problem of matching service capacity to the needs of the public is a process analogous to the marketing function of for-profit industries. Therefore, this section looks at strategic market planning to gain insights into how higher education can meet market needs under conditions of competition and overcapacity.

In the profit sector, corporations can be characterized as "leaders," whose prices and strategies dictate what is possible for the rest of the industry; "challengers," who are seeking to displace the leaders; "followers," content to do business under the conditions dictated; or "nichers," who seek out markets too specialized or too small for the others to occupy. In the 1960s private higher education in this country consisted of a few market leaders (such as Harvard University and Massachusetts Institute of Technology), some challengers, a large mass of I-want-to-be-like-Harvard followers, and specialists serving constituencies not reached by the others. As higher education moves into an era of massive overcapacity, the "followers" probably will compete more intensely and seek both new uses and more usage for the industry's products. These trends are already evident. Declining institutions can be expected to seek new market segments, as they have in the coeducation movement, or to reposition themselves through changed programming, new images, and other marketing techniques. Under such a strategy, agreements might be sought with nearby institutions that offer dissimilar programs. Such agreements—in the form of consortial arrangements, federations, new affiliations, or consolidation mergers—would constitute a form of controlled shrinkage in the industry. Under a different strategic approach, troubled institutions might look for niches where they can concentrate their efforts according to specific competencies; an institution seeking to enter some new realm of service might unilaterally undertake a change of affiliation, a change of mission, or even reincorporation for different purposes. Merger by acquisition represents a third strategy for radical change—and a very powerful one—but only if the institution seeking merger is willing to use it for this purpose.

Despite the overall decline predicted for higher education, some institutions will find themselves growing if trends toward technical education and certification continue (see Chapter Two). Such institutions and programs will expand—especially in urban settings, where individuals caught in the "baby-boom" population are struggling to improve their job opportunities. Large universities and urban technical schools may seek new sites from which to distribute their services as they expand. They may also wish to expand their programming and diversify their activities so that they are less vulnerable to shifts in demands for particular programs. Such impulses will make these institutions amenable to merger agreements under properly attractive conditions, but they will seek agreements that impose no programmatic commitments or that bring them only complementary programs. They may find that geographical distance is an advantage well worth the managerial cost it imposes. As states strengthen regulations of off-campus instructional programs, institutions offering such programs across state lines may find that ready-made campuses are the cheapest way to meet requirements for library facilities and support services. The financial troubles of some institutions will mean bargain opportunities for others—those with sufficient cash to underwrite new units. All this implies that large institutions with strong cash-generating programs will be considering merger agreements in the 1980s but that these agreements will amount to some form of acquisition.

Understanding the strategic planning of stronger institutions will be vital to the success of weakened ones seeking merger partners beyond the two or three that readily come to mind. One of the best sources of insight may be an institution's own board members. In one case, merger between schools sixty miles apart was suggested by a trustee active on both boards. If there is sufficient time to plan ahead, a weakened institution might even recruit trustees and administrators from strong schools in order to obtain the connections and understanding needed to negotiate later with stronger partners. Then, even if a logical partner can be found locally, interest exhibited by other buyers can be used to strengthen the desirability of the hoped-for merger. Although no specific bidder of this sort was on the scene, Norwich University's acquisition of Vermont College in 1972 was partly motivated by concern for potential competition if someone else were to acquire the site. Likewise, the merger of George Peabody College for Teachers with Vanderbilt University in 1979 crystallized only after it became clear that others might mount their programs on the adjacent acres (see Chapter Seventeen).

While retrenchment mergers in the past have taken place among small, geographically close institutions, the more promising opportunities in the future may be found in strategic moves made by large organizations seeking geographical expansion, broader programming, and diversification. But these may prove surprisingly unattractive to the trustees of troubled institutions. The buying institutions will most certainly be thinking in terms of radical change for the colleges they acquire. Only rarely will synergy and minor economies of consolidation reverse the financial posture of programs unable to support themselves. Nor can a troubled institution expect an act of pure charity from a responsible board serving in a highly competitive climate. Change will be part of the package even if it is not negotiated as such, and it will usually come quickly. If institutions in trouble fail to understand that radical change is inevitable, they lose a great opportunity to help shape that change according to their missions and beliefs.

Cases from the 1970s

Cases in this section illustrate the complexities involved in merger between private colleges. Even though institutions will have somewhat different needs in the next decade, these cases may suggest approaches worthy of emulation by those interested in merger.

Research University and Doctoral-Granting University. The Vanderbilt University–Peabody merger represents the sole instance in the 1970s of merger between a research university and a doctoral-granting university. Peabody had been troubled by falling enrollments for a number of years when its board decided to seek merger. A history of cooperative programs on campuses adjacent to one another made Vanderbilt University a logical candidate. But Peabody approached Emory, Duke, George Washington University, and finally Tennessee State University, a historically black unit that had just been integrated under federal court order by merger with the predominantly white University of Tennessee at Nashville (Bogue, 1980). Discussions with those institutions stimulated action at Vanderbilt. Within a short period of time, an acquisition agreement was reached whereby Peabody became a professional unit of Vanderbilt responsible for supporting itself on its own income and endowment, following the elimination of the music program and most of the liberal arts faculty. Arrangements were made for students to continue at Vanderbilt, but approximately one third of the Peabody faculty lost their positions (Ferris n.d.; "The Memorandum of Understanding," 1979). Under these arrangements Vanderbilt essentially acquired a specialized college rather than a university. In the future other institutions unable to continue as a whole may find that such partial arrangements provide a way for their basic missions to survive.

Doctoral-Granting University and Liberal Arts College. Newton College in suburban Boston was a religiously affiliated women's college with about 1,000 students when it began to have trouble meeting its mortgage payments. It approached Boston College to arrange merger because Boston College needed land and buildings, making Newton's campus an attractive asset. In arranging a dissolution merger, Boston College agreed to assume about $4 mil-

lion in secured and nonsecured debts. It agreed to give severance
pay to staff and to faculty, for as much as two years in some cases.
Some staff continued with Boston College, and about one third of
the former Newton students transferred to the successor institution. Boston College underwrote placement services for faculty to
aid them in seeking positions elsewhere; very few continued with
the successor institution. Following the merger Newton's campus
was used to house about 750 freshmen and a law school. Except for
the benefits received by discontinued faculty and staff, this merger
resembled a property purchase rather than a perpetuation of institutional mission (see Millett, 1976).

Merger between St. Mary's College and Notre Dame University never took place. In the late 1960s, concerns over single-sex
education led these adjacent schools to consider a coeducation
merger. Although neither school was financially pressed, the boards
agreed in principle that merger would be worth discussing. Talks
proceeded and some administrative functions were combined before a lack of agreement over administrative and financial structure halted the merger. Notre Dame then opened its doors to
women; and St. Mary's suffered enrollment losses, from which it
has since recovered. Proximity and the trend toward coeducation
were not enough to overcome difficulties that merger represented,
at least not in the absence of financial compulsion to do so.

Comprehensive University and Liberal Arts College. The most
common form of merger in the 1970s for a liberal arts college was
one with a comprehensive university. (The three Pace cases mentioned earlier are in this category.) In the 1980 merger of Edgecliff
College with Xavier University in Ohio, church-related institutions located two miles apart had complementary missions. Xavier,
which had originally been a men's school, concentrated on business,
science, and secondary education, while Edgecliff, originally a
women's college, concentrated on arts, language, and primary education. Through a regional consortium, the schools had arranged
cross-registration but had no combined programming. As Edgecliff's enrollments declined to about one third of their 1960s' level,
it sought further forms of cooperation with Xavier University. This
led to the dissolution of Edgecliff College, the acquisition of most
of its campus by Xavier to serve as a complementary unit within the

university, and the continuation of students for the Xavier degree.
Institutions that had originally served the separate needs of men
and women for a religiously oriented education had changed first
to coeducational institutions and then united their missions in the
face of severe financial pressures on Edgecliff College.

In the merger of Eisenhower College in New York with
Rochester Institute of Technology (R.I.T.), financial pressures on
the liberal arts college provided the basic impetus toward merger.
Distance and legal restrictions imposed both by the Eisenhower
trustees and by competitive institutions in the region made it impossible for R.I.T. to use the campus as a feeder site for its existing
programs. Instead, a new set of programs had to be designed and
mounted.

Two Liberal Arts Colleges. While few mergers between liberal
arts colleges came out of the 1970s, the Hamilton College–Kirkland
merger in New York is an example of one that *was* completed.
Kirkland was established as a coordinate college in 1965 on land
donated by Hamilton, with loans cosigned by Hamilton, and with
Hamilton supplying $2.5 million in operating funds between 1965
and 1978. By 1977 Hamilton's financial exposure on behalf of Kirkland amounted to roughly one third of the older institution's endowment. At that time Hamilton's trustees were asked to commit
up to $3 million more over the next five years, so that Kirkland
could build its endowment. During its short independence, Kirkland had developed governance patterns and programs markedly
different from those at the more traditional men's college. The
Hamilton trustees faced a choice of continuing to support an educational cause that they did not think would work financially or of
undertaking merger with an institution quite unlike itself. The
cosigned loans made closure of Kirkland unacceptable, and its location made Hamilton the only reasonable buyer. After some equivo-
cation Hamilton decided to impose a dissolution/acquisition merger
on Kirkland, in which property, students, and faculty transferred
to Hamilton amidst "near riot conditions on both campuses" (Baker,
1978, p. 34).

Specialized Schools. Specialized schools that have merged into
private comprehensive universities in the 1970s include two law
schools, a teachers college, and a business school. The merger of

Peabody turned out to be of this sort, as did the more recent merger between Vanderbilt and the Blair School of Music, a non-degree-granting conservatory. These moves suggest that some institutions may adopt a strategy to diversify their research orientation with more professional units. As research universities continue to feel the uncertainties of federal support, schools with high-quality, specialized programs might seek merger with the universities, at least for programs offering some research or enrollment potential.

In the past, specialized institutions—especially the seminaries—have been more inclined to seek merger with one another. The mergers involving Colgate Rochester Divinity School mentioned earlier were of this sort. Shared philosophies and a need for economy were necessary in both of those cases. In the unsuccessful negotiations between Mannes College and the Manhattan College of Music, difficulties in raising sufficient financial support led Mannes to seek merger, but broadly differing instructional and artistic philosophies led to the undoing of negotiations. Perhaps for specialized schools with distinct philosophies or beliefs, merger cannot tolerate less than a meeting of minds. If that cannot be arranged, the best alternative for such institutions may be either merger with a diversifying university or an orderly closure.

Problems in Negotiating Mergers

Despite the variety of circumstances and outcomes illustrated by these cases, some problems are common to the process. The following sections draw on case material and managerial techniques to suggest ways in which buyers and sellers might approach the analysis of a merger proposition. It should be clear from the cases outlined that the most important factor colleges need to know about when negotiating a merger is the basic financial structure that underlies the process. In reviewing any agreement reached, courts will be concerned that all parties with veto power over a merger have been informed and have agreed to the outcome. In simplified form these parties with primary legal interests are (1) the distressed institution, (2) its secured and nonsecured creditors, (3) the strong institution and possibly some of its creditors, and (4) any public agency charged with protecting the public's interest in educational nonprofit organizations. Since state governments generally retain legal power over changes in the nonprofit corporations they have authorized, they may ask whether the change being suggested is good for the people of the state, whether it fulfills the trustees' fiduciary responsibilities, and whether it has any drawbacks that justify interference. Normally, mergers will be considered constructive alternatives unless they involve moving assets out of state, as was contemplated in the Crozer merger, or lead to closure of a campus in some politically desirable location. In order for a merger to take place, then, each of these four parties must be at least minimally satisfied with the agreement. This minimum can be expressed most readily in financial terms.

Not only must there be a set of financial gains agreeable to all, but there must be enough extra value for the successor institution to make the project worth all its risk and bother. When merger negotiations collapse, it is usually because the stronger party cannot anticipate financial gains from the merger and therefore cannot see how purely academic changes could offset the inevitable difficulties, the added risk, and the reduced flexibility. The following analysis seeks out a set of prices within which the institutions and the other parties can reach agreement. If such a set exists, merger negotiations can work toward a mixture of these and other considerations, which will actually form the agreement. Each party will do what it can in the way of a financial analysis, depending on its time and managerial resources.

Accepting Social Responsibility. In planning for merger, trustees are obligated to provide as nearly as possible the benefits underwritten by their institutional trust. All other interests can be measured against this goal. For instance, it would be closest to the goal of educating students to ensure that current students not be harmed. On the other hand, severance pay beyond what is contractually required actually may be against laws forbidding assets of nonprofit corporations to be used for the benefit of individuals. Therefore, trustees should not make the assumption that a year or two of pay is owed to those displaced by a merger. Specific contracts must be honored if possible, but tenure alone does not establish a vested interest in future employment and is an especially tenuous economic claim under conditions of financial exigency (see Chapter Ten). Beyond this, boards will be justified in making such settlements only to avoid rancor or law suits, which could damage or delay the merger. By the same measure, arrangements where property continues to be used for educational purposes may be more attractive than sale for commercial purposes, even if the resulting funds were put to educational use. In general, the trustees will fulfill their obligations by bargaining to dedicate the assets of their school as closely as possible to their original purposes, and by providing for some mechanism (such as board membership, contract, or a holding company structure) that will ensure this outcome. Trustees are the only ones in a position to take this long view on behalf of the trust. Constituencies of the school—including its administrators—can be counted on to raise their individual concerns. Confusion and a violation of trust can result if the board does not adhere to its primary responsibility in governing the situation.

Establishing Property Value. A basic source of confusion in negotiating any agreement can be the value placed on the weaker institution's assets. It is not unusual, for instance, to hear how some school "got a $70 million campus for $15 million in debts," when the figures are based on the historical "book value" of the physical plant. Book value is the figure least relevant in negotiations. Institutions may also talk of the physical plant in terms of its replacement value: what it would cost today to build a similar facility. This is also a misleading figure, since the buyer probably would not want to build a facility in the same location and exactly like the one being acquired, especially with today's higher energy costs. Market value is a usable figure but is difficult to estimate. It represents the price for which the campus could be sold within a year or two of being placed on the open market. Under bankruptcy or closure, the funds available to meet the school's obligations after costs would be less than this value. Negotiated value will lie somewhere between the market value (the assets could be purchased and liquidated) and the price the stronger school would pay to build exactly what it wanted for its own educational goals, unencumbered by the obligations and risks of bargaining with another institution. To bargain effectively, boards must realize that book value and replacement value are best saved for press releases, that market value may be minimal unless the campus is in a desirable location, and that the stronger school will value the facility only in comparison with the other options available to it within its position of strength.

Paying Creditors. Nonsecured creditors, such as suppliers or employees working without pay, should be regarded first in terms of contractual obligations and then in terms of fiduciary and other considerations. When Pace paid off Briarcliff's suppliers, it understood that it had no formal obligation to do so; over time, however, the reputation and good will generated by the act will probably prove to be a worthwhile investment. Secured creditors, such as banks, insurance companies, and governmental agencies acting as lenders, can be dealt with more easily. Their interest in the institution is primarily commercial. Where loans have been secured by endowment placed in escrow, creditors will be paid in full. Where loans are secured by real property, however, the resulting notes or bonds have a monetary value somewhere between the sale value of the property and the full amount due on the loan, as adjusted for the risk that the institution may not meet its full obligation. Because of this, the value of dormitory bonds depends on the stability of the institution responsible for debt service on them. Merger of a weakened institution with a stronger one actually increases the cash value of this paper. For instance, when Kirkland merged with Hamilton, its dormitory bonds became a "bargain" on the securities market (Bullard, 1979). Most institutions arranging merger in the past have not realized that this jump in value, which occurs whether or not the securities are traded, amounts to an unwitting gift to whoever holds the weaker school's loans. If trustees of the merging institutions suspect that secured creditors will benefit in this manner, they may be able to bargain for a restructuring of debt, which will make the succeeding enterprise more workable. Government agencies, which are also sensitive to the nonfinancial costs of closure, may agree to an extended debt moratorium while the new enterprise gets under way, especially if their alternative is to acquire empty dormitories and the ill will of a financially damaged community. If a region is already financially distressed, the Economic Development Corporation also may be asked to assist in restructuring debt.

Differences in attitude on this point can change the shape of a merger. According to Millett's account of the Western College merger with Miami University (in Ohio), Miami paid Western College for its property in an amount sufficient to repay loans from the state government, the federal government, an insurance company, and a bank. "A year spent in arranging details convinced Miami University that it alone was in a position to pay off the college creditors, and that it had to make few if any concessions in the process" (Millett, 1976, p. 42). Because these institutions apparently felt that repayment in full was necessary, Miami may have paid more cash for the property and Western may have received fewer benefits than if they had used their bargaining position to gain concessions from the creditors. On the other hand, in the Eisenhower College–R.I.T. merger, three federal agencies and two banks were for the most part delighted to avoid foreclosure, allowing R.I.T. to negotiate an extended moratorium on principal and interest, low interest rates, and no extension of claims against the other assets of R.I.T. Not only did this help lower actual costs of the merger, but it substantially reduced the merger's risk.

Assessing Risks. For its financial analysis, the stronger school will probably look at several alternative uses for the merged institution, consider the cash flows and likelihood of launching each, and assess the risks involved. If there are other options close in cost, such as building its own facility, the institution may do a rough capital-budgeting analysis to compare options. If there is only one realistic opportunity, however, and little time to make a decision, an institution is likely to use something similar to Bayesian analysis to arrive at a "go" or "no-go" financial decision. The essentials are (1) a rough figure for what the unit's enrollment must eventually be in order to cover costs; (2) extra costs of launching the plan until this enrollment is reached; (3) an estimate of any merger-created differences in the gifts and related income the institution hopes to receive; (4) an estimate of the likelihood of reaching the break-even enrollment figure in a given number of years; and (5) the interest rate an institution gets on its investments (in order to equate all the dollar figures to their value in some common year). With these rough figures, the stronger institution can estimate whether different possible uses of the campus are likely to become financial liabilities. If some attractive use turns out to be financially promising, the question then becomes one of risk taking.

Sooner or later, negotiations will face the question of risk. In the profit sector, risk is often handled through a "portfolio" approach, where more risky ventures are undertaken only if they promise a commensurately higher rate of return. Trustees may be influenced by this kind of thinking; but, because of their responsibilities to preserve the funds invested in the school, they are more likely to follow conservative investment approaches. They will want to know what can go wrong—with the figures and otherwise. A financial analyst can provide information by changing the figures to reflect different contingencies. The analyst can then estimate whether the project would still be desirable under a variety of "what ifs," such as changing interest rates. The analyst can also look for a potential cash squeeze, a situation where the cash demands of separately wise undertakings coincide to make the whole unworkable. Some risks cannot be assigned a monetary value, however. Those upset by a merger can tie up negotiations or alter the nature of personnel relations for years to come. Delays and misunderstandings in negotiations can also be costly. For instance, when the R.I.T.-Eisenhower merger missed a deadline for state approval, R.I.T. underwrote Eisenhower's new academic year without having any legal guarantees. It was also forced to reopen negotiations with creditors just as interest rates jumped. In the long run, a "hunch" about such risks may determine the outcome of merger negotiations.

In addition to the four parties with legal veto power over a merger, a number of secondary parties affect the process indirectly. These are the constituencies that provide resources to private higher education; their perception of the merger can alter the flow of personnel, gifts, or students to the successor institution. Because gifts from private sources cover on an average about one quarter of a year's expense for private colleges (Nelson, 1978, p. 98), the strong institution must take into account (1) how much risk it can undertake before it undermines its own fund-raising credibility, (2) whether merger will sufficiently stabilize the acquired operation to make it attractive to donors, and (3) whether the proposed merger will so confuse the image of the successor institution that its former friends no longer see how it serves their needs. A merger agreement may include adjustments worth millions in future gifts if these sources are considered when programs and traditions are negotiated. For instance, the Case Western merger was motivated in part by a felt need to consolidate fund-raising efforts in the Cleveland community (Millett, 1976), yet program changes that took place as a result of the merger alienated alumni reaching a point in life when they could make generous donations to the successor institution.

This illustrates a key problem in estimating the financial outcome of a merger: the important financial factors are interactive. For instance, enrollment projections depend on the mix of programs offered, and financial stability depends on enrollment; gifts depend on public perception of that stability and also on the mix of programs offered. For this reason a financial analysis must be undertaken for each of the programmatic alternatives being considered for a successor institution.

Seeking Legal Counsel. Because each institution's legal structure and setting are distinctive, merger requires early involvement of counsel appropriate to the task. The type of counsel needed will depend on the role the institution will take. In the Crozer merger, for instance, attorneys for Crozer drafted most of the legal documents because the corporation would continue in Pennsylvania and had to follow Pennsylvania laws. Under these circumstances the stronger institution was able to use existing counsel to review the documents Crozer prepared. In the Eisenhower-R.I.T. merger, however, complexities of the acquisition/dissolution merger had to be handled by an attorney for the stronger institution, who had special expertise, while Eisenhower's general counsel reviewed the plans.

Attorneys may find important legal restrictions among the following: charters of the institutions and their bylaws; the original documents for gifts and bequests, including those defining affiliation with church organizations; terms of anticipated bequests; contracts with federal and state agencies; personnel contracts; the expectations of accrediting agencies; zoning laws and building codes as they may affect changing use of the site; service contracts; IRS restrictions protecting the nonprofit status of an institution;

property deeds that may restrict use; trust indentures for dormitory bonds; and the legal timing for informing state officials (for more complete discussions, see Meyer, 1970; O'Neill and Barnett, 1981; Haines, 1980). Restrictions not only may affect the uses made of the merged college, as they did in requiring the continued appropriateness of Eisenhower's program to the memory of President Eisenhower, but also can determine the legal structure of the merger itself, as in the divinity school mergers.

Dealing with Labor. Even where merger brings an infusion of funds and facilities, discontent can arise from unmet expectations or the simple discomforts of change itself (Bennis, 1977). Most mergers bring far less favorable situations. Where unionization exists, faculty and staff have a forum for expressing their fears. Most private institutions are not unionized, however, and herein lies an additional risk for college mergers. Regulations designed to ensure fair labor practice in going operations may so complicate relationships that a merger becomes far more difficult to negotiate. Other forms of organized dissent can also be disastrous.

Strategies to avoid such problems are varied. In the Crozer merger, the faculty were asked to decide who would travel with the school's income and students to the successor institution; after a day's debate, faculty asked the administration to settle the question and asked their dean to negotiate severance pay for those who would pursue jobs elsewhere. The Newton merger was negotiated as a merger rather than a property purchase, primarily to provide a transition period for faculty to arrange their futures (O'Neill and Barnett, 1981). In the Eisenhower merger, faculty placed on one-year contracts were soothed by intensive involvement designing new programs that would require their services. In the Briarcliff purchase, a militant faculty was one of the assets Pace chose not to acquire. In general, approaches that generously support faculty or those that separate them straightforwardly seem to work best. The most significant outcome of the conflict resulting from this approach could be a committee resolution under consideration by the national AAUP regarding treatment of faculty members in college mergers ("On Institutional Mergers," 1981, p. 85).

This resolution could attain a significance of its own for merger negotiations if it ever becomes part of contract language between institutions and their faculties. It states, in part, that faculty cuts in a financial exigency merger should be balanced between the schools if they are of equal strength but otherwise may fall "more heavily" on the weaker school. By moving away from a strict financial yardstick for tenure dismissals, this approach leaves room for arbitrary dismissals at both institutions. Even strong institutions cannot afford to upset their own faculties by threatening their security through such an arrangement. Moreover, with provisions for adequate notice, hearings, relocation assistance, retraining, and severance pay, the resolution precludes the kind of timely personnel selection that makes some mergers workable. As a result, strong schools may avoid mergers that would retain at least some faculty positions and wait instead for less binding bankruptcy dispositions. Whether or not this particular resolution finds its way into legal interpretations of the academic contract, faculty and administrators should consider its effect on their ability to survive the times. While flexibility still exists to do so, perhaps the AAUP and other faculty groups should develop their policies to increase, rather than decrease, the overall ability of institutions and their faculties to survive the times, even at the expense of short-run job security for faculty at troubled colleges.

Estimating Regulatory Costs. One final constraint may have a significant effect on the willingness of two institutions to negotiate a merger: the cost in managerial time and forgone income of any delay in negotiating or mounting programs for the successor institution. An example of such cost can be found, for instance, in the time required to meet state regulatory requirements and judicial review. In the Eisenhower merger, new programs required careful and lengthy state review before the institution could begin recruiting high school students. Regulatory delay in the first year alone cost over $7 million in forgone income, while fixed costs for the campus and its faculty continued. Whether caused by regulation, administrative problems, or legal difficulties, delay in turning around a failing campus can be a costly disincentive to merger (see Chapter Seventeen).

Changing Academic Programs. Merger brings a major opportunity to change academic offerings. In marketing terms the academic planning problem is one of identifying and "positioning" an appropriate mix of programs for the successor institution, and deciding which of these programs should be offered at the merger site. Any single academic program must be responsive to potential income from contractors and donors as well as to student demand. Support from these additional sources may significantly alter the number of students needed to break even. For instance, because funded research at Peabody would continue after its merger with Vanderbilt, that aspect of the original college's work has been encouraged by postmerger changes. Institutions more dependent on enrollment alone will look to unmet needs of the student constituency. Careful consideration must be given to launching new programs, however, unless they clearly fit a "hole" in the market. Even in better times, launching experimental programs after merger has seldom succeeded. A more promising strategy is to select for the successor institution those programs that might be kept viable in a new setting, as was done in the Peabody merger, or to transfer currently successful programs to the new location, as Boston College did.

Along with program changes, a key issue underlying merger discussions is the question of faculty quality and orientation (Haines, 1980). If the programs offered by institutions before merger are similar, differences in faculty quality may suggest forms of merger in which faculty at the weaker institution are not continued. The educational philosophy of particular programs may also determine the outcome. The Carnegie-Mellon merger came about largely because the faculty at Carnegie were becoming increasingly research oriented while researchers at the Mellon Institute were increasingly interested in training researchers (Millett, 1976). On the other hand, in one merger the fact that the successor institution had no aspirations toward becoming a football power created negotiation problems for an institution whose traditions and loyalties were tied to the sport (Hodgkinson, 1971).

Recommendations for a Successful Bargaining Structure

An attorney with much experience in college corporate change states that the merger decision is usually made on the basis of three factors: financial projections, programmatic questions, and hunch. If one thinks of negotiations as taking place between adversaries who must mutually "buy" a deal, it is easier to understand what these factors mean at the bargaining table. The strong institution will probably be considering several options, including the various uses it could make of the planned merger. Using data that are rough, subjective, and frequently only directional, this buyer considers the following attributes for each of its options:

- *Strategic advantages,* such as expanding program or geographical range.
- *Value,* in terms of faculty quality, physical plant, and good will.
- *Financial projections* of the investment needed, the possibilities of a cash squeeze, and other opportunities forgone.
- *Overall risk,* including potential problems in negotiation, legal and labor risks, room to adjust or escape the deal, and the lack of any special competencies needed to succeed.

The selling institution will also consider a set of options, including various forms of merger, Chapter Eleven bankruptcy, an orderly closure, and pursuit of the status quo in hopes that the future will somehow brighten. The sellers will evaluate such options according to the following attributes:

- *Ability to meet obligations,* including fiduciary responsibilities, needs of students, aid to faculty and staff, debts, and service to the community.
- *Control* over the mission to which assets will be applied, in terms of academic traditions and governance structures.
- *Overall risk.*

Since each option will look different to different board members and each attribute will carry more or less weight depending on the background of the trustee, reaching consensus within a board may be as difficult as reaching consensus between boards. Laying out options according to such a list may help speed the process, but eventually a decision will be made on the basis of judgment rather than analysis. Unless there are clear gains that create enthusiasm for the merger on both sides, a plan for the successor institution will lack the broad support needed to see it through the difficult period of postmerger change. Mergers that should have succeeded have failed because they did not satisfy key individuals. This suggests that negotiators should conscientiously seek out items to trade that cost little to the offering party but have potential benefit to one or more of the other primary and secondary parties. Continued support of alumni organizations, for example, is almost always negotiated into a merger agreement. In essence, bargaining opens a market that did not exist before, and colleges have an unusual ability to trade in reputation and influence as well as in cash. Once it is realized that "a close and fruitful relationship" is possible, all parties involved directly or indirectly in the negotiations may realize gains beyond those necessary for an agreement to be reached. What is needed is an imaginative and cooperative approach, giving due recognition to financial and legal constraints but looking beyond them from the beginning to the possibilities of a constructive mutual effort. It will be more difficult to adopt such an attitude where the strength of the parties is unequal, as it is in the financial exigency merger, but doing so is necessary for a successful merger effort—or even for a harmless disengagement.

For Further Reading

A listing of mergers and closures in the 1970s by Fadil and Thrift (1978) provides a good starting point for further research. Bugliarello and Urrows (1976) describe the process of merging the New York University School of Engineering with the Polytechnic Institute of Brooklyn in 1973. In his discussion of mergers of the 1960s and early 1970s, Millett (1976) generalizes about conditions and methods of merger; but only five of his ten cases involve merger between private institutions. Meyer (1970) discusses the legal aspects of merger, and Steiner (1975) discusses sources of synergy in corporate mergers, showing some similarity to mergers undertaken by highly diversified universities. Kotler's (1975) work on marketing provides insight into the strategic goals of a college merger. Finally, O'Neill and Barnett (1981) include advice for trustees and administrators on merger, bankruptcy, and closure.

ᑒ 7 ᑒ

Managing
Faculty Resources

Eugene C. Craven

The academic vitality of a college or university depends on the quality of its faculty. Projected conditions of the next decade, however, do not appear hospitable for faculty development and, hence, academe. The long-awaited demographic impact is just beginning to manifest itself in higher education. Equally threatening is the prospect of further decline in real financial support. The combined effects of slowed economic growth, continued inflation, and greater competition for scarce financial resources could lead to staff reductions despite stable enrollments. In addition, colleges must respond to public and legislative pressure for further productivity while trying to address shifts in student academic interests, continued expansion of knowledge, and changing needs of society. All this must be accomplished with professionally less mobile, aging faculty and with fewer opportunities for new faculty appointments. Clearly, the way in which institutions of higher education manage their faculty resources during this period of decline will determine, to a considerable degree, the health of their academic programs, if not their very survival, by the decade of the 1990s.

Three tasks are central to effective management of faculty resources. First, institutions must maintain flexibility to meet changing program needs and potentially declining levels of financial support while, ideally, preserving some measure of tenure opportunity for probationary faculty and avoiding the layoff of tenured faculty. Second, institutions must ensure an acceptable level of faculty intellectual vitality and, thereby, safeguard and advance the quality of instruction, research, and public service programs. Third, institutions must respond to public and legislative demands for increased productivity, particularly in instruction (Smith, 1978; Mayhew, 1979).

Sound management of faculty resources is only one element of the broader academic and fiscal planning that institutions should undertake. Colleges should in fact establish their academic goals first; decisions on personnel practices will then follow. Furthermore, despite the generally austere prospects for higher education in the next decade, not all institutions will face the same circumstances. Although most institutions will experience some effects, it is healthier to adopt the broader perspective of strategic planning and contingency budgeting, in which retrenchment is only one of several possible institutional outcomes (Frances, 1980a).

This chapter provides an overview of various strategies for managing faculty resources, especially in a period of decline, and examines certain issues and tradeoff considerations that can arise from potentially conflicting objectives among the alternative approaches. The extreme condition of institutional fiscal exigency and tenured faculty layoff is treated separately in other chapters.

Policies and Practices: Who Should Do What?

Individual Faculty Members. The primary role for ensuring a high level of intellectual vitality on campus belongs to the faculty. Traditionally, faculty members have accepted the professional responsibility for keeping current in their own fields, adding to the knowledge in their fields through research and other scholarly contributions, developing and improving curricular offerings, learning new teaching skills and instructional technologies, counseling and advising students, participating in institutional governance activities, and serving the public through outreach programs. To lay claim to the title of *academic* is, at the same time, to be obligated and committed to the pursuit of scholarly excellence.

It is important, especially in a period of declining resources, that faculty members recognize the mutuality of institutional interest and self-interest. There is a clear tie between the intellectual vitality of the faculty and the academic reputation of an institution, by which students may be attracted to enroll in that institution. The tie between teaching excellence and the retention of students is even more firmly established. Furthermore, the nature and range of faculty academic interests can shape the responsiveness of an institution to public issues and concerns, which, in turn, can affect public moral and financial support for the educational enterprise (Mayhew, 1979).

But there are inherent limitations in academic self-renewal. The scope of some revitalization efforts is beyond the resources of the individual faculty member. For example, in certain fields knowledge has been expanding at such a rapid rate that it is becoming increasingly difficult for faculty members to stay abreast of the latest developments. Also, selective curriculum changes that would enhance the quality of program offerings transcend the efforts of any given individual, or even department, and can be undertaken only on some broader institutional basis. In addition, self-renewal efforts may be hampered by a lack of institutional resources or incentives, such as a lack of selected library materials, special laboratory equipment, sufficient computing resources, or adequate travel funds to attend professional conferences. Finally, faculty members are not immune to potential psychological and sociological foibles that can undermine self-renewal efforts. There is the fear of trying to master a new academic competency and possibly failing or doing poorly before one's colleagues. Or there is the matter of faculty parochialism (Honey, 1972; Seldin, 1976). Occasionally, certain faculty members become wedded to familiar practices or become convinced of the merits of a particular viewpoint and are reluctant to explore new approaches to the study and teaching of their disciplines.

Though indispensable, the efforts of individual faculty members are insufficient. It remains for other organizational units of the higher education community to complement those efforts in addressing the challenging issues of faculty resource flexibility, vitality, and cost.

Academic Departments. The academic department is the organizational unit where decisions can be made that most directly affect faculty resource management. A sampling of the alternatives available to the academic department can be grouped loosely into personnel practices, program and professional development activities, and other management practices.

In the area of personnel practices, a natural starting point is to tighten the academic standards of appointment and promotion. This is probably the single most important step in assuring academic excellence and, over time, in renewing the intellectual vitality of the faculty. Since opportunities to make new appointments probably will be reduced substantially in the next few years and since a new appointment could result in a lifetime commitment, each new appointment must contribute to the long-range intellectual growth of the department. Consideration also should be given to the balance of such factors as age and faculty rank. The age mix of the faculty has important implications for the timing of position vacancies, while the faculty-rank mix can affect instructional costs.

Other personnel actions concern the use of the probationary period and the timing of tenure decisions. An early decision not to renew a probationary faculty member decidedly unqualified for tenure probably is in the best interests of the individual and the institution, since an early decision minimizes the lost investment of both. However, care should be taken to provide a fair opportunity for probationary faculty members to demonstrate their academic potential. Under most typical circumstances, where a probationary faculty member does possess the academic qualifications to be considered for a tenured appointment, it may be advisable to observe a full probationary period of six or seven years, since this period of time offers individuals a greater opportunity to develop their potential and a longer period during which vacancies in tenured positions might occur. From the departmental perspective, a full probationary period is preferred because long-term commitments are not made prematurely and program disruptions caused by more frequent probationary appointments are minimized. A word of caution, however: it is not generally advisable to extend the maximum probationary period. Six or seven years is sufficient time within which to judge the academic merits of probationary faculty; delaying that decision may increase the pressures finally to grant a tenured appointment to a "nice" person of modest academic ability (Kurland, 1972).

In earlier days the tenure decision would have rested largely on considerations of scholarship. Today rigorous academic standards are still being applied to the decision; but careful scrutiny also is being given to anticipated turnover in the tenured ranks, to the projected work-load trends within the department, and to the academic specialty of the candidate (to determine whether it is a growing or a stable subdiscipline). Another factor—which, unfortunately, is beginning to demand more attention—is the estimated ability of the institution to afford the future salaries of faculty members on permanent appointments in light of declining resources (Bailey, 1974).

The desire to avoid the resource inflexibilities of a highly tenured faculty has led to a policy that has become quite controversial—the use of tenure quotas. The most common notion of a tenure quota is represented by the ratio of the number of tenured faculty members to the total number of faculty (Simpson, 1975). Proponents of tenure quotas argue that their use gives an institution the flexibility needed in the allocation of resources and that the quotas contribute to institutional innovation and vitality through the infusion of new, young faculty (Dill, 1974). Studies conducted at such institutions as the State University of New York at Buffalo, the University of Pennsylvania, and Stanford University indicate that a tenure quota of 70 to 75 percent seems to provide adequate faculty mobility and financial flexibility (Allshouse, 1975).

There are several technical objections to this concept of tenure quotas. First of all, some believe that a tenure-prospect ratio—estimating the probability that a new appointment to the tenure-track faculty will gain tenure by the end of the probationary period—is more important than a ratio of tenured faculty to total faculty. When a tenure-prospect ratio is used, a management objective might be to ensure each probationary appointment a 50-50 chance of tenure. Interestingly, such a management practice eventually would lead to a tenure quota of approximately 70 to 75 percent (Dill, 1974). Others assert that a tenure quota based on the percentage of faculty holding tenure is imprecise and possibly misleading. More important is knowledge of the level of financial flexibility in the department or the institution. For example, highly paid professors reduce an institution's financial flexibility more than lower-paid faculty do. Thus, a financial-tenure ratio is proposed—the ratio of the total tenured-faculty salaries to the total "hard-money" budget (West, 1974). A number of concerns can be raised about the potential programmatic implications of any quota system; these concerns will be discussed later in the chapter.

Another personnel option is to make greater use of part-time faculty appointments. Part-time faculty can provide expertise in specific curricular areas, often at a proportionally lower cost than full-time faculty members and without long-term commitment. Another alternative is to use non-tenure-track instructional staff. For example, a department could employ a greater number of qualified instructional staff on fixed-term, non-tenure-track appointments, with limited instructional responsibilities; or in graduate institutions, departments could increase the use of graduate teaching assistants in lower-division courses.

Among the tenured faculty, departments could offer an early-retirement option. Contrary to early speculation, this alternative will not contribute to extensive faculty turnover. However, its selective use can be very important in making timely qualitative improvements in the faculty and academic programs (Patton, Kell, and Zelan, 1977). Some institutions with successful early-retirement programs offer preretirement seminars to explain the benefits and problems of retirement and to prepare prospective retirees for eventual retirement by dealing directly with the fears and stigma sometimes associated with early retirement (Bouchard, 1980). Older faculty members may accept part-time appointments if retirement benefits can be structured so as not to jeopardize Social Security benefits and/or possible tax advantages (Hample, 1980).

In the area of program and professional development, the academic department can make the faculty aware of the full range of educational and financial issues confronting the department and the institution, by involving faculty meaningfully in ongoing strategic planning of the department (see Chapter Eight). Departments also can contribute directly to the faculty's intellectual vitality by reinstating such traditional practices as inviting visiting speakers and holding departmental colloquia and symposia. These practices can be enhanced by inviting a visiting scholar to lead a series of seminars on a theme of interdepartmental interest throughout the academic term or year. Departments also can create endowed chairs for outstanding visiting scholars and can add vitality to their programs by participating occasionally in direct faculty exchanges with corresponding departments in peer institutions.

Another essential component of faculty development is a comprehensive program for the evaluation of instruction. As one dimension of a comprehensive evaluation program, many departments design and implement a mechanism for student evaluation of instruction on a regular basis. Although student evaluations are not without problems of validity and objectivity, a well-designed evaluation instrument and proper instruction of the students in the use of the instrument can alleviate many of the perceived shortcomings. Faculty members also can engage in a form of self-evaluation as well, by filling out the same form as the students and comparing the results. Another effective method of instructional evaluation is class visitation by colleagues. Faculty members can receive helpful feedback by asking trusted colleagues to attend one or more of their class sessions and provide informal assessments of their teaching styles. Additionally, departments can provide systematic, on-the-job training for graduate teaching assistants in order to improve the quality of instruction in lower-division courses taught by the teaching assistants.

Several other management practices supportive of faculty intellectual renewal can be pursued at the department level. Centra (1978b) and Furniss (1981a) suggest that a department head can conduct annual conferences with each faculty member of the department. The purpose of these annual conferences might be to review the accomplishments of the prior year, to examine possible problems concerning the faculty member's performance or departmental operations, to explore future professional needs and aspirations of the faculty member, and to discuss the academic goals of the department. One result of such an annual conference could be a "growth contract" drawn up by the faculty member and approved by the department head. The growth contract could build on the faculty member's academic strengths and could address weaknesses by establishing specific objectives of professional development in the year ahead. Such a contract could provide a basis on which to evaluate a faculty member's academic progress during the annual conference in the following year. The practice of growth contracts could be reinforced by a department-wide policy aimed at setting aside an established percentage of each faculty member's work load for teaching improvements and professional development activities.

Annual conferences and growth contracts can contribute to sound management practice, particularly in organizations with clear hierarchical relationships. There is some doubt, however, whether these practices are feasible or appropriate in a collegial structure where the department head, often elected for limited service on a rotating basis, is at most "first among equals" and is not likely to be accorded such review authority by peers.

Finally, departments, insofar as possible, should protect the faculty travel budget for professional conferences. In a time of austere budgets eroded by inflation, the travel portion of departmental budgets often is one of the first casualties in budget adjustment exercises. Faculty participation in scholarly conferences is so important to the intellectual life of the higher education community, however, that departments should even consider the unpleasant possibility of releasing someone in order to maintain an adequate travel budget (Bailey, 1974).

Institutions. The role of institutions (and schools and colleges within institutions) in the management of faculty resources is to facilitate the work of the academic departments and to achieve those objectives of resource flexibility, intellectual renewal, and fiscal accountability that are beyond the capabilities of individual departments. Like the academic departments, institutional contributions to faculty resource management can be summarized in three categories: general management practices, personnel practices, and program and professional development.

Of highest priority are the general management tasks of informing the faculty about the issues facing the institution and of seeking greater faculty involvement in the institution's destiny. The faculty can be informed properly on the issues only if the administration and faculty governance bodies communicate regularly with the academic community. Periodic updates on the state of the institution—focusing on selected data indicators, such as those identified in Chapter Three—can effectively illuminate the issues. Some institutions prepare and distribute quarterly reports for this purpose (Toombs, 1975). Increased faculty enlightenment on matters of institutional concern is of little value, however, unless it leads to the productive involvement of faculty members in the future of their institution.

A number of steps can be taken at the institutional level to improve the quality and responsiveness of the curriculum and to deal with rising instructional costs. In times of change, it is prudent for an institution to assess its environment and to review the appropriateness of its mission. When the institution has developed a clear sense of mission, program offerings should be evaluated in light of the stated mission. Programs essential to that mission can then be enhanced or added, and more peripheral programs can be cut back or eliminated. Institutions can make specific program offerings more cost-effective and, at the same time, preserve or even improve quality by (1) eliminating course duplication, such as discipline-specific courses in descriptive statistics; (2) making reasonable use of independent study; (3) allowing short-term experimental course offerings as an incentive to faculty creative interests, where such courses need not require approval through normal review channels; (4) introducing minicourses on a faculty overload basis; and (5) offering needed special courses by means of adjunct faculty, if necessary. Since institutions will continue to face public and legislative pressures to increase productivity, institutional policies may be required to increase average class sizes and the average teaching load to levels somewhere between those of the 1940s and the late 1960s (Mayhew, 1979). The combination of a firmed-up curriculum and increased productivity, in turn, could spell the need for fewer instructional staff.

Two other measures can aid in achieving more effective fiscal management of faculty resources. The first is to consolidate all funds currently being applied to faculty development activities, so that the dollars can be administered, at least in part, on a proposal-and-peer-review basis for the most pressing needs within the institution. Toombs (1975) has recommended that 1 or 2 percent of the institution's base budget be reallocated for faculty development purposes. The second measure, appropriate only for larger, research-oriented institutions, is the financial self-sufficiency approach of "every tub on its own bottom," as practiced at Harvard University. This approach decentralizes resource decision making and places even greater authority and responsibility for faculty resource management in the organizational units engaged directly in day-to-day academic program planning and implementation.

Probably the most fundamental management practice is the development of an effective information system and analytical capability. Institutions must have at their disposal information with which to answer such questions as these:

- What is the projected enrollment level for the institution over the next ten years? What are the anticipated academic program enrollments in the next three or four years? What is the expected mix of students in terms of full-time/part-time status, student classification, and age distribution? What have been the retention rates for various groups of students and how might these be improved?

- What are the student-credit trends by department, and what are the projected student work loads by department during the next three or four years? What is the anticipated service load of each department? What is the trend in average section size by type of instruction in each department? What are the unit costs of instruction by department and by degree program?

- What are the historical and projected rates of faculty appointment, promotion, tenure granting, and separation? What is the current profile of faculty resources by rank, tenure status, and age? What is the ratio of all faculty to non-tenure-track instructional staff? What is the trend in faculty average work loads by department?

- What is the average compensation by faculty rank and department, and are these compensation levels competitive with those of faculty in peer institutions?
- What are the projected revenues by source for the institution? What are the expenditure patterns by category? Is there a more mission-effective way to allocate funds within the institution?

Ideally, the information necessary to answer such planning and evaluation questions is valid, reliable, timely, and available in a form useful for decision making. To ensure responsive information systems, top-level administrators should learn the rudiments of what constitutes effective information decision systems, should support their development, and should insist on their effective performance (Craven, 1975).

Several analytical tools of particular value in managing faculty resources should be noted. With the use of computer-based models, patterns of faculty appointment, promotion, tenure granting, and separation can be analyzed at the institutional or the school or college level. Decision makers can model various future states by adopting different assumptions. (See Oliver, 1969; LaSalle, 1972; Hopkins, 1973; Scott and Taylor, 1973; Nevison, 1980.) Another useful analytical tool is the Education Financial Planning Model (EFPM) developed by the Interuniversity Communications Council (EDUCOM). The name of this analytical package is a misnomer in two respects. First, it is not a fixed model, designed only for a single purpose. Rather, it is a computer-based modeling language. The language contains features that permit a user to define relationships among selected variables and to project the results over a ten-year horizon. Second, the flexibility afforded by the modeling language does not limit its application to financial planning. Thus, this software offers a quick and flexible tool for projecting and analyzing a wide range of quantitative relationships.

Fewer personnel practices for managing faculty resources are available at the institutional level than at the department level. Principal among the institutional alternatives are the practices of reclaiming vacant faculty positions and of requiring departmental rejustification of these vacated positions. Institutional administrators can then assess the relative priority of claims on those resources across the entire institution and make better use of those resources by reallocating the positions to program areas of greatest need. The practice of allowing faculty members who are nearing retirement the option of working part time has been discussed in regard to the departmental strategies. A variation on this practice is to provide some opportunity for part-time faculty employment in nonacademic jobs on campus.

Normally, the institution is the agent responsible for seeking adequate compensation for the faculty, except perhaps in multi-campus systems. The compensation provided must be competitive nationally with that of peer institutions; otherwise, the institution will be unable to safeguard the quality of its programs by attracting and retaining young faculty members with scholarly promise and senior faculty members of established academic stature. This challenge will become increasingly difficult to meet in the foreseeable future.

Finally, the institution can exercise several personnel measures under emergency conditions short of those requiring faculty layoff. The institution can issue a temporary freeze on all hiring of personnel. Faculty also can be placed on reduced appointment, such as working a four-day week. And, although it seems out of character with current societal values, a faculty also could opt to receive a reduced salary in the interest of maximizing continued employment for the greatest number of its members. During the economic depression of the 1930s, faculty frequently chose this course of action. It is questionable, however, whether this alternative is viable in an inflationary economy. Furthermore, the increased emphasis on the legal protection of individual rights might diminish the corporate legal authority of institutions to take such collective action.

In the area of program and professional development, most institutions of higher education administer a sabbatical leave program and grant leaves without pay to faculty for purposes of further study, research, and academic renewal. In some instances, these traditional approaches to faculty development may not be used to best advantage, either by individual faculty members or by the institution. The availability of these programs should be communicated widely to the faculty, so that there is a high utilization of such opportunities. In addition, the interests of the institution might be better served, perhaps, if the purpose of these programs were defined in such a way as to encourage a balance between the interests of the individual faculty member and the programmatic needs of the institution.

In a review of current institutional practices, Centra (1978b) found that one of the most effective approaches to faculty development and teaching improvement is a program of small grants, since the relatively modest investment required to establish such a program produces tangible results and boosts faculty morale. Typically, awards are made to faculty members whose grant proposals have been favorably reviewed by their peers. Here again, the institution has an opportunity through policy action to define the general purpose of a grant program (for example, teaching improvement) and, in this way, to ensure that institutional priorities will be addressed while providing grantees latitude of inquiry within the general parameters of the program.

Whereas faculty often use sabbatical leaves, leaves without pay, and small grants to renew themselves in their primary fields, there is an increasing institutional need to offer faculty members opportunities to increase their range of academic expertise or intellectual mobility, so that faculty resources may be shifted to meet changing program needs. For example, institutions could encourage faculty members to develop and participate in multidisciplinary programs and could assign faculty members to joint appointments between academic departments. A more radical alternative to overcoming the limitations sometimes posed by the departmental structure is to encourage a collateral system of colleague groups and allow faculty members to devote a portion of their assigned time to work in a colleague group. Each colleague group would be defined by the shared academic interests of the participating faculty members; the focus of a colleague group typically would be multidisciplinary and problem oriented. Such information groups would be dynamic—forming, evolving, and disbanding in response to scholarly needs unmet by the work of the academic departments. One practical difficulty with this approach, however, is that current tenure and promotion criteria might not recognize the scholarly value of such interdisciplinary activity and thereby discourage the participation of untenured faculty (Group for Human Development in Higher Education, 1974).

A more direct approach to match an existing faculty with changing student interests is faculty retraining, where selected faculty members are given the opportunity to become proficient in additional academic fields, usually through a period of graduate study. The exact nature and length of a retraining program required to prepare a faculty member to teach in a different field are dependent on the "academic distance" traveled. An institution is probably well advised to initiate a faculty-retraining program by selecting a few cases where the academic distance involved is relatively short and, consequently, the transition easily facilitated. As an institution encounters increased disparities between patterns of student demand and available faculty resources, more extreme examples of retraining may be required. The inherent nature of faculty retraining prevents it from being used on a broad scale. In addition, faculty members may be reluctant to retrain, or a receiving department may initially be reluctant to accept a retrained faculty member. Despite its limited application and other potential difficulties, however, its impact on human resources and program quality can be significant.

Some institutions have sought to increase faculty mobility by increasing their public service mission. An expanded commitment to better serve the needs of society also enables faculty members to engage in outreach activities, providing a possible bridge to new careers outside higher education. Faculty members who become interested in considering a career change should be given access to counseling services to support them in such a move (Alm, Ehrle, and Webster, 1977; Bess, 1975).

One practice that gained significant momentum in the 1970s as part of the faculty development movement was the establishment of offices or centers on campus for the purpose of instructional improvement or professional development (Gaff, 1977). Such centers generally conduct activities directed toward (1) curriculum and instructional development, (2) organizational development, and (3) personal and professional development. Bergquist and Phillips (1975) provide a comprehensive model for a professionally staffed center incorporating these three dimensions of activity. As one of the services geared to curriculum and instructional development, the staff of the center can contract with individual faculty members to diagnose their teaching ability. Instructional skills identified as needing improvement can be developed by means of microteaching and videotaping feedback techniques. In addition, the staff can acquaint faculty with different educational methodologies and technologies. With regard to organizational development, staff can help faculty develop new skills in managing intradepartmental conflict and in building mutual trust and professional commitment, so that departments are better able to make planning decisions and curriculum changes. The staff also can work with department heads to develop new management skills. The staff of the center can promote personal and professional development in several ways: through structured interviews concerning a faculty member's vocational role, through training sessions in interpersonal skill development, through personal-growth workshops, and through programs designed to help faculty members who want to leave higher education for nonacademic employment. Institutions also may need to provide therapeutic counseling for faculty members who have significant emotional problems (Mayhew, 1979).

Multicampus Systems. The role of the multicampus system in faculty resource management is at least threefold: (1) to establish a context within which the campuses will recognize the need for prudent faculty management, will be encouraged in their attempts, and—if necessary—will be required to address these issues; (2) to monitor the institutional trends in program and resource management and, where resources are becoming inflexible and insufficient, to join with the affected institutions in determining appropriate planning activities; and (3) to protect institutions from unwarranted interventions by external agencies.

Donald Smith, in Chapter Fifteen, discusses the management practices and planning activities developed by the University of Wisconsin System to establish a context favorable to effective faculty resource management: precise mission statements for its institutions, a long-range planning cycle, a system of ongoing program evaluation established by the institutions and monitored by the system, fiscal and enrollment targets, and special institutional reviews triggered by indicators of institutional distress.

In the area of program and professional development, only a relatively small range of programs can be advanced by a system administration in support of improved faculty resource management. Though few in number, these program opportunities can make a difference. A system administration can establish a policy framework for institutional development of faculty renewal and retraining programs. It can seek state financial support for faculty development and then foster faculty development activities among the institutions through a competitive grant program.

A teaching improvement council composed of two or three faculty representatives from each institution and supported by the system administration can sponsor system-wide faculty colleges, administer a grant program, offer special workshops, arrange for consultants or visiting speakers, and publish a newsletter on instructional improvement and faculty development activities within the multicampus system. Over time, the council representatives would become a growing faculty nucleus, experienced and interested in promoting program and professional development activities at each institution.

A limited number of system-wide regent professorships for visiting scholars can be established to provide program enrichment and to stimulate faculty renewal. Regent professors would share their disciplinary expertise at several of the institutions during the course of their appointments and could lead system-wide seminars for faculty in their academic fields.

Finally, an interinstitutional program of faculty transfer and exchange can be formulated to make better use of existing faculty resources within a multicampus system. A policy of "courtesy of first consideration" for available faculty members within the system by institutions seeking to fill faculty vacancies could supplement the transfer and exchange program.

A system administration can take the leadership role in establishing comprehensive, system-wide personnel policies and procedures. In doing so, it should take special care to clarify potential ambiguities in the personnel rules or procedures before they are tested by litigation. Two areas that generally require clarification are (1) the policies and procedures governing declaration of fiscal emergency and layoff of tenured faculty and (2) the use and rights of non-tenure-track instructional staff. A system administration also should seek improvements in personnel benefits and faculty development programs provided by the state. Competitive compensation, reasonable retirement benefits coupled with options for early retirement and part-time employment, and adequate funding for faculty retraining and renewal programs are necessary components in the effective management of faculty resources.

State Government. Almost everyone will agree that state government has a difficult role to play in a time of scarce resources. Seemingly endless numbers of causes press their demands for priority consideration—and higher education is no exception. Despite the reality of increased competition for limited financial resources, state government is able to assist higher education in meeting some of the problems of faculty resource management. But whatever useful measures can be provided by the state must be initiated and persistently pursued by the higher education community.

What can be done? Higher education must help state government develop a better understanding of the problems facing higher education. With the frequent turnovers in state government and the competing claims, it is difficult to communicate the fact that the problems of higher education are real and not imagined, and that state support for faculty development programs is not an unwarranted "fringe benefit" for faculty but an investment in the maintenance of valuable faculty resources and in the quality of higher education services within the state.

David Spence and George Weathersby, in Chapter Thirteen, and Donald Smith, in Chapter Fifteen, discuss the necessity for reform of state funding practices, noting the detrimental impact of funding on an average-student-cost basis, when in fact many costs are fixed irrespective of enrollment levels. There is also a pressing need, as James Furman illustrates in Chapter Fourteen, to stop the erosion of faculty salaries caused by inflation.

One area of legislation that is beginning to attract increasing interest in higher education is "teacher mobility" legislation. The Minnesota legislature considered such a bill. It would have permitted extended leaves of absence—up to five years with re-entry rights—to assist faculty members wishing to explore a career change and would have provided early-retirement incentives for faculty and staff. Faculty or staff with twenty or more years of service in the state university could have been assigned, if they wished, to a part-time appointment at reduced salary without a loss in benefits (Hays, 1980). Multifaceted legislation of this sort would make possible a continued, even though modest, flow of bright young faculty into institutions of public higher education.

Another initiative that state government could take is the deregulation of excessive accountability requirements—in this case, as they might pertain to faculty resource management. For example, in Wisconsin a state administrative guideline required public higher education institutions to match state funds for faculty retraining and renewal purposes. The institutions in greatest need of faculty retraining, however, were least able to meet the matching requirement. Hence, an elimination of the matching requirement permitted more effective use of available state funds for faculty development.

Finally, state government could join with higher education, industry, and business to institute a state "talent bank" program, through which available faculty resources could be borrowed for specified periods by the participating sectors to address selected problems of state economy and welfare. Such a program would enrich the academic perspective of faculty members and, perhaps, offer a career alternative outside of academe.

National Associations in Higher Education. Through the cooperation and the combined leadership of national associations, several initiatives could contribute to the increased mobility and academic renewal of faculty members nationwide. The American Association of University Professors (AAUP) has suggested the establishment of a national information bank that would offer information and guidance to faculty members seeking nonacademic jobs or overseas academic jobs, particularly in the Third World countries (Jacobson, 1980). Second, national associations can enhance the career mobility of faculty by increasing the portability of non–Teachers Insurance and Annuity Association (TIAA) pension systems, establishing an insurance program for mid-career change, and organizing a time-off credits plan (Group for Human Development in Higher Education, 1974). Third, the national associations can take the leadership role in seeking congressional support for the rejuvenation of study-travel fellowship programs and research grant programs for faculty. Finally, these associations can sponsor a variety of forums in which members of the higher education community share experiences and ideas in adjusting to a period of decline.

Conflicting Goals—External Constraints

A number of problems can occur when various strategies of faculty resource management are pursued. Some difficulties arise from inherent conflicts in the objectives of certain strategies, while other problems result from factors external to higher education. Whatever the source of potential conflict, both faculty and administrators should be aware of the issues involved in faculty resource management, so that they can choose the strategy most appropriate to their program needs.

Fiscal Constraints. Underlying most of the problems associated with faculty resource management are the twin realities of changing program needs and declining real-dollar resources. Ironically, faculty resource management and development programs are needed most when the financial resources required for such programs are least available. As Furniss (1974b) has pointed out, some institutions are beginning to recognize that they might not be able to afford to move from a largely young (and consequently lower-paid) faculty to one balanced by rank and age. Also, inflation and the revision in the mandatory-retirement-age limit (age seventy, effective after July 1, 1982) are severely reducing the viability of the early-retirement programs offered at many institutions. The mandatory-retirement legislation presents institutions with unanticipated additional costs, complicates the process of making individual judgments about the performance of older faculty members, and potentially reduces even further the opportunities for new faculty appointments (Ford, 1978).

Financial pressures also restrict an institution's appeal to new clientele markets through the development of new academic programs. Rather, the inclination is to consolidate and prune programs in order to reduce instructional costs. Financial pressures also can make the already difficult decisions of academic program essentiality even more complex. At what point can a program still be regarded as essential to an institution's mission despite its high costs?

Individual Versus Institutional Interests. In a period of declining resources, there is an increased probability that the intellectual interests of the individual and the department may be brought into conflict with the purposes of the college or the institution, or even with the expectations of the larger society supporting the enterprise (Smith, 1978). In faculty development programs, for example, faculty members might wish to pursue self-renewal projects in their own primary academic fields, whereas the institution might want them to participate in a retraining project enabling them to serve in additional disciplinary fields.

Faculty autonomy in academic program and personnel matters has been a tradition of long standing. It is presumed, and correctly so, that faculty are the best qualified to determine what academic programs should be offered and who should be appointed to the faculty, who should be promoted, and who should be granted tenure. Faculty autonomy in program planning, however, has led to course proliferation based on self-interest, which, in a period of fiscal constraint, operates against institutional economic interests. Furthermore, faculty might feel compelled—for reasons of departmental survival rather than educational merit—to increase degree requirements for courses offered in the major departments. The authority of the faculty to make faculty appointments also can conflict with the desire of system administrators who wish to encourage interinstitutional transfers (see Chapter Nine).

With fewer opportunities for faculty appointments to tenure, the pressures among probationary faculty to qualify for the limited number of tenured positions have been increasing in recent years. Many institutions place a high value on a publishing record as evidence of the scholarly potential required for a tenure appointment. Consequently, some probationary faculty might become so absorbed in establishing a publication record for tenure review that they neglect their responsibilities for teaching, student advising, and committee service—to the detriment of instructional quality.

Non-Tenure-Track and Part-Time Appointments. Institutions can achieve greater flexibility of instructional resources by appointing an increasing percentage of the teaching staff to fixed-term, non-tenure-track positions or to part-time positions. Although this alternative does lead to increased resource flexibility, it may be achieved at the expense of program quality. Also, increased reliance on non-tenure-track or part-time instructional staff might generate feelings among students and full-time faculty that the part-timers are a second-class faculty.

Although part-time faculty can play an important role in institutional economies and often can provide essential academic expertise, employment of part-time faculty can create administrative difficulties. High turnover among part-time staff can require frequent attention to recruitment and orientation, sometimes making it difficult to provide continuity among courses. Part-time staff also may need to develop instructional skills. From an administrative perspective, reliance on part-time instructional staff can increase the burdens of record keeping and can complicate labor relations (Leslie and Head, 1979).

Furthermore, current institutional practices raise serious questions about the rights of non-tenure-track and part-time instructional staff. Should they be eligible for tenure? Are they receiving adequate guarantees of due process? To what extent should they be allowed to participate in academic governance? The American Association of University Professors (1981b) is grappling with these issues and has prepared several recommendations for institutional practices.

Affirmative Action. The increased employment of ethnic minorities and of women into the faculty ranks became a priority goal in higher education during the last decade. The future prospect of reduced opportunities for new faculty appointments, however, likely will slow the rate of continued affirmative action. Faculty tenure openings also will become more scarce, making it extremely difficult to alter significantly the profile of the tenured-faculty ranks. In addition, a retrenchment policy of "last hired/first fired" would have a disproportionately high impact on minorities and women, thus jeopardizing the affirmative action gains of recent years. One solution is for institutions to use a combination of seniority and programmatic considerations applied to ethnic minorities and to women separately from the general case, thereby ensuring reductions among these groups in proportion to those made among the nonminority male faculty population.

Discipline/Department Structure. Over the years the progressive structuring of knowledge by disciplines and departments has facilitated the advancement of scholarship in specific, focused areas of inquiry. Now it is questioned whether the discipline/department structure has become an artificial division of knowledge, posing an obstacle to the solution of scholarly problems that transcend discipline boundaries and to the flexible use of available faculty resources (Honey, 1972). In order to make more effective use of faculty in a period of decline, institutions must offer their faculty members opportunities to extend their intellectual mastery beyond the boundaries now defined by rigid departmental monopolies (Group for Human Development in Higher Education, 1974).

Faculty Tenure. Faculty tenure long has been a cornerstone of academe. The combination of scarce financial resources and the changing needs of scholarship requires that institutions establish a degree of flexibility in the assignment of faculty resources—"a need which will inevitably confront the inflexibility of the tenure system in highly tenured departments and institutions" (Smith, 1978, p. 13).

Advocates of the tenure system point out that tenure protects academic freedom and ensures program quality through an extended probationary period of peer review. Critics of tenure question the lack of similar guarantees of academic freedom for probationary faculty, point to the protection of due process through the civil courts, and assert that academic quality in the faculty ranks can be achieved by other means. Most observers of the tenure debate acknowledge that tenure historically was not intended as a guarantee of lifetime employment (see Chapter Ten). At the same time, most agree that length of service probably will play an important role in determining who among the faculty will be retained and who will be laid off, regardless of tenure.

Thus, the lines have been drawn. While perhaps a handful of institutions are experimenting with alternatives to tenure, most institutions will retain the tenure system and will choose between two basic strategies of faculty resource management. The first strategy seeks resource flexibility by maintaining a limit on tenure appointments and/or by maintaining a margin of non-tenure-track, fixed-term instructional staff. Although this strategy may provide the desired flexibility, it may lower the morale of probationary faculty facing a restricted number of tenure appointments. It may also interrupt the continuity of academic programs, since instructional fixed-term staff and probationary faculty would constantly be replaced. Moreover, there is concern, as expressed by Furniss (1974b), that this general approach to faculty resource management might establish a "revolving bottom" and contribute to the creation of an itinerant academic class.

The second strategy seeks to ensure program quality by promoting qualified probationary faculty to tenure without much regard for tenure numbers and by minimizing non-tenure-track appointments. The philosophy underlying this approach is that the normal functioning of the tenure system is the best guarantee of academic vitality and that tenure does not ensure job security when changes in programs or in funding levels dictate a need for terminating faculty. This approach to faculty resource management tends to reject the notion that the quality of an institution's academic program will suffer with a highly tenured, aging faculty. In any event, Mayhew (1979) believes that the problems of a highly tenured faculty will last at most only ten to fifteen years at many institutions before retirements (and perhaps renewed enrollment growth) will create new appointment opportunities. From a historical perspective, ten to fifteen years is a relatively short time; and, in his opinion, the problems of tenure density probably will pose a minimal threat to intellectual vitality.

Collective Bargaining. The actual or anticipated decline in enrollments and financial resources, among other factors, has spurred the faculty of some institutions to seek the perceived benefits of unions and to engage their administrations in collective bargaining. Advocates believe that collective bargaining establishes an open and systematic process and a new approach to the problems of retrenchment and tenure-related resource inflexibilities (Habbe, 1980). Critics of faculty collective bargaining state that negotiations usually focus on economic improvements for faculty, even when an institution may lack the resources required for such improvements, or that collective bargaining sometimes emphasizes economic concerns to the detriment of important educational matters. Opponents also argue that collective bargaining introduces adversarial relationships, which may undermine collegial relationships. Furthermore, collective bargaining may limit the use of part-time or non-tenure-track instructional staff and make seniority the dominant consideration in issues of faculty resource management (Mayhew, 1979).

External Intervention. In recent years state government and other regulatory agencies have tended to encroach on matters of faculty resource management in their efforts to ensure program accountability and economic productivity in higher education. A new "social contract" is needed—one that will reestablish the delicate balance between state government's right to ensure public accountability and higher education's need for protection from external interventions in academic program planning and personnel decisions. Such a contract will be difficult to establish in a period of fiscal austerity. Nevertheless, institutions can begin by doing a better job of long-range academic program and fiscal planning, taking into account relevant social, economic, and political factors in the larger environment. State government, in turn, should recognize the primacy of the faculty/institutional role in matters of internal management. Although it may not be possible to reach consensus on a new social contract, an effective balancing of public accountability and academic judgment is the goal—one that ultimately best serves public interests (Smith, 1980a).

No Single Answer

No single policy can solve all the problems of resource decline. More likely, successful efforts will occur in the broader context of academic program and fiscal planning and will consist of several interrelated approaches at various levels of the higher education enterprise. The general manner in which institutions approach the task of faculty resource management can determine the essential success or failure of their endeavors. Mandatory programs often are not successful. Faculty members should be educated to the programmatic and fiscal realities of the institution and should be included in determining the appropriate strategies for developing adequate resource flexibility, ensuring intellectual vitality, and coping with rising instructional costs. Openness and participation are key ingredients to faculty understanding and support of retrenchment measures. The top levels of administration must then support the selected management practices—including, if necessary, retrenchment to an equal or even greater extent than that required of the academic departments.

In all these matters, there must be a sensitivity to the human dimension. Certain approaches will generate unavoidable anxieties among the faculty. Increased attention, therefore, should be given to the personal implications of faculty resource management, and, wherever possible, measures should be taken to minimize the trauma of uncertainty or of denied aspirations. Once these steps have been taken, however, those responsible for decisions should resolve to live with the results.

Not all the alternatives presented in this chapter will be needed or even appropriate in every situation. And, as has been indicated, certain alternatives contain tradeoff considerations. Ultimately, the choice of an appropriate approach to managing faculty resources depends on the program needs, academic values, and resource constraints pertaining to each situation.

The decade of the 1980s will test the adaptive capabilities of institutions of higher education. For institutions that have not begun to prepare for a period of potential decline, the time is late. But much can still be done. For institutions that have been planning for the contingency of decline, their efforts have been well spent. Central to the question of institutional survival and the preservation of a healthy enterprise will be the wise management of faculty resources.

For Further Reading

Several different perspectives on current issues pertaining to faculty resource management are offered by Furniss (1974b), Gaff (1977), Mayhew (1979), and Smith (1978). The reports of two surveys (Centra, 1976; Nelsen, 1979) present a comprehensive overview of current institutional practices in faculty development. Suggested alternative approaches to faculty resource management are provided by Bergquist and Phillips (1975), Brown and Hanger (1975), Furniss (1973, 1981b), the Group for Human Development in Higher Education (1974), and Gaff (1975).

❧ 8 ❧

Faculty Responsibilities and Rights During Retrenchment

Paul Strohm

Views on retrenchment are a matter of perspective. Those who deal with it at the general level of resource allocation, institutional management, and enrollment projection are fulfilling a needed role—but one that encourages them to soar at a high altitude over the field of strife. Even provosts and academic deans remain comparatively insulated from the consequences of their decisions; the administrator who can handle an occasional red-faced chairperson in the office or sharp retort at a cocktail party need not live with a daily reckoning of the human costs of a retrenchment program.

Such policy makers are visible mainly by their vapor trails to potential retrenchees—the faculty—who wait at ground level for the next bad news. The experience of retrenchment is naturally very different to the troubled administrator wrestling with alternative forms of curtailment before deciding where the blow must fall, and the panic-stricken faculty member whose career hangs in the balance. This book would, needless to say, have a very different configuration if written from below, with chapters by an advanced graduate student, best in his doctoral program but despairing of employment; by a part-timer, for whom teaching must remain an underpaid avocation rather than a career; by a young scholar accepting a one-year replacement position with the knowledge that the job search for the following year must begin even before the suitcases are unpacked; by a young faculty member lucky enough to be on a tenure track but unlucky enough to see standards shift from year to year, always to her disadvantage; by a forty-year-old faculty member whose credentials surpass those of most tenured faculty but who is refused for tenure in a tight year; by a productive senior faculty member whose program is discontinued according to procedures he at best dimly understands.

That would be quite a book—but it would be different from the present one and would serve a different purpose. One purpose of this book is to anatomize the crisis at a point where some choices remain. My own contribution will be to address the crisis not as a retrencher (since as a department chairman I hardly wield such power) or as a retrenchee (since as a tenured member of a relatively essential department I appear unlikely to suffer that fate) but simply as a faculty member, writing from "ground level." While I cannot speak for individual faculty members, I can identify some of the harm done in the last half-dozen years to faculties as entities—as partially self-regulating polities of teachers and scholars. More important, I can make a series of suggestions about how faculties can and must involve themselves—as faculties—in the wrenching decisions that will be made in the remaining years of the decade.

Erosion of the Faculty Position

Faculties are suddenly being bombarded with new and ominous terms like *retrenchment, cutbacks,* and *reduction in force.* These terms have a quasi-official sound, which puts faculties immediately on the defensive, undermines their confidence, and mystifies the objective situation. *Retrenchment,* for example, can refer to almost anything from a mildly restricted financial situation requiring prudent economies to a state of grave emergency requiring the dismissal of tenured faculty and probationary faculty in mid-contract. Thus, when a president or provost mentions to a faculty body that retrenchment will be inevitable in the years to come, faculty members have no way of knowing whether to expect modest austerities, such as curtailment of travel funds and limitation of long-distance phone calls, or a major threat to the continuance of faculty contracts. Retrenchment in its "hard" sense has affected enough faculties to remind us that the threat is real. And it has affected almost all of us in its "soft" sense, introducing us to a period of hard times or, in the words of the old blues song, "dry spell blues."

This dry spell has already had adverse effects on the confidence and vitality of faculties at the most diverse institutions. Whether or not we experience financial exigency in its formal sense, all of us will be more deeply affected during the next ten years. My own institution, for example, is a large research campus within a comprehensive state university and has known nothing like retrenchment in its hard sense. With intelligent management and proper continuing support from our state, we should weather the next ten years without repercussions as dire as the financially motivated dismissal of tenured faculty. Nevertheless, we have already had an ample taste of the circumscriptions that come with hard times, and we are rapidly learning about the costs of even relatively mild forms of retrenchment to the delicate network of relations that permit an intellectual community to flourish.

One problem experienced by faculty on every campus is our dwindling compensation compared to that of other professional workers in our society. Faculty members in humanities, education, and the library have been harder hit than their peers in business, law, and applied science, but all of us have lost considerable ground in the course of the 1970s, in relation to our own salaries at the beginning of the decade and to the salaries of all other identifiable occupational groups. According to a recent AAUP salary survey, professors as a group lost 18.4 percent of their real income between 1969–70 and 1979–80, while most other occupational groups recorded substantial gains and no major group lost more than 11.1 percent (Hansen, 1980, p. 271). Losses like these—including a 5.5 percent decline in real salaries in 1980 alone—mock the traditional distinction between cost-of-living and merit salary increases, when virtually no one is receiving an increase equivalent to the rise in cost of living, and even the highly meritorious must accept a decline in living standards from year to year. Beyond its inevitable impact on morale, this salary situation has highly adverse practical consequences. Almost everybody in my department now applies for a full load of courses in our optional and relatively low-compensated summer session, and before long junior faculty will undoubtedly be forced to begin moonlighting during the academic year. Faculty members in business and some of the sciences will be able to moonlight without loss of professional esteem by consulting, but those in the humanities and some of the pure sciences might not be so lucky. I know one junior faculty member in the humanities who spends his weekends working as a waiter in a restaurant. The reader can imagine the impact of such readjustments on the self-regard of once-proud academic professionals. Even those who cheerfully accept added employment will pay a price in the loss of time for reading, research, and reflection, and this is a price that will affect us all as the quality of faculty research begins inevitably to decline.

Lost positions are another symptom of our plight. Even when they are lost through attrition or the simple expedient of leaving vacated positions unfilled rather than through termination, a superficially minor contraction in positions can cut deeply into the vitality of a program. In the last six years, my own department has contracted from seventy-one to sixty-six members—not a dramatic shift to an outside observer, and undoubtedly rather typical of the soft retrenchments going on in humanities and social science departments at most universities. Yet, pausing to reflect on the five potential colleagues lost, one realizes that they represent a loss of a great deal more than five lines or positions. Our institution, like most, has only recently developed a fully operative affirmative action plan, and hiring on affirmative action principles has just begun to affect the composition of our faculty. We cannot make headway without new appointments, and five lost positions represent a considerable step not taken in the direction of racial and sexual diversification. Similarly, we depend on a constant recruitment of young scholars from the graduate schools in order to maintain a vital mix of younger and older, junior and senior, fresh and experienced colleagues. Most of the five lost positions would have been filled with faculty in their twenties and thirties, and these appointments would have done much to alleviate a decided concentration of our faculty in the forties and fifties. Concern about a range of ages in the department is not, of course, simply an abstract impulse toward demographic tidiness. We have traditionally looked to new colleagues to keep us fully abreast of new areas and methodologies in an ever changing field. We can and must begin in the future to find new ways to promote mid-career development of continuing faculty. In the meantime, five lost colleagues represent not only five lost workers in an already crowded vineyard but also a lost reservoir of interest in writers beyond our accepted canon, in new techniques of literary analysis, in expanding areas like composition theory and teaching of English as a second language.

A related problem, also shared by most institutions, is that the faculty still in the nontenured ranks perceive a year-to-year shift in tenure standards, always in the direction of greater stringency. Quantitatively speaking, the shift at my own university has been gradual; more persons eligible for tenure receive it than not. Still, the atmosphere is uneasy and leads to tension between those still to face the decision and those who received tenure in admittedly more favorable circumstances. One hears the suggestion that a certain amount of pressure on nontenured faculty might lead to improved performance, but I am not persuaded. Scholarship, in the humanities in particular, is a slow-maturing enterprise requiring some security—or at least predictability—in external circumstances for best results. Junior faculty members who must worry about reappointment from year to year, or who have no clear idea of the standards on which they will ultimately be judged, are unlikely to complete research of much originality. When early publication of a considerable volume of research is required, the result is predictable: young faculty invest their time and hopes in the backward-looking enterprise of revising the doctoral dissertation for publication or "mining" it for articles, or reworking a restricted body of materials or data, when they should be seeking new directions and applications.

Undoubtedly, the most distressing consequence of this dry spell is the broad national proliferation of part-time, temporary, visiting, term, and other teaching appointments whose common denominator is the explicit denial of any possibility of tenure. My own university has resisted any large-scale commitment to such positions and continues to appoint on the "tenure track." Even a casual glance at national job listings in the humanities, however, reveals that well over half of the new positions opening up in college and university teaching include an explicit denial of eligibility for tenure. Numerically speaking, my own department's placement of recent Ph.D.s has not been bad, implying that a national need still exists for teachers in the humanities. We placed twenty-three persons for 1979–80 and twenty-one persons for 1980–81. Unfortunately and typically, though, only four of the twenty-three and six of the twenty-one were on tenure tracks; most of the rest will shortly reenter the job market, and most of them will fail ultimately to achieve a career in college or university teaching. This large-scale refusal of institutional commitment to new appointees is comprehensible in the light of budgetary uncertainties and the need to preserve year-to-year flexibility. Yet institutions considering this "option" must understand its costs. Teachers hired on such contracts are usually hired for heavy introductory teaching duties only; and they often teach increased loads, so that their own professional development is effectively curtailed. Employing institutions should not be surprised when such cut-rate teaching—conducted by people without any expectation of a continuing career and without the nourishment of research and reflection—turns out not to have been a bargain in the long run. We know already that our traditional notions of collegiality have been deeply compromised by such teaching arrangements. Faculty participation in governance is in sad shape on many campuses today and can hardly survive the development of a two-tiered system in which growing numbers of teaching personnel are excluded by definition from full participation in departmental and institutional decision making and from any personal sense of sharing in the consequences of decisions that are made.

This sad enumeration undoubtedly sounds familiar to all readers in higher education. It is intended as an illustration that— whether or not we are ultimately to be retrenched—"dry spell blues" have already affected us all. Even if nothing worse happens to us than has already happened to us, we will go through the remainder of the 1980s less prosperous, less numerous, more senior, more white, more male, and less intellectually venturesome than should have been the case.

Unfortunately, many of us *will* experience worse things. Substantial cuts in direct federal aid and in indirect support for student aid, research grants, and guaranteed loans are now inevitable. Recent reductions in funding for public education in Michigan, Wisconsin, Oregon, and other states warn us that state legislatures will not only be unwilling to take up the slack but will engage in substantial budget cutting of their own. We are now only a year away from a long-predicted major downturn in matriculations of eighteen-year-olds. Acute as the discomforts of the last half-dozen years have been, relatively few institutions have been forced to abandon academically sound programs or to dismiss tenured faculty. Under coming conditions of stringency, many faculties will find themselves under pressure to approve, or at least acquiesce in, such steps. In some disarray already, faculties must nevertheless regroup to face more numerous and more intense challenges throughout the next ten years.

What Can Faculties Do?

Most of the occurrences I have described seem to have happened *to* college and university faculties. We must now begin thinking about what we can do *for* ourselves, as faculties, to limit the further erosion of our position.

Like any other constituency, faculties must act in concert to protect interests that they hold in common. An ironic barrier to such concerted action has been erected, however, by the very difficulties in which we find ourselves. As I have suggested, the present hard times have had a disintegrative effect on the ideals of collegiality. Budgetary pressures have opened up rifts between younger and older, junior and senior, nontenured and tenured faculty. These rifts are minimal, however, compared to the alienation of those non-tenure-track teaching personnel who can hardly be called "faculty" at all, since they are denied the rights and privileges attached to the word. This centrifugal effect is further enhanced by the widely differing situations of component units of colleges and universities, with financial burdens seeming to fall heavily on areas with steady or diminishing enrollment (such as arts and sciences and education) and lightly if at all on areas that are the focus of particular student demand (such as business, law, and applied sciences). Readers of this volume need hardly be reminded of the further estrangement of teaching faculty from administrators and the damage dealt by this period of hard times to the traditional concept of shared authority in decision making.

In spite of these powerful centrifugal forces, faculties have much to gain by recognizing their common interests and by organizing to protect those interests. Whether within the framework of a faculty senate or other governing body, or within a collective bargaining agreement, or within the mixed form of a collective bargaining agreement that supports the authority of traditional governance bodies, faculties can address issues of common concern. We have acquiesced far too passively in the difficulties described above, many of which are still open to modification. While united faculties cannot single-handedly overcome problems of underfunding, they can address some of these problems at their source. At my institution, for example, local units of the American Federation of Teachers and the American Association of University Professors cosponsored a "Faculty Action Day" during each of the last two legislative sessions, including extensive person-to-person lobbying for personnel compensation increases in the university budgets. Although the administration of my university remains unconvinced, members of the faculty believe that these efforts have had an impact, particularly in 1979–80. Faculties can also do much more to emphasize the value of their services. One irony of our situation is that public support of higher education has declined during the last ten years, even before the ostensible cause—a decline in available eighteen-year-olds—has made itself felt. In my own department, for example, shifting patterns of choice have reduced enrollment in preprofessional graduate courses but have actually increased demand for courses in advanced composition and professional writing skills; had we received support commensurate with the value of and demand for our services, we might actually have *grown* in the last five years. All of us stand to gain by working through speakers' bureaus and other means to emphasize the importance of our curricular services and our research to the increasingly wary taxpayers and potential donors whom we serve. The full agenda for faculty attention is too long to summarize here. Certainly, faculties must resist the dilution of faculty status by non-tenure-track appointments. Certainly, faculties must defend allocations for faculty development (including funds for research, course development, travel, and symposia) as long-term economies at a time when the stimuli associated with growth have been lost. Most of all, though, faculties must involve themselves in the crucial areas of short-term and long-term budgetary planning.

Faced with the prospect of a worsening economic situation, faculties cannot afford to wait passively for a desperate administration to invite them to certify a state of emergency or to endorse a plan for reducing tenured staff. We must involve ourselves actively in "preexigency planning"—in preventive budgetary planning designed to avert a state of emergency before it occurs. Organizing to exercise such responsibility can be arduous, especially with many traditional agencies of faculty governance in disarray. Still, faculties must make the effort—when possible, with the assistance of enlightened administrators, who realize that they have much to gain from encouraging their faculty to become full partners in the budgetary planning process. Administrative cooperation can make a crucial difference in the vitalization of the faculty role; bodies accorded significant participation based on freely shared data are inevitably more likely to flourish than those screened off from significant budgetary information or merely invited to offer token "input" prior to actual decision making.

Depending on the size and traditions of the campus, significant budgetary responsibility might be exercised by periodic faculty meetings or an executive committee of the faculty (on a college campus) or by an academic senate or a budgetary affairs subcommittee of an academic senate (on a university campus). The fact that a faculty is in a collective bargaining relation with its administration or board need have no bearing on such an arrangement. Many faculties with collective bargaining agreements maintain traditional governing structures that include such committees; at the University of Cincinnati, for example, the negotiated contract has been used as a way of specifying and augmenting the powers of the budget committee. Such bodies will necessarily work closely with their campus administrations, since budgetary planning can succeed only as a joint enterprise that respects the views and perspectives of both faculty and administration. When well conducted, such bodies can quickly establish their worth by communicating faculty views, ideas, and priorities in ways that will enhance the efficiency and effectiveness of their institutions.

One of the more obvious ways in which faculty bodies can be involved in the budgetary process is by participating in the regular review of both degree-granting and non-degree-granting units. A baseline established by periodic reviews will be valuable if hard priority decisions must eventually be made. In the shorter run, reviews of degree-granting and other academic units can alert decision-making bodies to overlapping programs, to redundant staffing, and to other problem areas. Such reviews can positively encourage faculty to move into adjacent teaching areas of greater demand. In my own department, for example, demand for relatively sophisticated, upper-level composition courses has increased even as certain graduate teaching possibilities have contracted. A good review can identify such a trend and encourage a department or program to redeploy its teaching assignments to its own advantage. Other redeployments that might occur to a reviewing body touch on such areas as class size—where, for example, middle-sized classes could be eliminated in favor of a balanced mixture of lecture classes and seminars, thereby accommodating more students and providing better circumstances for teaching. Reviewing bodies should not, of course, confine themselves to academic programs. Non-degree-granting units, including administrative offices and other support activities, should also be open to scrutiny, and proper faculty bodies should have an opportunity to weigh their costs together with their institutional responsibilities. Such bodies will learn that many support services are in fact revenue generating, as in the recruitment functions of a good admissions office or the retention functions of minority programs and career-counseling centers. In such cases the end result of such reviews may simply be better understanding—but usable suggestions may often emerge as well.

The largest and most sensitive issue connected with the faculty role in budgetary planning is the relation between financial considerations and decisions on the continuation of entire academic programs. Faculty bodies have always had the authority to recommend the discontinuance of programs that fail to meet appropriate academic standards. Institutions may also discontinue programs on grounds of demonstrable financial exigency—particularly, according to the AAUP, when the state of exigency threatens the survival of the institution as a whole. The dilemma for a faculty budget committee or senate arises when financial stringency falls short of ultimate exigency—circumstances where elimination of a faltering program might help to avert a threatened state of exigency that has not yet occurred. The idea of lopping off a program or two to save the institution as a whole has some attractive aspects, but it also raises the disturbing possibility that academically sound programs might be sacrificed to momentary financial panic or to short-term enrollment cycles. The responsibility for finding the right balance point between sound financial planning and the protection of distinctive academic programs obviously lies with the faculty; if we do not make the argument that excellence might entail financial sacrifice, we cannot expect others to do so.

Fearing abuse if anything other than academic grounds were admitted relevant to program decisions, the AAUP has drawn an emphatic distinction between terminations in a state of exigency (which are spread across the institution as a whole and are subsequent to a demonstration that a state of exigency actually exists) and terminations resulting from discontinuance of a program (which occur in that program only and are subsequent to a decision "based essentially upon educational considerations") (American Association of University Professors, 1977c, pp. 17–18). Furniss (1977, p. 136) has argued that this distinction is unrealistically tidy in a context of budgetary stringency, which requires that institutions operate somewhere in the middle ground between normalcy and exigency. The AAUP has acknowledged this problem and sought informally to resolve it. Writing in the *AAUP Bulletin,* Brown (1976) has reminded us that the AAUP's word choice is deliberate when it says that program discontinuance is to be based "essentially" on educational considerations. If the considerations are to be "essentially" educational, what others are then admissible? He concedes somewhat wryly that hard times are likely to encourage a more rigorous application of academic standards: "It is entirely natural that the educational value of fields of instruction or research should be viewed with a colder eye in bad times than in good" (p. 13). May the "cold eye" include considerations of enrollment and cost, as well as academic quality? My own answer (and *not*, I emphasize, the official stance of the AAUP) is that such considerations may have a contextual bearing, though academic considerations must still be central in the final decision. One way of seeing that both the financial context and the academic quality of the program are given their due is to assign each its proper place in the process. Operationally, this position might suggest that a budget committee would question the status of particular programs but that final decisions on continuance of the programs would be made by an academic senate or a policy committee or another body sensitive to academic considerations. Such a division of responsibilities would concede the bearing of financial circumstances on educational programs even as it insisted that academic strength is the "bottom line" of consideration when the final recommendations are made. Another approach to the weighing of both financial and academic criteria in program decisions is embodied in the standards of the Vanderbilt Reassessment Panel, described in Chapter Four of this volume. However program decisions are made, the crucial point is that predictions of financial distress must not overbear the process of academic decision making. As long as this caveat is observed, and as long as decisions with manifest academic implications are made by appropriate faculty bodies, the discontinuance of particular programs may well have less adverse impact on an institution than the more generalized loss of vitality attending the across-the-board dismissal of junior or nontenured faculty.

No wonder faculty committees have tended to avoid such issues; innocuous-sounding suggestions like "reassignment of faculty" can generate considerable rancor in the working out. Still, measures such as these are obviously preferable to their alternative, if that alternative is a state of full-blown economic emergency or outright institutional collapse. Now that faculties have been educated to the possibility of financial emergency and have even tasted some of the privations that such a state would entail, they may be ready to accept more real responsibility in planning to avoid ultimate emergency.

Politics of Financial Exigency

Despite all the preplanning in the world, some institutions will still experience financial exigency. Faculties in institutions where a condition of exigency seems imminent must nevertheless assure themselves that exigency is not declared prematurely, or declared as a convenient ruse for eliminating an unpopular program in an otherwise flourishing institution.

Why might an administration favor a premature declaration of exigency? At the risk of sounding oversuspicious, I would point out that a state of exigency has some analogies with a state of siege or a decree of emergency powers in statecraft; its most noticeable effect is a radical centralization of administrative authority over budgets and academic programs. So convenient are states of financial exigency or impending exigency for justifying wide-ranging actions that the sense of these already amorphous phrases is being debased to serve all sorts of dubious tactical purposes. I recently saw a letter from an administrator to a faculty member which began breezily, "Due to the present financial exigency . . ." It went on to inform her that she would be placed on a leave of absence without pay, on the evident assumption that a fleeting reference to exigency could justify any action whatever. Most administratively promulgated documents make the president the sole judge that a condition of financial emergency does in fact exist. A draft document circulated by the administration of a private university in Illinois makes the president the judge of whether a condition of "stringency" exists and stipulates that "faculty members' contracts, whether tenured or nontenured, and whether written or unwritten, or for a specific term or indefinite as to term, may be terminated and a faculty member laid off in the event of financial stringency or elimination or curtailment of an academic program or discontinuance of particular courses of instruction." This document is more muddled than most, in its lumping together such diverse conditions as a broad perception of stringency, on the one hand, and a particular decision to eliminate a course, on the other. It is nevertheless valuable as an indication of the extent of authority that some administrators seek. Particularly disturbing is the rigidity with which this document would apply narrow financial considerations to academic decision making. Listed as cause for "reduction in forces, programs, or academic divisions," for example, are these considerations:

- An average class size of less than fifteen in any program area.
- A pattern of difficulty within a program area, with respect to the program as a whole or of individuals within it, to maintain the required load of courses or an adequate student credit-hour load (for example, an average class size of eleven students) for full-time members of the faculty.
- Serious and continuing difficulty in supporting expanding programs in the university.

Under these guidelines the failure of a program to expand or to contribute to expansion, or even the failure of an individual faculty member to maintain sufficiently large classes, could lead to an administrative recommendation of termination under conditions of stringency.

Administrators like these, envying the broad range of initiatives granted to administrations under conditions of bona fide exigency, are seeking to claim similar powers in situations that fall far short of exigency in its traditional sense. In its traditional sense, as defined by the AAUP, financial exigency remains "an imminent financial crisis which threatens the survival of the institution as a whole and cannot be alleviated by less drastic means" (American Association of University Professors, 1977c, p. 17). This is a strict definition, and rightly so—a bona fide state of exigency is a terrible thing, opening the way to actions including dismissal of tenured faculty of an institution. Thus, any faculty that would maintain reasonable control over its circumstances must be prepared to resist effectively the improper or promiscuous declaration of a state of financial exigency on its campus. Exigency is *supposed* to be hard to establish, and is *supposed* to be considered in the context of the entire institution, precisely to protect individual programs from excessively crass cost-effectiveness formulas or shifting political currents.

Faculty members should know that a faculty body must participate in any decision that a condition of financial exigency exists; this is the position of the American Association of University Professors (1977c, p. 17); and, as John Gray points out in Chapter Ten of this volume, it is the position of the courts as well. Both the AAUP and the courts agree that, when evaluating a condition of alleged exigency, a faculty has the right to insist that such a condition actually exists; that any measures proposed as a result of exigency be reasonably calculated to relieve it and not directed toward some other end; and that, if dismissals of tenured faculty are contemplated, they reflect fair standards of selection and reasonable efforts to find alternative employment. These are welcome supports to the faculty position—though disturbing shortcomings in decisions on exigency cases continue to remind faculty that they must not simply rely on legal redress but must work for enlightened policies on their own campuses. While the AAUP has insisted that a state of exigency must threaten the survival of the institution as a whole, several recent court decisions (discussed in Chapter Ten) have watered down the description of exigency to a simple inability to meet current expenses from current operating income, without regard to other institutional assets. While the AAUP has insisted that exigency must be considered in the context of the whole institution, the court held in *Scheuer* v. *Creighton University* that the term may apply to a department or college of a university. The problem with such findings is that they facilitate—or even invite—relatively easy demonstrations of exigency, thereby opening a "shortcut" to the elimination of temporarily undersubscribed programs or programs in various states of political disfavor or eclipse, without adequate attention to the question of their academic quality and importance. The *reductio ad absurdum*—which fortunately has not often occurred—would be the elimination of a single, distinguished program in a flourishing institution on grounds of exigency, simply because a fluctuation in enrollments had temporarily impaired its status as a net money maker.

If faculty members stand their ground on the definition of exigency as "survival threatening" and "institution wide," the number of exigency cases to be faced in the coming hard years can be held to a minimum. Still, cases of bona fide exigency will occur. Bearing this fact in mind, faculties may wish to consider drafting a set of guidelines that define a state of exigency, specify faculty involvement in certifying a state of exigency as bona fide, and determine the steps to be followed if dismissals of tenured faculty are to occur. Inserted in faculty handbooks or negotiated contracts, such guidelines can significantly fortify both the practical and the legal situation of a faculty should exigency occur. Of course, such provisions must be carefully formulated. Crudely written contract articles on "layoff and recall," which simply set an order of retrenchment without specifying conditions under which retrenchment can appropriately occur, seem more likely to weaken than to strengthen the faculty position. The state of the art in the preparation of careful and effective guidelines is undoubtedly represented in the 1979–1981 agreement between the University of Cincinnati and the AAUP. Those actively interested in such matters should seek their own copies of the full agreement, but I might point out some of its remarkably comprehensive provisions.

The agreement draws a clear distinction between (1) retrenchment under conditions of financial exigency and (2) termination because of program discontinuation, physically separating them into different articles. The article on financial exigency begins with a definition of exigency as "an imminent financial crisis which threatens the survival of the institution as a whole." If exigency is anticipated, the administration is to present to the AAUP "the data on which this anticipation is based, including the amount of savings which it deems is necessary to effect. . . . The administration and the AAUP shall then agree to submit either a joint recommendation or separate recommendations to the board of trustees as to whether a condition of financial exigency exists. . . . Retrenchment of faculty may not take place until the formal declaration of financial exigency has been made by the board of trustees, which must include a statement of the amount of money needed to relieve the exigency. . . . Following a declaration of financial exigency, a joint financial exigency committee shall be formed and shall consist of seven members appointed by the administration and seven members appointed by the AAUP. . . . The purpose of the financial exigency committee shall be to develop recommendations to provide sufficient savings for relieving the exigency." The article urges reallocations, budget cuts, and normal attrition as measures to be explored short of termination and includes extensive faculty safeguards in the event of termination. The article on program discontinuation because of educational considerations is, if anything, even more tightly conceived, with provision for a faculty senate committee with full authority to consider any administrative recommendation in the light of such considerations as the historical role of the program, its interdependence with other university programs, and the stature of its faculty (University of Cincinnati and AAUP, 1979, pp. 39–50).

A faculty handbook or a collective bargaining agreement is a product of a unique set of circumstances, and the particular features of the Cincinnati agreement might not be transferable to every campus. As I have suggested, some campuses may be unable to divorce entirely the consideration of the academic merits of individual programs from the financial situations in which they find themselves. But the Cincinnati agreement seems particularly valuable in its clear and rigorous definition of financial exigency and in its insistence that decisions on individual programs are to be made within a context that is ultimately academic.

Suppose that an institution finds itself in a state of bona fide exigency. Despite natural human tendencies to withdraw from the arena where hard decisions on termination of appointments are being made, the faculty must remain actively involved. The American Association of University Professors (1977c, pp. 17–18) has offered detailed recommendations, and I will not seek to equal their refinement here. As a general rule, though, one might suggest that terminations for reasons of exigency should normally be made across the entire institution (except as modified by considerations of educational policy) and should normally give maximum protection to tenured faculty (except as modified by considerations of affirmative action). The concept of spreading cuts across an institution rather than concentrating them in a single program makes particular sense in a college where programs may already have been reduced to an essential core. If elimination or reduction of particular programs seems desirable in a large and diverse university, then those selecting the programs to be eliminated or reduced should give full weight to academic as well as financial considerations. Any decisions on particular terminations are bound to be anguishing, and a decision to protect tenured faculty at the expense of those just beginning their careers is no exception. Not only must one be concerned about the plight of terminated junior faculty in an unfavorable job market; one must also be wary of devitalizing an institution by eliminating its developing faculty. Nevertheless, tenure is more than a simple system of job security. Tenure is a status consciously and affirmatively conferred by an institution after intensive screening, and its guarantees should not lightly be set aside. Protection of tenure rights must therefore be a central priority of any faculty policy on retrenchment in a context of financial exigency.

Conclusion

Our intellectual enterprise has been wounded by the "soft" retrenchment that most of us have experienced already, and it could suffer still more from the "hard" forms of retrenchment that might lie ahead. Rather than waiting passively for worse things to come, faculties must seek a more active role in "preexigency planning" on their campuses, even to the extent of participating in hard decisions about the future of academic programs. Certainly, they must resist premature or unfounded administrative attempts to declare states of exigency. But they must also consider preplanning, in the form of careful guidelines to cover states of retrenchment under exigency on their campuses. Finally, should a state of bona fide exigency occur, faculty must accept a proper share of responsibility for determining the criteria for necessary terminations.

For Further Reading

A fine point of departure for discussion of the role of faculty in governance is the "Statement on Governance of Colleges and

Universities" by the American Association of University Professors, the American Council on Education, and the Association of Governing Boards (see American Association of University Professors, 1977c). For other basic studies and discussions, see American Association for Higher Education, Task Force on Faculty Representation and Academic Negotiations (1967); Millett (1962); and Mason (1972). For a good short survey, see Wilson (1979, pp. 100–121). For two broadly based studies of the last decade, see Corson (1975) and Millett (1978).

✎ 9 ✎

Procedures and
Criteria for
Faculty Retrenchment

Kenneth P. Mortimer

Enrollment uncertainty, growing student preference for professional as opposed to liberal arts programs, and the gap between revenues and expenditures—all these conditions combine to challenge the creativity and ingenuity of administrators in postsecondary education (Mortimer and Tierney, 1979). In its final report, the Carnegie Council on Policy Studies in Higher Education (1980, p. 1) argues: "During the next twenty years, enrollments may fall even as the total population continues to rise; real resources available to and used by colleges and universities also may decline, even if and as the total GNP keeps increasing. This dramatic new situation has given rise to a great sense of uncertainty within higher education, to many fears, and to some hopes."

As this volume illustrates, faculty retrenchment is only one of the responses to enrollment decline and financial stringency, although the most visible and controversial. This chapter reviews the experience with faculty retrenchment in postsecondary education, especially in the public sector. It also outlines the procedures and criteria that should be followed in the dismissal or termination of faculty in mid-contract for other than medical or just-cause reasons. Collapsing vacant positions, using more part-time faculty, imposing tenure quotas, or raising the standards for achieving tenure may constitute important ways of coping with enrollment problems and financial stringency, but the dismissal of tenured or tenure-eligible faculty involves a host of special legal, procedural, and policy issues.

The experience with faculty cutbacks in the 1970s was substantial. As early as 1971, in a survey of the membership of the Association of American Colleges, Gillis reported that seven of fifty-four respondents had already found it necessary for reasons of financial exigency to terminate one or more tenured members of the faculty (p. 367). It is difficult to unravel the rather serious conditions that prevailed at the City University of New York (CUNY) during 1975 and 1976, but an investigating committee of the American Association of University Professors (1977a, p. 80) reported that there were 1,000 terminations: "The retrenchment was accomplished without terminating the appointment of any full-time teaching faculty with tenure as recognized by the statute and by-laws governing the university. The appointments of a number of counselors, administrative officers, laboratory technicians, and other nonteaching staff with tenure were terminated. Also terminated were the appointments of an unknown number of full-time lecturers with a hybrid sort of tenure that this association would characterize as an entitlement to unqualified tenure. Finally, the appointments of about ten professors who were informed that they would be granted tenure were terminated before the statutory date—September 1—when their indefinite tenure would have commenced."

Faculty terminations at the State University of New York (SUNY) have received less attention than those at CUNY but have involved more tenured full-time faculty. According to the AAUP's investigating committee, 103 faculty at SUNY were terminated on the grounds of retrenchment from September 1974 through September 1976 (American Association of University Professors, 1977b, p. 244). Of these terminations sixty-two involved tenured faculty, only thirty-four of whom were reemployed elsewhere within the system.

In Wisconsin in late 1972, the legislature mandated successive 2.5 percent cuts in the personnel budgets of the university system for the years 1973–74 and 1974–75. The regents of the university decided that the faculty members affected were not to be terminated but, rather, were to be laid off. According to Furniss (1974a, p. 164), they "would retain their titles and rank . . . [but] were to be without salaries and duties; for two years they were to have first chance of reinstatement if their positions reopened; and assistance was to be given them in finding other employment within the system." The university created a procedure for determining faculty members who could be laid off; it also created an appeal procedure. It then laid off eighty-eight tenured faculty members. In May 1974 thirty-four additional tenured faculty were laid off, effective May 1975. (An eventual court decision, *Johnson* v. *Board of Regents,* sustained the faculty dismissals; see Leder, 1975, for a discussion of the case.) According to Pondrom (1980), many of these layoffs were later rescinded.

Case Study: Pennsylvania State College and University System

The Pennsylvania system of fourteen campuses had been in the "retrenchment era" for the entire decade of the 1970s but until 1979 had succeeded in avoiding the actual termination of tenured faculty. The details of this experience from 1974 to 1980 are summarized in the following discussion.

The 1975–76 Retrenchment. The series of events that engulfed the Pennsylvania State College and University System from 1971 to the fall of 1976 have been recounted in some detail elsewhere and can only be summarized here (Johnson and Mortimer, 1977, pp. 47–68). This fourteen-campus system was organized for collective bargaining in 1971, and the bargaining unit consisted of almost 4,000 faculty. The colleges are owned by the state of Pennsylvania, and, although they have both a separate system board and local boards of trustees, the essential details of their operation are controlled by the Pennsylvania Department of Education. In late 1974 the Department of Education, facing a probable revenue-expenditure gap of some $16 million in 1975–76, began to consider retrenchment. Since, in November 1973, the Department of Education and the faculty union had signed an agreement providing for a moratorium on retrenchment through the end of the academic year 1974–75, and had later agreed to extend this ban through 1975–76, the Department of Education and the separate colleges were obligated to live with the legislature's appropriations for the 1975–76 year and to plan any retrenchments for the 1976–77 year.

In early 1975, partially because of its dissatisfaction with the retrenchment provision in the 1974 contracts, the Department of Education conducted retrenchment simulations at two of the state colleges. At the time the governor's budget request was released, in March 1975, the department was well on the way to understanding how retrenchment could be achieved. Based on the *assumption* that the colleges might be operating on a budgetary "deficit" of $16.7 million during 1975–76, which would carry over into 1976–77, the department proceeded to develop guidelines for personnel retrenchment, to be effective September 1976. The twelve retrenchment guidelines are too detailed to be cited here in full, but the four more important provisions are listed below.

First, retrenchment projections for 1976–77 were based on the *projected* discrepancy between funds needed and funds available for 1976–77. Each college was given a prorated budgetary "deficit," for which it would have to compensate by personnel cutbacks. If actual salary increases were higher or lower than projected for the coming year, retrenchment requirements might be decreased or increased as appropriate. This link with salaries was to prove crucial in later negotiations.

Second, the following priorities were to be considered in the retrenchment of teaching faculties: (1) protection of new state college missions approved by the state college planning commission and the Board of State College and University Directors in January 1975; (2) affirmative action; and (3) other programmatic considerations, including complementarity of academic programs among the various state colleges in a given geographical area of the state. Seniority appeared to be given fourth priority.

Third, retrenchment of management and nonteaching professional positions was to occur at approximately one and a half times that of the teaching faculty (later changed to a rate equal to that of the teaching faculty), and nonacademic personnel would be retrenched in direct proportion to the total number of all positions to be reduced at the college.

Fourth, after the submission of retrenchment lists on June 30, 1975, each president could submit a statement concerning alternative cost-saving approaches designed to reduce retrenchment. The retrenchment plan was subsequently labeled Plan A, and the alternatives to retrenchment, Plan B.

The state college presidents pressed the Department of Education to allow the alternatives (Plan B) to be submitted before the retrenchment list (Plan A), but the department remained convinced that significant economies no longer could be achieved in nonpersonnel areas. (Significant reductions in nonpersonnel areas had been made in previous years.) One president indicated that he could achieve the cost reduction required of his college without retrenchment, and that the manner in which savings could be accomplished should be left to the individual institutions. He publicly announced his intention not to submit Plan A and was threatened with dismissal if he did not comply with the department's directives.

On September 8, 1975, the deadline for retrenchment letters, two hundred personnel (including eighty-two faculty) were informed that they would be involuntarily retrenched as of September 1976 unless budgetary conditions improved. Seven of the state colleges achieved sufficient cost savings in other areas to avoid involuntary retrenchments altogether.

The faculty union protested this retrenchment of eighty-two faculty members and proceeded to contest several aspects of the retrenchment process via the contractual grievance procedure. After a series of maneuvers on the part of both management and the union and separate rulings by the Pennsylvania Labor Relations Board, an arbitrator ruled in January 1976 that "the commonwealth was not required to prove financial exigency in order to proceed with retrenchment." Because, according to the arbitrator, there is a difference between retrenchment and termination, "tenured faculty were therefore unprotected by the provision in the faculty contract concerning termination of tenured faculty"

(Johnson and Mortimer, 1977, p. 53). (This last ruling was on the substance of the contractual language itself.)

Although the details concerning the eventual settlement of these grievances are rather complex, the commonwealth agreed to rescind the eighty-two retrenchment notices in exchange for a union agreement to hold across-the-board faculty increases to 3.83 percent for 1975–76 and 4 percent for 1976–77. Subsequent contract negotiations resulted in delaying further retrenchments for the 1977–78 and 1978–79 academic years.

The 1979–80 Retrenchment. In January 1979, however, the specter of retrenchment raised its head again when the commissioner of higher education issued a new set of guidelines for retrenchment, to take effect at the end of the 1979–80 academic year. The guidelines specified that all existing documents relative to a retrenchment discussion would be made available to the union, that procedures to identify the faculty to be retrenched would be instituted, and that any retrenchment decisions would be discussed with the union beginning in February 1979. These guidelines also pointed out that, in order for a faculty member to be retrenched in the fall of 1980, notices would have to be sent by September 8, 1979.

In September of 1979, ninety-nine faculty on four campuses received retrenchment notices, to be effective at the end of the 1979–80 academic year. Again the union was galvanized into action. It filed a grievance case, arguing that the commonwealth had violated the contract by failing to "meet and discuss" with the union prior to the notices.

In March of 1980, twelve of the eighteen retrenchments at East Stroudsburg were rescinded when the administration found out that the financial picture for 1980–81 was not as bleak as it had originally thought. Four retrenchments at Edinboro were rescinded for somewhat similar reasons. In May of 1980, the union was successful in getting the commonwealth to designate a full-time person to look for jobs for the terminated faculty. The union was also able to identify forty-six existing vacancies for which the terminated faculty might be qualified under the negotiated transfer policy. By July of 1980—because of a revised financial picture, resignations, retirements, transfers to other campuses, and so forth—the number of faculty designated for release had been reduced to fifty-nine. In the fall of 1980, an arbitrator was considering the cases of the remaining faculty slated for termination.

Lessons from the Case. The Pennsylvania case is intertwined with a number of other developments in the commonwealth's post-secondary education scene, but some specific points can be made.

First, the specter of retrenchment caused the campuses to look very carefully at staffing and financial patterns and resulted in severe reductions in nonpersonnel areas. In fact, it was embarrassing to the administration to uncover what cost savings could be made without retrenching.

Second, the issue of the transfer of faculty between campuses was brought to a head by the retrenchment experience. The system-level parties (the commonwealth and the union) negotiated a policy that specified procedures for the transfer of faculty among the campuses. This policy became part of the collective bargaining agreement.

Third, the political milieu of the Pennsylvania system during the 1975–76 retrenchment was quite different from that of the 1979–80 incident. All the chief protagonists at the system and state levels were different (the governor, the secretary of education, the deputy secretary, the commonwealth's chief negotiator, and the commissioner of higher education). The new commissioner left retrenchment decisions to each campus and specified only that procedural regularity be observed.

Fourth, whereas the campus presidents and the Board of State College and University Directors opposed the earlier retrenchment and believed that there were other alternatives, by 1979–80 they believed it to be necessary. Presidential support for faculty retrenchment was based, at least partially, on the rebudgeting incident of 1978–79. In August 1979, after the fiscal year had begun, the Department of Education announced a "rebudget," which reassigned $2 million of the appropriation from five campuses to nine others. A number of presidents became convinced that "inefficient" or "deficit" campuses should be forced to retrench rather than be carried by the stronger campuses.

Fifth, the contractual requirement of a year's notice prior to the layoff's taking effect pushed some administrators to issue hasty retrenchment notices, apparently in an attempt to increase their flexibility in the face of *possible* or projected financial crises. The retrenchment notices themselves put immense pressure on administrators to justify the projections and/or predictions. In the University of Wisconsin System, by contrast, state law requires that campus budgets be reduced as enrollment declines. In order to observe the one-year, timely-notice requirement of university policy, special funding was necessary, since the state requires that the university begin to repay funds in installments to the state as soon as fall enrollment is determined to be less than projected in the budget (Lee and Bowen, 1975, p. 105).

By way of summary, retrenchment in the Pennsylvania system has been regarded as the last straw in a long string of financial stringencies. It became a reality only after alternative actions had stripped the system of its flexibility.

Conditions Necessary for Retrenchment

The American Association of University Professors identifies four legitimate bases for terminating tenured faculty: cause, medical reasons, bona fide financial exigency, and bona fide program closure (Mortimer and Tierney, 1979, pp. 41–42). Cause and medical reasons are not of concern in this chapter, since they are usually confined to a single individual and apply only in the given case.

Financial Exigency. The AAUP's 1976 "Recommended Institutional Regulations on Academic Freedom and Tenure" (RIR) (American Association of University Professors, 1977c) states that financial exigency should be an imminent financial crisis that threatens survival of the institution as a whole and that cannot be alleviated by less drastic means. The Commission on Academic Affairs of the American Council on Education has prepared a critique of the RIR (Furniss, 1977). The commission's concern arises from three circumstances. First, since the term *financial exigency* is imprecise, courts may provide their own definitions, which might be quite different from the definition the institution in good faith was following. Second, the commission does not believe that the AAUP's definition should be accorded the status of common and accepted practice, as other AAUP documents are. Rather, it should be regarded as *one source* of suggestions that institutions should consider when they seek workable ways to meet financial problems. Third, the commission argues that the document makes termination for financial exigency legitimate only when an entire institution is on the brink of bankruptcy and makes terminations for program change legitimate only when no financial considerations are involved—that is, when the terminations are essentially an educational matter. There are, the commission believes, many intermediate positions between these extremes. In short, experience with difficult financial conditions is too limited and the issues are too complex to have the AAUP or anyone else produce a good *universal* policy and procedural statement.

These criticisms focus attention on the usefulness of the AAUP's entire range of statements—first, as guidance for institutional policy; second, as documents explicitly developed for adaptation as institutional policy; and third, as guidance about standards of academic customs for use by a court of law (Furniss, 1978). In contrast to the concern expressed by the commission, Brown and Finkin (1978, p. 44), who are advocates for the AAUP point of view, argue: "To the extent the standards of academic freedom and tenure built up by the AAUP over the past sixty years represent a body of persuasive professional opinion, the courts should give weight to them; if the standards are arbitrary or unreasoned, they should not." (For discussions of court definitions of *exigency,* see Mix, 1978; Holloway, 1980; and Chapter Ten of this volume.)

Program Discontinuance. In a time of declining resources, the discontinuance of some academic programs is an almost inevitable outcome of budget gaps and of such processes as academic program review (described in Chapter Five). The decision whether to retain programs that do not meet or are low on specified criteria is an integral part of the entire academic review process.

Program closure is not *necessarily* a decision to dismiss tenured faculty. Indeed, the University of Michigan's policy on discontinuance of academic programs specifically states that the university has never released tenured faculty members because of program closure (see Davis and Dougherty, 1978). Furthermore, if it should become necessary to release tenured faculty within a program to be discontinued, every effort would be made to place tenured faculty and staff in other suitable positions, perhaps through retraining.

It is equally clear that a decision to reduce the faculty or engage in reductions in force need not be a decision to close programs. As shown in the Pennsylvania State College and University case, the maintenance of program vitality is often a specific goal in retrenchment guidelines. The AAUP's report on the mass dismissals at the City University of New York (American Association of University Professors, 1977a, p. 72) indicates that only one of the stages in a five-stage decision-making process was the abandoning or curtailing of programs. Davis and Dougherty (1978) have discussed alternatives to program closure, including merger, transfer to another unit, joint programs with another institution, and transfer to another institution.

It is also apparent that substantial technical, bureaucratic, and emotional barriers confront an administration attempting to phase out programs (see Chapter Five).

Procedures Required in Faculty Retrenchment

Due Process Requirements. Due process and legal requirements constrain but do not cripple administrators considering retrenchment decisions. Terminating a tenured faculty member's contract for reasons of financial difficulties or program closure in a public institution is not the same formidable undertaking as dismissal for cause. "The necessity for reduction must be shown and certain considerations of due process come into play, but it is neither required nor desirable in such cases to demonstrate that an individual once judged fit to occupy a permanent position on the faculty no longer possesses such fitness" (Kurland, 1972, p. 306).

While the conditions of a given situation will dictate the specific reasons for retrenchment, the institution should make sure that (1) the reasons cited for retrenchment are demonstrably bona fide and not arbitrary or unreasonable; (2) individuals are not identified for retrenchment by constitutionally impermissible reasons, such as the exercise of First Amendment rights; (3) there is adequate consultation with existing faculty bodies; (4) the terminated faculty member is given written notice of the decision, the information on which the decision is based, and an opportunity to respond (Mix, 1978, p. 16); (5) reasonable attempts are made to place the retrenchees elsewhere within the institution or system when that is feasible; (6) recall procedures and criteria are specified.

Bona Fide Action. The concept of bona fide action is not an easy one to document, since the "good faith" of an action often depends on the intent of the actor. The issue is whether administrations in financial difficulties have made reasonable efforts to find alternatives to retrenchment. Peterson (1976) suggests that the courts should allocate the burden of proof regarding the existence of exigency and of good faith dismissal: "In view of the institution's reliance on the existence of a financial exigency as grounds for dismissal and its possession of the records necessary to prove such a condition, the institution should be required to prove that an exigency actually exists. However, if the institution meets this burden, the faculty member should then be required to establish that he was dismissed for reasons other than financial exigency" (pp. 431–432).

Of course, one of the most obvious standards as to whether dismissals were bona fide is the extent to which the institution has followed its own previous policies in the staffing reductions that normally precede retrenchment of tenured faculty. For example, there should be no suspicion that the dismissal of a tenured faculty member is simply an attempt to gain flexibility in resource allocation and/or subsequent staffing decisions. (See Chapter Ten for examples of "good faith" and "bad faith" as interpreted by the courts.)

First Amendment Rights. The requirement that constitutionally impermissible reasons for retrenchment not be used is obvious. Due process rights cannot be violated, nor can the retrenchment be a result of a faculty member's exercise of free-speech rights. The corollary, however, is that criteria be identified well in advance, a subject to which we return later.

Adequate Consultation. The requirement for adequate faculty consultation is also obvious, but its implementation may be difficult in state systems of postsecondary education where faculty governance mechanisms at the state and/or system level are not well developed. The consultation will take different forms at the varying levels at which faculty are affected. A system-level union may negotiate general procedures for retrenchment, whereas a campus local will be more specific about the matter. The union may insist, for example, that the administration at the local campus must specify the criteria for identifying academic units to be the targets of retrenchment.

The existence of a unionized environment may be a crucial ingredient in attempts to involve faculty in retrenchment decisions in a meaningful way. In the Pennsylvania State College and University System, the union decided not to take part in the individual decisions on retrenchment. A system-level policy was negotiated, but the specific retrenchment decisions were appealed under the contractual grievance procedures. From the union's point of view, refusing to participate in individual campus retrenchment decisions may be a wise political strategy. Union members identifying other union members for the axe would be extremely disruptive to the organization.

Political tension between faculty and administration will affect the retrenchment process, whether or not the faculty are unionized. But the union contract would seem to require the administration to negotiate some type of agreement on retrenchment. (Lozier, 1977, p. 237, reports that about 60 percent of the contracts have retrenchment clauses.)

Minimal Procedures. The minimal procedures requirement set forth in *Johnson* v. *Wisconsin Board of Regents* (see Leder, 1975) specifies that each faculty member to be laid off must be furnished with a reasonably adequate written statement, an adequate description of the manner in which the decision has been arrived at, and an adequate disclosure of the information and data on which the decision is based. The faculty member also must be given the opportunity to appeal. Institutional attempts to find alternative employment for retrenchees often go beyond these minimal requirements, however. Some institutions have decided that they have an obligation to help retrenched faculty members be retrained, find new positions, and so forth. According to Pondrom (1980), the University of Wisconsin System has had some success in placing retrenched faculty members elsewhere in the university.

Recall. Whenever reasons other than program discontinuance are given for retrenchment, there is an implication that dismissed faculty members might be rehired if conditions should change. Procedures for rehiring or "recall" should be formulated at the same time that retrenchment decisions are being implemented. Recall policies should specify the criteria and procedures by which faculty members will be recalled.

Retrenchment Criteria

Establishing retrenchment criteria requires determining the units to be retrenched, the categories of personnel involved, the locus of tenure, affirmative action goals, the relative priority of these criteria, and the order of layoff.

Retrenchment Unit. The retrenchment decision must include definitions of the appropriate retrenchment unit. In Pennsylvania, for example, the secretary of education allocated retrenchment-planning targets to each campus. College administrators had a degree of flexibility in deciding how the targets would be implemented. These campus retrenchment targets were based on budget assumptions that honored the "extraordinary needs of colleges such as California, Cheyney, and Mansfield for a 'greater share' of the regular allocation of the total state college budget distributed on the basis of enrollment. To do otherwise would probably force a level of faculty reduction at each of these colleges that could weaken their ability to survive as institutions with comprehensive higher education programs" (Pennsylvania State College and University System, 1975, p. 3). This is an explicit recognition of the smaller size of these units and the difficulty in absorbing across-the-board cuts that a small campus suffers. It also preserves the integrity of Cheyney, the only predominantly black college in the system.

The same principle would apply to institutions as they seek to assign retrenchment targets to schools, colleges, divisions, departments, and/or programs. Other things being equal, the larger the unit, the more likely it is to be able to absorb retrenchment targets without a serious impact on educational programs.

Administrators should be aware that the definition of an appropriate retrenchment unit is one of the more controversial elements of a retrenchment policy. Many institutions have been operating with very small departments and/or programs. To define a very small department or program as the appropriate retrenchment unit may have the impact of identifying a specific person to be retrenched. A narrow retrenchment unit may limit the possibility of finding alternate employment for the terminated employee.

Personnel Categories. Retrenchment targets should be spread among the various categories of employees. The quickest way to get and sustain faculty antagonism about retrenchment is to avoid the retrenchment of nonacademic and administrative employees. The policy should establish roughly equivalent retrenchment ratios for these other employees. In Pennsylvania the original guidelines called for management positions at each college to be retrenched at a percentage rate of approximately one and a half times that of the teaching faculty.

Another issue is the extent to which administrators are teaching courses and performing other faculty duties. In a union environment, administrators doing faculty work will be the subject of intense bargaining.

Locus of Tenure. Retrenchment decisions will force institutions to reexamine whether tenure is based on a campus or in a system. Lee and Bowen (1975, p. 109) point out that two prestigious groups have reviewed this matter and arrived at diametrically opposed conclusions. The Carnegie Commission on Higher Education has suggested that employment contracts and tenure should be based in a multicampus system rather than on a particular campus, whereas the Commission on Academic Tenure in Higher Education believes that academic tenure should be held in the institution and not in the system as a whole. "The same uncertainty is found in the nine multicampus systems under study. In general, unless the decision has been forced upon them, multicampus administrators have attempted to avoid the issue. The reason is obvious: campus-based tenure runs counter to the concept of a single university, which most systems espouse. But system-wide tenure poses so many practical problems as to appear unrealistic" (p. 110).

A faculty transfer policy will be an important ingredient in any multicampus or system-level retrenchment policy. The likelihood of an effective transfer policy is directly related to the complexity of the system involved. For example, it may be possible to negotiate a transfer policy in the Pennsylvania State College and University System because the campuses have somewhat similar teaching missions. It would be quite difficult if not impossible to negotiate such a policy in a multicampus system composed of two-year community colleges, four-year technical institutes and liberal arts colleges, and major university centers. The politics of such transfers as well as their substantive soundness would be seriously called into question.

Affirmative Action Goals. Those responsible for formulating retrenchment policies must consider their impact on affirmative action goals. Unfortunately, minority and women faculty are likely to be among those most recently recruited and therefore most subject to being retrenched. Therefore, institutions may need to consider the extent to which retrenchment based strictly on seniority will damage the diversity—both racial and sexual—of the faculty.

Seniority Versus Other Criteria. Institutions must determine the relative priority to be given to the separate criteria in arriving at the order of retrenchment. Common criteria are employee status—part-timers are normally retrenched before full-timers; seniority (last in, first out); and program need, cost, and quality. The following quotation, from the University System of Georgia's 1980 draft policy, is illustrative: "In determining which faculty member's employment is to be terminated, consideration shall be given to tenure status, years of service to the institution, and to other factors deemed relevant, but the primary consideration shall be the maintenance of a sound educational program that is consistent with the mission of the institution and the affirmative action goals of the institution" (p. C-8).

A judgment about program balance and vitality is best made by people close to program decision areas. To quote Furniss (1974a, p. 167): "Despite efforts to keep a retrenchment policy objective, some kinds of judgment are not only necessary but also inevitable in the complex of decisions leading to faculty terminations and layoffs. The relative desirability of one course of action over another must be evaluated, the relative attractiveness to potential students of one program over another must be estimated, and so on. . . . These kinds of evaluations and decisions are both necessary and appropriate as triggers for layoff or termination actions and are not challengeable on Fourteenth Amendment grounds as long as the decisions are objective in the sense that they deal with numbers or classes of persons rather than with individual cases."

After consideration is given to the criteria outlined above, one suggested order of layoff would be as follows:

1. Faculty members on part-time/temporary appointments.
2. Faculty members on full-time/temporary appointments.
3. Nontenured faculty in inverse order of continuous service within the institution.
4. Tenured faculty in inverse order of continuous service within the institution.
5. When two or more faculty members in 2, 3, or 4 above have the same amount of continuous service, the faculty member with the lesser rank shall be the first to be laid off.

Finally, retrenchment puts great pressure on procedures for evaluating tenured faculty. It is deceptively easy to argue that retrenchment decisions should take into account the relatively superior performance of one faculty member as opposed to another. But the issue of evaluation of tenured faculty is itself controversial and probably would not survive being tied to issues of retrenchment.

Concluding Remarks

This chapter has discussed retrenchment as an isolated and fairly limited response to conditions of enrollment decline, program discontinuance, and financial stringency. There are four points to be made in conclusion.

1. *Retrenchment is a solution looking for a problem.* Many other strategies have been followed by colleges and universities seeking to cope with environmental turbulence. These include greater use of part-time faculty, raising tenure standards, decremental budgets, and so forth. While the AAUP's "institutional survival" test appears

too severe, dismissing tenured faculty merely to gain additional flexibility seems too cavalier. The establishment of vital faculty development programs and better planning to avoid overstaffing are more humane solutions.

2. *Faculty do more than teach.* In research- and service-oriented institutions, faculty have more complex functions, and student contact hours are not the only measure of their worth. The decision to lay off faculty because there are not enough students to teach requires institutions to place greater emphasis on the teaching than on research or service functions. In research-oriented universities, there are *no* standardized teaching loads and *no* uniform standards of research productivity.

3. *Most retrenchments have to be made on projections rather than on actual conditions.* Timely-notice requirements make it necessary to issue notices at least a year before the action is to take place. Most projections are not accurate enough for this purpose.

4. *Retrenchment notices or the threat of retrenchment notices can have unanticipated consequences.* Not all of them are bad. Mankato State University in Minnesota found it necessary to reduce its faculty by 150 positions from 1970 to 1975 (Alm, Ehrle, and Webster, 1977). The university received its faculty allocation from the legislature through the State University Board on the basis of projected enrollments. When the enrollment decline hit, two problems became evident: (1) the notification requirement dictated that faculty had to be removed from the positions on the basis of *projections;* (2) microprojections for individual departments had to be made. Interesting coping strategies developed at Mankato: "A faculty member in the mathematics department asked if there wasn't some way that faculty could offer short-term minicourses. If these were taught as overload with no additional compensation, credit hours would be produced, faculty positions saved, and a lot of educational excitement generated as well. With the support of the administration, the idea quickly spread through the faculty, who heartily endorsed it. At the high point, some 600 minicourses were being offered each quarter. The additional credit hours supported an average of seven positions a year" (p. 160).

As Eugene Craven describes in Chapter Seven, numerous alternative strategies can be attempted prior to retrenchment.

The dismissal of tenured faculty should remain the "court of last resort."

For Further Reading

For a more complete description of the retrenchment process in the union environment of Pennsylvania, see Johnson and Mortimer (1977). Similarly, Alm, Ehrle, and Webster (1977) provide an analysis of the faculty reduction process at a public institution in Minnesota. Readers can familiarize themselves with the positions of the American Association of University Professors on dismissal of tenured faculty by reading the analyses by Furniss (1974a, 1977, 1978). See also various chapters in Hample's (1981) *New Directions for Institutional Research: Coping with Faculty Reduction.*

❧ 10 ❧

Legal Restraints on Faculty Cutbacks

John A. Gray

When a college is forced by financial difficulties to reduce the size of its full-time faculty, ordinarily it does not reappoint probationary faculty and does not fill vacancies created by retirements or resignations. If it decides to go further and to reduce the number of tenured faculty, legal restraints and consequences arise. When dismissing tenured faculty, members of governing boards and senior academic administrators have to deal with difficult issues and should resolve them primarily on the basis of sound educational and financial policies and not on the basis of legal considerations. At the same time, if they are to safeguard the rights of all parties and prevent unnecessary, acrimonious, and expensive litigation, they will need to be aware of the legal consequences of their decisions.

This chapter focuses on the legal restraints decided on by the courts as a matter of contract law when colleges release tenured faculty because of financial exigency. Although the cases reviewed

This chapter is a revision of an article originally published as "Higher Education Litigation: Financial Exigency," *University of San Francisco Law Review*, 1980, *14* (3), 375–402. Copyright, *University of San Francisco Law Review*.

involve private, independent institutions of higher education, the issues discussed are also relevant to state institutions. That is, although the discussion focuses on contract law and not on the due process requirements of constitutional law triggered by "state action," it has value for state institutions because the relationship between faculty and institution at state institutions is also contractual. The faculty contract is the starting place for determining both public and private institutions' financial exigency responsibilities. The courts have attempted to balance the need and ability of an educational institution to cope with a financial crisis against the contractual right of a tenured faculty member to be safeguarded against a "bad faith" dismissal. The courts have been asked to determine (1) whether a financial exigency exists, (2) whether the dismissals were demonstrably bona fide, (3) which party has the burden of proof, and (4) the appropriate remedy in the event of a "bad faith" dismissal. There is no "law of the land" regarding the issues discussed. Court decisions are controlling precedents only within the jurisdiction of the deciding court. At the same time, a court does review and is guided by the judicial opinions of other jurisdictions, especially when there is no mature body of law on the issues available in its own jurisdiction and especially where the issues touch on well-established and widely shared principles of law, as in contract law.

The Tenure System

The tenure system came into existence in the early twentieth century, as a result of numerous complaints by college and university faculties that faculty members had been dismissed or were in jeopardy because trustees, administrators, other faculty, or powerful external parties disliked the content of their teaching and scholarship. The faculties' conviction was that a democratic society requires institutions of higher education characterized by academic freedom. More than any other higher education organization, the American Association of University Professors (AAUP) has historically been the forum, formulator, advocate, and monitor on issues of academic freedom and tenure. The AAUP's 1940 "Statement of Principles on Academic Freedom and Tenure," drafted jointly with the Association of American Colleges and endorsed by more than ninety educational institutions and disciplinary societies, asserts that academic freedom "is fundamental to the advancement of truth" and "is fundamental for the protection of the rights of the teacher in teaching and of the student to freedom in learning." The 1940 statement defines tenure as "a means to certain ends; specifically: (1) freedom of teaching and research and of extramural activities and (2) a sufficient degree of economic security to make the profession attractive to men and women of ability. Freedom and economic security, hence, tenure, are indispensable to the success of an institution in fulfilling its obligation to its students and to society" (American Association of University Professors, 1977c, p. 2).

Most public colleges and universities have tenure systems, although only one state has a statute providing tenure for its entire university system (Peterson, 1976, p. 419). State institutions that enact a tenure system are engaged in "state action" and have created a "property interest" subject to federal constitutional restraints under the Fourteenth Amendment (*Board of Regents* v. *Roth,* 408 U.S. 564 (1972); *Perry* v. *Sindermann,* 408 U.S. 593 (1972)). At private institutions tenure is created by decision of the board of trustees and normally is considered an integral part of the institution's contract with its faculty. Courts have consistently held that an institution's tenure policy is part of the faculty employment contract even where not specifically mentioned in the contract. "There is extensive authority in accord with the proposition that university rules, regulations, bylaws, and policies become implied terms of faculty employment contracts and thereby give rise to protectable rights" (*Rehor* v. *Case Western Reserve University,* 43 Ohio 2d 224, 240 (1975)). Thus, academic freedom and tenure are legally protected at private institutions by contract and at state institutions both by contract and by state and federal constitutions.

Tenure status is a legal entitlement to continuous employment terminable for cause or by reason of disability, mandatory retirement, program discontinuance, or financial exigency. Specifically, tenure status brings with it a legal entitlement to certain due process requirements prior to dismissal. These requirements, both under contract law (governing private institutions) and constitutional law (governing state institutions), differ, depending on whether the dismissal is for cause or by reason of financial exigency. AAUP dismissal procedures for cause are found detailed in Regulation 5 of the AAUP's 1976 "Recommended Institutional Regulations" (RIR), and procedures for dismissals based on financial exigency are discussed in Regulation 4(c) (American Association of University Professors, 1977c). The courts have recognized that there is a distinct difference between those two kinds of dismissals and correspondingly a difference in procedural safeguards (*Browzin* v. *Catholic University of America,* 527 F.2d 843, 846–47 (D.C. Cir. 1975)). To dismiss for cause is a direct challenge to the personal competence or conduct of the faculty member and requires stricter safeguards than dismissal for financial reasons, which is impersonal.

Defining Financial Exigency

In its "Recommended Institutional Regulations," the AAUP defines financial exigency as "an imminent financial crisis which threatens the survival of the institution as a whole and which cannot be alleviated by less drastic means" (1977c, p. 17). The meaning of the AAUP's "survival" standard is that the institution would have to close if it did not dismiss tenured faculty. This "survival" standard also implies that, before deciding to dismiss tenured faculty to prevent closure, a college has first tried other remedial measures (presumably less drastic than terminating tenured faculty) to alleviate its severe financial difficulties.

In the cases where the college's contract did not expressly adopt the AAUP's "survival" standard for defining financial exigency, the courts have not used the "survival" standard in determining whether a financial exigency exists. Determining whether a financial exigency exists also entails the question of how much deference a court may or must give to the discretionary judgment of a college's board of trustees. In assessing the reasonableness of a board's determination of financial difficulties, may a court review all capital assets and analyze their potential alternative uses to alleviate the college's financial difficulties? The cases reviewed below indicate that the courts have preferred to leave the determination of financial exigency to the judgment of a college's governing authority and have accepted as financial exigencies situations that would not meet the AAUP's "survival" standard.

In *Lumpert* v. *University of Dubuque*, 225 N.W.2d 168 (Iowa Court of Appeals No. 2-57568, April 14, 1977) (Table of Unpublished Opinions), the contract under which the tenured faculty member had been dismissed included the following provision: "It is understood that continuous appointment is based upon the need for the services of the appointee and the financial ability of the institution to continue the appointment." The trial court defined "financial ability" and "financial exigency" as follows: "financial ability: the ability to provide from current income, both cash and accrued, the funds necessary to meet current expenses, including current debt payment and sound reserves, without invading or depleting capital; financial exigency: an urgent need to reorder the nature and magnitude of financial obligations in such a way as to restore or preserve the financial ability of the institution" (255 N.W.2d 168). For the trial court, the university's inability to meet current expenses from current income constituted financial exigency. On the question of the permissible scope of review, the court of appeals held: "Whether a financial exigency existed is primarily a matter of subjective judgment to be exercised by the officials charged with . . . operating the university . . . [and] not . . . a question of fact to be determined by the jury. Moreover, we do not believe it is a matter for the substitution of the court's judgment . . . for that of an administrative body" (225 N.W.2d 168).

In contrast, in *AAUP* v. *Bloomfield College*, 129 N.J. Super. 249, 332 A.2d 846 (Ch. 1974), the trial court accepted the AAUP's "survival" definition of financial exigency. In June 1973 Bloomfield College dismissed thirteen tenured faculty. On June 26, 1974, the New Jersey trial court ordered reinstatement with back pay of full salaries. "Tenure should be vigilantly protected by a court of equity except where . . . the survival of the college is imperiled and then only where the good faith of the administration in seeking the severance of tenured personnel has been clearly demonstrated as a measure reasonably calculated to preserve its existence as an academic institution . . . and not simply in some degree advance the financial fortunes of the institution" (332 A.2d at 854). The trial court took the position that the determination of whether the current financial difficulties of the college constituted "extraordinary circumstances," which under the contract would allow the dismissal of tenured faculty, should include an analysis of the college's capital assets and alternative possible uses of them to solve the college's cumulative deficit, liquidity, and cash-flow problems. Because the college had assets in the form of real property (the Knoll Country Club purchased by Bloomfield College in 1966), which could be sold to alleviate the liquidity problem, the trial court found that there was no financial exigency (332 A.2d at 857).

The court of appeals rules that the trial court had erred in its interpretation of the meaning of financial exigency. "The interpretation of 'exigency' as attributed by the trial court is too narrow a concept of the term in relation to the subject matter involved. A more reasonable construction might be encompassed with the phrase 'state of urgency'" (*AAUP* v. *Bloomfield College*, 136 N.J. Super. 442, 446, 346 A.2d 615, 617 (App. Div. 1975)). It further ruled that the trial court had erred in not finding a state of financial exigency "in view of the admitted absence of liquidity and cash flow" (346 A.2d at 617) and that the trial court had overstepped the proper bounds of judicial review by its analysis of alternative uses of the capital assets of the college as a way to resolve its financial difficulties. "It was improper for the judge to rest his conclusion in whole or in part upon the failure of the college to sell the Knoll property . . . the exercise of the business judgment whether to sell or retain this valuable asset was exclusively for the board of trustees of the college and not for the substituted judgment of the court" (346 A.2d at 617).

In *Krotkoff* v. *Goucher College,* 585 F.2d 675 (4th Cir. 1978), one of the four issues that the federal district court submitted to the jury was whether the trustees reasonably believed that a financial exigency existed at Goucher. The plaintiff argued on appeal that the jury was entitled to determine "whether the trustees acted unreasonably in failing to secure judicial permission to invade these assets [namely, a large endowment and valuable land] and whether the trustees should have sold land which they were holding for a better price" (585 F.2d at 680–81). Goucher College, like Bloomfield College, had capital assets available, the disposition of which arguably would have been a less drastic way of alleviating its financial difficulties than terminating tenured faculty. The 4th Circuit, noting the *Bloomfield* case, concluded that "the existence of financial exigency should be determined by the adequacy of a college's operating funds rather than its capital assets" (585 F.2d at 681).

In *Scheuer v. Creighton University*, 199 Neb. 618, 260 N.W.2d 595 (1977), the court held that the term *financial exigency*, as used in the professor's contract of employment, was not restricted to a financial crisis threatening the institution as a whole, but that a financial exigency in a department or college of a university is sufficient cause to terminate employment of tenured faculty. The court argued that a close analysis of prior cases supported this conclusion.

> We do not accept the 1976 recommendations of the AAUP defining "financial exigency" so as to limit that term to an imminent crisis which threatens the survival of the institution as a whole. . . .
>
> . . . To accept plaintiff's definition would require Creighton to continue programs running up large deficits so long as the institution as a whole had financial resources available to it. The inevitable result of this type [of] operation would be to spread the financial exigency in one school or department to the entire university. This could likely result in the closing of the entire institution.
>
> . . . Common sense dictates that plaintiff's contention is untenable. To sustain it, we must hold no tenured employee in any college may be released until the institution exhausts its total assets or at the very least reaches the point where its very survival as an institution is in jeopardy [260 N.W.2d at 600–01].

Courts have accepted the following as financial exigencies sufficient to warrant the termination of tenured faculty:

- Legislatively mandated budget reduction, which necessitated reducing the number of faculty members (*Levitt v. Board of Trustees of Nebraska State Colleges*, 376 F. Supp. 945 (1974)).

- Current $100,000 operating deficit (*Lumpert* v. *University of Dubuque,* 255 N.W.2d 168 (Iowa Court of Appeals No. 2-57568, April 14, 1977) (Table of Unpublished Opinions)).
- Legislatively mandated 2.5 percent budget reduction plus reduced enrollments (*Johnson* v. *Board of Regents of the University of Wisconsin System,* 377 F. Supp. 227 (1974)).
- Cumulative operating deficits, no cash, loss of credit, declining enrollments (*AAUP* v. *Bloomfield College,* 136 N.J. Super. 442, 346 A.2d 615 (App. Div. 1975)).
- Stipulation that the School of Engineering and Architecture was faced with a severe budget reduction (*Browzin* v. *Catholic University of America,* 527 F.2d 843 (D.C. Cir. 1975)).
- Situation in which the School of Pharmacy had had an operating deficit for six years, anticipated another, and was facing a reduction in funds after having adopted other remedial measures (*Scheuer* v. *Creighton University,* 199 Neb. 618, 260 N.W.2d 595 (1977)).
- Six years of operating deficits, expendable endowment diminished, declining enrollment (*Krotkoff* v. *Goucher College,* 585 F.2d 675 (4th Cir. 1978)).

However severe the financial difficulties of any of these institutions, it is difficult to characterize any of these situations, with the exception of Bloomfield College, as an imminent financial crisis threatening the survival of the institution as a whole. It seems that the courts are unlikely to apply the AAUP "survival" standard of financial exigency as contractually binding unless this standard has been explicitly adopted by an institution. The 4th Circuit's "operating funds" standard seems more likely to prevail.

Tenure: A Matter of National Understanding

Prior to the *Krotkoff* v. *Goucher College* decision (1978), no court had decided whether termination of tenured faculty by reason of financial exigency is permissible in the absence of a financial exigency clause in the tenure contract.

One major issue in the *Goucher College* case was whether, as a matter of law, the tenure contract inherently permitted termination because of financial exigency when there was no provision concerning financial exigency in the contract or in relevant college policies. The 4th Circuit (Butzner, Circuit Judge) held that, even without a contract provision regarding financial exigency, a college may terminate tenured faculty on the grounds of financial exigency.

The significance of the 4th Circuit's decision in the *Goucher* case is that it relied on "the national academic community's understanding of the concept of tenure" as the basis for its decision. The 4th Circuit held that, in the absence of any evidence of a different understanding or practice in the Goucher academic community, the Goucher contract must be interpreted consistently with the understanding of the national academic community about tenure and financial exigency. This approach further reinforces the legal trend toward a common law of academic status (Finkin, 1973).

Neither the Goucher College contract nor other relevant faculty policy statements referred to or incorporated by reference any of the AAUP's policies. The question raised by the 4th Circuit's approach is: How far will a court go in importing AAUP statements and regulations into a faculty contract in the absence of a specific reference? In the *Scheuer* case (1977), the supreme court of Nebraska refused to accept the AAUP's 1976 "Recommended Institutional Regulations" (RIR) defining financial exigency, since that definition was adopted several years after the execution of the contract, which explicitly incorporated the 1940 statement and the 1968 RIR. The District of Columbia circuit court, in the *Browzin* case (1975), stated: "It is entirely proper to look to the 1925 statement and indeed to other material cited by *amicus* [AAUP] in interpreting the contract before us. . . . This does not mean, however, that all of the AAUP's proffered documents necessarily control the disposition of the case at hand. Determining the relevance of each requires a sensitive exploration of its impact on the academic community, assessing whether it represents accepted norms of conduct or has founded widely shared expectations" (527 F.2d at 847–48). It seems that the courts will attend to AAUP policies and regulations and give them significant weight as indicators of the national academic understanding and practice, but not in an undiscriminating or automatic way.

The 4th Circuit relied in part on the expert testimony of Todd Furniss, director of the Office of Academic Affairs of the American Council on Education, who testified that the "common understanding" was that a tenure contract could be terminated in an instance of financial exigency. He based his opinion partly on the AAUP's 1940 "Statement of Principles on Academic Freedom and Tenure," which states: "After the expiration of a probationary period, teachers . . . should have permanent . . . tenure, and their services should be terminated only for adequate cause, except . . . under extraordinary circumstances because of financial exigencies" (585 F.2d at 679). The 4th Circuit's analysis of the primary purpose of tenure showed that a concept of tenure permitting dismissal based on financial exigency is consistent with tenure's primary purpose. "Dismissals based on financial exigency, unlike those for cause or disability, are impersonal; they are unrelated to the views of the dismissed teachers. A professor whose appointment is terminated because of financial exigency will not be replaced by another with more conventional views or better connections. Hence, bona fide dismissals based on financial exigency do not threaten the values protected by tenure" (585 F.2d at 680).

Dismissals Demonstrably Bona Fide

The 4th Circuit accepted "the understanding of the national academic community," as expressed in AAUP statements, as allowing dismissal of tenured faculty by reason of financial exigency, even without a contract provision regarding financial exigency. At the same time, the courts have not accepted the AAUP's standard of "survival of the institution as a whole" as the test of financial exigency unless there was an express contract provision adopting the AAUP standard. However, the courts have consistently accepted the AAUP position that dismissals of tenured faculty by reason of financial exigency must be demonstrably bona fide.

A review of the cases indicates that while dismissed faculty have challenged an institution's declaration of financial exigency, most often their principal challenge has been to the "good faith" aspect of the dismissals. They have complained that the dismissals were motivated by an antitenure bias and that financial exigency was a subterfuge used to defeat the purpose of tenure *or* that the criteria and methods of determining who should be dismissed were arbitrary and capricious in general or as applied to specific individuals *or* that the college failed to make a reasonable effort to provide alternative positions for which the dismissed faculty were reasonably qualified.

An Illustration of "Bad Faith." AAUP v. *Bloomfield College,* 129 N.J. Super. 249, 322 A.2d 846 (Ch. 1974), provides an excellent illustration of "bad faith" dismissals, despite a genuine situation of financial exigency. Bloomfield College's board of trustees had dismissed thirteen faculty members and offered the remaining faculty one-year terminal contracts, which in effect abrogated their tenure status. Bloomfield College was in a situation of financial exigency that justified under the contract the dismissal of tenured faculty, and the college could show that the dismissals were a measure reasonably calculated to alleviate its financial exigency. While the *Bloomfield* appellate court ruled that the trial court had erred in not finding financial exigency, it upheld the trial court's finding that the dismissals were not demonstrably bona fide (136 N.J. Super. 442, 346 A.2d 615 (1975)). "The existence of the 'financial exigency' per se does not necessarily mean that the termination of tenure was proper. The key factual issue before the court was whether the financial exigency was the bona fide cause for the decision to terminate the services of thirteen members of the faculty and to eliminate the tenure of the remaining members of the faculty. . . . Causation and motivation therefore emerged as the prime factual issue for determination by the trial judge" (346 A.2d at 617–18).

The following considerations were the bases for the trial court's findings of "bad faith."

1. The college had failed to show how abrogation of its status of tenure for the continuing faculty was a measure reasonably calculated to alleviate the college's financial exigency. There was no showing of an immediate financial benefit from the abrogation of tenure. "It was a gratuitous challenge to the principle of academic freedom" (322 A.2d at 856). If Bloomfield College had not abolished the tenure system itself for continuing faculty, an action with no immediate financial consequences, other evidence in the record suggestive of a lack of "good faith" might not have had the same persuasive impact.

2. After the dismissals Bloomfield had appointed new full-time faculty members to twelve of the fifty-four positions mandated by its new curriculum. The trial court found that the college

had failed to explain convincingly why the thirteen dismissed faculty members were not reasonably qualified to fill the twelve new positions (333 A.2d at 856). Furthermore, these dismissed faculty apparently were not given the opportunity to show that they were qualified for some or all of the positions filled by the newly appointed faculty. At least, the trial judge was not convinced that the college had shown in court what its criteria were for filling these positions and that the dismissed individual faculty had had an opportunity to show that they met those criteria. If Bloomfield College had shown this convincingly in court, perhaps the court might simply have ordered the reinstatement of tenure status to continuing faculty and at the same time upheld the specific dismissals.

3. Another indicator of "bad faith" was the timing of the board's decisions. In the fall of 1973—*after* the initiation of the suit and *after* the June dismissals—the board formally made its decision to adopt the new academic programs that were the educational basis for the full-time positions available. This "backward" timing apparently created a suspicion in the mind of the trial judge that the new curriculum was adopted as a subterfuge to rationalize earlier actions (332 A.2d at 856). The college might have appeared in a better light if the timing of these formal decisions had been reversed; that is, if it had first determined academic program needs and then, on that basis, decided how many and what positions to authorize in order to meet those needs.

4. Relying on the expert testimony of William Keast, chairman of the Commission on Academic Tenure (AAUP/AAC Commission), the trial court found that the college had failed to follow "standard academic procedure." "Termination of tenure based on changes in academic programs can be justified only after a faculty evaluation of the problem" (332 A.2d at 856–57). "The 'standard practice' is to involve the maximum amount of faculty participation to ensure sound professional judgment that the long-term purposes of the college will be fulfilled, to ensure that the new programs are clearly desirable educationally, that the financial considerations are clearly bona fide, and that the best professional judgment is made as to those places in the faculty where reductions should be made in order to achieve the long-term purposes of the college" (332 A.2d at 857). Apparently, the college had

failed to introduce evidence, if there was any, that the faculty had participated in an evaluation of the problem.

5. Before dismissing tenured faculty, the college had failed to use alternative remedial measures—such as across-the-board salary reductions for all faculty members or nonrenewal of probationary faculty's contracts—to alleviate its urgent financial difficulties (332 A.2d at 858). This consideration of the trial court again indicates its adoption of the AAUP's definition of financial exigency as "an imminent financial crisis which threatens the survival of the institution as a whole and which *cannot be alleviated by less drastic means*" (Italics mine). The AAUP standard asserts that the most drastic means, the ultimate measure, to be adopted by an institution to alleviate financial exigency is to dismiss tenured faculty. If the college had adopted less drastic remedial measures reasonably available to it within the restraints of its operating budget, the "good faith" of the dismissals might not have been suspect.

6. Internal memoranda introduced into evidence indicated to the court an antitenure position on the part of the college's president (332 A.2d at 857–58).

An Illustration of "Good Faith." While the *Bloomfield College* case illustrates what counts for "bad faith," *Krotkoff* v. *Goucher College,* 585 F.2d 675 (4th Cir. 1978), illustrates "good faith." In addition to implying the institution's contractual right to dismiss tenured faculty on the grounds of financial exigency, the 4th Circuit also implied as an inherent part of every faculty contract at an institution with a tenure system the contractual right of the faculty that the dismissal be demonstrably bona fide. According to the 4th Circuit's opinion, this right includes the right (1) that the institution use fair and reasonable standards in determining which faculty will be dismissed and (2) that the institution make reasonable efforts to provide dismissed faculty with alternative suitable employment at the institution. Just as it did for the institution's right to dismiss on grounds of financial exigency, again the 4th Circuit relied on "the national academic community's understanding of the concept of tenure" (585 F.2d at 682) to justify making this corresponding faculty right an inherent part of the contract.

Goucher had had a serious cumulative operating deficit and declining enrollments for over six years. Furthermore, Goucher's board of trustees had adopted a more aggressive investment policy to seek a higher rate of return on endowment and had promoted rental of Goucher's auditorium and excess dormitory space. It also had adopted the remedial measures of freezing salaries, cutting administrative and clerical staffs, deferring maintenance, and not renewing the contracts of eleven untenured faculty. A faculty committee, elected by the faculty, had recommended elimination of the classics department and of the German section of the modern language department except for a service program in German, to be staffed by one teacher, for students majoring in other disciplines who needed German as a research skill. The college, in addition, had made an effort to provide the plaintiff with an alternative position.

The "Suitable Position" Requirement. Directly at issue in *Goucher College* was the plaintiff's contention that her contract as a tenured faculty member and her seniority entitled her to be preferred for the remaining position in German over another tenured faculty member with fewer years of service or, alternatively, to be retrained at the college's expense for a position available in another discipline. "The German faculty consisted of Krotkoff, who taught mostly advanced literature courses, and another tenured teacher, Sybille Ehrlich, who taught chiefly introductory language courses. The dean, concurring with the chairman of the department, recommended retention of Ehrlich primarily because she had more experience teaching the elementary language courses that would be offered in a service program and because she was also qualified to teach French. The president followed this recommendation" (585 F.2d at 678). Following the college's decision to abolish her position, the college had given a list of all vacant positions at the college to the plaintiff. She declined to be considered for any position other than a full-time tenured position at her same level of pay. The only such position was in the economics department, an appointment that would require two to four years of additional training.

The 4th Circuit court ruled that nothing in the plaintiff's contract gave her precedence (585 F.2d at 682). "Nor was the college under any contractual obligation to retain Krotkoff by demoting Ehrlich to part-time teaching and part-time administrative work" (585 F.2d at 682). "No evidence suggested that the head of [the economics] department or the president acted unreasonably in assessing the time and expense of retraining Krotkoff for the [vacant] position or in deciding that her transfer would not be feasible" (585 F.2d at 683). In the absence of an explicit contractual provision, tenure does not entitle faculty to training for appointment in another discipline.

In *Browzin* v. *Catholic University of America*, 527 F.2d 843 (D.C. Cir. 1975), the court also addressed the "suitable position" requirement. Judge Shelly Wright provided this perspective:

> A university must have some flexibility to respond to drastic reductions in funds or to the need for a change in curriculum. . . . In these situations, the same elaborate procedural safeguards [that are required when a faculty member is dismissed for cause] do not apply because they are not entirely suitable to the issues arising when the university changes its curriculum or reacts to reduced funding.
>
> But the obvious danger remains that "financial exigency" can become too easy an excuse for dismissing a teacher who is merely unpopular or controversial or misunderstood—a way for the university to rid itself of an unwanted teacher but without according him his important procedural rights. The "suitable position" requirement would stand as a partial check against such abuses. An institution truly motivated only by financial considerations would not hesitate to place the tenured professor in another position if one can be found, even if this meant displacing a nontenured instructor [527 F.2d at 846–47].

And in a footnote the court states, "Although the most likely place to find other positions which will prove suitable is, of course, the department or school the professor formerly served, the university's obligation is not discharged unless it has considered other departments and schools as well" (527 F.2d at 846–47, n.7).

In this perspective the "good faith" indicators or requirements are necessary as a check against the potential for abuse of the purpose of tenure. "Bad faith" is the use of financial exigency as a "too easy excuse" to violate academic freedom.

The major issue on appeal in *Browzin* involved an interpretation of Regulation 4(c) of the 1968 AAUP "Recommended Institutional Regulations," which both parties stipulated were binding under the contract by specific reference (527 F.2d at 846). The federal district court ruled that the language of the 1968 RIR required the university to make a reasonable effort to find alternative suitable employment *only* in the case of discontinuance of a program of instruction and *not* in a situation of financial exigency. Since both parties had stipulated that this was a financial exigency situation, the district court ruled that the university had no contractual obligation to find alternative "suitable employment" (527 F.2d at 846). On appeal the AAUP *amicus* brief contended that the history of the formulation of the 1968 RIR clearly indicated that the intent of the 1968 RIR was to make the "suitable employment" requirement mandatory in situations both of financial exigency and of discontinuance of a program of instruction (527 F.2d at 846). The circuit court held that the interpretation issue was not decisive for establishing the university's contractual obligation, since the facts clearly indicated that the situation included both financial exigency and discontinuance of a program (527 F.2d at 848).

More important, the plaintiff in *Browzin* had accepted the burden at the trial level of proving that an alternative suitable position was available and/or that the university had failed to make a reasonable effort to find alternative suitable employment for him. The federal district court ruled that he had failed to make a prima facie case, and this decision was sustained by the court of appeals (527 F.2d at 849–50).

Right of First Refusal. Does a tenured faculty member dismissed because of financial exigency have the right to be the first person offered the position in the event that it would again become available? While the *Goucher* case did not address this issue, *Browzin* did. In *Browzin* both parties stipulated that the contract incorporated the AAUP's 1968 RIR. Regulation 4(c) provided that "the released faculty member's place will not be filled by a replacement within a period of two years unless the displaced member first has had an opportunity to accept the post." Another professor joined the department a year and a half after Browzin was dismissed. Browzin was never offered the opportunity to return to his former position in the department. Although the plaintiff had competence in two of the three areas assigned to the new professor, the circuit court sustained the federal district court's finding of fact that the new professor had not been hired to fill Browzin's place, since the *third* area was the *critical* area in the program and the program of courses as a whole was significantly different from what Browzin had been teaching (527 F.2d at 850–51).

Burden of Proof

Kaplin (1978, pp. 163–164) has noted that the allocation of burden of proof "has critical practical importance; because the evidentiary problems can be so difficult, the outcome of financial exigency litigation may often depend on who has the burden of proof." Does the college have the burden of proving that it has fulfilled all explicit and implicit contract provisions that justify termination of tenured faculty? Or do the dismissed faculty members have the burden of proving that contractual conditions have not been met?

In *AAUP* v. *Bloomfield College,* 129 N.J. Super. 249, 322 A.2d 846 (Ch. 1974), the trial court assigned the burden of proof to the college on all issues. The appeals court sustained this allocation. "[Tenure] was their [that is, the faculty's] vested right, which could legally be divested only if the defined conditions occurred. The proof of existence of these conditions as a justifiable reason for terminating the status of the plaintiffs plainly was the burden of the defendants" (346 A.2d at 616). As a prerequisite for dismissing tenured faculty, the college had the burden of proving by a preponderance of the evidence (1) that there were extraordinary circumstances because of financial exigency and (2) that the dismissals were demonstrably bona fide.

In *Browzin* v. *Catholic University of America,* 527 F.2d 843 (D.C. Cir. 1975), the federal district court placed the burden of proof on the plaintiff to demonstrate that Catholic University had violated his tenure contract by failing to make a reasonable effort to place him in another suitable position. Apparently, the district court relied on the contract law principle that usually the burden rests on the plaintiff as to all elements of his action for breach of contract. The district court held that the plaintiff had failed to make a prima facie case on the "suitable position" issue. On appeal the plaintiff-appellant argued for reversal on the grounds that the district court had erroneously allocated the burden of proof. The court of appeals for the District of Columbia did not directly settle this issue but did sustain the district court because of the appellant's failure to object at trial to the allocation of the burden of proof (527 F.2d at 850).

In *Krotkoff* v. *Goucher College,* 585 F.2d 675 (4th Cir. 1978), the federal district court placed the burden of proof on the college on all issues: (1) whether the college was entitled to read the condition of financial exigency into its contract; (2) whether the trustees reasonably believed that a financial exigency existed at Goucher; (3) whether Goucher reasonably used uniform standards in selecting the plaintiff for dismissal; and (4) whether the college made reasonable efforts to find the plaintiff alternative suitable employment at Goucher. On appeal, no issue was raised regarding the allocation of burden of proof.

On the basis of these cases where the allocation of burden of proof has been addressed directly *(Bloomfield College)* or indirectly *(Browzin, Goucher College),* it is reasonable to conclude that the college has the burden of proving (1) that it was faced with financial exigency and (2) that the dismissals were demonstrably bona fide.

Specific Performance Remedy

The usual remedy at law for breach of contract is compensatory money damages. In special situations where money damages are inadequate to remedy the wrong done, courts will grant the equitable remedy of specific performance of the contract subject matter—in the case of improper faculty dismissals, reinstatement. In the *Bloomfield College* case, the trial court reinstated the plaintiffs to their full-time faculty positions with tenure. On appeal Bloomfield College attacked the propriety of the remedy of specific performance, whereby plaintiffs were reinstated to their positions, but the court of appeals affirmed the remedy: "In view of the uncertainty in measuring damages because of the indefinite duration of the contract and the importance of the status of the plaintiffs in the milieu of the college teaching profession, it is evident that the remedy of damages at law would not be complete or adequate" (346 A.2d at 618).

Legal Conclusions

Both the academic community and the courts recognize that financial exigency is a legitimate ground for the dismissal of tenured faculty. The 4th Circuit has held financial exigency to be an inherent term implicit in every tenure contract, unless a particular academic institution shows that it has had an understanding or practice different from that of the "national academic community." The courts are not likely to apply the AAUP's "survival" standard of financial exigency unless this standard has been explicitly adopted by an institution. The 4th Circuit's "operating funds" standard seems more likely to prevail. The *Scheuer* court applied this standard to a division of the university and did not restrict its application to the operating budget of the university as a whole.

More precisely stated, courts do not determine whether an institution is in a situation of financial exigency—institutions do. Rather, if a plaintiff chooses to challenge an institution's decision that it is in a state of financial exigency, the court will review, based on evidence presented by the parties, whether the institution's decision has been arbitrary or capricious. To decide this "arbitrary or capricious" issue, the courts need a definition of financial exigency, a standard against which they can compare the institution's assessment of its situation.

The cases show that the courts have adopted an "operating funds" standard and rejected the AAUP "survival" standard. They have limited their scope of review to the financial needs of the institution in terms of its operating budget and have rejected an approach that would include an analysis of the institution's assets.

This "operating funds" approach is similar to the "business judgment" rule. Just as courts (theoretically) do not decide what is the *best* or the *wisest* legislation or agency rule or contract provision, but only whether the statute is rationally related to a permissible state purpose, or whether an agency's action is reasonable (that is, based on substantial evidence in the record considered as a whole), or what was the intent of the parties (who are free to enter into a foolish contract)—so likewise courts do not second-guess the wisdom of a company's board of directors but only review whether their decision was not arbitrary or capricious (that is, whether it was reached in good faith and for the good of the business). A court is not to second-guess a board's decision about the disposition of assets for the long-term good of the institution. *Legally,* Congress, agencies, businesses, and the like are entitled to make mistakes (by hindsight) or decisions that do have consequences that hurt people (for example, layoffs).

In effect, these courts are saying that a college can lay off tenured faculty for financial reasons (to balance its operating budget). However, in doing so, because tenure is so important to academic freedom and is a contractual commitment, the college must comply with certain procedural safeguards to ensure good faith. That is, it is not sufficient that an institution is in a situation of financial exigency. The courts uniformly insist that the dismissals be bona fide; that is, motivated and caused solely and exclusively by considerations of financial exigency. A dismissal decision is in bad faith if motivated by an antitenure bias, with the financial situation used as a subterfuge. A dismissal decision is also in bad faith if, although properly motivated, the college failed (1) to adopt and apply uniformly reasonably objective standards and/or (2) to make a reasonable effort to find an alternative "suitable position" for the dismissed faculty. The "suitable position" requirement does not entitle the dismissed faculty to training for appointment to a position available in another discipline.

When there is an issue over which of two tenured faculty members to retain to fill an authorized position for which both are qualified, there is no inherent, implicit right to be preferred by reason of seniority of service.

The cases have not addressed the question whether a tenured faculty member dismissed by reason of financial exigency has an implicit, inherent right of first refusal. The logic of the courts' reliance on "the understanding of the national academic community," in the absence of express contract provisions, and the fact that a financial exigency dismissal is impersonal suggest that courts would include the right of first refusal as part of the "good faith" requirement.

As for the burden of proof, the courts have ruled that in litigation the institution must show (1) that the institution is in a situation of financial exigency, (2) that the termination of tenured faculty is a measure reasonably calculated to alleviate the financial exigency, (3) that those terminated were fairly selected, and (4) that the institution made a reasonable effort to find an alternative suitable position. The burden then shifts to the plaintiff to prove by a preponderance of the evidence that any one or more of the four assertions stated above are not true. If the plaintiff prevails on any one of the four, the plaintiff is entitled to the remedy of specific performance.

Future Issues

This chapter has assumed the existence of a tenure system at institutions of higher education. In contract law the intent of the parties to the contract is controlling and the express terms decisive. Governing boards, administrators, and faculty should be clear about the contract and the faculty policies and procedures at their particular institutions. If these documents incorporate the 1940 AAUP "Statement on Principles of Academic Freedom and Tenure," this incorporation does not bind the parties to other AAUP policies (for example, the 1976 RIR's definition of financial exigency). If these documents do incorporate the AAUP "survival" standard, the parties are bound by that standard.

While it is almost impossible to predict with certainty the outcome of future litigation, in general it is reasonable to assume on the basis of the cases reviewed that the courts will sustain dismissals of tenured faculty because of financial exigency as long as three essential conditions are met: (1) The faculty have been informed of and have participated in decisions regarding the educational mission, educational programs, qualifications for staffing, and criteria to determine which programs and faculty will be terminated. (2) There has been no antitenure animus on the part of the governing board and/or administration. (3) The governing board's decisions regarding the educational mission and financial situation of the institution are not arbitrary or capricious. The AAUP policy on financial exigency itself allows the retention of nontenured faculty over tenured faculty where not to do so would entail "a serious distortion of the academic program."

It remains to be seen whether the *Scheuer* court's decision— that financial exigency in a department or unit of the college or university is sufficient to warrant financial exigency dismissals— will be adopted in other jurisdictions. The AAUP "survival" standard limits financially exigent situations to those affecting the institution as a whole. If an institution, in its academic planning and budget process, were to hold each unit accountable for its revenues and expenditures and on that basis from year to year authorize faculty positions, in the absence of any express contrary contract provisions, the *Scheuer* court approach might very well be adopted.

Future litigation will further refine a number of issues already litigated and resolve new issues. It is clear that the courts accept financial exigency as a valid contract excuse for dismissing tenured faculty. But will the courts allow an institution to dismiss tenured faculty in order to avoid financial exigency? A number of institutions may find themselves in a nondeficit but precarious operating budget situation. In order to maintain their nondeficit posture and to enhance their educational and financial vitality, these institutions may initiate a process of redefining their basic educational mission. And the result of this newly defined mission may entail the dropping of some programs, with dismissal of program faculty, and simultaneously the initiation of new academic programs, with the appointment of qualified faculty. On the one hand, sound management requires that the institution be managed in such a way that it will not become an educational "Chrysler Corporation." On the other hand, the situation of these institutions meets neither the AAUP's "survival" standard nor the courts' "operating funds" standard. A solution to this situation might be to appeal to the 1976 AAUP RIR, which allows dismissal of tenured faculty "as a result of bona fide formal discontinuance of a program" (American Association of University Professors, 1977c, p. 18). The discontinuance is to be "based essentially upon educational considerations," which are to be "determined primarily by the faculty as a whole or an appropriate committee thereof" and which must reflect "long-range judgments that the educational mission of the institution as a whole will be enhanced by the discontinuance." The problem with this solution is that the "educational considerations" are "not to include cyclical or temporary variations in enrollments." Courts may view this restriction as an unrealistic restraint on the institution's need and ability to change its curriculum, just as they have rejected the AAUP "survival" standard while affirming the AAUP's basic policy that financial exigency is a valid basis for dismissing tenured faculty.

During hard financial times, individuals and institutions are inescapably confronted with difficult "philosophical" issues. These issues are not and should not be primarily legal decisions. Faculty, administrators, and governing boards must work thoroughly through the root questions of mission and integrity: "Who are we? What are we doing? Why? Should we be doing it or something else?"

For Further Reading

For comprehensive coverage as well as detailed analyses on legal issues affecting higher education, two works that can profitably be used as basic, up-to-date starting points are *The Law of Higher Education: Legal Implications of Administrative Decision Making* (Kaplin, 1978), together with its update (Kaplin, 1980); and *Higher Education and the Law* (Edwards and Nordin, 1979), together with its cumulative supplement (Edwards and Nordin, 1980).

❧ 11 ❧

Enrollment Management

Frank M. Bowen
Lyman A. Glenny

One form of enrollment management—a term that encompasses many different concepts and activities—is the planned and controlled distribution of students among campuses within a state. In most states the existing distribution of students is not the product of deliberate planning and enforcement of size limitations; instead, with few exceptions, student choice has determined campus size. But with prospects of a declining enrollment pool, some state and higher education administrators see the use of ceilings, quotas, or "caps" as a means of limiting the possibly adverse results of increasing institutional competition.

Ceilings or quotas have the appeal of apparent simplicity. The most visible and easily quantified impact of a declining enrollment pool will be the unevenness of its effects among campuses. We expect large campuses and those in major population centers to be more attractive to students—part-time ones in particular—than small institutions in isolated locations. Large, popular, and well-situated campuses will maintain and perhaps increase enrollments at the expense of less popular ones. As critical as a statewide decline of, for instance, 10 percent might be, it pales by

194

comparison to the greater impact that its disproportionate distribution could have on individual institutions. For example:

	1980–81 Enrollments	1990–91 Enrollments	Percent Difference
Campus A	15,000	15,000	0
Campus B	10,000	9,000	10
Campus C	5,000	3,000	40
Total State	30,000	27,000	10

The unfortunate results of a 40 percent decline at Campus C could, some might argue, be avoided if enrollment ceilings—of perhaps 14,000 students at Campus A and 9,000 at Campus B—were imposed. The assumption would be that students who could not enroll at Campuses A and B would attend Campus C. This type of enrollment management is discussed in this chapter.

Enrollment Management During Growth

In the 1950s and 1960s, state policy focused on accommodating the unprecedented number of applicants to colleges and universities. Rapid growth was as much of a new problem then as the projected period of decline is now. "Swelling enrollments, mounting budgets, competition for funds among public services, and the establishment of new institutions" were conditions that even the most ardent defenders of institutional autonomy saw as requiring state intervention "by some kind of coordination" (McConnell, 1962, p. 143). Between 1950 and 1970, twenty-six states adopted various agencies for coordination (Berdahl, 1971, p. 35), usually over the objections of institutional leaders but with the statewide objective of maintaining "orderly growth" in higher education. Orderly growth required state higher education agencies to manage factors directly related to enrollments: to review and sometimes approve institutional budgets, campus locations, new physical facilities, and new programs. While the limits on the exercise of this authority are not fixed to the satisfaction of all, these forms of enrollment management clearly remain part of current relationships between higher education and the state.

Institutions changed during the period of growth. Some became remarkably large. Halstead (1974, p. 266) attributes "the gigantic size of some mature institutions . . . to the fact that, for all practical purposes, size as a constraint has been ignored." Growth also meant the establishment of small institutions that were widely dispersed, in order to achieve the goal of access. Millett (1970, p. 48) suggests that the "inclination for geographical dispersion has probably been the most powerful single influence in state government for development of higher education in the . . . twenty-five years following World War II."

State concern with enrollment numbers grew in the 1960s and 1970s as state legislatures, budget offices, and higher education agencies increased their reliance on enrollment-driven formulas to allocate state funds (Boutwell, 1973, p. 41). The extent to which campuses adhered (or were expected to adhere) to enrollment estimates or "targets" used in the formulas varied from state to state. Adherence was expected, for example, in Illinois in the mid-1960s, for targets were intended to discourage overambitious building plans, and institutions were warned that the added costs of students accepted above targets would have to be absorbed indefinitely. Other than temporary overcrowding, however, campuses incurred few penalties for exceeding their enrollment targets. Demand for places continued, campuses were reluctant to turn away applicants, and the prior year's budgetary targets were usually submerged in the heat of the current year's negotiations. The "institutional memory" of a state agency is usually short because of personnel turnover, reorganizations, and the volatile saliency of policy. Good campus administrators in Illinois and elsewhere were aware of this, and most eventually found funding for actual enrollments regardless of budgetary targets. As factors in budget formulas, enrollment targets undoubtedly had some influence on the distribution of students among campuses. But where such targets were intended to set actual enrollment limits—to be ceilings—they seem rarely to have been successful. Target numbers tended to reflect compromise between optimistic institutional enrollment projections and pessimistic estimations of available state resources. Monitoring and enforcement, if any, were fragmented among the many participants in the state budget process. *Distribution of funds,* not of stu-

dents, was (and will remain) *the major objective of state budgeting.*
Budgetary enrollment targets were seen as transitory and negotiable means to fiscal ends. Targets were neither seen nor implemented as long-term objectives with justifications unrelated to
the current budget.

The past period of growth was a "seller's market," in which
the student was the buyer. With loosely controlled eligibility standards, institutions could pick and choose among applicants. Expansion, necessary for access, was encouraged by enrollment-driven
budgetary formulas that generated dollars on an average-cost
rather than a marginal-cost basis. Some legislative authority was
shifted to the new state higher education agencies in attempts to
ensure that size and diversity of demand would be matched by
location, capacity, and diversity of institutions. For other than the
most poorly located campuses, the only real limits on size were
fiscal. Most states (although not all) have met their obligations to
provide a sufficient number and variety of places for students.

During growth, states seldom tampered with the authority
of each institution to accept as many students as its physical capacity
allowed. Enrollments *were* managed, but they were managed *for
growth* by specification of broad policies on location, eligibility, and
institutional missions and programs. In most states the share of
state enrollment a campus now has is its "market share," as determined by institutional attraction, student choice, and the competing political pressures of large institutions and local communities
that wanted new or expanded local campuses. Past state enrollment
management practices—budget review, budgetary enrollment targets, campus and program control, statewide planning—undoubtedly will continue into the projected period of decline. The
question is not really whether enrollment management will take
place but whether fixed enrollment ceilings will serve as tools to
achieve the state objectives of student access, institutional diversity, and program quality.

Enrollment Ceilings in Four States

Experience with enrollment ceilings has not been extensive,
and we could not study all states that currently have or plan such

limits. Instead, we present summaries of how ceilings have been imposed and are operating in four states: California, Colorado, Maryland, and Wisconsin. Although experience in one state is never fully transferable to another, some aspects of the experience in these four states deserve more general consideration.

California: Multicampus Administration of Ceilings. The 1960 *Master Plan for Higher Education in California* established a three-tiered structure through differentiation of segmental functions and eligibility standards. Control over additional campuses was given to a new state higher education agency, but the *Master Plan* permitted growth within the segmental structure. Minimum, maximum, and optimum enrollments were suggested for campuses in all three segments (Liaison Committee . . . , 1960, p. 111), with responsibility for enforcement left to the segmental governing boards. The *Master Plan* enrollment ceilings apparently were developed primarily to determine the need for additional campuses. However, campus ceilings were already part of long-range planning at the University of California, based on perceptions of relationships among maximum size, quality of instruction, controlled growth, costs, and community impact. It is the University of California experience that is of interest here.

University policies for maintaining ceilings first developed in the mid-1960s, when enrollments at Berkeley reached the suggested limit of 27,500. The policies, as they emerged, became applicable to both ultimate limits and interim quotas for controlled growth of new campuses. In the beginning the University of California Academic Senate (1964, p. 54) recommended random selection (and rejection) of applicants: "One student's claims are as good as another's, and, since there are not places enough for all, random selection would seem to offer the best chance to avoid bitter feelings when some are retained and others are redirected." A minority of faculty wanted only scholastic criteria to be used. But neither random selection nor wholly scholastic criteria were instituted by the systemwide administration.

Current university procedures, which have remained substantially unchanged since 1970 (Kidner, 1971; University of California, Berkeley, 1979), are designed to assure every qualified applicant a place at one of the university's eight general campuses. Applicants are not merely rejected after a ceiling is reached but are given redirection to other campuses. When a student applies for admission, his application form—a uniform application for all campuses—is filed at the campus of first choice. The applicant also can designate second- and third-choice campuses and state particular reasons why it would be a hardship to attend a campus other than that of first choice. The month of November is an open-filing period, and all applications that a campus receives during that period are given equal consideration. About two months are allowed for screening applicants and notifying them of their status, and delays are not uncommon.

The first step in campus enrollment planning is to estimate the number of continuing students for the following year and to reserve places for them. The second step is to translate the number of places available for new students into the substantially larger number of applications that must be processed to fill those places. At the university slightly more than half of the students who file applications eventually enroll at their campuses of first choice. If, during the open-enrollment period, a campus receives more applications than are required to fill the places available, then university policy specifies criteria both for selection among applicants and for redirection of those not selected. Campuses receiving more applications than places available must select among them as follows: 50 percent are selected on the basis of high school grades—the best academically of all applicants; 45 percent are selected on the basis of "criteria not wholly academic," such as academic interests, campus programs, hardship factors, selective recruiting efforts, and special awards; and 5 percent of the open places are reserved for appeals.

Those whose applications are not selected for processing are redirected to their second-choice campus, if designated, and their records are forwarded to that campus. Redirection causes at least three problems for the second-choice campuses: uncertainty over the coming fall enrollment because of unexpected increases or decreases in applications to the University of California as a whole; uncertainty regarding continuing students, since a substantial number may be simply biding time until they can transfer to their first-choice campus; "image and quality-of-life problems, which are the result of having a large proportion of students who would rather be somewhere else" (McGuire, 1974).

The ceilings and redirection procedures have kept popular campuses from growing beyond levels perceived as appropriate and have probably increased enrollment at less popular ones. Data indicate, however, that only 27 percent of redirected applicants actually register at a second-choice campus, whereas 53 percent register at their first choice (McCorkle, 1974). But redirected students can be a substantial proportion of the new undergraduate enrollment of a second-choice campus. The only incentive for a redirected applicant was assurance of a place later at some other campus in the same system. In 1979, however, a new incentive was added for those seeking admission to the popular Berkeley campus. At that time the University of California approved a bilateral agreement between Berkeley and Santa Cruz that would assure participating students, on successful completion of lower-division work at Santa Cruz, a place in the upper-division programs at Berkeley (Doby, 1980, p. 17). Under these still-experimental procedures, Berkeley increased the percentage of successful redirections to Santa Cruz from about 30 to about 40 percent. Although of limited scope thus far, the new procedures provide options that were not previously available to students. It is unlikely that they would have been adopted, however, in the absence of expected enrollment and budgetary pressures on the entire university system.

Colorado: Bilateral Administration of Ceilings. Enrollment limits were first imposed by the Colorado legislature in 1971. They remain in effect, substantially unchanged, for the state's two major university campuses—the Boulder campus of the University of Colorado and Colorado State University at Fort Collins. A recent legislative staff memorandum states the reasons for the original imposition (Colorado State Legislative Council Staff, 1980):

> To control growth in keeping with each institution's stated role and mission. . . .
> To curtail new capital construction programs on these campuses.

To reduce the type of uncoordinated growth which had resulted in duplications of facilities and course offerings.

To respond to local communities concerned about unbridled expansion of institutions.

To "redirect" those students who were refused admission at a "capped" institution to one of the state's many underenrolled institutions. . . .

To achieve a balance between the senior research institutions and those other sectors of the state's higher education system which had experienced disproportionately low enrollments.

To anticipate a decline in enrollments due to reduced populations of college-age peoples, expected to occur in the mid- and late 1970s.

Another staff report suggests that the objective of curtailing capital construction was attained but notes the difficulty of determining the success of redirection: "The success of this 'capping' policy from this perspective has been harder to measure, and may have been partially thwarted by the refusal of the higher education 'system' to provide any incentive to 'redirected' students to attend underenrolled institutions, in the form of 'guaranteed transfer slots' at the senior capped institutions" (Colorado State Joint Budget Committee Staff, 1980). The second staff report notes the paucity of data in Colorado for evaluation of redirection, refers to California data, and pointedly calls attention to the Berkeley–Santa Cruz arrangements for guaranteed admission of redirected students seeking transfer.

Contrary to the staff comments, Colorado State University (1976) has responded to the problems of rejected students. The admissions director initiated two types of contracts with underenrolled institutions: contracts with eight rural community colleges but with no guarantees of eventual admission to Colorado State (although preference is routinely given to all community college transfers who have attained their associate degrees) and contracts with four-year colleges and community colleges that have programs comparable to Colorado State's engineering and forestry degree offerings—with guaranteed admission to Colorado State on completion of course prerequisites. Under both types the nonadmitted applicant's credentials are forwarded, with his or her permission, directly to a campus that has places available, and the costs of administering the referral or redirection are shared by that campus.

About 30 percent of the Colorado State applicants who are referred to a less popular four-year campus enroll at that institution. On the other hand, only some 10 percent of the applicants referred to community college campuses actually enroll at them. Assistance to nonadmitted applicants is only now being implemented on a statewide basis. Responding to legislative direction, the state higher education agency has developed a program to inform rejected students of the availability and benefits of several small four-year and two-year institutions (Colorado Commission on Higher Education, 1979). As at the University of California, ceilings have successfully kept enrollments at Colorado State within bounds perceived as appropriate. Assessments have not been made of the impact of the ceilings on the enrollments at other campuses.

Maryland: State Quotas on Freshman Numbers. In Maryland enrollment management by use of ceilings was instituted as a result of the *Statewide Plan for Postsecondary Education,* issued by the Maryland State Board for Higher Education (1978). In the *Statewide Plan,* the state board noted that earlier institutional emphasis on freshman enrollments and undergraduate education had resulted in large undergraduate enrollments at several institutions, particularly the College Park campus of the University of Maryland. Because enrollment projections in Maryland, as in other states, indicated that the era of expanding undergraduate enrollments was coming to an end, the state board examined the results of the earlier emphasis. It reported the following findings: (1) Enrollments of new full-time freshmen in Maryland concentrated on the College Park campus, some 21 percent of such students being enrolled there in fall 1977, while the two next-largest percentages were 8 percent (Towson State) and 6 percent (Montgomery Community College). (2) Lower-division students constituted almost half of the enrollment at the College Park campus, in contrast to about a third at major university campuses in other states. (3) Although less extreme than for lower-division students, College Park's proportions of both upper-division and graduate students were well below those proportions in comparable institutions. (4) College Park enrollment exceeded its planned physical capacity by about 15 percent, and about $64 million in capital construction would be needed to serve current enrollment. Other campuses had excess space. (5) Overall enrollment trends affected unit instructional costs and effective use of physical facilities; campuses suffering enrollment losses had higher costs per student and more unused physical capacity than campuses whose enrollments had not declined.

On the basis of its findings, the board concluded: "The problem confronting the state is how to increase enrollments where additional plant capacity exists while at the same time eliminating overcrowding at schools where their plant is insufficient, so that the quality of education can be improved" (Maryland State Board for Higher Education, 1978, p. 44). To resolve the problem, the state board proposed that the enrollment of first-time, full-time freshmen at four campuses be limited. By imposing the ceiling on full-time freshmen, the board avoided disruption of continuing students and recognized the dependence of part-time students on nearby institutions. It did not assume that limiting enrollments at some campuses would automatically result in increases at others but, rather, sought to ensure that an adequate enrollment pool would be available if underenrolled campuses could improve programs and reputations to attract more students. Although not explicit in the *Statewide Plan,* it seems assumed that the College Park campus would reduce the number of new full-time freshmen by increasing scholastic admission requirements.

The first annual review of the *Statewide Plan* (Maryland State Board for Higher Education, 1979) showed mixed results among the four campuses in the first year of ceilings. Two campuses, including College Park, admitted fewer new full-time freshmen, roughly meeting the 1978 ceilings. In contrast, the other two campuses had difficulty in meeting ceilings; one was 19 percent below and the other 21 percent above the respective ceilings. In both cases the ceilings were changed to reflect more accurate estimates of physical capacity and admissions experience. In general, assessment was complicated by an unexpected decline in freshman enrollments that Maryland shared with other states. In addition, the College Park reduction was accomplished mainly through limiting out-of-state enrollment.

In the fall of 1979, the College Park campus substantially exceeded the ceiling because of miscalculation of acceptances. During the summer of 1980, new ceilings were being negotiated for all public four-year campuses; but, with the exception of two or three of the four on which ceilings were originally imposed, the ceilings are said to reflect enrollments that the campuses would find difficult to exceed. The ultimate ceiling originally set for the College Park campus is not expected to change, but the campus will be given more time in which to reach it.

In reviewing the impact of ceilings, the state board reportedly uses an enrollment information system—implemented in 1978—that contains data on individual students and provides information on student movement among campuses.

Wisconsin: Ceilings, Quality, and Access. The University of Wisconsin System comprises all public higher education in the state other than two-year vocational and technical schools. Admissions policies are largely the responsibility of the campuses. The governing board requires only that campuses have evidence that applicants are prepared to do satisfactory work; each campus sets specific requirements by way of class rank, course credits, submission of national test scores, and exceptions. The only routine involvements of the central administrative offices with the admissions process are in updating a uniform admissions and financial aid form; in publishing a detailed information brochure for high school students and counselors; and in operating a toll-free telephone information service, called the Higher Education Location Program (HELP).

The system is allocated state funds under a statutory enrollment-driven formula. When this formula was suspended by the legislature for the 1975–77 biennium, the system found that it was unable to provide additional instructional funding for its most rapidly growing campuses. Moreover, because the system projected a decline of some 19,000 full-time-equivalent students by 1993, the wisdom of expanding physical facilities and staffing for what appeared to be a temporary enrollment bulge was questioned (see Chapter Fifteen). In the face of fiscal stringency and perceptions that current enrollment growth was temporary, ceilings were imposed at four of the university's thirteen degree-granting campuses in the fall of 1975, the system electing to limit access rather than to reduce quality: "Thus, the policy issue was framed in Wisconsin: that in attempting to balance the demands of student access and fiscal austerity, educational quality must be preserved" (Craven and Becklin, 1978, p. 106). The ceiling levels were derived from already existing and relatively complex management tools that related enrollment "targets" to funding on student-credit-hour, disciplinary, and instructional-level bases (Bowen and Glenny, 1976, p. 231; Bowen, 1976a, p. 13). These "targets" became "ceilings" for those institutions that were required to control enrollments at or near the targets (Smith, 1980b, and Chapter Fifteen).

In response to concern that ceilings had an adverse effect on educational opportunity, the central administrative offices questioned a stratified random sample of 539 applicants out of some 2,900 who had been denied admission in fall 1976 because of ceilings. From analysis of 460 usable responses, it was concluded that the enrollment ceiling policy appeared to have only a minimal impact on access. More than half of the respondents had not been affected by the ceilings, for they were either enrolled at a first-preference campus or had been accepted by such a campus and decided not to attend school. (Multiple applications are possible in the Wisconsin System, and campus preference does not appear on applications, as it does, for example, at the University of California.) About 27 percent of the respondents were attending campuses of lesser preference. About 14 percent were not attending school, having been rejected by the only campus to which they applied, or by all such campuses, or, after acceptance by a lower-preference campus, having decided not to attend any school. Students attending school, regardless of preference, were substantially more satisfied with their choices than those who were not in school. Those at campuses of first choice were only slightly more satisfied than those at lower-preference campuses (University of Wisconsin System, 1977).

The study indicates that applicants to the Milwaukee campus (an urban setting with a relatively large proportion of minority and disadvantaged and part-time students) were most affected by the ceilings. Only 23 percent of the rejected applicants had made multiple applications—an indication that this place-bound student body perceived few other higher education options open to them. At the other campuses with ceilings, multiple applications were far more common, with 90 to 97 percent of the rejected applicants applying to at least one other institution.

Ceilings were imposed in Wisconsin not to redistribute students but to maintain quality in the face of fiscal stringency. The analysis, therefore, stresses the implications of ceilings on access to a campus with a ceiling, rather than the impact on enrollments at other campuses. It did find, however, that, as a result of the ceilings, students were shifted to a public campus without a ceiling (Craven and Becklin, 1978, p. 106). Loss of access and choice by a relatively small number of applicants may be the price of maintenance of quality. Given the mutual dependence of student numbers, financial support, and program quality, one of these must yield if another changes. It does not seem inappropriate, however, to suggest additional investigation of the impact of ceilings on the urban campus at Milwaukee. It will be unfortunate if quality can be preserved only at the expense of those whose location and financial circumstances are such that denial of choice means denial of access.

Ceilings and Fair Practice Codes: Overlapping Alternatives

We believe that institutional competition for students will increase over the next decade, for the following reasons:

- Higher education's competitive position relative to other state services will neither increase nor decrease substantially during the next decade.
- Total funds for public higher education will continue to vary with total state enrollments, even though funds may not decrease as rapidly as enrollments do.
- The distribution of state funds among public institutions will be closely proportionate to their enrollments.

Each institution will struggle to maintain a historical "fair share" of the state enrollment pool, and many will have to increase their fair share to avoid program and service reductions. The strategy of enrollment maintenance is not, of course, the only one open to institutions, nor is it exclusive of other strategies (Academy for Educational Development, 1979, pp. 143–169). Nevertheless, institutional survival ultimately will depend on the numbers of students enrolled. We have elsewhere stated our belief that increased enrollment stress may tempt institutions to adopt inappropriate competitive means, to lower admissions standards, to dilute program rigor, and to engage in dubious recruiting practices (Glenny, 1978). We have also warned of the dangers of the "used-car salesman techniques that will be used to proselytize students" (Bowen and Glenny, 1980, p. 58). The danger of unrestricted competition for students has been recognized by others (Carnegie Council on Policy Studies in Higher Education, 1979; Breneman and Nelson, 1980), but little agreement exists on how the danger might be met or who has primary responsibility for meeting it.

Of the several agencies proposing means for containing destructive competition, only the Carnegie Council on Policy Studies in Higher Education (1980) appears explicitly to favor continuing reliance on the student marketplace over planned enrollment ceilings. In *Three Thousand Futures*, the council advises state planners "that creation and use of fair competition in the student market is a better alternative than increasingly detailed state control in managing a decline in enrollment. . . . We question the advisability of setting enrollment quotas for individual continuing institutions to spread out enrollments among them, preferring instead that they be allowed to compete in the student market" (pp. 6, 125).

The council qualifies its position somewhat by noting that a better case can be made for reliance on student choice when declines are moderate than when they are severe. It cautions that essential program balance within institutions should not depend on student choice alone. But it argues that students, by and large, can probably make as good decisions as state planners, and that it would be "easier politically" if they did so. On the other hand, a state planner may make a different and better decision from the broader perspectives of institutional diversity, program quality, and all students for whom the state has responsibility. Although state planners may not *always* make "objectively correct" decisions, the planners do deliberately consider critical state policy issues of which students are unaware and which faculty and campus administrators sometimes succeed in ignoring.

Our major concern is with the apparent universality of the advice of the council that codes of fair competition are more likely to serve state higher education objectives than are planned enrollment ceilings. Codes may be preferable in some states, but not in all. We are sufficiently doubtful about these codes of competition that we would urge all states to consider enrollment ceilings as partial alternatives. We do so because we share with the council the serious concern that enrollment decline may encourage state agencies to penetrate "even farther into the internal life of institutions" (1980, p. 3). But we believe that the council's "codes of fair competition" may constitute a greater threat to institutional autonomy, a greater intervention into the "internal life of institutions" than would enrollment ceilings.

In its *Fair Practices in Higher Education*, the Carnegie Council (1979, p. 72) recommends that regional accrediting associations, serving "as the primary external actor in matters of institutional rights and responsibilities," should develop and enforce "general codes of ethical academic conduct," including a review of institutional advertising, catalogues, and similar "full-disclosure" statements. A more likely "external actor," we suggest, would be a state higher education or consumer protection agency (see Academy for Educational Development, 1979, pp. 176–177).

We see a parallel between the development and enforcement of a code of fair competition and the affirmative action laws, regulations, and procedures designed to protect the rights of women and minorities. In these cases unquestionably desirable objectives are stated in necessarily general terms to limit institutional activity and to protect individual rights. Effective enforcement requires formal administrative action to balance institutional activity against individual rights. Even though the impact on college and university autonomy has been substantial because of affirmative action (see Bailey, 1978; Lyman, 1979), this action has been necessary under the federal Constitution. But constitutional protection does not shield students against questionable recruiting practices; codes of fair competition could so do. Under such codes, and in a manner similar to affirmative action, disaffected students could ask a state agency—probably the state higher education agency—to rule on questions such as the adequacy of information about employment opportunities, the sufficiency of remedial assistance, and the truth of statements about competing institutions or the claims about the quality of particular programs or their suitability to the individual's particular needs. Also, to protect students from unfair competition, every effort should be made to assure honest and informed high school and internal counseling. Under general state laws, courts should protect students against recruiting practices that cross a reasonable threshold of propriety. Student rights should be protected, but protection need not require the creation of a code of fair competition with elaborate and almost inevitable quasi-judicial and bureaucratic procedures.

We do not know with certainty whether enrollment ceilings would be less intrusive on institutional autonomy than the enforcement of codes of fair competition would be. There is far too little experience with either in a period of decline to measure one against the other. Experience does indicate that ceilings and redirection of students have not negatively affected institutional quality in California, Colorado, Maryland, or Wisconsin. We believe that the *possibility* of ceilings' being less intrusive than codes is sufficiently great that extensive and detailed analysis should be undertaken before a state rushes into reliance on the student marketplace alone to contain the threat of destructive, uncontrolled institutional competition.

Final Observations

"Cures" for the ills of enrollment decline are at least as numerous as the people writing about them. No one proposes any single or simple remedy. Assuredly we do not. Our comments are not based on formal research into enrollment management; but they do reflect earlier, related studies of fiscal stringency and enrollment decline, as well as the opinions of administrators who are currently working with enrollment ceilings and redirection. Our observations:

1. The complexity and expense of enrollment management will be increased by ceilings, codes of fair practice, modified budgetary formulas, and other devices intended to restrain institutional competition. The fiscal and procedural impacts of state intervention into the flow of students should be fully explored, and such exploration will require individual student data, which few states now collect or analyze.

2. Enrollment ceilings can inhibit large, popular campuses from recruiting students at the expense of less popular ones. Although the evidence is drawn from only a few instances, some applicants do shift to second-choice campuses, probably more do so when referred or redirected, and still more do so when given the promise of eventual transfer to their campus of first choice.

3. Ceilings on more popular campuses and redirection may increase enrollment at less popular ones but are unlikely to do so to the extent of reducing competition among the second-choice campuses themselves. Codes of fair competition might do so, but implementation of such codes should guard against (a) bureaucratic, quasi-judicial intrusion into internal campus matters, and (b) unintended discouragement of active recruiting as opposed to prevention of deception and fraud. The line between acceptably aggressive recruiting and that which an administrative agency might consider too aggressive is not one that a campus should be required to draw at the peril of protracted litigation.

4. The close relationship between the mission of a campus and the characteristics of its students can change if ceilings are imposed. *First*-choice campuses may or may not become more selective, depending on criteria for limiting access. *Second*-choice campuses may find that additional students are less qualified scholastically and more difficult to retain. Four-year campuses of second choice may assume missions as two-year feeder campuses for the more popular institutions with ceilings.

5. Concern about declining enrollments would abate to some extent if budgetary formulas distinguished fixed from variable costs and limited reduction of funding because of enrollment losses—to marginal rather than average costs. But funding by program regardless of enrollment is highly improbable, even though some argue that stable funding of lower enrollments would be a painless way for the state to improve quality. Legislators and state budget officers are not likely to abandon totally the enrollment numbers that represent a reality to which they have long been accustomed.

6. Faculty and administrative concern over program quality is real and should be respected, but preservation of quality should not be a cause for ceilings and the denial of access unless quality is

evidenced by the results of rigorous assessment of existing programs against campus missions and staffing needs.

Our final observation above may go beyond the focus of this chapter, but we urge its importance. Whether enrollment management during decline relies on ceilings, fair practice codes, or other procedures, care should be taken that the procedures support planned, statewide institutional balance and diversity. Orderly growth was the objective of state control and coordination for some twenty years, and balance required that the aspirations of a number of four-year campuses to become research universities be held in check. Orderly growth is now giving way to contraction and consolidation—"orderly decline," perhaps. Many institutions may now tend to overemphasize certain programs, such as business administration, at the expense of statewide diversity and balance.

The first line of defense against distortion of campus missions is within the institutions themselves. Most will attempt to maintain the internal balance of program offerings that the Carnegie Council (1980, p. 99) urges, but we are not optimistic that all will do so. Regardless of the form of enrollment management, states and multicampus systems should set rigorous program review standards and closely monitor them. Perhaps most important of all, state and multicampus administrators should encourage realistic program assessment by providing financial and other support for programs of proven quality and by requiring the reduction or elimination of poor ones.

For Further Reading

Enrollment management at the system or state level is a new concept in higher education. As background, readers are referred to the literature on the admissions process. See, for example, the Carnegie Council on Policy Studies in Higher Education (1977a) and Shulman (1977). For an analysis of enrollment's relationship to state budgeting for higher education, see Bowen and Glenny's (1976) *State Fiscal Stringency and Public Higher Education,* which is part of a series of publications on state budgeting from the Center for Research and Development in Higher Education at the University of California at Berkeley.

❧ 12 ❧

Program Evaluation as a Tool for Retrenchment

Robert J. Barak

The problems created by an inappropriate response to financial cutbacks in higher education have become painfully apparent during the past decade. In a comprehensive study of the impact of budgeting and management practices during periods of retrenchment, Frank Bowen and Lyman Glenny noted in 1976 that governors and legislatures rarely specify criteria in making reductions and that, almost universally, public higher education has simply been assigned a proportionate share of an overall state reduction. Unfortunately, the response of managers in public higher education has all too often been simply to extend these across-the-board cuts down to the various units of the university. Rarely did Bowen and Glenny find evidence of a realistic integration of program planning and evaluation with budgetary procedures, even when time permitted. While such practices had not been harmful when resources were plentiful, Bowen and Glenny suspected that, in the future, poorly managed institutions would be unable to maintain their quality and vitality.

Little has changed since 1976. Higher education still desperately needs an ongoing and continuous strategic approach to management. Such an approach would integrate academic planning, evaluation, and budgeting in a single, meaningful process and provide decision makers with adequate tools to reduce expenditures and minimize the potential negative effects of retrenchment while preserving or even enhancing academic quality.

This chapter describes two forms of evaluation: the first, evaluation of proposed instructional programs—often referred to as "program approval"—and the second, evaluation of existing programs—referred to as "program review." Both types of evaluation take place at various levels of the higher education structure—ranging from departments, schools, and colleges within institutions to system offices and state-level coordinating and governing agencies. These evaluations often utilize multiple criteria, with several types of indicators or proxies for each criterion. The typical criteria for program review and approval at most levels include cost, need/demand, centrality to the mission of the institution, and quality (although each of these may be defined differently at different levels).

Program review and program approval are not new; in fact, they have both been around for many years. Recently, however, these two processes have become increasingly utilized by colleges, universities, systems of colleges and universities, and statewide coordinating and governing boards for higher education. For example, according to a recently completed study for the National Center for Higher Education Management Systems (Barak, 1981) on program review and approval, only about 24 percent of the colleges and universities surveyed had conducted reviews prior to 1970, but 76 percent had initiated such activities since 1970. At the state level, only a handful of state coordinating/governing agencies conducted program reviews ten years ago; today approximately twenty-eight state-level agencies have authority to review at least some existing programs, and seventeen have authority to discontinue at least some existing programs. Nearly all the state coordinating and governing boards are currently conducting some form of program approval.

The expanded use of program review and approval at all levels has been an outgrowth of complex societal and educational factors, which have been amply described elsewhere (Peterson, 1977; Hill, Lutterbie, and Stafford, 1979; Harcleroad, 1980). Suffice it to say that these developments have occurred as a result of a combination of the following factors:

1. Concerns about the quality of education.
2. Financial strains on higher education caused by tighter or reduced resources, declining enrollments, inflation, and increases in energy and other costs.
3. Improved academic management techniques, including the adoption of strategic approaches to planning and budgeting.
4. Widespread duplication of academic offerings and increased competition.
5. Recent demands for accountability at all levels.

Program Approval

In institutions the process of gaining approval for new instructional programs usually begins at the departmental level. In large universities the program proposal is forwarded through a labyrinth of committees and administrative officers until it is either turned down, approved, or revised, and then, if not turned down, is presented to the chief academic and executive officer and/or the board of trustees for final institutional approval. In smaller colleges the procedure is usually less formal and less complex. In many community colleges and some other types of institutions, the process may begin with the administration's proposing the program as a result of an identified need or institutional planning process. Regardless of whether the proposal procedure is formal or informal, the proposal is ultimately judged on the basis of its consistency with institutional priorities, its cost, its quality, and the anticipated demand for the program.

Colleges and universities that are a part of a system usually must obtain approval of proposed programs at the system level. In states with coordinating or governing boards for higher education, proposals from public institutions—and in some instances from independent institutions as well—must conform to prescribed procedures and often must be submitted at a specified time for approval. The statutory powers, organizational structures, scope of authority, and procedures used vary greatly among the state higher education agencies. Depending on the state, the state higher education agency will either *approve* or *reject* the proposed program or, if limited in authority, will make recommendations for acceptance or rejection to the institution and/or the legislature.

The state higher education coordinating/governing boards have developed three general approaches toward program approval: an incremental approach; a planning approach; and an eclectic approach, which utilizes elements of the other two types. The incremental approach reviews new instructional program proposals one at a time or in small numbers of proposals at a time. No specific times or deadlines are prescribed in states using this approach, and the colleges and universities are free to propose new programs either individually or in groups at any time (a variation of this approach limits new program proposals to certain time periods). The planning approach generally makes program approval an integral part of the planning and/or budgeting cycles, and program proposals must be submitted in a manner consistent with these cycles. The difference between these two approaches, then, is the degree to which program approval is integrated into a planning and/or budgeting process.

The planning/budgeting approach is often used by the regulatory coordinating and governing boards (as opposed to those with only advisory powers). These agencies often have strong mandates or interest in statewide master planning and/or strong budgetary responsibility. In these agencies programs must first be integrated into a planning/budgeting cycle and then are eligible to come forward as new program proposals. Oklahoma's board of regents uses a planning/budgeting process that ties together program planning and fiscal budgeting. No new educational program is approved without funds placed in the budget for its implementation. Consequently, institutional requests for new educational programs must be submitted on or before July 1 of each year. Such requests are acted on by the state regents at their November meeting. Programs approved become effective at the beginning of the fiscal year, July 1, following their approval (Oklahoma State Board of Regents, 1977).

Agencies using the incremental approach do not openly ignore the planning and budgetary aspects of new program proposals, but they may do so in a less discernible way. Obviously, new programs requiring additional financial resources must be integrated into the budget in some way. Generally speaking, the planning and budgeting approach—because it is a more comprehensive and strategic approach to resource allocation—appears to have certain advantages over the incremental approach in times of retrenchment.

Program Review

Most program reviews attempt to make a judgment regarding the need, quality, and cost of the program and its relation to the mission of the institution. The focus of reviews at the institutional level is frequently program improvement. At the system or state level, the focus shifts from a developmental evaluation (often referred to as a formative type of evaluation) to a more critical assessment of the need for a program at the state level (sometimes referred to as a summative type of evaluation) (Barak, 1977).

The statutory or constitutional authority of state agencies for undertaking program review, like that for program approval, varies greatly among the states and ranges from no authority, to limited authority for reviewing certain programs at certain levels, to broad authority to review all programs for all institutions at all levels—such as the authority of the New York board of regents. Not all agencies with authority for program review exercise, or fully exercise, that authority, however; and some agencies without specific program review authority do conduct reviews and implement their findings through their budget or planning authority.

Some state agencies directly review existing programs—sometimes with the aid of outside peer consultants (that is, academic peers to the program under review who are engaged by the state agency). Other agencies rely, either largely or entirely, on program reviews conducted internally by the colleges and universities; these agencies may also conduct special studies or lateral reviews of similar programs across institutions. Both of these state-level approaches, if undertaken carefully, have been found effective in achieving the various objectives relegated to program review.

Problems and Benefits of Program Evaluation

Advocates of program evaluation claim a wide range of outcomes from the process. Among the potential benefits are improved, higher-quality instructional programs; improved faculty morale and self-esteem; enhanced educational experiences for students; more effective use of resources; and improved accountability of postsecondary education to state officials and the general public (Feasley, 1980; Craven, 1980; Barak and Berdahl, 1978; Barak, 1981). During periods of retrenchment, however, evaluation may well result in the termination of programs; the displacement of faculty, students, and staff; and, in the case of institutional closure, the economic and social disruption of local communities. If care is not taken, an evaluation under these circumstances quickly changes in perspective from a positive, nonthreatening process to one viewed as negative and highly threatening. In a retrenchment context, program evaluation can change in people's perspective from an objective, neutral process to a highly political one. Neutral parties frequently cease to exist under these conditions as the sides take the view that "you are either with us or against us," making reconciliation more difficult.

The retrenchment environment also makes the development of the review and approval process itself (if one was not already in place prior to the onset of retrenchment) extremely difficult, if not impossible. Collegial approaches become bogged down in endless debates, and attempts at arbitrary approaches merely aggravate the situation. Consensus on the evaluation process, criteria, supporting data, the data collection process, and so forth, becomes very difficult to achieve. All these factors point to the need to establish the entire evaluation process—including criteria, administrative process, and procedures—prior to the onset of retrenchment.

Even when a process is in place, there are significant limitations in applying program review to retrenchment. Good program review takes time. Colleges and universities and state agencies often review programs in cycles over a five-year period. If cutbacks were needed before a cycle of reviews had been completed, judgments could not be made on an equal basis for all academic programs. Furthermore, if the primary financial advantage of cutting back programs is found in the reduction of faculty lines, most institutions would want—either out of a concern for faculty welfare or out of the need to meet the contractual requirements—to give appropriate advance notice to the faculty being terminated.

Other legal restraints would complicate and in some cases actually prevent the effective use of program review as a tool for saving money. Recent court decisions support the requirement that colleges and universities provide appropriate due process under such circumstances. If, in its contracts with faculty, an institution has accepted definitions contained in the *Statement on Financial Exigency* (American Association of University Professors, 1976) or the *Statement on Financial Exigency and Staff Reduction* (Association of American Colleges, 1971), for example, rather lengthy proceedings would be necessary before a faculty member, especially a tenured faculty member, could be laid off. The restrictions imposed by contractual relations with faculty, either collectively or individually, provide other restrictions as well. Some collective bargaining agreements specifically prohibit layoffs; others make the layoffs based on program review an unrealistic approach to budgetary savings because an institution is restricted either to laying off nontenured faculty or to laying off on the basis of seniority rather than program priorities. Still other contracts require such elaborate layoff benefits that it is simply cheaper for an institution to maintain the faculty status quo.

At the state and system levels, there is also the problem of the legal authority of the agency to require the elimination of specific programs. As noted earlier, the authority of the state agencies varies widely from specific authority to deregister or terminate programs to authority only to advise or recommend that programs be terminated. A state agency with only the latter authority could find its effort to select programs for reduction or elimination virtually thwarted by institutional resistance or legal impediments.

Probably the greatest hindrance to the successful use of program review and approval is the external and political intrusions into the review process. There is hardly a program in higher education today that does not have some proponents—students, faculty, parents, local business people, or others. Almost from the moment a program is proposed for reduction, those favorable toward that program can be rallied on its behalf. Their actions can range from emotional appeals to political power plays on behalf of the threatened program. The same kinds of actions can be rallied on behalf of newly proposed programs. All too often, program reduction decisions are reversed, frequently for the wrong reasons.

In spite of all the difficulties noted, program approval and review—if implemented properly and combined with other retrenchment strategies—can be a major tool for effectively reducing expenditures while maintaining essential program quality. Almost no other retrenchment strategy offers that important combination of benefits. The combination is achieved because program evaluations set priorities among programs, so that decision makers have a legitimate basis for resource allocation and reallocation. Program evaluation thus becomes a management tool to counteract the tendency toward across-the-board cuts, which frequently reduce all programs to a mediocre level. Instead of a "hatchet job," "delicate surgery" is used to "prune out" poor, duplicative, and unnecessary programs and to select or improve programs that are central to the mission of the institution.

Can Program Evaluation Save Money?

There is some disagreement over the ability of program evaluation to save money. Some institutions and state agencies clearly have *not* saved money as a result of their evaluations. The cost of program evaluation itself may eat up any marginal savings. Other institutions and agencies, however, *have* saved money—by not approving new programs, with their increased expenditures, and by eliminating existing programs and their associated costs. The past history of experience with program review provides a partial explanation of these mixed results (Mingle, 1978). At the institutional level, and even at the state and system levels, "saving money" has not been a major purpose of program evaluation. For example, the goal of program review has generally been program improvement, which often resulted in requests for additional resources, *not* fewer resources. This was especially true during the growth years of the 1960s and early 1970s. The very nature of these reviews was usually contrary to the concept of saving money. Even where "saving money" was a goal, the major source of the savings, laying off of faculty, was unthinkable and to be avoided; so savings tended to be minimal. Given the circumstances, it is no wonder that program reviews by and large did not result in money saved. At the state level, it is true that savings—defined as identifiable dollars that can be returned to the state treasury or other sources—have not accrued as a result of most state-level reviews to date. It is also true that most state-level reviews did not have as a primary goal "to save money" but rather to ensure minimal quality.

Two other factors help explain the lack of identifiable dollar savings as a result of many state-level reviews: the absence of retrenchment conditions in most of the states and the nature of the first rounds of state-level reviews. State coordinating and governing agencies for higher education only recently undertook the task of program review, building on earlier experience with program approval. Most have recognized the sensitivity of program review and have entered into the effort with considerable caution due to a respect for institutional autonomy and/or a desire to avoid major challenges to their authority. Consequently, the programs under review tended to be those that were widely duplicated in other institutions or were extremely small in enrollments and/or degree recipients. The programs singled out for reduction or elimination were often "paper programs"—programs with few students and few, if any, full-time faculty—resulting more in a cleaning up of the catalogue than in locating funds for reallocation or reversion to the state.

Melchiori (1980) has identified four useful levels of program discontinuance at the state level, based on the severity of the impact of the discontinuance:

> Level I. Elimination of a program that, at the time of elimination, existed only on paper.
> Level II. Release of lecturers and untenured faculty; budget reductions; no new students admitted; phase-out closure planned.

Level III. Release of some tenured faculty; no new students admitted; date set for future closure.

Level IV. Release and/or transfer of all faculty; enrolled students transferred to other programs; no new students admitted; date set for closure.

Most program discontinuance activities of state agencies and institutions have been Level I and II types. A notable exception is the experience of the State University of New York at Albany, where drastic reductions in the budget were carried out programmatically (Shirley and Volkwein, 1978; Fields, 1976). Albany's experience shows that a program review process in place can result in definite dollar savings. (See Chapter Five for further discussion of the Albany cutbacks.)

Another aspect of "savings" needs to be noted. Savings can be of several types: (1) funds not spent, (2) funds saved over the long term, and (3) funds immediately freed for a reversion back to the source or for other use, such as reallocation. In a period of retrenchment, all three kinds of "savings" can be achieved, to some degree, as a result of the program review and approval process. Effective program reviews can identify programs that have adequate funding and those that could operate with the same quality and effectiveness on a smaller budget. Savings effected thereby, as well as savings from programs cut (even those with modest resources), also result in savings over the long term. Funds can also be saved over the long term on equipment, books, salary increases, and other line items not spent. Finally, immediate savings (that is, those resulting from equipment sold, faculty not hired, or faculty terminated) can be used for other critical purposes or, if need be, reverted to the state or other source.

The single largest category of expenditure in a college or university budget is for faculty salaries. An institution, system, or state can in the short run defer maintenance and purchases and institute hiring freezes to curb expenditures. But if the need to reduce expenditures is serious enough or takes place over a long enough period of time, cutting back on faculty is the only sure way to effect substantial dollar savings. Although one approach to faculty reduction could be to terminate all adjunct, part-time, and nontenured faculty, it might be in the best interest of the state, the institution, and the students to terminate faculty on the basis of priorities determined through a vigorous process of program review.

Some in academe would regard this approach as heresy, since tenured faculty could be terminated before nontenured faculty. As noted earlier, some collective bargaining contracts prohibit laying off tenured faculty while there are still nontenured faculty employed, but such a policy or contract provision may be unwise from a qualitative perspective. Such actions may be greeted with dismay and hostility by tenured faculty. Volpe (1977, p. 155) notes, however, that "in a period of contraction, no intelligent or rational plan to revise or cut academic programs can be devised unless the academic community, specifically the faculty, is ready and willing to confront the issue of tenure by separating its current interpretation as a guarantee of job security from its original and only justifiable intent as a guarantee of academic freedom."

As Volpe has written about his experience in the City University of New York, where one cutback has followed another in recent years, the "inescapable choice between maintaining a balanced academic program or dismissing tenured faculty creates a paralyzing dilemma" (1977, p. 158). If programmatic considerations are not given first priority, the credibility of higher education may eventually deteriorate. As difficult as some termination decisions are, the viability of the program must be maintained.

Conclusion

Program approval can effectively be administered at any level and can be as strict or as lenient in its application as the procedures and standards by which programs are evaluated. In a period of retrenchment, the standards at all levels are usually strict, as they probably should be. The burden should be on those proposing any new program to prove that the program is needed and that its fiscal requirements are justified. The program approval process should begin with the lowest administrative level. Ill-conceived programs should be discouraged quickly, and faculty should not be given false promises regarding programs they seek to develop. The conservation of resources (and faculty energy is an important one) should begin early. Courses leading to a new program but not needed for existing programs should not be added, and faculty not needed for existing programs should not be hired. Similarly, library holdings, equipment, and such should not be allowed to be purchased for potential new programs whose likelihood of being approved is low.

The above advice is relatively easy to implement with an institution whose own board makes decisions about new programs. Such an institution will mainly need to develop its internal administrative or governing mechanism so that it can make these decisions without stifling faculty vitality and the development of critical new programs. For an institution that is part of a system, however, efforts must be made to tie the institution's program approval process more closely to the system-level process. Two methods to bring these different approval processes closer together have worked in a number of states. First, some state agencies require some form of early-warning system, ranging from a "letter of intent" to elaborate planning mechanisms, in order to advise the state agency when programs are being strongly considered for development. The agency can then give the institution some indication of the likelihood of approval and possibly even suggest modifications that would make the programs more palatable. Second, to increase the likelihood of eventual approval, many colleges and universities have adopted the state agency's program approval standards as a part of their own approval standards. In order to prevent the premature development of new programs without state authorization, some state agencies have gone so far as to require the approval of every new course. Course approval can also be used to give early advice regarding the acceptability of new program development. At the same time, however, it can create a substantial paperwork burden on both institution and state agency staff.

In a time of limited or declining resources, statewide program approval takes on added significance because of its potential to enhance the effective management of a state's available resources through the prevention of unnecessary program duplication and through qualitative control over program offerings. In such times someone needs to look beyond the institutional perspective and view the "big picture" of the state as a whole, but individual institutions and their boards are not likely to take the broad view. For this reason additional layers of review, especially in periods of limited resources, seem to be amply justified.

While there is a degree of consensus regarding the advisability of the state higher education agencies' role in program approval, this seems to be less true regarding their role in program review. Many institutions, especially the better ones, have been reviewing their existing programs for years, and many are doing a good job. These institutions view the state agencies' role as duplicative, sometimes inferior, and a real threat to institutional autonomy. The state officials, however, note that programs are seldom if ever terminated as a result of institutional program review and that some control is necessary in order to maintain minimal standards, eliminate unnecessary duplication, and protect consumers. As discussed earlier, state and institution reviews do serve different purposes; and, taken together, they can be complementary (Barak, 1977).

Whether the reviews are conducted internally, internally with system- or state-level oversight, or by a state-level agency, the program review system must be credible. That is, the system and procedures must be based on some degree of consensus of those encompassed by the system, must be fairly and equally applicable to all, and must provide for due process or appeal for those who feel wronged by the system. With these basic components in place, the procedures and criteria agreed to need not be perfect (in fact, they never are), but the review system has the strength of a broad consensus. (At the state level, this could well include some degree of consensus among influential legislators and the governor.) Such consensus will provide strength to the process when it faces the test of controversial program closures. Any weaknesses in the review system will surely be highlighted in such situations.

Regardless of who undertakes the review in a period of retrenchment, the review is a tool that can be used for the purpose of a qualitative approach to budget cutting. The word *tool* should be emphasized here, since the review is only one tool and should be used in combination with other tools in a strategic approach to planning and budgeting.

For Further Reading

Arns and Poland (1980), Barak (1981), Craven (1980), Gentile (1980), Shirley and Volkwein (1978), Mims (1978), and Heydinger (1978) have written about specific approaches to institutional-level program review that have been time-tested and useful approaches. Barak (1977, 1980, 1981), Barak and Berdahl (1978), and Craven (1980) also provide examples of the various approaches to program review at the state and system levels. The general literature on program evaluation is also full of theories, models, and approaches to program evaluation in general which some may find useful in developing a review system (Stufflebeam and others, 1971; Scriven, 1967, 1972; Tyler, Gagné, and Scriven, 1967; Alm, Miko, and Smith, 1976). Several writers—including Heydinger (1978), Micek (1980), Lawless, Levi, and Wright (1978), and Stevenson and Walleri (1980)—have written about the integration of planning, evaluation, and budgeting.

✌ 13 ✌

Changing Patterns of State Funding

David S. Spence
George B. Weathersby

Changing enrollment patterns are already having a marked effect on higher education funding, and the pace of these changes may be expected to quicken through the 1980s. With both growth and decline expected to occur at the same time within a state, policy makers are faced with new funding problems, which call for new approaches. Complicating the situation is the presence of different perspectives on the expectations of postsecondary education in the 1980s. From the student perspective, as the Carnegie Council on Policy Studies in Higher Education (1980) has noted, the next twenty years hold every promise of being a golden age. The number and diversity of academic program offerings are far greater than ever before. This generation of college-age youth is likely to be the most sought after, the best served, and the highest rewarded in recent history. And all this will be available at a net price that will probably continue to decline relative to the price of other services. For the student the real cost of college attendance has declined almost steadily since the 1960s, not only in proportion to family income but also as a consequence of the tremendous expansion in student aid financing at the federal and state levels (Breneman and Finn, 1978).

Institutions, however, may have doubts about the prospects of their future. As a service industry dependent for its funding largely on public appropriations and the fees it charges, higher education is particularly susceptible to inflation in the prices of goods and services that it must purchase. And because higher education is not capital intensive in the traditional sense and is not able to pass along increased prices to consumers, the choice in the coming years may have to be between increased productivity and decreased quality of program offerings. Increasing productivity will be difficult because of faculty and disciplinary prerogatives and values. The challenge is for institutions to provide incentives to faculty which will raise both productivity and quality.

For many institutions the 1970s were a period of declining real resources per student. Inflation—particularly in the costs of energy, periodicals and other paper products, and higher salaries—has more than offset monetary gains for all but a few institutions. Budgets have been "cut, squeezed, and trimmed," "fat" has been eliminated, and "accountability" (read "frugality") has been demanded. In a few cases, lower spending limits have been mandated by law. All too often colleges and universities have drawn down their invisible reserves (deferring maintenance, not replacing obsolete instructional equipment, increasing faculty work loads, not investing in faculty renewal), leaving them less capable of providing high-quality services as future enrollments decline from the current historic highs (Bowen, 1980).

Higher education is already responding to the new enrollment outlook by developing new rationales to increase funding so that income, adjusted for inflation, will decline at a slower rate than enrollment decreases. These include (1) using higher cost allowances for the same work load (the marginal-cost approach), (2) supporting new services and new priorities, (3) improving the quality of existing services, (4) charging consumers higher prices, and (5) "unbundling" services.

Using Marginal-Cost Formulas

Until recently most formulas for state support were based on an average cost per student—that is, the formula would generate the same funds for each additional student. Thus, formulas added or reduced funding at the same rate as enrollments increased or declined. As enrollments decline, many institutions believe that quality will suffer if student-based funds are withdrawn at the same rate that they were added. Generally, however, enrollment-based subsidies during growth were in excess of efficient costs. Higher education usually claims that this extra income was used to enhance the quality of institutions and that this funding margin for quality would not only be lost but would be reversed if resources were withdrawn at an average-cost-per-student rate. However, given limited state resources, funds provided to ease the transition of institutions losing enrollment may reduce the rate of increase in funds for growing institutions. Institutions continuing to grow may well object to diversion of their "quality surplus" to declining institutions.

In many states higher education and state government are studying marginal-cost approaches and the more precise costing of continuing activities that may have been underfunded in the past. Formulas are being redesigned to differentiate between fixed costs and variable costs. In a marginal-cost approach, fixed costs would be funded at the same level as the previous year, and funding would be adjusted only for items that actually change, with greater or fewer numbers of students.

One way to employ these marginal adjustments is to establish nonenrollment criteria as bases for funding noninstructional activities. Most funding formulas now separate libraries, academic and student support, and administration from enrollment. For instance, funds for plant maintenance are typically based on square footage, intensity of usage, type of construction, and age; research funding is based on the amount of nonstate funding received and on graduate program emphasis; utilities are based on actual cost estimates; and libraries are based on the number of different programs by level. In Indiana the marginal-funding approach results in adding only about one third of the state dollars that would normally follow additional students if all costs were assumed to increase at the same rate as enrollments increase. At the same time, when only variable costs are considered, an institution—if it loses students—loses only one third of the average total cost per student.

A less precise way to employ marginal-cost principles in funding is to establish ranges of yearly enrollment changes within which no new resources would be withdrawn or given. For example, Tennessee uses a 2 percent plus or minus range. If an institution should have, for example, a 4 percent decline in enrollment, only a 2 percent adjustment would be made in its formula-based budget; similarly, an institution increasing by 4 percent would be granted additional resources of only 2 percent.

The percentage of fixed costs in an institution typically is arrived at either by estimating from the actual costs of an institution over time or by comparing costs across many institutions with different enrollments for the same time period. The central issue, however, is not what costs institutions have built up during the years when enrollments and funding were increasing rapidly, but what costs are really essential for sound educational programs to meet state needs. Perhaps the most basic problem is how to define a "core curriculum." At one extreme is the claim that, to simplify matters, all courses now being offered should be assumed as constituting the core required, regardless of student numbers. Two questions need to be answered in constructing a more reasonable response to the core curriculum question: (1) What resources are necessary to provide quality programs at various levels of enrollment? (2) Is there an enrollment minimum below which a program should be eliminated? These questions concern educational policy and should be the basis of costing practices. Too many times the answers have evolved or been inferred from actual practice. Curriculum experts have argued that many programs have over twice the number of different courses being offered as are needed (Meeth, 1974). In their view, the proliferation of courses is related more to faculty needs than to student needs—a finding that is troublesome, especially at the undergraduate level, where instruction is supposed to be of higher priority than faculty research. The question of how small a program can become before its value falls below its cost is especially crucial for higher-cost graduate programs. The related issue is how many programs can be eliminated before a whole institution no longer has the critical core of necessary programs which justify its existence.

The state of Virginia has established funding floors, in which institutions dropping below set levels of enrollment (2,500 students for four-year institutions and 1,000 students for two-year colleges) still receive a certain level of funding, presumably to cover fixed costs. Wisconsin provides detailed information on what should be included in a core curriculum, regardless of the number of students. The implication is that its formula should recognize that a larger proportion of instructional costs should be assessed as fixed than is now the case. Florida recently has begun an effort in program budgeting, in which a major step is the examination of the appropriate relationship between enrollments, resource costs, and state needs in major program areas. The purpose is to develop enrollment limits and ranges to which funding can be pegged but which also are sound educationally. The following questions are being asked:

- Why should this program be offered by this institution? What state needs will be met?
- What is the minimum cost to operate this program with a basic core of faculty, and how many students can be accommodated at this level of funding?
- If projected enrollment exceeds the number that can be accommodated by base-level funding, what factors justify the expanded enrollment?
- What level of enrollment is so small as to render this program ineffective with regard to the satisfaction of state needs?
- What objectives are intended to be achieved by funds requested beyond the base-level funding?
- What standards of quality have been determined for this program? What evidence can be presented to ensure that these standards have been achieved?

While marginal costing is portrayed as an attempt to lessen the strict reliance on student numbers as a funding base, on closer examination the reverse actually holds. The real aim is to make the relationship between enrollment numbers and state funding *more* exact and reflective of actual needs. Enrollments will continue to provide the major justification of funds. This link may not appear every year, but over a period of years it will be evident.

A different dimension of the state's effort to assess the appropriate costs of needed educational services and programs is the formulation of indicators, which define limits on efficiency outside which the state will raise questions about support. These limits may concern minimum institutional or program size. For example, Minnesota is considering establishing a 400-student minimum for community colleges—the rationale being that this is the number of students that could be supported by the core resources. For 400 students or for any smaller number of students, all costs are fixed, since the same resources would be required. Other indicators used by states relate to costs, faculty tenure rates, or enrollment trends. In Wisconsin, for instance, the state government and the university system agreed on several indicators, which, if surpassed, automatically trigger special studies of state support for certain institutional operations (see Chapter Fifteen).

Supporting New Services

Higher education may counter the loss of revenue due to enrollment decline by proposing new kinds of services or redefining services now offered. New degree programs are being proposed to meet changing manpower needs of the states. Universities are calling for new public service relationships with private industry and state government agencies and would like to be the source of needed research to solve energy, health, and urban problems.

Institutions also cite the higher support of services needed for the different kinds of new students. As part-time students increase as a percent of all students, colleges are proposing that these students should be subsidized at a higher rate. Studies from Wisconsin indicate that a part-time student may require nearly as much funding support and service as are required by a full-time student. The board of regents in Ohio suggests that full-time students who live on campus should be funded at a higher level than for full-time students living off-campus, due to the extra services needed daily by the campus residents and the need to subsidize excess capacity in the dormitories. Higher education also is asking for more support to educate the increasing numbers of students requiring remedial education. As the pool of traditional college students shrinks, it is likely that larger proportions of enrollment will be composed of students who need basic skills. Another frequent response by institutions facing enrollment slowdown has been to emphasize the vast reservoir of older people who could benefit from lifelong education. The next step is for institutions to request broader state support of these older students, to include heretofore noncredit and unfunded programs or courses. Institutions also lay special claim to funding even in the face of enrollment decline when they serve a specific student body that is either place bound or racially identifiable. And an institution may be allowed to become inefficiently small because of state political interests and priorities.

But the claims by higher education to meet new needs call for clearer statewide policy and priorities concerning what those needs are and by whom and how they are to be determined. Increasingly, the state's interest and an institution's interest in postsecondary education may be diverging. When the demand for postsecondary education was growing rapidly in the 1960s, states focused on providing enough institutions and programs to guarantee access. New needs were identified annually, and mistakes in overbuilding or in misplacement of programs tended to be hidden by the increasing numbers of students. By the mid-1970s, however, much had changed. The demands on other state services increased; and, although in many states student demand stabilized or began to decline, demands from institutions increased. Campus requests called for more funds for new programs, significant salary increases, and quality improvement in order to cope with increased institutional competitiveness. This widening gap between state and institutional perceptions of need means that there must be a clearer separation between policy and management. Policy on needs for higher education must be set at the statewide level, and those needs must be compared to the needs for other state services. A state's legislators and executive officers must be able to judge all needs together and in forms that permit the different services to be compared. The clearer identification of state needs for higher education provides a base on which institutional claims may be assessed and the following question answered: Who is funded to do what?

States have considered several alternative approaches: (1) to plan and regulate institutional roles and services more carefully, (2) to reduce statewide regulation so that institutions may compete and the best win out, or (3) to provide for a combination of incentives that will allow enough competition to ensure quality services but will also place limits on unnecessary duplication. The financing policies and procedures that would support these three alternatives would vary considerably.

State Management. States may regulate the use of resources by differentiating institutional roles more clearly. In anticipation of increased competition, states are seeking more carefully to define institutional missions in order to prevent unnecessary duplication. The plans for clearer institutional differences, however, depend on the capacity of financing policies to accommodate them. These financing procedures will be judged by their sensitivity in distributing funds to each different institution. States can accommodate institutional differences in several different ways. For example, to distribute state funds for salaries, a state may use institutions with similar roles in other states as comparative standards. Or a state may compare its faculty salaries in various disciplines to those in other states. Just how much difference there should be in salaries for faculty of the same discipline but in institutions with different roles is a controversial issue. Many believe that higher salaries are needed for faculty in research and in graduate institutions because they must be prepared and qualified to teach and conduct research with the most advanced students. Several states provide special funding of research and public service activities for institutions with those missions. These funds are over and above the regular faculty salary support. It is well to remember that states actually provide the largest share of support for research through base salaries, since faculty are assumed to conduct research as well as teach. In addition to base salaries, Kentucky and Texas add funds for research, based on the amount of research support obtained from the federal government and other sources. Tennessee is proposing distinct funding for the public service activities of community colleges and urban universities. Once such roles have been established, financing can be tailored to fund institutions in ways that reinforce the differences among them.

The Market Approach. An alternate way for a state to decide what kinds and levels of services to fund is to establish an economic market system for higher education, in which all institutions are treated as if they were "private" and in which institutions are increasingly responsible and accountable for managerial decisions. The role of state government in this approach is to (1) establish the legal framework for public and private institutions; (2) establish public priorities for educational services, and set prices to be paid by the state for the services rendered; (3) provide consumer information about educational services available; and (4) regulate destructive, expensive competition.

The economic market approach presumes that individual and community needs will be expressed through the willingness of students or organizations to pay for educational services— assuming there is a choice of at least two programs. The price of these services is jointly established by the institution (tuition or contract price), the state (institutional subsidies, student grants, contract price), the federal government (student grants), and the consumer's willingness to pay. For decentralized market decisions, there must be several institutions capable of acting independently to decide the quality and quantity of services to be offered for all the state's major population groups.

Mixed Approach. A third way for a state to respond to higher education's claim for funds to support changing roles and services is a combination of policies, including state regulation and market principles. Such an approach focuses on the importance of funding institutions according to their ability to meet the needs of students and other clientele, while promoting enough competition to increase quality but not unnecessary duplication. An issue in this approach is the extent to which institutions and their programs must be regulated to ensure efficient size and quality.

As David Breneman indicates in Chapter Two, the market's advantages are that students may be able to indicate in a more direct and politically acceptable way what institutions and programs are needed. One disadvantage is that the efficient use of resources may require minimum enrollment levels in various programs and institutions—levels that may not be reached without some state direction. The second disadvantage is that it is uncertain to what extent the increased competition for students actually improves the quality of programs. Many believe that most student consumers are more interested in a credential than in a quality education; if that is true, unregulated competition might well lead to lower standards. The key question is: What funding procedures would capture the advantages of the student market, keep state regulation to a minimum, and create incentives to increase quality?

States have taken several approaches to limit destructive competition. More specific role and scope designations and, perhaps, enrollment limits at major universities are two steps that some states already have taken (see Chapter Eleven). Enrollments may also be directed through differential tuition rates. The tuition share of institutional revenue may be allowed to increase while the percentage of state support made directly to the institution declines. A greater share of state support may thereupon shift to student aid to cover the higher tuitions. Alternatively, states may move toward limiting the programs for which direct state support could be used. Institutions could establish new programs but, if the programs are not approved by the state, could use only tuition money to cover the costs.

States could also require that each new program proposed by an institution go out for bid to other institutions and that the program be awarded on the condition that a review would be made of the program's value within three years. The review would be based on specific qualitative and quantitative criteria established at the time of the award, and the result would be used to assess whether to continue or to transfer the program to another institution. The aim is to place responsibility for the quality of a program with the institution's leaders in such a way that the results will directly affect future financial support. Because an institution would be competing with itself or against standards set by its own leaders, such a process might produce competition that helps to maintain, instead of diminish, quality.

Improving Existing Services

Perhaps the most popular strategy to justify increased funding as enrollments decline is based on the improvement of the quality of programs now offered, not a shift to different services. However, higher education has not been clear about the nature of quality and how to improve it. During the growth period of higher education, quality improvement was not used frequently as a distinct funding rationale. Presumably, institutions supported quality improvement measures with the constantly increasing funding margins provided by the average-cost formulas. Now, as enrollment growth has slowed, higher education has reacted by highlighting quality improvement as an area that requires special funding. The most difficult task of a state seeking to accommodate enrollment decline is determining how to respond to these demands for dollars to improve quality. A clearer definition of *quality* is needed—a definition that may differ from state to state and across institutions within a state. Quality will have to be better expressed in terms of student outcomes and the meeting of state needs than was the case in the past. Instead of measuring quality solely by the level of faculty salaries, the attractiveness of the facilities, the rigor of admissions standards, and the student-faculty ratio, institutions and states should move toward value-added definitions of quality. Quality would then be measured by the social and academic achievements of students between admission and graduation. Furthermore, quality would be judged by comparing program outcomes, such as graduation and placement rates, with state needs.

One way of thinking about quality improvement is to begin with institutional objectives. These objectives should differ substantially among institutions—from community colleges to major research universities, from residential liberal arts colleges to professional schools, from public service–oriented extension programs to fundamental research in the basic sciences, and from developmental education to advanced academic achievement. In essence, requests for "quality improvement" are ways proposed to enhance the attainment of institutional objectives. Changes in institutional objectives or changes in clientele served are not necessarily improvements in quality; these new objectives and clientele may be preferred to the old ones, but this choice still begs the question of how well the new objectives are attained or the new clientele is served. Some reordering and clarification of institutional roles may be required as a first step in quality improvement. The result will be more distinct missions among a state's institutions and a more effective use of state funds. The emphasis will be on providing fewer diverse programs and doing a better job on what remains.

As a state is presented with requests for quality improvement that vary significantly from one institution to another, it will need to develop new review processes. Institutions will have to frame funding requests in greater detail, to specify exactly how the requested funds will be spent and how institutional activities will be improved qualitatively because of certain expenditures. Claims that increases in salaries of existing faculty will lead to quality improvement will be viewed skeptically by legislatures. A stronger argument is to justify the need for increased funds in order to change the faculty work load or to hire new faculty. With requests for quality improvement expected to be justified more fully than base requests, the greater detail in budget requests is likely to lead to closer postaudits. Being held to the letter of their request will be the price institutions must pay for quality-improvement money.

While the typical method of funding improved quality still is to add funds directly in the formula through increased dollar rates per student, more states are shifting to nonformula categorical grants for special programs to enhance quality. The distinct grants have the advantages of separating funding for base-level services from qualitative improvements and of enabling a more accurate accounting of the use of funds. Some states, such as Indiana and Virginia, already administer a separate funding process in which institutions propose specific programs or activities to improve quality. The proposals are made to a state agency, which has established a distinct fund and guidelines for evaluating the various institutional proposals. The process is competitive, and subsequent evaluations determine whether or not the funds should become part of the future base budgets.

Charging Consumers Higher Prices

If state resources are limited, why not charge the student a higher proportion of the total cost? In fact, almost all colleges and universities have raised tuition to some degree as costs increased. A few have raised prices even faster than the general inflation rate, but on the whole prices have increased at slightly lower rates (Breneman and Finn, 1978). But the brake on tuition increases is the belief that high prices will reduce student demand. When income falls at an average price per student (tuition and fees plus state appropriations) and costs can be contracted only at the margin, plummeting enrollments are to be avoided by institutions—at almost any cost. Even though federal and state student financial aid programs would greatly mitigate any tuition increases for almost all students from families of modest means, most institutions have still been unwilling to take the risk of being perceived as "high priced."

As higher education considers raising tuition, state policy on financial aid must be examined. Certainly, the area of state and federal appropriations for higher education showing the highest percentage of growth in the 1970s was student financial aid (Breneman and Finn, 1978). Direct grants from state or federal sources are now provided to probably 50 percent or more of all undergraduates enrolled at least half time. Low-interest loans have been available to all students enrolled half time or more; even the interest accrued at subsidized rates is forgiven while the student is in school or in a deferment period. State student assistance often is granted to students in independent as well as in public institutions. Student aid is the major area of support of higher education by the federal government and is an area of increasing state emphasis. The state role may be expected to become more crucial in the wake of new federal policies on student assistance.

As colleges and universities raise their prices to provide adequate operating income, some individuals are "priced out" of attendance. These individuals often are the very ones for whom low-price access is essential—individuals from families of modest financial means. If tuitions rise, as they have done and will continue to do, financial aid must rise consistently. Therefore, while increasing public tuition may appear to relieve the public treasury, this can be only partially true because increased public student aid will be needed to offset the tuition increases for students from low-income families—the higher the tuition increase, the higher the proportion of all families who qualify for state financial assistance.

Higher tuition in public institutions, along with increased student aid that is portable across sectors, will have a positive impact on private colleges. By recognizing the important contributions made by independent colleges in meeting state needs, such policies to reduce the cost gap between public and private education will result in the more effective use of resources statewide. As competition is increased—and perhaps quality—student choices are effectively widened. Of course, as James Mingle has noted in Chapter One, thorny issues remain concerning a state's role in evaluating or assuring the quality of these institutions. Also, as enrollments decline statewide, state funds diverted to the nonpublic sectors may increasingly be resented by the public institutions and their legislature.

"Unbundling" Services

Another strategy for coping with declining traditional demand for higher education is to "unbundle" some of the services that institutions of higher education now provide and to create a capacity for distributing these services separately. The services provided by higher education include assessment of prior learning or knowledge, career counseling, academic counseling, direct instruction, evaluation of direct instruction, certification (awarding a degree), linkage to further education or employment, research and development, and library and information services. Most colleges and universities provide all these services but will not provide any of them separately. A student who requests career counseling will usually be told, "You should apply, be admitted, pay your tuition, show up next fall, and we'll try to help you." A student trying to get certification without taking instruction is told, "You're questioning the very ethic and ethos of an institution that just doesn't simply give away degrees." But if certification is something that is valued by society and is a key to a wide variety of employment and other opportunities, should not access to that certification also be available, independent of the means by which learning is achieved?

Each function could be priced, managed, and delivered separately and independently of other functions. In fact, there are organizations—public, nonprofit, and profit making—that specialize in each one of these separate functions without providing the others. By constraining itself to think only of "whole dinner menus" and not "à la carte," higher education has limited greatly both the sources of expertise to which public enterprise turns for these services and the opportunities of students and other clients to avail themselves of these services.

Congruency of state policy objectives with the actual use of appropriated dollars could occur either through greater state managerial control—that is, to replace the decision-making process within institutions by the decision-making process of the state—or through greater unbundling of higher education services, which would allow a differentiation in the kind of state support provided. States would then pick and choose among the services they wished to support, leaving the others to institutional discretion and institutional ability to gain other sources of support. The effectiveness and efficiency of the use of state dollars will not increase with state control of institutions of higher education—unless state government agencies and organizations are more effective and efficient than is traditionally observed. However, the unbundling of services enables both students and the state to choose the services they wish to purchase—and greatly increases the array of organizations capable of providing one or several of those services.

Keys to the Future

As a way of summarizing the state's and postsecondary education's financial responses to enrollment decline, two points need to be emphasized—one having to do with statewide coordination, the other concerning institutional initiative.

Statewide Coordination. To respond effectively to enrollment decline, state coordination procedures will have to become more sensitive and more able to address discretely the complex demands of postsecondary education. These demands are certain to include not only requests for expansion of new programs but also rationales for quality improvement as well as for retrenchment of existing programs—an array of decisions reflecting a much more complex agenda for statewide coordination than existed in the 1960s and 1970s. To accommodate this greater complexity, coordinating functions should be reexamined. Besides more effective and distinctive planning as a foundation, perhaps the most essential component of coordination is a procedure that combines program and budget review at the state level. Institutional requests for funds will be more diverse in the 1980s. Some requests will continue to emphasize enrollment-based reasons; others will focus on quality improvement or the need for new programs or for the provision of new services by faculty. The great diversity of requests requires a review procedure that is sensitive to these differences.

Formula-based review of budgets will not be as helpful in the face of such diversity. Budget review in the 1980s must incorporate more comprehensive judgments of the need for specific programs and activities and of an institution's capacity to meet those needs. In short, state-level program review must be related to budget review.

The increased amount of time involved in such reviews requires a reexamination of the state's approach to program and budget review. One possibility is for coordinating agencies to focus on program review and for the legislature to focus on budgets. Since the legislature's chief interest lies in budgets and appropriations, coordinating agencies could devote more of their resources to developing the kind of program evaluation that could be merged with budget assessment. This division of labor would come together when program priorities are compared to budget possibilities. The result could be a workable form of program budgeting and would depend on the ability of the coordinating agency and the legislative and executive staff to work together effectively. Without such an effective combination, states are unlikely to be able to make a sufficiently sensitive response to postsecondary education's differentiated strategies to counter enrollment decline.

Increased Institutional Productivity. Institutions can also do more to develop creative and effective responses to enrollment decline. On the surface increasing productivity appears to be a self-defeating proposition for institutions faced with enrollment reduction. As enrollments decline, raising productivity normally would mean an even larger reduction in the number of faculty. However, productivity also may be viewed as including all the activities in which faculty participate—not only instruction but student advising and counseling, scholarship and public service efforts, research, and institutional administration. In other words, productivity could be increased with the same number, or even fewer numbers, of students. The aim could be to identify outcomes that could be increased—such as the improvement of the basic writing, speaking, and mathematical skills of students, with special attention given to the disadvantaged and the gifted students.

There may be opportunity for faculty to build a relationship with nearby elementary and secondary schools—an activity that could result in higher-quality education at all levels. The possibility of faculty involvement with social agencies, especially in urban areas, could be explored, despite warnings that faculty are out of their element in such environments. Expanded service to business and industry is another source of increased productivity of faculty.

These potential services will not come easily to faculty because the current discipline-based professional structure does not reward such activities. However, with the threatening decline in the numbers of students, the time may have come for these activities to be taken as serious options. Of course, state legislatures will have to be persuaded that such activities are in the state's interest and that they will be done well. The initiative must be taken by faculty. The result will be faculty who have closer ties to the institution and to the needs of the surrounding community than to their own disciplines.

For Further Reading

The series of reports published by the Center for Research and Development in Higher Education at the University of California at Berkeley, under the direction of Lyman Glenny, remains the most comprehensive and detailed study of state budgeting for higher education. Meisinger (1976) analyzes the uses of formulas in the states; Purves and Glenny (1976), the application of information systems; and Bowen and Glenny (1976), budgeting under conditions of fiscal stringency. More recently Bowen (1980) has studied *The Costs of Higher Education,* including an analysis of economies and diseconomies of scale and, after a historical analysis of costs, offers some conclusions on what higher education programs *should* cost.

❧ 14 ❧

State Budgeting and Retrenchment

James M. Furman

The financial security of public higher education is intimately linked to the prosperity of the states, since about half of the current fund revenues of public institutions now come from state and local appropriations (National Center for Education Statistics, 1980a). Thus, as state tax collections rise and fall with the business cycle, so does the prosperity of public higher education. The combined impact of double-digit inflation and high unemployment rates in 1980 and 1981 revived once again (as it did in the 1974–75 recession) the necessity for midyear budget cuts in state after state, as revenues fell short of expectations. This chapter examines the roles typically played by state government and by university officials who, faced with constitutional requirements to balance state budgets and with resounding expressions of voter resistance to higher taxes, must respond to the reality of having insufficient funds to meet prior commitments.

Double-digit inflation, while a severe problem for higher education and for other state agencies, has not been the condition

that required cutbacks in state appropriations to higher education
and other governmental services. In the late 1970s, annual inflation
rates of 12 percent, when coupled with relatively low unemployment, were actually a boon to governors and their budget directors.
As inflation drove up the cost of consumer goods, sales tax receipts
increased; and as inflation pushed wages and salaries to higher
levels, progressive state income taxes produced unexpected yields.

   This ever-escalating and essentially unpredictable inflation
rate, however, did cause problems for the spenders of tax dollars.
A budget drawn up by higher education officials and state budget
officers one year in advance of the actual appropriations failed to
take accurately into account the runaway inflation that occurred
one to two years later. Education and government administrators found, much to their chagrin, that in actual experience inflation had exceeded their expectations, and it became their task to
operate programs on a dollar that had shrunk even more than
anticipated. In each year following the one in which inflation
and revenues had been underestimated, state budget officers felt
the wrath of managers required to make cutbacks because of an
unanticipated increase in inflation, but fortunately state budget
officers were receiving one year's grace period from the consequences of inflation.

   The problems of state government and higher education
have been greatly compounded with "stagflation"—the combination of high inflation and high unemployment. When, in 1980,
unemployment began to climb steeply in many states, the result was
lower-than-expected revenues from income taxes. In addition,
consumer sales were off, producing lower sales tax receipts than
anticipated. The state treasuries of midwestern and northeastern
states were particularly hard hit by the rapid increase in unemployment, and states like Michigan and Ohio, which look to the
automobile industry as a major underpinning of their economies,
were dealt an especially heavy blow. The state universities in Ohio
received the first reduction in their appropriations almost immediately after the beginning of the 1981 fiscal year, and the second followed at midyear as the Ohio economy worsened. The
midyear reductions were especially difficult because institutions

had to absorb the entire impact in the course of six months, thus magnifying the budget loss by a factor of two.

Budget Reduction: The Players and Their Roles

Office of the Governor. Few will deny that governors and their budget directors are in key positions to anticipate and respond to declining state revenues. As an employee of the governor, the state budget director constantly monitors the indicators of the state's economic well-being and relates them to the accuracy of revenue projections. The budget director is the person with the responsibility of warning the governor of an unexpected downturn in revenues. If convinced that a substantial decrease in revenues has occurred and that the state budget is out of balance, the governor must take remedial action to correct the problem.

Correcting the problem may well involve several different but equally important strategies. One obvious approach is for the governor to impose spending cuts. In departments and agencies under the governor's direct control, budget reductions are often imposed simply by executive order and implemented by the budget director. These reductions can be and often are quite specific: a freeze on employee hiring, cutbacks in travel, and delayed purchase of equipment. The relationships between the governor and department heads are reasonably clear; if the governor orders a cutback in funding for the corrections department, the department director follows through on the task, no matter how unsavory the assignment.

The working relationship between the governor and the state's higher education system, however, is less certain and more obscure. In states where university governing boards have constitutional status, a governor may not have the authority to mandate specific budgetary reductions; but even in the vast majority of states where institutions do not enjoy constitutional status, traditions affecting the relationship between government and education have made the matter of cutting education budgets a delicate exercise. Even though governors normally have the authority to direct higher education budget cuts by discreet distinctions of program and object of expenditure, they are unlikely to do so. The most likely scenario is for the institutions to receive a single total dollar or percentage figure for reduction and then be allowed to decide where and how the reductions are to be achieved.

Institutional Boards and Administrators. In general, institutions have been permitted to determine how and where budgets are to be cut because education administrators have been successful in their warnings that government interference in the day-to-day affairs of universities impugns the integrity of the institution and inhibits it from acting in the best interest of the society it serves. The assertion that education and politics should not be mixed underpins the argument of those who call for insulating many of the higher education budget decisions from state budget offices. Also, universities are different from the typical state agency in that they are governed by policy-making boards of trustees. These trustees in most instances are appointed by the governor, with the understanding that they have the responsibility for implementing policies governing the universities. Though it is considered appropriate for the governor to decide how much of the burden will be shouldered by each of the tax dollar spenders, it is generally left to the universities' governing boards and administrators to make the specific line-item budget reductions within the system. The most appealing way to make a budget reduction for a university or perhaps any agency of government is simply to make an across-the-board reduction. This is the usual method applied by governors in distributing cuts among agencies. If the method were applied to the internal budget of an agency or a university, it would result in the same percent reduction for salaries, equipment, operating and maintenance, and other functional areas. But such an approach is ill advised, simply because it forfeits any recognition of the need to develop spending priorities in an individual budget plan. Fortunately, universities seldom choose across-the-board budget reductions—but for reasons that unfortunately do not relate to good budgeting practices.

Higher education budget reductions during the last decade consistently have been in areas of nonpersonnel spending. When reductions must be made, the first response typically is to postpone equipment purchases and defer maintenance. Invariably, the budget line for salary increases is protected at all costs. The elimination of programs and positions is resisted in every way possible. The resistance to taking a part of the budget reduction out of the salary-increase line is understandable in light of the impact of inflation on faculty salaries. The resistance is also understandable when one considers the political realities involving the president's relationship to the faculty and the pressures that can emanate from any suggestion that salaries bear a portion of the cutbacks to be made. There is little reason to believe that cutbacks of the future will be handled differently, and equipment and maintenance spending categories will continue to fare badly in any analysis of higher education's spending patterns.

Statewide Coordinating or Governing Board. A statewide coordinating or consolidated governing board can assume an especially important role when the state political leaders decide that the budget-cutting decisions are to be made by higher education officials. An invitation to the administrators and trustees of individual institutions to divide the cuts among themselves without the involvement of a statewide board would cause warfare without benefit of the Geneva Conventions. Once the magnitude of higher education's cut is known, a statewide coordinating board is in the best position to allocate reductions among the various segments of higher education. If this task is performed skillfully, with frequent consultation and an emphasis on the equitable treatment of the affected colleges and universities, the worth of the coordinating agency in the cause of higher education will be apparent.

In many ways the process used to make these cuts is as important as, if not more important than, the cuts themselves. Participation and discussion need to be emphasized repeatedly in this connection, just as they do in the development of a statewide master plan for higher education. As onerous a task as the implementation of appropriation cutbacks is, the requirement for involvement and participation in these is as important here as in the building of the annual higher education budget by a coordinating agency and the individual institutions of higher education.

As it develops its cutback strategies, the coordinating agency must establish and recognize priorities among the various sectors of higher education as well as among the objects of expenditure within the various colleges and universities. The coordinating board has the obligation to weigh the relative needs of private higher education, the student assistance program, and public higher education, with distinctions being made between types of institutions. If the coordinating board has the confidence of the governor and the legislature, the board is performing one of its most important tasks in developing statewide higher education policies through the setting of such priorities. In doing so, whether in budget making or in budget cutting, the coordinating board is lessening the political load of the governor and the state legislative leaders. The board is also performing a service that, if left to the individual institutions, would inevitably lead to mutually destructive warfare. With a reasonable amount of good faith on the part of the state's political and educational leadership, the tasks performed by the coordinating board in the cutback process should lead to a result that will receive general, if not unanimous, support.

The Legislature. When it becomes necessary to make cuts in appropriations in midyear, after the legislature has completed its regular appropriation process, the initiative for such cuts most often rests with the governor and the state budget director. As a consequence, the legislature frequently finds itself in a reactive mode to the fiscal emergency that has resulted after the fiscal year has begun, the appropriation has been made, and the legislature has adjourned.

In this set of circumstances, a key decision for the legislative leadership is whether to support the governor's position regarding the need to make cutbacks or to call for emergency tax increases to offset the declines in revenues. The prospect of midyear tax increases is usually met with a decided lack of enthusiasm by legislators whose career plans include remaining in public office. If the leadership, therefore, declines the midyear tax increase option, it finds itself primarily in a "watchdog" role during the cutback process. Subsequent surveillance tasks are most often performed by legislative staff and committees through the hearing process.

Even though a legislative body may delegate to the coordinating agency the responsibility of deciding where budget cuts are to be made among the institutions of higher education, hearings held by legislative committees play an important role in influencing the decision-making process. Although unanimous legislative agreement is seldom achieved because of the wide variety of conflicting pressures and opinions presented to a legislative body, few higher education officials would be so bold as to ignore a strong expression of intent about where and how to make midyear cutbacks. The virtual certainty of retribution at the next regular appropriation session of the state legislature looms large.

Conclusion. Politically and educationally, the most prudent way to reduce budgets is to have the specific decisions affecting programs and personnel made at the institutional level. Thus, the governor and the legislature have responsibility to determine higher education's share of the statewide cut; the state coordinating or governing board develops the general priorities concerning cuts among the sectors of higher education and among the major program categories; and the officials at the institutional level carry out the cuts, using their specialized knowledge of programs and personnel.

For example, a coordinating board may decide that the universities will receive a 5 percent reduction for salaries, but the institution's board of trustees and administration decide how this reduction will be allocated among various types of personnel; that is, faculty, administrators, and support staff. In this way the special circumstances of each institution can be recognized, and the persons responsible directly for the administration of the individual institution can make their decisions accordingly. Each major participant has an important responsibility and role to assume in the process of an appropriation cutback. The danger inherent in a breakdown of this process is evident: a centralization of the decision-making process so that detailed decisions that should be made by the institution are made instead by the state.

State-Level Budget Strategies

The key to accommodating to midyear reductions in appropriations with a minimum of disruption is contingency planning that prepares a strategy for rapid implementation when revenue shortfalls occur. Recent experiences regarding revenue shortfalls in 1980 for the state of Washington provide examples of how advance planning can cushion the blow of unexpected budgetary cutbacks.

As a first step, when the Washington legislature enacted its biennial appropriation bill early in 1979, it provided a reserve of 3 percent of the general revenue fund to be expended only on the authorization of the governor (*Laws of 1979*, sec. 213, chap. 270). The language of the law charged the governor with the responsibility for monitoring the state's fiscal health on an ongoing basis and gave her the authority to respond to threatening conditions. The state's fiscal director, armed with the reserve set-aside directive, could then make decisions to release this reserve on a quarterly basis, provided revenue projections held up to expectations. In the state of Washington, the decision was made to release the reserve for the first year of the biennium; but as economic conditions worsened for the state in the second year, the governor stopped the release of reserve.

If simply holding back the allotment reserve fails to bridge the gap between state spending and revenues, a governor can supplement the freeze on reserve funds by ordering additional stringencies in expenditures. In Washington, when it became apparent that additional expenditure cuts would be necessary, the governor issued on April 30, 1980, Executive Order 80–06, placing a freeze on the hiring of state employees. Included in the order were the following administrative measures:

1. *Staffing Freeze.* Agency directors are instructed to establish no new positions and to fill not more than 50 percent of funded positions now vacant or vacated during the period of enforcement of this order. Exceptions to this directive will be granted only for critical or emergent situations for which there is clear evidence that compliance with this directive could be detrimental to the best interest of the state, or in cases where a letter of intent has been signed prior to this order. The budget director shall establish criteria and propose procedures for the granting of exceptions to this directive subject to approval by me.

2. *Overtime.* Agency directors are instructed to reduce wherever possible the use of overtime and other premium pay and to avoid the use of these

compensations as a means of circumventing the staffing directive of this order.

3. *Exceptions.* All exceptions to this directive will be made by me and are to be requested only by the agency director to the budget director.

When the above executive order and a previous one reducing by 20 percent the reimbursement for automobile travel were coupled with the decision not to release the 3 percent reserve during the second year of the biennium, the result was a carefully drawn state government strategy to curtail spending incrementally, responding with greater severity as the state's fiscal plight became more serious.

For those who thought that retrenchment initiatives had run their course in Washington, state agencies received yet another jolt on September 29, 1980, when the governor issued another executive order, requiring an additional 1 percent reduction of general revenue fund dollars. The impact of this executive order was magnified by the fact that the 1 percent holdback was applied against a biennial appropriation base during the second year of the biennium, thus requiring a reversion of over 2 percent. The State Budget Office eased the problems associated with the reversion requirement of September 29 by alerting state agencies as early as July that an additional 1 percent reduction of their budgets might well be forthcoming. On July 17, 1980, the budget director circulated a memorandum to all agencies, requiring plans to be developed for a possible 1 percent allotment revision, effective October 1, 1980.

In the best of all worlds, the State Budget Office and the Legislative Appropriation Committees in Washington would have been able in 1978 to make accurate revenue forecasts for the 1979–81 biennium. However, given the wild gyrations of the economy nationally and in the individual states, accurate revenue projections are frequently not achievable—especially when forecasts are required for a two-year period. Accordingly, the state legislature and the office of the governor acted responsibly in providing themselves with the tools to make mid-course corrections when revenue forecasts did not live up to expectations. Because state revenues were monitored on an ongoing basis, spending revisions could be made in a gradual way, given the severe downturn in the state's economy, so that single massive cuts, leading to severe dislocations, were not imposed. The very significant dislocations that have occurred in some states could have been avoided with substantive advance planning.

A state's budget makers also should consider the need for an adequate working-cash balance. Statistics projected for 1980, compiled by the National Governors' Association and the National Association of State Budget Officers, show that there are wide variations among the states in the percentage of funds set aside as a cushion for a working-cash balance—from Alaska's 124.3 percent of expenditures to Alabama's 0 percent. A rule of thumb frequently applied is that a state should end its fiscal year with 5 percent of its general revenues as a cash balance. A reserve significantly less than 5 percent immediately places a state in a position of peril as the new budget year develops and deviations in spending and revenue estimates become apparent. Many of Ohio's current budget problems can be traced to its practice in recent years of dividing up its budget surpluses, primarily among the state's school districts.

At the institutional level, the most important consideration again is to have contingency plans that chart a course of action for handling cutbacks in state funding. With good contingency planning, institutional officials can avoid having to stumble from one crisis to the next and instead can respond quickly according to predetermined priorities. The state's educational leaders, including representatives of the coordinating board and the individual colleges and universities, must demonstrate that they are fully able and willing to assume the burden of making the budget cuts called for in higher education. This responsibility requires the ability to establish priorities among levels and types of institutions and the willingness to make choices among categories of expenditures.

Changing State Priorities

While unexpected requirements to reduce state appropriations demand considerable attention and receive the newspaper headlines, a far more serious problem for higher education is its declining share of state revenues. During the past decade, higher education has been the victim of a change in state spending priorities, a change whereby colleges and universities receive a smaller percentage of the total state dollars available (Ruyle and Glenny, 1980). Illinois, for example, received 17.5 percent of general revenue funds in 1970 but only 12.7 percent in 1980. While falling state percentages for the support of higher education are not as yet the rule in the Sun Belt states, the Illinois experience is a typical one for the large midwestern and northeastern states of the country.

Population changes for the 1980s and for at least a part of the 1990s suggest that higher education will have even more difficulty in the years ahead in maintaining even its current share of total revenues. A fact that should strike fear into the hearts of higher education officials is that the lower priority given to higher education by state governors and state legislatures came about at the very time that higher education enrollments were increasing. If higher education could not maintain its share of total state revenues during a ten-year period of enrollment increase, what fate awaits it during the budget struggles of the 1980s, when enrollments are declining?

What factors have contributed to higher education's declining share of state revenues, and what programs apparently have assumed a higher priority in the minds of state legislative and executive budget makers? Interestingly enough, state support for elementary/secondary education presents a paradox when compared with appropriations for higher education. Elementary/secondary education has not experienced a decline in the percentage of state revenues in any way similar to that of higher education in the 1970s (Ruyle and Glenny, 1980). This is all the more amazing when one realizes that during the 1970s elementary/secondary education experienced the enrollment declines projected for higher education in the 1980s. Not only has elementary/secondary education done a better job of holding on to state revenues, but it has done so at a time when its work load was decreasing and higher education's was increasing.

Higher education is faced with a number of new competitors for state funding—in addition to its historic competitor, elementary/secondary education. Energy, environment, mass transportation, and Medicaid have emerged as relatively new and significant priorities for consideration by state officials. These new programs, which may have been started when state treasuries were growing, must be abandoned when revenues decline, or their support must come at the expense of other established programs. In many states the higher education budget represents one of the largest discretionary state expenditures and is therefore a likely program to shift money *away* from. Also drawing down the balance remaining for higher education are the entitlement programs, such as welfare and retirement, and the health and corrections programs, the expenditures for which are frequently increased by court mandates for better or expanded services.

There are other reasons why higher education has failed to compete effectively in the quest for tax dollars. In many ways it has become its own worst enemy. Higher education officials in a state often find it difficult to make a strong and united stand for their common needs. They fail to support the state coordinating board, which, because of its position within state government, is a uniquely credible advocate for higher education. The resulting fractures and fissures between the private colleges, the public universities, and the community colleges take place in full view of state budget makers. As long as the various higher education sectors are unable to reinforce each other in their presentation of budgetary needs, the effectiveness of their case for increased funding is seriously undermined. Unless higher education representatives from all sectors realize that they have much more to gain than to lose in presenting a common front and that the most serious challenge is to present effectively all of higher education's needs, in contrast to spending programs and priorities outside of higher education, the painful erosion of support for higher education is likely to continue throughout the decade of the 1980s.

Inflation's Impact on Faculty

It often has been said that inflation is the cruelest tax of all, and this is especially so when one examines higher education's funding experience. Report after report in recent years demonstrates that faculty salaries have not kept pace with inflation

(Hansen, 1980; Illinois Board of Higher Education, 1980). The wage earners in this country might well exclaim that the ravages of inflation are not unique to college and university faculty; but, in fact, their relative suffering at the hands of inflation has been greater than for most of the other professional and wage-earner employment groups used for comparative purposes. Federal government employees, nonagricultural workers, and various professional groups have experienced a much happier situation than have college and university faculty in the quest to maintain real income.

In Illinois faculty salaries in public higher education increased 66 percent between fiscal years 1972 and 1981, while during the same interval the consumer price index increased 108 percent. Even the gross national product implicit price deflator (a more conservative measure of cost increases) climbed by a factor of 90 percent between 1972 and 1981 (Illinois Board of Higher Education, 1981). Few employee groups in the labor sector have a worse record of decreased earnings as measured in real income than the one experienced by faculty; and since spending for salaries typically reflects 75 percent of all higher education spending, the end result is that higher education generally has not maintained its share of state revenues.

Achieving real increases in faculty salaries is crucial to improving higher education's competitive share of state resources. Thus far the collective bargaining process can point to little in the way of strategies and accomplishments that have led to higher salaries. Instead, the opportunity for maximum effectiveness lies within the institutions of higher education themselves. They are in a unique position to control the market forces that have contributed to depressed salary scales. Colleges and universities are the sole producers and primary employers of Ph.D.s. In the face of declining enrollments, the institutions are presented two options: they can limit the number of Ph.D. graduates by limiting admissions or eliminating programs (that is, control the supply), or they can effectively show political leaders how higher education and the work of its faculty relate to and support the social and economic needs of the state (that is, increase the demand). A combination of both tactics will probably be most effective in generating the support required outside the higher education community for activities taking place within. Universities that reach out into their communities and apply their resources to the problems besetting the citizens will be doing more than enhancing public relations. The university that shares the expertise of its urban transportation specialists with the political leaders of a city whose bus and rail system is facing imminent bankruptcy will be creating new consumers of its services, to replace the eighteen-year-olds who used to sit in its classrooms. Schools that develop programs that increase the access of blacks and Hispanics to the legal and medical professions will find new and important advocates in the state legislature.

The inflation squeeze and the overall competition for public funds have led also to damaging consequences for nonpersonnel spending items. An examination of university budgeting practices in recent years clearly reveals that campuses have fallen far behind in maintaining buildings and replacing equipment. An examination of cost patterns for utility expenditures, equipment needs, and library books demonstrates that inflation has been even more severe in these areas than might be imagined. Studies published by the U.S. Office of Education (Halstead, 1979) and by the National Association of College and University Business Officers (1980) indicate, for example, that utility costs for higher education between 1967 and 1980 soared by a factor of 309 percent. The annual percentage increase for utility costs in three of these years was more than 20 percent, reaching a single-year high of 28.2 percent in 1975, followed closely in 1980 with a one-year increase of 27.5 percent. Since 1973 the average yearly increase for utility costs in higher education has been more than 18 percent. Using another comparison, while the consumer price index rose 108 percent between fiscal years 1972 and 1981, the higher education utility costs index climbed by a spectacular 234 percent during this very same period of time.

While rising utility costs are no doubt one of the most dramatic examples of inflation, the higher education price index for nonpersonnel spending overall has its own steep rate of ascent. For example, from 1967 to 1980, nonpersonnel spending in higher education for all components increased by 161 percent. During this same period, the index for books and periodicals soared to 364 percent, using 1967 as a base year of 100 percent. There is little wonder that library acquisitions have had to be trimmed when the forces of inflation fueled cost increases of more than 10 percent per year for eight of these thirteen years (Halstead, 1975, 1979).

Conclusion

All the preceding statistics on the various aspects of inflation in higher education simply reinforce the fact that colleges and universities during the past decade have found themselves caught in a two-way squeeze in their search for adequate funding. Changing state priorities and inflation remain the culprits that confront higher education in the battle of the budget. Unfortunately, the decade of the 1980s holds little, if any, promise of relief from these pressures.

Some claim that colleges and universities have always competed for funds with other state agencies and services, and that inflation is no more a problem for higher education officials than for anyone else. Those assertions, however, are not completely true. The statistics show that higher education in the 1970s received a disproportionately smaller share of total state government funds expended and that higher education has been relatively harder hit by the effects of inflation than have many other areas of government service and sectors of the economy. Again, while midyear decisions to reduce appropriations are heralded by dramatic announcements, the methodical grinding effects of changing state priorities and inflation do far more damage to the very fiber of our colleges and universities.

The growth and prosperity of higher education in the 1980s will depend not on its ability to reverse the potentially crippling effects of inflation and declining enrollments but on its ability to serve society's needs in spite of them, and in some cases because of them. The opportunity to concentrate on improving the quality and effectiveness of the educational program is a potential reality when universities are no longer being hard pressed simply to provide minimal services to ever-growing legions of students.

It is wrong, though, to portray this enhancement of quality as an opportunity; it is, in fact, a necessity. Educators must take a lesson from America's recent recognition that the natural resources needed to produce energy are limited. In a very real sense, the willingness of American taxpayers to support education from their earnings can be viewed as the natural resource that catapulted this nation into worldwide prominence within 150 years of its birth; and that willingness, like our energy supply, is not limitless. Taxpayers and their elected representatives will increasingly demand that higher education prove its ability to address and solve the myriad of social and economic problems contributing to the decline in the quality of American life. It can do so by skillfully implementing decisions arrived at through critical self-appraisal of its goals and operations. Underlying all this is the absolute necessity for the individual members of the higher education community to understand their commonality of needs and to act in a manner that responds to the legitimate demands of the public—namely, that resources be used in a planned and shared manner to produce an efficient *system* of quality higher education.

For Further Reading

The most complete analyses of state budgeting practices can be found in Bowen and Glenny (1976) and in Meisinger (1976). For a review of the literature on financing public higher education, readers are referred to Stampen (1980). Bowen (1980) discusses the impact of inflation on faculty salaries, and Bouchard (1980) discusses the impact of "Proposition 13" legislation on higher education. For a more general review of the relationship between higher education and the states, see the Carnegie Foundation for the Advancement of Teaching (1976). Millard (1976) and the Southern Regional Education Board (1978) provide discussions of the role of statewide boards in budgeting.

❧ 15 ❧

Preparing for Enrollment Decline in a State System

Donald K. Smith

Since 1975 the University of Wisconsin System has been developing its internal planning and budget management systems with an eye to the probable decline in enrollments in the decade 1983 to 1993. The system and its institutions assume that substantial enrollment decline will be accompanied by a decline in state subsidies. This assumption is supported by common sense. Lower instructional work loads imply lower costs for instruction. However, it is not easy for a university system and state government to agree on the appropriate method of calculating the fiscal decline that might follow enrollment decline. For example, the university believes that resources should not be withdrawn because of enrollment decline if at the same time they are being withdrawn indirectly because the costs of inflation are not funded. This is fiscal double jeopardy, and the university has had experience with its impact in the past decade. Moreover, the university believes that those responsible for funding reductions must take into account the fiscal impact of

259

shifts in student preference from lower-cost to higher-cost programs, the potential impact of serving a higher proportion of adult and part-time students, and the possible long-term effect of fiscal austerity on the quality of programs. While willing to listen to such matters, state government remains cautious about making policy commitments that might draw heavily on future resources.

In Wisconsin the assumption that enrollment decline will be accompanied by fiscal decline is valid because the institutions are funded through an enrollment-driven formula. In theory an increase or a decline in enrollments is accompanied by an increase or a decline in state support for instruction. In fact, the formula has worked erratically. In 1975–77, faced with university projections of substantial enrollment increases, the state suspended the formula. Substantial enrollment increases did materialize. The resulting fiscal stress accelerated planning by the university to effectively address fiscal decline, or enrollment decline, or both.

The 1975 SCOPE Report

The university system's first comprehensive document on the management of decline was produced in 1975, although many of the 1975 planning assumptions had been anticipated in occasional papers and fiscal actions undertaken in earlier years. The 1975 SCOPE Report (University of Wisconsin System, 1975), as it became known, was produced with unseemly haste in response to a request from Governor Patrick Lucey that the university system report on how it proposed to reduce its scope in light of prospective fiscal stringency and enrollment decline. Would it close campuses, colleges, or programs, or all of these? Given its genesis, the report is in considerable measure a political document, analyzing and taking exception to the assumptions underlying the governor's request. However, it also develops in some detail the principles and procedures that the system would use to address questions of efficiency and educational quality, as well as enrollment and fiscal decline if these conditions should occur.

Two basic positions on effective academic planning were put forward in the SCOPE Report, and these continue to be articles of faith for the system as it further refines and develops its plans for the management of enrollment and fiscal decline. First of all, noting the twofold historic instructional mission of public higher education—(1) to provide access to higher education for all persons wishing and able to benefit from it and (2) to provide high-quality education, since access to a bad education is not access at all—the SCOPE Report asserts that the system should continue to seek both maximum access and maximum quality but that, if a choice must be made, quality should be protected—even at the expense of access. The second basic position of the SCOPE Report is that, for effective mid-range and long-range academic planning to occur, universities must be reasonably free from repeated fiscal crises, and faculties must be involved in the major decisions about decline. (For a more detailed description of the genesis, contents, and aspirations of the SCOPE Report, see Smith, 1977.)

Planning in 1979: New Initiatives

In 1979 two circumstances accelerated planning for prospective enrollment and fiscal decline. First, the university system decided to reexamine the enrollment funding formula, to determine whether it grossly overstated the level of budgetary change that should flow from changes in enrollment if the budget for instruction were to show reasonable fit with costs. With legislative encouragement in the biennial budget bill, the system engaged in a major study of instructional costs, particularly to determine the proportional relationships of fixed and variable costs, as well as the broader question of the financial conditions under which the system could manage most efficiently and effectively. Through the Office of the Legislative Council, hearings were held with a committee of the legislature on the university's findings. The university held that, whereas the formula assigned 10 percent of the direct costs of instruction to the category of fixed costs, a closer approximation would be that 50 percent of such costs were substantially fixed.

The second planning initiative of 1979 came in a report to state government on the specific topic of the management of decline (University of Wisconsin System, 1979). This has been commonly known as the "November 30 Report." However, I think our universities generally regard this euphemistic use of a calendar date as simply a variant form of the "Ides of March." The November 30 Report emerged from a legislative mandate in the 1979–81 biennial budget bill asking that the system specify further the procedures and criteria by which it would meet the problem of enrollment decline and associated fiscal decline in the 1980s. But the legislature also specified a cost criterion, which would require the regents and the system to reduce the instructional costs of any institution whose unit instructional costs exceeded the average unit costs of all institutions with similar missions by 30 percent or more. The cost criterion was not inherently severe, although it did serve as a springboard for planning steps vis-à-vis one of the thirteen universities of the system, the University of Wisconsin at Superior, and several of the two-year transfer centers. The way in which the legislative criterion was integrated with a broader set of system planning criteria and the impact of immediate implementation will be considered subsequently.

Ongoing Management Instruments

I am occasionally bemused by the way in which the university since 1975 has linked enrollment decline in the 1980s to fiscal decline. The two phenomena *can* operate independently. They did so in Wisconsin in the 1970s, when the system faced progressive fiscal stringency in the presence of enrollment increase. Moreover, the widely heralded enrollment declines of the 1980s may or may not occur. In fact, the American Council on Education (ACE) (Frances, 1980b) predicts that—instead of the long-awaited declines of the 1980s—enrollments will be relatively stable. All this will happen, thinks the ACE, because of prospective improvements in high school graduation rates, in college attendance rates, in retention, in continuing education demands by older populations, and in demand from foreign students. If the ACE is right, then our elaborate planning efforts in Wisconsin may turn into a management version of Samuel Beckett's play *Waiting for Godot*. The two characters in this play carry on their extended conversation under the dramatic pressure of an awaited appearance of Godot. But Godot never arrives. However, I suspect that the analogy ends there. Beckett's people were both hoping for and fearing Godot's arrival. Those of us in Wisconsin will be so relieved if enrollment decline does not arrive that we will be quite willing to overlook small questions of excessive or disproportionate advance effort.

The system's 1975 SCOPE Report observed that the level of higher education enrollments in the 1980s was much more likely to be affected by public policy decisions on the support of students and institutions than by the past relationships between demographic data and enrollments. This seems to me an almost self-evident truth, and one that adds uncertainty to the work of projection. Nevertheless, the November 30 Report put aside speculation about whether enrollment declines would occur. The report projected that they would occur and that the declines would be substantial—about 19,000 full-time-equivalent (FTE) students by 1993, or about 15 percent of current enrollments—and would be accompanied by some level of constant dollar decline for the support of instruction. The linkage of fiscal stringency and enrollment decline for planning purposes makes sense, since the probability is inescapable that the system will be facing some level of fiscal austerity in the 1980s. Several or many of the institutions will also be facing some level of enrollment decline, and these events produce interrelated and complicated problems of academic program and fiscal administration.

Some of the major management instruments developed by the system to address fiscal stringency or enrollment problems have obvious value even in the absence of stringency. Others specifically address the problem of early identification and response to problems. Some of these instruments are in rather widespread use across the nation; others seem to me to undertake approaches not found widely elsewhere.

1. *Mission Statements.* Each of the system's thirteen universities, its set of two-year university centers, and the extension institution has a mission statement established by the board of regents. This statement sets boundaries within which an institution can plan academic programs and offer academic degrees. The institutions are categorized in clusters. For example, the two doctoral institutions are in one cluster, and the eleven baccalaureate-master's degree institutions are in a second cluster. Each cluster has a mission

common to member institutions, but each institution also has a special mission, defined by the program areas within which it may seek approval for new offerings.

We have faced the possibility that some institutions, absorbing a disproportionately large rate of enrollment decline, may have to reexamine their missions. In this sense a change in mission may enable a particular institution to meet unusual problems of declining resources while still maintaining the quality of the services that are continued. A fundamental change in an institution's mission, however, is the most drastic surgery for meeting decline that we can envision, other than the outright closing of a campus. With effective planning, it is hoped that the use of either medicine will be, at worst, infrequent.

2. *Constraining, Altering, or Reducing Program Arrays.* Since 1973 we have been using two processes to slow down and selectively reverse academic program growth, which proceeded so freely in the 1950s and 1960s. These processes are (1) a rigorous review process before an institution is given the go-ahead to plan and implement a particular new program and (2) a process for the systematic evaluation of all existing academic programs, in order to decide whether to continue, modify, consolidate, or discontinue each program. Many states now have a version of this latter process in operation.

The current difficulty most universities face in coping with enrollment and budget decline flows from a history of excessive program specialization in American higher education, particularly at the undergraduate level. As a result, when sudden or systematic shifts occur in student program choices, universities cannot react to these shifts because their resources are tied up in personnel who are often too specialized in their interests and preparation to serve alternative instructional needs. I do not want to seem too critical of our history of program specialization, even though in the 1980s it will account for some of our most severe management problems. Specialization was a way to fulfill the public university dream of bringing the "blessing" of higher learning to bear on the educational needs and occupational interests of all people. It was a way of coping with the current reconfigurations of particular knowledge. But, aided by the perfect vision available to hindsight, we now can see that higher education perhaps went too far too fast.

In Wisconsin we assume that, to cope with enrollment and fiscal decline, universities will need to move toward two goals: (1) the elimination and consolidation of courses, in order to protect against the inefficiencies of excessively small classes; and (2) the changing of program arrays, including the elimination or consolidation of programs not essential to the fulfillment of the institution's mission. This process should also be used to provide for resource reallocation needed to support the development of new courses and programs, which will be essential to respond vigorously to the demands of new knowledge and new societal needs, even in the presence of fiscal austerity.

The instruments of curricular and program consolidation will, we believe, enable most of our institutions to meet the problems of enrollment and related fiscal decline in the 1980s and enter the 1990s with undiminished quality and vigor. When the weather is right, one can even dream that the whole process of adaptation may strengthen institutional purpose and quality. But such a dream involves the unlikely assumption that fiscal decline related to enrollment decline is the only, or major, fiscal uncertainty we will face. We also assume that some institutions may face problems of decline of such severity that they will no longer be able to respond in ways that protect either the continuity or the quality of their enterprise. Additional instruments are available for such circumstances.

3. *Enrollment and Fiscal Targeting.* Since 1976 the University of Wisconsin System has provided the regents with a four-year enrollment forecast for each university, updated annually. In the November 30 Report, provisions were made to extend projections over a six-year period. These projections are called *targets* rather than *forecasts*. The enrollment target figure is related to a fiscal target figure. For institutions whose enrollments steadily fall behind earlier targets, which had been reconciled with their resources, lower enrollment target figures are projected and schedules are established for phased reductions in their instructional budgets. In theory the phased funding reductions for institutions experiencing enrollment decline can be used to increase targets for institutions experiencing heavy pressure on admissions. In practice this has been erratically possible. The suspension of state enrollment funding increments in 1975–77, the effect of inflation on budgets

generally, and the unusual volatility in changing student prefer-
ences for institutions and programs have all created a state of almost constant crisis and have greatly impeded the application of
the enrollment and fiscal targeting plans.

In effect, enrollment and fiscal targeting have been developed to permit institutions greater latitude to protect the quality
of programs by restricting enrollments to a level consistent with
their resource base. Targeting also allows for phased reallocations
of instructional funding *from* institutions whose enrollments fall
below targets *to* those facing demand for admission in excess of the
funded target. The decision to manage enrollment and fiscal
targets in this way was consistent with the planning position of the
system: that universities cannot effectively and quickly respond to
sudden withdrawals—or, for that matter, to sudden increases—of
instructional funding. Faculty commitments cannot be turned on
and off if one expects to maintain an effective community of scholars. Programs cannot be closed overnight, and should not be, unless decisions are to be based on the vulnerability of politics and
personnel of the program rather than its order of worth in the
university as a whole.

In 1973, when the system began analyzing instructional
costs, it was clear that wide differences existed in unit instructional
costs among institutions with similar missions. The system set as an
objective the narrowing of this gap—not to achieve homogeneity,
which would substitute formula-driven budget decisions for academic judgments, but to establish a set of relationships that could
be defended as reasonably equitable and educationally responsible.
In the four years after initiating enrollment and fiscal targeting,
the system took $5.5 million out of the instructional budgets of
seven institutions and added $4.1 million to the budgets of seven
others. The difference in these two numbers reflected an effort in
part to restore a contingency account against unanticipated fee
revenue shortages and in part to compensate for deficiencies in
state allocations.

In support of our enrollment and fiscal targeting procedures, we have also developed an index called the Composite Support Index, or CSI. (A brief technical description of the CSI is
maintained by the Office of Analysis Services, University of Wisconsin System, Madison, Wisconsin 53706.) It reflects the effects of

all decisions on the relative strength of fiscal support for the instructional mission of institutions in the same cluster. Essentially, this index measures the number of dollars behind each weighted credit hour of degree instruction offered by each institution. It takes into account the differences in costs for instruction at four different levels (lower division, upper division, first-level graduate, and second-level graduate); the differences in costs for six disciplinary areas (ranging from the high-cost engineering and physical sciences areas to the lower-cost social sciences and humanities areas); and the difference between each institution's FTE and head-count enrollments. The index gives a quick and consistent way of looking at relative support levels for institutions, which is much more informative than simple unit costs. It would be difficult to manage enrollment funding decisions without such an index. At the same time, the system has resisted tying allocation decisions simply to the CSI levels. The system's enthusiasm for the CSI is not shared, however, by administrators and faculty at many University of Wisconsin institutions. The institutions from which funds have been withdrawn have little trouble discovering numerous reasons why the index inaccurately portrays the relative adequacy of their support.

Thresholds of Concern

The management instruments described thus far have been developed over a period of several years. In 1979 the university system added a new process, designated "Special Planning," for the few institutions where normal planning and reallocation procedures will be unable to cope with the severity of enrollment and fiscal decline. The president of the system, as well as the chancellor and faculty of an affected institution, should have available "indicators of trouble," which suggest that intensified communication between the institution and the president should be undertaken. We named these indicators "thresholds of concern." This is a euphemism, although it is true that an institution could cross one or more of the thresholds without any great indication that it was heading for serious trouble. Among the thresholds is one indicator called a "trip wire." It relates to the legislative mandate that if the instructional costs of any institution, as measured by the CSI, exceed the average costs of institutions in its cluster by 30 percent or more, then the regents shall undertake a special study to determine what changes in mission or program array, or both, are needed to bring the costs of the institution back to an appropriate level. In cases where, in the judgment of the system president and regents, conditions are extremely severe, an external task force appointed by the president is asked to make recommendations. The president and the regents then develop directives or action to follow from the task force recommendations. In 1979 two presidential task forces were established to assist the president and the regents in responding effectively to the legislative mandate.

The thresholds of concern established in the November 30 Report as possible triggers for the special planning process are as follows:

1. An institution's actual or projected Composite Support Index exceeds its targeted CSI by at least 6 percent.
2. Actual or projected enrollment or related fiscal decline exceeds 5 percent in one year or 12 percent over the six-year planning period.
3. The institution's fixed instructional cost exceeds 65 percent of total instructional cost in the current year or has increased by more than 10 percent in the previous two years.
4. The projected percentage of faculty, teaching academic staff, and graduate teaching assistants whose contracts terminate in any one year is less than twice the percentage of projected enrollment decline in that same year.
5. Highly tenured institutions (institutions with 35 percent or more of their instructional staff in departments where at least 80 percent of the faculty are tenured) register significant enrollment declines (more than 5 percent for any one year or 12 percent over the six-year planning period in at least half of the departments).
6. An institution's Composite Support Index is projected to exceed the weighted cluster average by 30 percent or more. (This threshold is the legislatively mandated trip wire.)

There is little point in speculating about how well these indicators will work to tell the president, the chancellors, and the regents when an institution is headed for trouble and when the trouble is so serious that intervention will be required. The indicators assume that universities can adjust to declining enrollments and associated fiscal decline if (1) they are not the object of other kinds of severe budget cuts; (2) they do not experience an atypically large decline; (3) they are able to protect as much flexibility in their personnel commitments as may be required to achieve staff reductions appropriate to work-load reductions; and (4) they can manage curricular and program array consolidations in ways that prevent both the erosion of program quality and cost escalations inherent in steadily declining average class size. By 1985 we will know whether the boundary conditions for these indicators have been wisely set or, for that matter, whether our fiscal environment is stable enough to make any kind of rational planning possible.

Presidential Task Forces

After the regents had approved the November 30 Report, the two presidential task forces called for in the report were established. The first task force was to examine the mission, structure, and program array of the University of Wisconsin at Superior, since legislative action had, in effect, mandated that the regents take prompt action to lower instructional costs at Superior. Although annual budget retrenchments had been undertaken at that institution under the enrollment and fiscal targeting procedures, continuing enrollment declines had made these insufficient to check relative growth in Superior's unit costs. In fact, enrollment losses in the fall of 1979 had caused unit costs at Superior to grow to 142 percent of the average for the eleven universities with comparable missions, and this was well above the 130 percent trip wire set in the 1979–81 budget bill. The task force was made up of administrators and faculty from other institutions of the system, but with liaison members from Superior, and had authority to engage such other consultative assistance as it might wish.

A study by the second task force was directed by the regents and related to the University of Wisconsin Center System of fourteen two-year, liberal arts transfer centers, headed by a chancellor and center system staff. Three of the smallest centers had developed unit costs in excess of 130 percent of the average for the center system as a whole, and the entire group of centers increasingly required resources in excess of the fiscal targets. Enrollment and fiscal projections through 1985–86 also indicated that the center system, in the absence of structural change, might confront an all but unmanageable rate of fiscal decline. It was arguable that the fourteen two-year centers were part of a single institution of the system, even though each had its own campus, and that the costs of one of the centers should not be compared to the costs of one of the universities. The regents thought otherwise, however, particularly because in earlier policy they had asked for continuing effort to keep the costs of individual centers within the range of 120 percent of average costs for the center system as a whole.

The task forces were charged with completing their reviews and recommendations before the end of the 1979–80 academic year, to give the president ample time for review prior to bringing his own recommendations to the board of regents. In November 1980 the system president brought his report and recommendations to the board of regents. The board also received reports from institutional planning committees. The regents approved the president's recommendation that the center at Medford be closed, and this recommendation was forwarded to the legislature, where, under state law, it must also be approved to become effective. The regents further endorsed the plan for the fiscal and academic steps that will be taken to lower Superior's instructional costs, primarily through a major reorganization of the program structure of the College of Letters and Science. This reorganization will shift the college from its traditional departmental structure to a divisional structure, deemed more appropriate to a small university. Curricular consolidation and staff reductions will accompany the change. This reorganization plan is endorsed by Superior's planning committee and chancellor and by the system's president and regents. It can be implemented without further approvals.

Conclusion

In 1981 the received wisdom of the higher education community of America is that the 1980s will bring to most states a decade of fiscal stringency. Enrollment decline will either induce the financial squeeze or be caused by it or appear with relatively little relation to it. For institutions such as the public universities of Wisconsin, already worried by a decade of tight dollars, this is not an encouraging outlook. There is only limited comfort in the fact that it is an outlook shared by a wide range of tax-assisted institutions and services across the nation.

Despite such general fiscal pessimism, the great range and variety of resources and missions now found among American universities make it probable that most universities will survive the 1980s, and many will be able to make this more than a decade of "reduction, reallocation, and retrenchment," to use the melancholy title of a recent American Association for Higher Education report (Mortimer and Tierney, 1979). The issue for reasonably mature universities with a taste and talent for intellectual quality is not really *survival*. The issue is whether they can maintain the vitality of their academic communities and can maintain the nation's resources of knowledge and highly educated citizens in an environment marked by sustained fiscal decline and erratic, crisis-ridden fiscal policy toward higher education. Can faculties growing old together, with their wisdom unleavened by a sufficient flow of newcomers, escape intellectual obsolescence? Can a profession facing a progressive decline in status, security, and income attract the best minds among today's students into the university vocation? If not, what does this say about the future quality of intellectual leadership? And if the intellectual resources of the nation are permitted to deteriorate, how can it reclaim the international leadership it once so unquestionably held? Or how can it generate either the knowledge or the educated leadership so clearly demanded by the seemingly intransigent problems of our age?

These are large questions. Yet they are questions that must be of as much concern to government and society generally as they are to the universities. Appropriate answers to such questions will not necessarily lead to the conclusion that *all* institutions, higher education missions, and programs need to be equally protected, or in some cases protected at all. But the questions will remain, and they cannot be pushed aside by government or society except at hazard to the nation.

In such circumstances I remain optimistic that the University of Wisconsin System's attempt to restore some measure of stability to its fiscal and governance relationships with the state of Wisconsin will bear fruit in the 1980s. Effective academic planning and resource management require such stability. The new social contract that emerges may well promise austerity rather than affluence. Universities can grow smaller and in relative terms less costly while remaining vital centers of intellectual life. But they can do this only if government respects the rhythms of university decision processes required by the structure of the academic communities. As of this writing, the prospects for an escape from crisis management in Wisconsin are not promising. But it is difficult to believe that any society will long persist in failure to invest reasonably and with prudent continuity in its own future and the future of its people. University administrators and planners should ask no more of government than this.

For Further Reading

Those interested in the relationship between large multicampus systems of higher education and state government should read *12 Systems of Higher Education: 6 Decisive Issues* (Kerr and others, 1978). For an understanding of institutional governance, familiarity with Millett's (1978) *New Structures of Campus Power* is essential. For an overview of planning activities in large public systems of higher education, see Lee and Bowen (1975). For additional discussion of events in Wisconsin and their impact on faculty, readers are referred to Pondrom (1981).

❧ 16 ❧

Political Realities of Statewide Reorganization, Merger, and Closure

James R. Mingle
Robert O. Berdahl
Marvin W. Peterson

In 1979 and 1980, the Southern Regional Education Board conducted two parallel sets of case studies on the response to decline. The institutional cases are discussed in Chapter Four. Three of the state cases (Alabama, Connecticut, and Massachusetts) are discussed here. In all three states, planning agencies were proposing some form of consolidation of governance structures and the merging or closing of public colleges. Like the planners in the states, the SREB research team began its study by asking whether administrative and governance consolidation, institutional merger, and closure in the public sector are viable retrenchment solutions to the problems of enrollment decline and financial cutbacks, and ended by examining the political response to these issues and the problems of statewide governance. The following questions guided the research:

1. What are the political dynamics that lead to proposals for reorganization, consolidation, or merger in the public sector? What reasons are advanced for any change? Who are the major proponents and opponents?
2. What are the expectations for the new arrangement? What is its legal mandate? What do the interested parties or political groups, affected agencies, and institutions really intend or expect to accomplish?
3. What are the likely future targets for public-sector consolidation? What is the likely impact on statewide coordinating mechanisms?

Background on Public-Sector Reorganization and Merger

The reorganization of statewide coordination and governance arrangements has a long-standing tradition in public higher education (see Table 1). In addition to the formal changes shown in Table 1, many unsuccessful efforts were made to change statewide structures. In recent years it seems that no sooner had legislators in some states settled on one form of coordination and governance than demands came for additional changes.

Table 1. Statewide Coordination and Governance in Public Higher Education, 1940–1980

	1940	1950	1960	1970	1980
No statewide structure	33	28	17	2	3[a]
Voluntary association	0	3	6	2	0
Advisory coordinating board	1	1	5	13	9
Regulatory coordinating board	1	2	6	14	18
Consolidated governing board	13	14	16	19	20
Total States	48	48	50	50	50

[a]The nonstatutory 1202 Commissions in Delaware, Vermont, and Wyoming.

From a look at the table, one readily sees that statewide coordination has generally become formalized and that coordinating boards, with their regulatory powers, have grown during the past forty years. Table 1 also reveals two other dimensions at the state level: the instability of the coordinating structures and the stability of the consolidated governing pattern. As advocates of institutional interests, the consolidated boards have had a fairly clear role identity. They are also a relatively understandable and simple mechanism for achieving clear accountability over the seemingly unwieldy structures of higher education. In contrast, the coordinating boards have often been unsure whether to act as advocates of institutions or as an arm of the governor or legislature or, even more difficult, as a "buffer" in no man's land—probably engendering criticism from both sides.

Historically, state higher education agencies were formed for a variety of purposes related to growth and expansion in the public sector. The new agencies were called on to coordinate the budget requests of an increasing array of institutions, to plan the expansion of their systems, to strengthen the case for higher education in dealings with the legislature, and to help ensure some equity of treatment for all public institutions in their states. While institutions often resisted coordination—especially when it involved losing governance powers to higher levels—they understood the purpose of coordination to be relatively positive; so during the growth period there was only limited institutional resistance to the formation of the higher education agencies. Times have changed, however. As David Spence and George Weathersby note in Chapter Thirteen, there is an increasing divergence in state and institutional objectives. The state agencies have become more concerned with improving efficiency by controlling new program expansion and by monitoring productivity, as well as with protecting consumers from qualitative declines. Consequently, institutions increasingly view state or system-level offices, with their larger and more bureaucratized staffs, as more supportive of state political concerns than of institutional objectives.

Public-sector reorganizations sometimes involve some form of merger, of individual institutions into systems or a more thorough organizational integration. As Gail Chambers notes in Chapter Six, the most common legal form of merger in the past has been the consolidation merger (sometimes referred to as just "consolidation"), in which all assets and liabilities of the institutions involved pass to a new successor corporation and the previous legal entities cease to exist. The second major form of merger is the dissolution/acquisition variety, in which one institution is dissolved and its assets and liabilities pass selectively to the remaining institution. In the public sector, consolidation mergers may refer either to system consolidations, as in the formation of the University of Wisconsin System in 1971, or to the combining of pairs of institutions, as in the 1975 merger of Lowell State College and Lowell Technical Institute (now the University of Lowell) in Massachusetts. The merger in 1974 of independent Western College with Miami University, a public institution in Ohio, is an example of a dissolution/acquisition merger (see Millett, 1976, for a discussion of this and other private/public mergers). Boberg (1979) reports 116 private/public mergers from 1941 to 1979, which reflects the way many states chose to expand the public sector during higher education's growth period. Consolidation of public institutions into "systems" is probably best reflected in the statistics reported by the Carnegie Foundation for the Advancement of Teaching (1976): in 1940, 70 percent of all public institutions were governed by individual boards; in 1970, only 30 percent of all institutions were so governed.

In the past, changes in governance arrangements for public higher education had only minimal impact on the day-to-day life of students, faculty, and administrators on campuses. But the reorganizations being proposed in response to no-growth and decline most certainly will have a more substantial effect. The program cutbacks, institutional mergers, and campus closings being proposed may involve personnel retrenchment and will raise questions of student access. The cases that follow illustrate how volatile such issues are likely to become in many states in the near future.

Alabama

In December of 1979, at a public meeting in Montgomery, the staff of the Alabama Commission on Higher Education (ACHE) introduced a draft of a new master plan for higher education to its commissioners. Elaborating on many of the recommendations of an evaluation team which had recently studied the commission, and with the anticipated support of a newly elected governor, the staff proposed a series of sweeping changes for higher education in Alabama, including the closing of an upper-division state college, the revision of the mission of a senior institution toward that of a comprehensive community college, the merger of groups of individual two-year institutions, and the reorganization of the statewide governance structure.

Proposal: Close Athens State College. Following a number of years of declining enrollment and declining financial support, Athens College, Alabama's oldest institution of higher learning (1822), was offered to the state in 1974 by the United Methodist Church. Despite a recommendation to the contrary by the Alabama commission, the legislature, in its 1975 session, included a $1 million appropriation to Athens in the budget bill, with a provision that the State Board of Education assume governing control of the college. In December of 1979, the staff of ACHE recommended again that the commissioners voice their opposition to state support of Athens College. The staff recommended that Athens be prohibited from accepting any new students beginning in the fall term of 1980 and that the physical plant be returned to the United Methodist Church in 1981.

The reason for the recommendations remained the same as in 1974: the Athens College programs were widely duplicated in other nearby institutions with excess capacity (there were three other public four-year universities within fifty miles). In addition, by 1980 Athens needed—according to ACHE—nearly $3 million in capital improvements and renovation just to make the campus minimally acceptable (Alabama Commission on Higher Education, 1980).

In arguing against the staff proposal during a public meeting of the commission, the Athens president asserted that (1) this upper-division college, with its unique program to prepare instructors for the technical colleges, was providing a needed state service that other institutions in Alabama were neglecting; (2) the needs for renovation and capital construction on the campus were far less than the commission staff claimed; and (3) actual per student costs were the lowest in the state, so that, rather than saving money, the closing of Athens College would mean added expenditures as students transferred to higher-cost institutions. Per student expenditures at Athens were low as the result of serious underfunding by the legislature, which had consistently failed to adopt ACHE's formula-generated recommendations for the college. If its programs and graduates were equal to or better than those of other institutions, the president could argue legitimately that the institution was the most cost-effective in the state. But the staff at ACHE believed that quality had suffered at Athens from this low level of state support and from questionable transfer practices in the recruitment of community and technical college students. However, no independent qualitative review was conducted; nor did any other public institution in the state publicly criticize the Athens program. The qualitative argument was further weakened when, in the midst of the debate, Athens received reaccreditation from the Southern Association of Colleges and Schools.

Support among the commissioners for the staff report was mixed. A few publicly expressed reservations about singling out Athens in the face of more obvious examples of duplication, especially between black and white institutions in the state. But the commission, in a close vote in February 1980, accepted the staff recommendations and forwarded to the governor and the legislature a recommendation that Athens College be closed. In the 1980 legislative session, however, the issue received little attention, largely because of the small annual state appropriation for the institution—about $1.6 million. Some legislators who had supported the Athens College takeover in 1975 had changed their minds by 1980 but were not ready to take any immediate action to close Athens. One said, "I voted for it [in 1975] out of emotion and sympathy. It was the oldest institution in the state. It seemed terrible that it would close. But now it's an albatross around our neck." Support for closing Athens was stronger in the executive branch. The commission's recommendation received the endorsements of the governor and the state finance director, but sentiment prevailed, and funding for Athens was continued.

Proposal: Revise the Mission of Livingston University. Livingston University enrolls approximately 1,200 students in three colleges— general studies, business and commerce, and education—and the school of graduate studies. In 1979, 65 percent of the degrees awarded by the institution were in the field of education. Twenty-five percent of the student body is black. Located in west central Alabama near the Tombigbee River, Livingston is in one of the poorest sections of the South. Per capita income in the county is only half the national average. Population projections show a continuation of the decline that occurred during the 1970s. With a drop in enrollment of a full 25 percent in the past decade, per student costs rose steadily. In 1979 these were 150 percent of the state average, and the institution was still "underfunded" according to the commission's formula.

While the "cost problem" provided an understandable rationale for considering changes in Livingston's mission, implicit in the recommendations of the commission was concern about the "inappropriateness" of its academic program, given the social and economic characteristics of the region and the absence of community or technical college programs in that part of the state. The recommendations included in ACHE's original master-plan draft called for the development of new technical programs at Livingston and a phasing out of graduate and upper-division programs if they could not be justified in terms of enrollment and cost. If such programs were eliminated, the institution would eventually become part of the proposed comprehensive community college system. Finally, if the change in institutional mission failed to produce additional enrollments, the institution would have to be closed.

When the Livingston issue was first discussed publicly, the possibility of closing the institution dominated the discussions. Press reports emphasized this aspect of the ACHE plan and, in the view of the Livingston president, created "dismay and panic" among students and faculty. Commission staff reassured the president that the intent of the plan was not to close Livingston but to change its direction in order to ensure its continued viability.

Livingston wanted two-year occupational programs but not at the expense of upper-division and graduate offerings. Cost considerations should not be a factor, the president argued, given Livingston's proximity to an isolated and economically disadvantaged population. The commission agreed to postpone the question of phasing out upper-level programs (it had only the power to recommend such action in any case) and to revise the language of the master plan. Having headed off these program retrenchment efforts for the time being, the Livingston president offered, if not his support, at least his acquiescence to the revisions.

Proposal: Merge Two-Year Colleges in Alabama and Reorganize Governance. The two-year college "system" in Alabama consists of forty-four separate institutions: fifteen junior colleges, twenty-two technical colleges, six community colleges, and one special-purpose institution. Governance is through the elected State Board of Education, and the state superintendent of schools serves as the equivalent of chief executive officer of the system.

The Alabama commission claimed that this "system" of junior, community, and technical colleges—which had grown rapidly under the sponsorship of former governor George Wallace— had been developed with little thought to coordination and planning. Other critics used harsher terms, noting the blatant political patronage that had determined the location of institutions, and the resulting widespread duplication and inefficiency of some very small operations. Some of the duplication had clearly been planned. Two-year institutions in Mobile and Birmingham were established in 1965 as legally segregated institutions for blacks— the last two institutions in the nation to be so designated. Enrollment in the two-year sector in Alabama peaked in 1975 and declined steadily during the remainder of the decade.

In its 1979 master-plan recommendations, the commission proposed the following:

1. Creation of a comprehensive community college system, in which forty-three separate junior and technical colleges would be consolidated into a system of not more than twelve district community colleges, each having one central administration.
2. Appointment of a twelve-member State Board for Community Colleges and a chancellor, to replace the elected State Board of Education and the superintendent of schools.
3. Development of district and state advisory bodies to provide local input into the new consolidated system.

The commission observed that, nationally, comprehensive community colleges had developed extensively and that the merging and consolidation of institutions would mean the elimination of numerous separately administered institutions of extremely small size (twenty-six of the colleges had enrollments of fewer than 1,000 students, and, of these, ten had fewer than 500 students). While the ACHE proposals specified no particular campus closings, the commission did suggest that such actions should be considered by the new board. It presented a number of alternatives for drawing district lines and merging institutions, and suggested that two basic criteria be followed: (1) each district should have at least 2,500 students, and (2) a comprehensive range of programs should be reasonably accessible to the district's population.

As for changes in governance, the staff noted that the new consolidated system would need a board that could devote its attention solely to the community colleges. This new board—to be appointed by the governor, the lieutenant governor, and the speaker of the house—"should be charged with the responsibility of viewing the community college system from a statewide perspective rather than representing a regional constituency" (Alabama Commission on Higher Education, 1980). The issue of elected board versus appointed board was perceived by many as the "real problem." One state official observed: "The junior colleges are the political arena of these state board members, their political operatives. When it comes time to appoint a new president, the courtesy system operates and board members defer to their colleague elected from the district in which the college is located. Rather than consider statewide concerns, the board members are parochial. Their selection of presidents is totally a matter of political patronage" (Interview, 1980).

As expected, the reaction of the state board and the superintendent of schools was negative. The board sought legislation to have ACHE removed entirely from the planning and program approval process in the two-year sector and at the same time took the offensive by calling for a gradual consolidation of the system as current presidents retired or resigned. (The *Birmingham News,* January 14, 1980, called this provision a "fairly transparent sop to those presidents, many of whom have political connections.") The

ACHE staff had estimated that savings from the consolidation plan would be at least $6 million, half from cuts in administrative salaries and a like amount from consolidation of other support activities. The superintendent took exception to these figures (which he nevertheless called "minor savings"), suggesting further that such centralization would most certainly increase costs by adding a level of bureaucracy. More importantly, he argued, there was a great advantage of an elected board over an appointed board; namely, its "responsiveness to the people."

In April of 1980, the Alabama commission, in an 11–0 vote (with one abstention), accepted the recommendations of its staff and passed the resolution outlining the reorganization and consolidation proposals for the two-year colleges. However, seeing little prospect for support in the legislature, the commission chose not to seek sponsorship for a bill reforming the two-year system. As one state senator put it, "I couldn't vote to close any of these two-year colleges. They are my base for political support. I would lose the next election for sure" (Interview, 1980).

Postscript. In the 1981 legislative session, no consolidation bills were considered. However, a bill was introduced to add program review and termination powers to the Alabama commission's authority. It also would have eliminated the requirement that the commission's executive director be reconfirmed every four years by the Senate (the only such provision in the nation). With opposition from all but one of the members of the State Board of Education and a majority of community college presidents, the bill went down to defeat. As for action to consolidate institutions themselves, the state board had merged Athens State College with a nearby community college and was considering one additional merger. In a move that further strengthened the two-year colleges' influence in the legislature, the state board appointed legislators to three of the four presidential vacancies that occurred in early 1981.

Connecticut

The Connecticut Board of Higher Education (BHE), established in 1977, serves as that state's chief agency for statewide coordination of higher education. It succeeded another statewide board which had performed similar functions since 1965. The four major segments of higher education in the state—the University of Connecticut and its branches, the four state colleges, the five technical colleges, and the twelve regional community colleges—are each governed by a statutory board. The establishment of the new coordinating board, with expanded powers and a change of name, had been in part a by-product of the failure in 1976 to create a single board of regents for governing all public institutions of the state. Proponents of the earlier regents idea, however, supported a legislative mandate for the new coordinating board to undertake immediately a study of further statewide governance changes. This requirement proved to be a difficult task for the BHE and its staff and consumed much of their energy during the first two years of the board's existence.

In its report and recommendations submitted to the legislature in September 1979, the BHE called for the following reorganization and governance consolidations:

1. A comprehensive two-year college system, which would include three of the University of Connecticut's two-year branch campuses, the regional community colleges, and the technical colleges under a single board appointed by the governor.
2. A single governing board for the University of Connecticut and the four state colleges, to be administered by a chancellor who at the same time would serve as president of the university. (While the proposed legislation did not mandate specific campus closings, it did call on the new board to "study the question and validity of the full integration of Eastern Connecticut State College with the university's main campus at Storrs, twelve miles away.")
3. A "reconstituted and strengthened" Board of Higher Education, which would have expanded power over budgets and over the monitoring of expenditures; the power to set "enrollment parameters" for each of the public institutions of the state; and the authority to award external degrees. The new BHE would now be constituted entirely of lay gubernatorial appointees and would exclude all institutional representation [Connecticut Board of Higher Education, 1979, pp. c-1–c-28].

Debate over the proposed changes took place first in a joint Education Committee meeting of the House and Senate. Public hearings and legislative committee meetings were held in late 1979 and in the spring of 1980. Despite strong interest expressed by members of the Education Committee, the reorganization proposals generated little public interest. Among the institutions, however, the reaction was intense. The objections to the BHE proposals illustrate the divisions in many states between the state and the institutional perspectives of the need for governance changes and their likely impact.

Enrollment Projections and Enrollment Planning. While the issue of statewide governance had been considered several times during the past twenty years, the BHE brought a *new* justification for reorganization; namely, the impending sharp decline in the number of high school graduates in the state (projected to be 25 percent by 1986, 43 percent by 1994). The board concluded, "If a laissez faire philosophy is allowed to prevail . . . institutions will be forced into a competitive mode of operation which can waste resources, deplete educational quality, and shortchange students" (Connecticut Board of Higher Education, 1979, p. 10).

The institutions disagreed. Rather than the 25 percent decline predicted by the BHE for 1986, the University of Connecticut expected declines of between 6 and 12 percent. The university also opposed the enrollment planning process proposed by the BHE, believing that it would impose on all public institutions a fixed share of the pool of high school graduates. The coordinating board claimed that it had proposed the establishment of enrollment targets for the institutions, not absolute quotas or ceilings.

Institutional Autonomy and Centralization. In a response to the BHE recommendations, the university asserted: "The thrust of all the recommendations is to place the trustees' present and already diminished authority wholly in the hands of BHE. Whether there are two boards of trustees as proposed, or several, BHE, with a much enlarged staff, would set policy for and govern all of public higher education" (University of Connecticut Board of Trustees, 1979, p. 3). As proof of this change in governance arrangements, the university noted the proposed expansion of the BHE's control over budgeting and expenditure of appropriated funds. The BHE staff disagreed and characterized the recommendations as consolidation proposals, not centralization. They noted that institutional boards would continue to have the power to set personnel policies, select institutional presidents, award degrees, and develop budgets and programs of institutions and subunits.

The state college system initially supported merger plans that called for a "neutral" chief executive over both the university and state college systems. But faced with university opposition and a desire not to create an additional administrative support staff, the BHE developed a compromise plan, whereby the president of the University of Connecticut would also serve as chancellor of the merged system. The result was the loss of support of the state colleges and continued opposition of the university because of the enhanced powers provided the BHE. The parallel proposal for creation of a merged two-year system received support of the regional community colleges but not the technical colleges. The community colleges had for some time advocated mergers because of the "commonality of interest" that could be enhanced through reorganization—the sharing of library and computer facilities, the coordination of curriculum, and the improvement of transfer provisions between the two sectors. (Several of the campuses were in close proximity.) Technical college spokesmen, like those of the university, pointed to the added layer of bureaucracy which they believed would follow consolidation.

Access and Status. The issue of access—specifically, access of community college transfers to the high-demand programs at the upper-division level of the University of Connecticut—was also a major point of controversy. The coordinating board argued that the university gave preference to students transferring from their own branch campuses over students transferring from community colleges. If the branches were combined administratively with the regional community colleges, this discrimination would end, the board asserted. The university did not regard branch students as transfer students but as "branchfers," who were moving from one physical location of the university to another and, if they maintained satisfactory progress toward a degree, should be allowed to continue at the main campus location in Storrs. In practice this policy meant that branch students, even those with much lower grade point averages than attained by some applicants from the community colleges, had preference in being admitted to the university's upper-division programs.

In a state and region of the country that draws clear, if not always accurate, distinctions in the pecking order of colleges and universities, the public colleges of Connecticut were especially concerned with the impact of reorganization on that order. The technical colleges, for example, opposed merger with the community colleges, for fear that such a merger would dilute the quality of their programs. (The much smaller technical college system has as its base the engineering and science technologies, which serve the state's defense and high-technology industries.) Status and its privileges had also been a stumbling block to even the mild forms of cooperation that had been attempted in the four-year institutions, and some legislators expressed their belief that "intellectual snobbery" was higher education's biggest problem.

Institutional Mission. The planners at the BHE sought some rationalization of the academic missions of the institutions, as evidenced in their proposals for comprehensive two-year colleges. For the university the BHE wanted less emphasis placed on lower-division undergraduate work—this would be the job of the two-year colleges—and more emphasis on graduate and professional studies. For the state colleges the BHE wanted some specialization, as protection against an enrollment squeeze from the universities on one side and from the community colleges on the other. While grateful for the BHE's support on specific program proposals, the state colleges sought not specialization but comprehensiveness as their hedge against enrollment decline.

The Hidden Agenda—Retrenchment? Although the BHE did not specifically recommend personnel cutbacks or institutional closings, many opponents of the reorganization suspected that retrenchment was in fact the hidden agenda of the BHE plan. All else was a "masquerade," technical college representatives asserted in the public legislative hearings. Although the BHE report raised the possibility that some campuses might eventually be closed and the administrative consolidations implied personnel retrenchment, the specifics were to be left to the newly organized boards, as with the review of the facilities at Eastern Connecticut. Presumably, supporters of the consolidation proposals believed that new boards governing merged systems would be more able to carry out retrenchment. The BHE staff noted that the governing board of the University of Connecticut had been unable to close its branch at Torrington—which had an annual state budget of $400,000 and fewer than 125 full-time-equivalent students. (During the 1980 legislative session, pressure built for the university to close the branch, but local community and political support resulted in a commitment by the university board to provide additional financial support to increase enrollment. The university did put the branch on notice that it would have to produce results within three years or face closure.)

   Legislative Reaction. The compromises and alterations in the reorganization plan—made first by the BHE and then by legislators—created legislative bills that found few supporters among the parties involved. The state colleges opposed merger with the university because of the absence of a "neutral" chancellor; the university opposed the new reorganization because it perceived that the BHE was still pursuing the regents idea, which its legislative supporters had sought for the state. Furthermore, some institutional opponents suspected that, in fact, the current BHE harbored strong private college leanings and was seeking a substantial diminishment of public higher education in the state. The focus of the legislative debate centered in the relatively noninfluential Education Committee. (One powerful legislative leader who earlier had supported the regents idea and served as the BHE's chairman in 1977 had retired from public office.) With little public interest generated by the reorganization plan and nothing but political liabilities following those who backed it, the BHE failed to gain endorsement from the governor, who in 1980 was occupied with tax issues and revenue problems. As the reorganization bills proceeded through the legislature, they received less and less endorsement. Reported favorably out of the Education Committee after additional compromises and dilution, the measures were blocked in a second committee by a delegation from Danbury, which opposed the BHE because of its failure to endorse capital expansion of their local state college. Brought to debate through petition, both the bill to consolidate the four-year colleges and the one consolidating the two-year institutions failed in the House.

Postscript. In the 1981 legislative session, the Board of Higher Education introduced and supported legislation that would revise the administration of the state's financial aid system. The BHE also supported the closing of the Torrington branch of the University of Connecticut (whose funding was continued in the appropriations bill). While no legislation on reorganization or consolidation reached a floor vote, twelve reorganization bills were introduced by individual members, and the Appropriations Committee was sharply critical of the redundancies in the community college system and in the five separate college operations in the greater Hartford area. Many legislative leaders believe that major reorganization will be considered again in the 1982 session; but without strong gubernatorial support—which is problematical in an election year—some observers are pessimistic about passage. Some believe that reorganization, if it should take place, will most likely originate in the Appropriations Committee rather than in the Education Committee and will be based mainly on the need to reduce expenditures.

Massachusetts

In 1980 the General Court of Massachusetts, in a quick and surprising move, reorganized statewide governance for public higher education in the state. Using language in the "outside section" of the appropriations bill, the legislature created a consolidated board of regents with governing powers over Massachusetts' twenty-eight public institutions. At the same time, all existing institutional and system boards were abolished and replaced by new boards of trustees, which would serve as management boards. Also eliminated were the state coordinating board (the Massachusetts Board of Higher Education) and the Office of Secretary of Educational Affairs—both pretenders for more than a decade to the title of statewide coordinator. The apparent suddenness of these changes, however, masked years of conflict and debate over coordination and governance—a debate that had greatly intensified since the end of growth budgets in 1974. Budget cutbacks in the mid-1970s were followed by, at best, level funding for the remainder of the decade. Legislative support eroded as an increasing number of elected officials viewed higher education as unresponsive to the fiscal belt tightening in the state. Many expressed their irritation over what they perceived as excessive administrative costs in the various system offices in the public sector. Among state planners and public higher education leaders, there was growing consensus by the end of the decade that statewide reorganization could eliminate obvious examples of duplication and achieve gains in political and financial support for the programs that remained.

The focus of greatest legislative discontent fell on the competing institutions in the city of Boston, which had suffered especially from the absence of a strong statewide coordinating mechanism. Apprehension about the future of Boston-area institutions was heightened by the projections of significant enrollment declines in the Boston area, which some analysts expected to be as great as 30 percent in public institutions by 1994 (Massachusetts Board of Higher Education, unpublished memorandum, May 8, 1979). The University of Massachusetts campus in Boston, opened in 1965, had never reached its planned capacity of 15,000 students (enrollments stood at about 8,000 in 1979). Boston State College was the object of special concern. A series of events in the 1970s had kept the college in the public eye and marked Boston State as a troubled institution. Enrollment declines in its education and liberal arts programs and cutbacks in state support were followed by retrenchment of nontenured faculty in the history department in 1974. In 1977 the faculty voted no confidence in the college's president and called for the resignation of other administrative officers, claiming that the officers had excluded faculty from important academic decisions, which had resulted in the diminishment of the institution's liberal arts orientation. In 1978–79 the administration proposed dismissal of unspecified tenured faculty because of insufficient credit load (the institution was over 90 percent tenured) but dropped the plan because of language in the faculty union contract. Despite its apparent competition for students with both the university and the city's two-year colleges, supporters of Boston State pointed to the institution's valuable service to the city's work-

ing adults who sought out its newly initiated occupational programs. With a substantial level of black enrollment (12 percent), it
was also said to be an institution sitting on "neutral ground"—a
place where both blacks and whites feel comfortable in this city with
distinct racial and ethnic neighborhoods.

In contrast to the four-year sector, the community colleges
of Boston had suffered from underdevelopment. Not until 1973
had the two Boston city community colleges been established. Roxbury, a predominantly black and Hispanic college, was still without
a permanent home in 1980. Its rundown facilities were in stark
contrast to the new physical plant that served the much larger and
overwhelmingly white student body of Bunker Hill Community
College in Charlestown. While a new location in the Roxbury community had been selected, no capital funds had been provided. As
the years progressed, estimates of the original $30 million cost
proved outdated by inflation.

Creation of Special Commission on Reorganization. The precipitous action of the legislature in 1980 was not without antecedent. A
legislative attempt to establish a "super board" had failed in 1976
but had prompted several agencies to examine the governance
question. Studies by the Board of Higher Education and the Sloan
Commission on Government and Higher Education added support
to the need for governance reform. In 1979 Governor Edward
King appointed the Special Commission on the Reorganization
of Higher Education, consisting of gubernatorial appointees and
legislators. By the end of the year, the commission's deliberations
were under way.

Despite the statewide implications of the Boston issues, the
commission chose to divide its work between a subcommittee on
Boston and one on statewide reorganization. Of the two, the Boston subcommittee was by far the more active and visible, proceeding throughout the first six months of 1980 to air the variety of
proposals for reorganization being advanced—including merger
of Boston State with the University of Massachusetts campus at
Boston, and the broader proposal to create a City University of
Boston, consisting of two-year and four-year institutions.

Paramount to the Boston State faculty were guarantees
of employment for all personnel in the event of any merger—

commitments which in fact they were able to exact from the sub-committee. Such conditions, however, were unacceptable to the University of Massachusetts, which would consider merger only if it could choose selectively from among the already overstaffed and underenrolled programs of Boston State.

The work of the subcommittee on statewide reorganization was proceeding at a far slower pace than that of the Boston sub-committee, and it became apparent to both the legislative leadership and the governor that the commission as a whole was unlikely to present a reorganization plan that the legislature could act on in the 1980 session. It was also unlikely, given the lobbying efforts of the Boston State faculty, that the legislature could act unilaterally to merge this institution with the university.

In early May 1980, without waiting for a report from the commission, the House Ways and Means Committee, with the support of the speaker, introduced a bill that proposed to combine the state colleges with the community colleges but left the university alone. The action served as a stimulus to the commission. The Governance Subcommittee quickly adopted a reorganization plan calling for a strengthened coordinating board for the state. But two influential gubernatorial appointees dissented; they issued a minority report asking for a consolidated system governed by a single board of regents. When the legislative leadership met to settle the House and Senate differences on the appropriations bill, the four members of this conference committee chose to include in the "outside section" the proposal for a single governing board of regents. Their action took the higher education community by surprise. Out of fear of budgetary retribution, the institutions remained silent through the brief House debate over the bill.

The swift action of the legislature was the result of the need for the state's political leaders to achieve some immediate reorganization, even if changes in Boston would have to wait. It also put some distance between themselves and the sensitive merger issues being proposed in that city. At the same time, the politicians received credit for some highly visible retrenchment of "excessive" administrative waste—a popular target for legislative cost cutters. System administrative officers were eliminated, as were two state planning agencies. The legislature's willingness to allow the new board budgetary control over the individual institutions through provisions for a consolidated budget surprised many people. As for the proposals for institutional mergers and closings, many observers believed that the regents had received a mandate to carry out these actions. The new fifteen-member board received explicit authority to close public institutions in the state upon a two-thirds vote of its membership.

Postscript. A year after the passage of the legislation, the full implications of the change to a consolidated board remained unclear. There were indications, though, that the new regents viewed themselves as being somewhat of a hybrid between *governing* and *coordinating* board. Statewide policy issues would be the focus of their activities, while the local boards of trustees would oversee institutional management. The manner in which the legislation for the regents had passed had not provided a strong constituency for the new governing board, and there were indications that the regents would again be the subject of legislative study and action if they did not act quickly to solve some of the Boston city issues. Amendments to the legislation passed in 1981 recreated the University of Massachusetts "system," and a single board of trustees was appointed to manage its three campuses. In 1981 the regents' staff undertook a new study of the Boston issues. In July the board voted to discontinue governance of Boston State and to merge it with the University of Massachusetts at Boston.

Public-Sector Reorganization: Short-Term Impact, Long-Term Goals

The three preceding cases were presented in more than the usual detail so that readers might draw their own conclusions about the applicability of the issues to their states. Our conclusions are offered with caution but nevertheless with the expectation that these issues and debates will be repeated in other states experiencing enrollment and fiscal stress.

1. Administrative and governance consolidations are likely to be a major element of the plans of statewide agencies to respond to enrollment and revenue declines. These consolidations will create new legal governing bodies and possibly merged administra-

tive staffs and services but will stop short of full organizational and academic merger. Proponents—of which the state coordinating boards will be among the strongest—will argue that, given limited state support and projections of enrollment decline, excessive competition is both wasteful and politically destructive. Despite claims to the contrary, supporters of consolidation will note the similarity of institutional missions rather than differences and will argue that these changes can take place without seriously affecting student access. Supporters of consolidation will claim immediate cost savings through cutbacks in administrative overhead and will promise future savings through the elimination of duplicative programs and services. Given the propensity of organizations to find ways to maintain and even proliferate administrative activities in order to protect turf, such cost savings may or may not occur. Without specific requirements and fiscal constraints, administrative and governance consolidations can create further layering of bureaucracy and its attendant costs.

2. Despite the minimal short-term impact of governance changes on institutions, advocates will view these reorganizations as a required first step toward institutional retrenchment. In our case studies, the plans for governance consolidations were combined with mandates for the new boards to eliminate duplicative academic programs and administrative support services, as well as the physical facilities at some locations. Once the new consolidated boards were created, supporters of these plans believed that the boards would have the political insulation to make the needed changes. There are no guarantees, however, that the agenda of the new boards will be identical to that of those who worked for the boards' creation, although strong expressions of legislative intent may provide the necessary incentive.

3. Institutional opposition to governance consolidations will center around fears about loss of autonomy, loss of identity, and loss of status. In Connecticut the state colleges opposed merger because the chancellor of the new merged system would come from the university; the technical colleges, in objecting to merger with the community colleges, feared for their special status as purveyors of high-quality technical programs. For institutions to support consolidation, there must be compelling reasons. The "costs" to the

institutions, even if no immediate personnel reductions are called for, will be in the form of conflict and disruption of the status quo. "Gains" will be viewed skeptically and, at best, as accruing over the long term. Arguments that consolidation will bring an end to political meddling and a beginning to renewed financial support through a united front will be generally unconvincing to individuals who fear for their status or job.

4. Strong public institutions will undergo the difficult and time-consuming process of full organizational merger only on their own terms—which means selectively choosing from among the weaker institutions' programs and faculty. Therefore, institutional mergers are likely to be of the dissolution/acquisition variety, in order to avoid the inflexibilities and cost burdens that led to distress in the first place. These proposals will meet with stiff opposition from labor and organized faculty, who are likely to view merger in this context as a closing of the college and a circumvention of contractual obligations.

5. While the merging or the closing of public four-year colleges in the next decade will be a rare event because of political constraints, our cases indicate that such actions will receive serious consideration. There will be continued pressure for closing down the facilities of some state colleges whose programs can be transferred to nearby universities or their branches. Two-year branch campus and community colleges with low enrollments will also be targets of closure movements. But it is doubtful that states will close institutions serving isolated communities or economically depressed areas unless state economic conditions are quite severe or the institutions shrink to an extremely small size. The cost savings from such closings would be minimal, the political costs high, and the impact on local economies sometimes substantial. In the South additional mergers of black and white institutions, similar to the 1979 court-ordered merger of Tennessee State with a branch of the University of Tennessee in Nashville, may occur. While program and personnel retrenchment may not be an objective in these cases, it could well be the result if enrollments drop following merger.

Institutions and their supporters will go to great extremes to avoid merger or closure. Institutional presidents and faculty groups will be joined by outside supporters. Businessmen who may be affected economically will oppose the closing of the local college, and politicians and powerful alumni will threaten political retribution for those who seek to do so. Black colleges and other institutions with special constituencies will strongly resist merger or closure. For example, when such merger possibilities were raised by coordinating boards in Maryland and in Alabama in 1979 and 1980, supporters of the black colleges filled the meeting rooms to overflowing and provided enough opposition so that the proposals for consideration were dropped or postponed.

Impact of Retrenchment on State Coordinating Boards

In our three case studies, statewide coordinating boards played important roles in bringing the questions of consolidation and cutbacks to the legislatures. But they were generally unsuccessful in gaining political support for their positions. They were, to borrow from Allison's (1971) terms, the "rational actors" analyzing the problems facing higher education and proposing their reasoned solutions. However, it takes more than an examination of the merits or shortcomings of these plans to understand the success or failure of a given proposal. The outcomes in these cases were also shaped—in some cases solely shaped—by intense organizational rivalries and by the force of individual personalities in the agencies, the legislature, and the institutions—each striving for enhanced power, prestige, and resources. It was the force of these institutional and individual wills that eventually determined the winners and losers.

Statewide coordinating boards should take warning from these cases. No matter how innocent the intentions of the initiators of a plan for contraction or consolidation, others inevitably will react to it as a "nonneutral" proposal—either supporting or opposing it according to its presumed impact on substantive issues, or on future distributions of powers over process, or both of these. This reaction will be even greater if the contraction/consolidation plan includes as an aspect, either planned or unplanned, an increase in the power of the statewide board proposing the changes. Rather than focusing on the need for and efficacy of the contraction proposals, the debate will switch to the "power grab" of the proposing agency. Given this phenomenon, and the probability of more immediate and more intense reactions from opponents than from proponents, it is no wonder that contraction and consolidation are viewed as volatile issues which state officials hate to see reach the political agenda. Coordinating boards should not expect to receive much credit for playing retriever and laying the dilemma dutifully at the feet of the governor or the legislature. Governance legislation generates low levels of public interest but intense reactions from vested interests. Furthermore, legislators thrive on bringing activities and funds home to their districts—whether the funds are for a new highway or for a new college. To ask legislators to acquiesce in the closing or contraction of higher education operations in their districts is to hope that water will run uphill.

One solution for keeping these issues out of the political arena is to provide greater incentives for campuses or systems to engage in serious self-contraction. When money saved must revert to the state—in contrast to the private sector, where a penny saved is a penny earned—institutions can rightfully argue that they need more incentive to undertake the unpleasant work. In our cases board members often had the power, but not the will, to carry out retrenchment decisions. (While structural impediments were advanced as the reason for reorganization, supporters of change were often seeking no more than a new set of individuals who, they hoped, would find this will.) Some state agency heads may be tempted to appeal directly to institutional board members, but this will engender hostility from presidents. The key lies in the quality of gubernatorial appointments to boards. Prestigious individuals with statewide perspective and a willingness to ask important policy questions of the presidents are absolutely essential.

The coordinating board or planning commission proposing changes will need to obtain firm gubernatorial support in cases where (1) reorganizing of governing boards is viewed as a necessity for carrying out consolidation, as in the merger of institutions under two separate boards, and (2) there is insufficient incentive for these boards to support such changes. A governor can provide valuable assistance in putting a legislative district's immediate loss in the broader context of the state's ultimate goal. But it is important that the work of the coordinating board staff be convincing and thorough. If the coordinating boards are going to take the "rational actor" approach and leave the politics to others, their plans must be well designed, well timed, and supported by data. If a governor does uphold the plan and then later finds it vulnerable to attack, both the plan and its designers may be in jeopardy. Called on to take the political risks associated with consolidation proposals, a governor may be tempted to reorganize the entire system, replacing the old members with new appointees. Thus, statewide boards, having raised awkward political issues, may find that the contraction they have initiated is their own.

For Further Reading

For a perceptive analysis of the political dimensions of higher education planning, readers are referred to Millett (1974) and to Mosher and Wagoner (1978). For a discussion of the role of statewide coordinating and governing boards, see Dressel (1980); essays by Kerr, Geiogue, and Weathersby in "Coordinating Higher Education" (1980); and Berdahl (1975b).

Readers interested in more detailed case studies of the state response to enrollment decline and financial stringency are referred to the SREB case studies on Alabama (Mingle, 1980) and Connecticut (Mingle and Berdahl, 1981), and the 1975 and 1979 reports of the board of regents of the University of Wisconsin System.

✑ 17 ✑

Public Policy Toward Private College Distress

Richard W. Jonsen
with E. Grady Bogue and Gail S. Chambers

The Carnegie Council on Policy Studies in Higher Education (1980, p. 64) identifies categories of vulnerability to enrollment declines, the most vulnerable being the less selective liberal arts colleges and private two-year colleges. Similarly, Mayhew (1979, p. 4) identifies four particularly vulnerable types of institutions: "(1) the small, little-known liberal arts colleges; (2) the private, single-sex two-year institution; (3) the small, recently created institution designed to serve a quite specific clientele; and (4) the middle-level private universities and perhaps a few of the more remote state colleges located in regions experiencing sharp population declines."

Observation of institutional performance over the past decade tends to support these judgments of vulnerability. The 141 private institutions that, according to the National Institute of Independent Colleges and Universities, closed in the 1970s were, typically, "small, church related, and coeducational: 87 percent had fewer than 500 students, 55 percent were church related, and 62 percent were coeducational" ("Private-College Openings, Closings, and Mergers, 1970–79," 1980, p. 8). Whereas 29 percent of *all* institutions experienced enrollment decline between 1970 and 1978, 39 percent of private institutions did so; hardest hit were the less selective liberal arts colleges, 47 percent of which declined in enrollment from 1970 to 1979 (Carnegie Council on Policy Studies in Higher Education, 1980, p. 75). Most of these highly vulnerable institutions—particularly, the less selective liberal arts colleges and two-year colleges—have limited resources. Minter and Bowen (1980) point to the growth of current liabilities and interfund borrowing as a sign of financial weakness.

It would be misleading, though, to suggest that institutional vulnerability can be characterized by a few programmatic and financial characteristics when the factors leading to decline are complex and numerous. Many colleges are likely to fail in the 1980s. Some estimates place the number as high as 200 or 300 during the decade (Breneman, 1979, p. 4), but the Carnegie Council cautions against putting an excessive emphasis on specific numerical predictions of college failures, because "too much depends upon private action and public policies that are yet undetermined" (Carnegie Council on Policy Studies in Higher Education, 1980, p. 63).

Evolution of State Policy Toward the Private Sector

The growth of publicly funded colleges and universities and of state support to the private sector has brought the private sector increasingly into state planning, policies, and programs for higher education. Many state planning documents written in the past twenty years attest to this. These documents set out the rationale for state interest in the private sector and describe the role played by the private sector in the total "system" of higher education in the state. But the real extent of state involvement with the private sector can be found in the operating policies and programs of the state and its agencies. Specifically, the state's relationship with the private sector can be measured by the extent to which the private sector is involved in its institutional and program approval practices, planning activities, and program of direct and indirect financial support, as well as in its policies that specifically concern troubled institutions.

The clearest evidence of a state's interest in and involvement with the private sector is found in programs of support to private institutions in the form of general institutional support, categorical institutional support (often achieved through contracts), or support to students attending private institutions through grants. These programs of support are the *practical* foundation of the relationship between the state and the private sector. They are also the foundation of any policy with respect to failing institutions. Indeed, most of the existing programs of support were established in recognition of the present or anticipated financial difficulties of private institutions and of the state interest in efficient utilization of resources of the private sector. According to many executive officers of state higher education agencies and their staffs, basic state policy is to help the private sector, through student or institutional aid, to compete fairly with the public sector for students. This "marketplace" approach, with its underlying idea that institutions unable to attract students do not serve society's needs and should be allowed to close, works only under conditions of fair competition—thus the private sector's strong interest in narrowing the cost gap through state financial aid programs for students attending private institutions.

Most states charter private institutions as nonprofit corporations, and private institutions may or may not fall under more specific licensing regulations. (Many states exempt regionally accredited private institutions, or those chartered before a specific year, from those regulations.) The private sector is often involved in statewide planning for postsecondary education through representation on planning boards or committees advisory to them, as well as through a variety of consultative mechanisms. Such involvement is less extensive where the statewide planning is conducted by the governing board for public institutions. Increasingly, the private sector is considered, and sometimes consulted, in the process of reviewing existing or newly proposed programs in the public sector. But state review of private-sector programs, either new or existing, is, at this point, fairly rare.

The responses thus far developed by states toward private colleges experiencing financial distress have been to monitor the extent of that distress and then to reach decisions about intervention.

Monitoring. A state, usually through its postsecondary agency, may systematically monitor the private sector, so that, under its planning responsibilities, it can assess the financial health of that sector and of individual institutions. Wing (1979) describes two levels of monitoring activity: *routine monitoring* and *case-study preparation.* Routine monitoring includes data collection and analysis, with a number of institutional and financial indicators used to group institutions according to degree of financial distress. Case studies, using more detailed data and information gathered from direct involvement with the institutions, are prepared for institutions shown by the routine screening to be in, or headed for, difficulty.

Intervention. While a state agency may monitor the health of the private sector as part of its planning responsibility for postsecondary education, intervention implies more extensive regulatory power and can be of several types and of varying levels of intensity. Systematic intervention may occur when a state having a monitoring procedure in place regularly initiates some action toward an institution judged to be in sufficient difficulty. In New York, for instance, an institution perceived to be in danger of failure is asked to submit a formal plan describing the way in which the institution intends to respond to its problems. The next step is to take some regulatory action. In New York the institution might be ordered to stop admitting students (Wing, 1979). Under the former Office of Management Services in New York's Department of Education, intervention at this point could also include helping the institution to close in an orderly way (as in the case of Bennett College) or working closely with the institution to consider alternatives to closure, such as merger with another institution. Haines (1980) describes several of these cases and discusses mergers, reorganizations, and affiliations. (Chapter Eighteen details the administrative provisions that states need to establish for private college closings.)

Few state agencies have the staff resources, procedures, and authority, however, to permit systematic intervention. Ad hoc intervention is a more typical practice. In response to clear signals of distress or to the pleas of the institution itself, a state postsecondary agency or another state office may intervene either to regulate or to help an institution. Measures to regulate institutions include requirements of some specific action on the part of the institution or revocation of the institution's license to operate. In many cases the state agency, responding to the perceived or acknowledged distress of an institution, has provided consulting assistance from its own staff or from outside experts. Such assistance was offered by the Board of Higher Education in Connecticut when Annhurst College was in serious financial difficulty during 1979. (It closed in the fall of that year.)

Some ad hoc intervention has gone beyond consultation to analysis and recommendation of significant state action. Sullins College in Virginia, prior to closing in 1976, requested that it be taken over as a state institution. The Virginia Council on Higher Education conducted a feasibility study, subsequently advising against acquiring Sullins but never publicly releasing its findings—at the request of the governor, who denied the Sullins request because of the state's fiscal problems (Meisinger, 1980). When Athens College requested state status from the Alabama legislature in 1975, the Alabama Commission on Higher Education conducted a study of the proposal and submitted a negative recommendation. The legislature chose to support the college, however, and in 1980 the commission sought to have the institution—now a public upper-division college—closed (Mingle, 1980). In contrast, Mayhew (1979) describes the positive support received by New College in Florida—formerly a private college but now functioning under the auspices of the state university system. Private institutions often were converted to state institutions in the 1960s and early 1970s (for example, the University of Buffalo, the University of Baltimore, and the University of Chattanooga); however, because of the extensive development of public systems in the past twenty-five years, cases involving such major institutions seem unlikely to occur in the future.

There are also cases of ad hoc state intervention through significant one-time support. In 1979 the Peabody Institute of the Johns Hopkins University, a renowned music conservatory, approached the Maryland State Board for Higher Education to request short-run financial assistance from the state. After reviewing Peabody's management plan, which called for $10 million in state assistance, staff of the Maryland board presented a request to the legislature for a $7.5 million loan to serve as an endowment. The measure was approved as an annually renewable grant, contingent on the institution's raising additional endowment funds (Maryland State Board for Higher Education, 1980, p. 1).

The following case studies (of Tennessee and New York) provide further examples of different approaches to involvement of the state in the issues of private college distress and institutional merger. In Tennessee the coordinating board, based on recent experiences, has formalized its policies toward ad hoc requests from the private sector for state assistance. The New York case outlines the regents' involvement in the merger and dissolution of private institutions.

Case Study: Tennessee*

The policy problem in Tennessee is a typical one: how to preserve for the state the diversity and independence offered by private higher education, given the competitive pressures these institutions will face during the 1980s. With fifty-five private institutions and total enrollment in fall 1979 of over 45,000, the private sector accounts for 24 percent of total enrollment in the state, which is near the national average and highest among the fourteen states of the southern (Southern Regional Education Board) region. Among the primary statutory responsibilities of the Tennessee Higher Education Commission (THEC) is the development of a master plan for public higher education. In a variety of ways, the

*This section was written by E. Grady Bogue.

commission has come to recognize the important role of the private sector in developing that plan. By 1979, with the publication of its second master plan, THEC recognized explicitly the need for consideration of the programs and offerings of the private sector in reviewing programs in public institutions. Furthermore, the commission chose to develop explicit policy for evaluating possible transfer or merger of private institutions into the public sector, an issue that had surfaced in recent years as the coordinating board and the state became directly and indirectly involved in merger issues and requests for transfer or merger of private institutions into the public sector.

For the past quarter of a century in Tennessee, the only instance of a private institution's coming into the public sector was the transformation of the former University of Chattanooga into a campus of the University of Tennessee in 1968—a change endorsed in a special study by THEC, conducted with the help of consultants provided by the Southern Regional Education Board.

While the 1979–80 THEC master plan was being prepared, however, at least two cases of private-public merger were under consideration, and another case occurred shortly after the master plan was published. Here is a brief description of these three merger possibilities and the public policy developed to anticipate instances of private-public merger.

The Southern College of Optometry (SCO) is an independent institution founded in 1932 and offering a major course of study leading to the Doctor of Optometry degree. The Bachelor of Science and Associate of Science degrees are also offered. With entering classes of approximately 150 each year, the college enrollment represents thirty to forty states but has historically served special needs in the South. The college has been successful in arranging contracts through the Southern Regional Education Board (SREB) with several southern states, including Tennessee. (As a way of avoiding unnecessary duplication in the region, states reserve spaces in the program for their residents and appropriate funds in support of the program.) Early in the 1970s, the SCO board of trustees authorized the president to pursue the possibility of state affiliation. But an informal assessment by THEC in 1975 concluded that the need for optometrists in the state was being adequately served through the SREB contract mechanism and that it would be financially inadvisable for the state to take on the operation of an entire school when its needs were being met through the contract arrangement. Again in 1979 the institution sought state affiliation. But with a declining state fiscal condition in 1980, a major study proposed by THEC was postponed, and the possibility of state support through merger, or status as an independent public institution, faded for the time being.

State policy makers were presented with a similar request from King College, a small liberal arts college located in upper East Tennessee and historically related to the Presbyterian Church. In recent years the college has experienced both enrollment and financial difficulty. In 1978 the trustees of King College had authorized its president to explore the possibility of merger with East Tennessee State University. After staff discussions and studies, a consensus developed among political leaders, executive officers of the board of regents, and the governing board of the institution that merger was not an appropriate step for the moment. Part of that attitude derived from the conviction that East Tennessee State had sufficient management problems on its hands in getting a new medical school started. However, East Tennessee State, King College, and Milligan College (another church-related private college) arranged for closer ties. Students at King and Milligan can now cross-enroll at East Tennessee State, with special opportunities in technical fields such as computer science. Likewise, students at the state institution can cross-enroll at the two private schools for courses in foreign and classical languages and religious studies. While a merger was not consummated, a specific and constructive program of cooperation was established.

George Peabody College for Teachers is a Tennessee institution that has played a significant national role in the preparation of professionals in the field of education. However, the decline in demand for such professionals, especially at the undergraduate level, and the growth of preparation programs in many public institutions produced an enrollment and financial trend that made it extremely difficult for the college to remain a strong independent institution. Consequently, in the summer of 1978, Peabody began to explore the option of merger with other insti-

tutions. Initial contacts were largely with other private schools—
Vanderbilt, Duke, George Washington, Emory.

In the fall of 1978, however, certain events produced a climate favorable for merger conversations between Peabody and
Tennessee State University (TSU), a historically black university in
Nashville. Closing a ten-year court suit seeking integration of the
state's higher education system, federal court rulings of 1978 and
1979 merged the former University of Tennessee at Nashville with
Tennessee State University, with TSU as the surviving institution.
This ruling created in Nashville an integrated public university
with significant resources and long-range potential as an urban
university. Despite this merger the Tennessee Higher Education
Commission was reluctant to approve a new Doctor of Education
degree program proposed by Tennessee State, both on the basis of
the lack of need for an additional degree program in the region
and in recognition of the program already offered at George Peabody. The initial rejection of the TSU Doctor of Education program proposal by the commission and the simultaneous search by
Peabody for merger possibilities produced a situation where conversation between these two institutions was mutually attractive. It
would have been a grand venture—the merger of a historically
black university, itself with a newly defined mission, with an institution having historic and significant strength in the preparation of
professionals in education.

A combination of factors—some internal to the institutions,
some public and political, and some related to the renewed interest
of Vanderbilt and the close physical proximity of Peabody to
Vanderbilt—resulted in the termination of merger discussions between Peabody and TSU and the eventual merger of Peabody and
Vanderbilt University on July 1, 1979. An interesting and pleasant
by-product occurred, however. With the support of opinions by the
federal court and Tennessee's attorney general, the state board of
regents and TSU resubmitted the Doctor of Education proposal to
the coordinating board. This proposal included a contractual and
supportive relationship with Vanderbilt University. The contract
provided for faculty and library support of Vanderbilt University
(utilizing faculty and library of the now-merged Peabody College)

in helping TSU get the program started over a five-year period. There were other features as well, including opportunity for cross-enrollments between the two schools. The Doctor of Education degree for TSU, with this contract support from Vanderbilt included, was approved by the commission in January 1980.

While the political debate surrounding the issue of merger and "takeover" by the public sector will no doubt be difficult and sometimes acrimonious, the evaluative questions developed in the 1979 master plan, which grew out of the commission's experience in these cases, will provide a rational starting point. The following questions are included in the plan:

- Can the program continue under private auspices?
- Why should the state assume the programs, facilities, and other resources involved?
- [Will] the programs involved . . . be lost to the state if either merger or long-term contractual relations are not accomplished? [If so, are the programs] needed by the state or region?
- What would be the long-term financial obligations incurred by the state in any action proposed?
- What would be the financial and programmatic effect on current public and private institutions and educational services offered in the state?
- Would the proposed action be the most cost-effective and educationally sound way of providing the services involved?
- Would the proposed action violate either the U.S. or state Constitution or state or federal laws?
- What changes in mission will result in the proposed action, and how will such [changes] relate to other institutional missions? [Tennessee Higher Education Commission, 1979.]

Tennessee is not an affluent state. Its principal tax base is a sales tax, and there is no state income tax at present. Major new obligations are being felt, including the opening of a second public medical school and a college of veterinary medicine, at a time when the state is experiencing revenue shortfalls. Thus, it is easy to discern that these policy questions are designed to establish a conservative posture on the future possibility of the state's assuming fiscal responsibility for private institutions or services.

Of equal concern to THEC is the protection of the autonomy and distinctive missions of private institutions. After all, among the major strengths cited for private higher education are independence from governmental influence, the nurture of religious and other special values, and the freedom to innovate. When a private institution proposes a merger or contract for service that strikes at any one of these strengths or that suggests a move to weaken the distinctive mission and heritage of the institution, careful evaluation is in order. These policy questions are designed to ensure deliberate evaluation early in that process.

Case Study: New York*

Governance of higher education in New York is distinctive because New York's regents are established by state constitution as the supreme board over all educational undertakings in the state, preschool through professional—including 135 independent colleges and universities. As such, the regents and their 3,000-member administrative arm, the State Education Department, are responsible for the promulgation, execution, and adjudication of a body of administrative law covering all aspects of education in the state. Their authority seems sweeping but is bound by both law and custom and is constrained by their limited role in the state's appropriations process. In the battle for funding, regents' recommendations have far less clout than do recommendations made by the powerful State University of New York and City University of New York interests. There is also a constant possibility that the legislature will undo the regents' plans, since their constitutional authority exists only "as modified by the legislature" (New York State Constitution of 1938, Article XI, sec. 2). Moreover, the state's highest court has cautioned them against interfering with the daily activities of the institutions they govern (*Moore* v. *Board of Regents*, 390 N.Y.S.2d 582 (1977)). To operate effectively within these constraints, the regents have developed a stance toward the higher

*This section was written by Gail S. Chambers.

education community characterized by close observation, coordination, and quality control, combined with an arm's length approach to institutional affairs.

But the stake held by state government in the fate of independent colleges is substantial and direct. Since New York City's financial crisis in 1975, New York has been particularly anxious to maintain faith in its fiscal practices. This poses a special problem in relation to enrollment decline. Much postwar building in the state's higher education system—public and private—was financed through bonds issued by the New York State Dormitory Authority and secured by assets, endowment in escrow, and cash reserves, but *not* by the full faith and credit of the state (Bullard, 1979). The credit it thus created is sustained by large enrollments at the independent institutions and indirectly by the state's obligation to cover debt service for the public institutions. Large-scale default due to enrollment declines in the independent sector could shake the financial institutions holding state bonds and create moral and practical obligations to back these bonds. On the other hand, large-scale enrollment losses in the public sector could create an additional net burden on the treasury. Thus, the fiscal interests of the state are tied to the problems of enrollment decline, regardless of whether decline occurs in public or private institutions. Pressures to maintain the fiscal structure could lead to an ad hoc approach in the future, as individual institutions face default.

A Controlled-Market Approach. Planners in the State Education Department anticipate a 33 percent drop in statewide enrollments by 1990 if there are no intervening changes in public policy (interview with David Nolan, New York State Education Department, July 1980). In all likelihood a large number of independent institutions will cease to exist by 1990. Shrinkage of the order of magnitude anticipated for New York—if it occurs—clearly will not be absorbed by incremental changes in existing institutions but will require some broader strategy. Realizing this, in 1977 the regents adopted procedures for monitoring institutional health; for consulting with those experiencing fiscal difficulties; and for suggesting resolutions, which might include state grants or loans, "state-related status," interinstitutional contracts, mergers, and closings (Hollander, 1977). Through this and related policies, the regents seem to be moving toward an overall retrenchment strategy based on the free-market tradition of economics. Under such a market theory, pressures of perfect market competition drive out only the least efficient units.

Elements of regents' policy that indicate this approach include efforts to narrow the public/private tuition gap by recommending a strengthened program of student-carried state assistance (the Tuition Assistance Plan), funded at $243 million in 1980; to keep competition fair through regional master planning and the regulation of off-campus instructional programs; to encourage the vitality of all institutions through even-handed monitoring and consultation; to protect students from the undesirable effects of competition by eliminating weak programs; and to encourage flexibility and variety when these are backed by sound educational planning.

The success of such a policy depends on the purity of the market and on whether buyers possess the kind of "perfect" knowledge and mobility needed to purchase in aggregate the best set of programs. Whether the market for higher education in New York State can be made to approximate these conditions is, of course, subject to serious question.

Merger Options in New York State. Not all the state's policies are consonant with the regents' controlled-market approach, but current practice with respect to mergers illustrates the advantages and drawbacks of such a strategy. Merger represents one form of institutional closure plus a source of innovation to meet changing market needs. Under New York's education law, procedures for merging educational institutions are more definitive than they are in other states (Meyer, 1970). There are two possible routes for colleges seeking mergers in New York State: the traditional consolidation of two or more institutions into one; and a rarer form, using laws designed for institutional closure, which dissolves one institution and transfers its assets to another. As noted in Chapter Six, the dissolution merger of independent institutions could be the type most frequently practiced in coming years, because assets and liabilities can be "selectively" acquired by the successor institution. The dissolution/acquisition route is not favorable to the dissolving institution, but it does provide continuity for current students and their records and also may provide in part for employment of faculty and staff, perpetuation of some goals and traditions, and—importantly—continued debt service supporting the dormitory bonds.

Under their monitoring policy, the regents may suggest to a distressed institution that it seek merger. The regents will continue to be involved with the merger by tracking the progress of a successor institution through its period of postmerger adjustment, and by requiring that programs previously approved in the merged institution must be reregistered with the regents by the successor institution. Negotiations with the regents' staff throughout the process can impose significant restraints on the surviving institution. Delays may increase both the real and the risk costs of mergers by extending the period of stress associated with transition. Furthermore, the successor institution may be constrained in the design of its academic plan by objections of other nearby institutions, both public and private, which can be involved in the negotiations and hearings. This was the case with the merger of Rochester Institute of Technology and Eisenhower College (see Chapter Six).

In addition to the policies discussed above, two other governmental practices in New York can alter the progress of a college merger. The first is the possibility of legislative override if a merger is politically sensitive and involves the public sector or public funds. The second is a new development, which provides a parallel override feature for the independent sector. It is the Mannes College decision, in which the regents took their first action to dismiss an active board of trustees under a long-standing law allowing them to do so (New York State Education Law, sec. 226). The law's scope is not exclusive to mergers, but in this case it had the effect of blocking a merger attempt.

Policy Effectiveness. Within their legal and political constraints, the New York regents have developed a large array of tools to deal with the problems of retrenchment, plus an overall strategy to guide their use. The state's involvement in mergers between private colleges reveals both the strengths and the weaknesses of this approach. Because there is no explicit merger policy, the state and the institutions can hand-tailor resolutions to the problem at hand. This provides for flexibility and the consideration of a broad range of interests, the obverse of which can be considered arbitrariness and interference. It also requires the aid of a well-coordinated, skilled state staff. These are manageable concerns. The policy's great weakness, however, is that it provides for fine-tuning the outcome of retrenchment competition but not for adequately balancing the overall competitive setting. Hence, the regents can effect only incremental changes in the state's higher education system and must hope that changing political forces will provide them with a market capable of closing only the least worthy programs, whether public or independent, during an era of distress.

A Framework for State Policy

In developing state policy toward the private sector, state decision makers should consider the following issues: (1) the role and contribution of the independent sector in the past, (2) current programs of support for independent colleges, and (3) policy options with respect to providing assistance to failing institutions.

Role and Contribution of the Independent Sector. The Education Commission of the States (1977, p. 4) has recommended that "Each state should construct a specific policy regarding the independent colleges and universities that serve its citizens. States should develop such policy in the light of clear state purposes and a detailed understanding of the role and condition of independent institutions." The development of such a policy should be based on the answers to four key questions: (1) What are the general policy objectives for postsecondary education within the state? (2) What is the role of independent colleges and universities, and how do they contribute to the accomplishment of those objectives? (3) Is there a consequent state interest in independent higher education? (4) What state policies and programs are appropriate in light of the state's interest in the independent sector (including, in this case, policies that specifically refer to institutions in danger of closing)?

Current Programs of Support for Private Higher Education. The most effective bulwark against losing the private sector's contribution to the achievement of state goals for postsecondary education is a well-conceived and effective program of state support for all of private higher education. The keystone of such a policy is an effective student aid program, broad enough to provide financial assistance to a significant number of students who attend or wish to attend private institutions. Tuition-offset grants, which six states now make available to all resident students attending private institutions (irrespective of need), go farther than need-based programs in "equalizing" tuition between the public and private sectors. The aid-to-the-student approach (whether need-based or not) recognizes that a state policy that seeks to ensure access to a diverse range of public and private institutions must create a reasonably fair market between the two sectors and among their institutions. This coincides with the first need of vulnerable institutions—to maintain enrollments.

Some states provide institutional aid either on a "per student" (Oregon), "per financial aid recipient" (Minnesota), or "per degree" (New York) basis, through institutional entitlements or contracts. Institutional aid provides direct support for institutions' finances and thus allows enrichment of the academic program without larger increases in tuition levels. Institutional aid can also relieve some of the effect of debt service for many institutions in financial difficulty, and thereby can be an important noncategorical contribution to their survival.

Nine states have programs that permit contracts for educational service with private institutions. Because many vulnerable institutions are geographically isolated and because direct programmatic competition with public institutions erodes their stability, contractual arrangements that allow them to use their resources more productively are a focused and imaginative means of ensuring their ability to survive and at the same time utilize state money efficiently. (For a good discussion of use of contracts, see Cooper, 1980.)

Assistance to Failing Institutions. In providing assistance to failing private institutions, the state may play a monitoring role, or it may give nonfiscal assistance, or it may provide fiscal support.

The extent of monitoring involvement will be determined by staff capacity and by the magnitude of the state's financial commitment to the private sector. Through existing data sources (such as the Higher Education General Information Survey), or through data collection designed for this explicit purpose (based, for instance, on audited financial statements), the state's higher education agency could monitor the financial condition of the state's private institutions, to identify sources of serious financial difficulty. Where financially troubled institutions are identified, additional information could be sought, to make it necessary for the institution's leaders—its chief administrators and board—to face implications of the institution's declining financial condition, if they have not already done so.

A monitoring role may be justified by the broad authority of a state postsecondary agency. More direct involvement or intervention requires more specific regulatory power on the part of that agency, which would normally be based on significant programs of state support to the private sector. Again, staff capacity is critical. Nonfiscal involvement and assistance could include consultation. Staff functions should be to examine the management structure of the institution and advise where it might be strengthened; to examine the short-run plans of the institution, in order to determine whether they appear adequate to "turn the financial situation around"; to consider the way the institution is positioned with respect to its programs and its present and potential clientele; and to determine its chances for survival under present or proposed conditions. Consultants could also act as third-party facilitators between the troubled institution and others with whom merger is a possibility. If failure is inevitable, the consultants could help the institution prepare a plan for orderly closure (see Chapter Eighteen).

Any direct fiscal support given troubled institutions should be given in light of policies clearly developed beforehand—overall policies with respect to the private sector. Alternative sources of funding should also be considered. States may decide to support, on a one-time basis, institutions that appear likely to survive if given short-term resources to enable them to move successfully in a new direction; or they may decide simply to allow troubled institutions to close. Resources for facilitating closing should be available at each institution. Institutions usually fail because their liquid assets are inadequate, not because their total liabilities exceed total assets. Funds needed to facilitate closing might be borrowed against the total assets of the institution; in most cases that would represent a secure loan. States may also wish to consider a revolving loan fund for this purpose.

Constructive state policies for dealing with colleges in danger of closing must include an allocation of tasks, with one agency—either the state postsecondary agency or a statewide governing board—made responsible for coordinating the tasks. Such agencies, in place in most states already, perform responsibilities such as monitoring and have the experience (if not the manpower) to consult with the institutions and to facilitate their relationships with other state agencies, other institutions, and interested organizations in the private sector.

The legislature will of course be involved in the development of the proposed policies and in translating them, when appropriate, into statutes. It needs to be kept informed because of the oversight role it will play in the execution of these policies. Any policies that involve financial support will also require legislative appropriation. Additionally, executive agencies other than the state postsecondary agency (such as economic development agencies if the failing college is located in a small town with existing economic problems) may have an interest in the matter. Lending or bonding authorities, such as state dormitory authorities or higher education facilities authorities, have a formal interest in institutions with obligations to them. It is appropriate for these agencies, in protecting that interest, to work directly with the institutions but also to coordinate their efforts with the state postsecondary agencies.

Concluding Observations

The foregoing policy options are meant to supplement policies and programs relating to the private sector that are already in place. As we have previously said, these existing policies, especially student-based financial aid programs, must be seen as the foundation for policies that directly relate to distressed institutions. If these programs, especially student aid programs, create a market in which private institutions can compete fairly with public institutions, their fiscal health can be largely assured. Those that cannot continue to attract students are thereby demonstrating that they no longer serve present purposes and should be allowed to close. The adequacy of *existing* policies is critical and should be periodically reviewed.

Even if existing policies and practices are well constructed, there may be pressure to respond in ad hoc fashion to the needs of specific institutions in trouble. Measures to provide "bail-out" support should be carefully considered and sparingly employed. The best way to avoid such pressure is to have policies and practices that specify procedures with respect to failing private institutions articulated in advance through board action or legislative decision. The state postsecondary agency will play a central role in this regard.

As states become more frugal and, in some cases, constrained by tax and revenue limitations in their ability to fund higher education, state postsecondary agencies will increasingly be seen as instruments of control. As more state support flows to the private sector, it too will be brought under the influence of the coordinating agencies. This has already happened, but the degree of control or regulation by the state is in step with the degree of support—that is, quite limited. At the same time, the policies developed by those boards, or by the state, toward *public* higher education are just as important to the private sector as policies directly bearing on it. The difficulty of closing a public institution is widely recognized, and public institutions that are kept open in spite of declining usefulness or efficiency may contribute to the difficulties of institutions in the private sector.

Finally, it is important to remind ourselves that state policy can never "save" the private sector. The best guarantees of survival remain (1) capable institutional management, (2) program flexibility to respond to new needs, (3) a sound fiscal base, and (4) the good fortune to be located in a part of the country where declines in the college-age population will be minimal or absent. This last point illustrates the chance element in institutional survival. As Howe (1979, p. 70) has pointed out, "The problems of the next fifteen years will not only result in the elimination of marginal private institutions we can get along without but also will cause the closing of many colleges that give American higher education important elements of quality, flavor, and diversity."

Breneman and Finn (1978, p. 51) support this point of view: "If substantial overall contraction does occur in a state's post-secondary system, and if the state does not intervene in that process, then (1) the 'wrong' programs and institutions will survive through their skill at political manipulation, (2) the private sector will suffer a disproportionate and possibly undesirable retrenchment, and (3) randomized, piecemeal erosion will occur, resulting in a large number of crippled institutions rather than a smaller complement of healthy ones."

This argues for the development of sound policies relating to retrenchment and the possibility of institutional closure. Those policies, however, should be designed to ensure not the survival of individual institutions but the vigor and effectiveness of a system, which includes the resources of both public and private sectors. Those policies, while they *affect* institutions, *concern* students and society—through the provision of access, equality of opportunity, quality and balance of program resources, beneficial research, public service, and freedom of expression and inquiry. State policies that involve institutions are directed toward the more effective pursuit of those broad purposes.

For Further Reading

More detailed discussion of the Tennessee and New York cases in this chapter can be found in the case studies by Bogue (1980) and by Chambers (1980) (available from the Southern Regional Education Board). A comprehensive examination of federal policy toward private higher education is found in *Public Policy and Private Higher Education* (Breneman and Finn, 1978). For recommendations on state policy, see the report of the Education Commission of the States (1977). Chronister and others (1978) discuss the involvement of independent colleges in statewide planning. For a detailed presentation of the monitoring policies of the New York Department of Education, see Wing (1979).

✑ 18 ✑

State Role in Private College Closings

Joseph P. O'Neill

During the academic year 1979–80, my colleague Samuel Barnett and I studied the merger or closing of thirty-four colleges. We reviewed case-study material; interviewed faculty, students, and staff at four colleges in the process of closing; and also interviewed a variety of administrators, including six presidents, from institutions that had closed earlier in the 1970s. Our purpose was to produce, under a grant from the Ford Foundation, a source book to help faculty and staff in future college closings to anticipate at least some of the difficulties that the dissolution of a college entails (see O'Neill and Barnett, 1981).

Some of the lessons that we learned in researching and writing the source book apply not so much to the colleges in question as to the agencies that accredit, license, and monitor them. If, as has been predicted, 200 or more colleges close in the period 1985 to 1995 (U.S. Department of Education, 1980), these state agencies and accrediting associations may well be forced to review and revise their procedures for dealing with colleges in distress. This chapter focuses on aspects of college closings that may be of interest to state postsecondary agencies, accrediting associations, and bodies that provide support to church-related colleges.

Until recently the states' interest in the opening and closing of private colleges was limited mainly to a state's jurisdiction over the chartering of corporations and the exercise of its police powers to prevent fraud or to check the abuse of a trust. Questions about the financial and academic stability of private colleges and universities were left to the monitoring process of voluntary accrediting associations. In the past fifteen years, however, state agencies have begun to take a closer look at the private sector. This change in attitude is due in large part to the rapid growth of state-sponsored student financial aid programs. In 1965 few states had grant or loan programs whose eligibility was not linked to some special purpose, such as war orphans' support or nurses' training. By 1978 every state had a general benefit grant or loan program (Suchar, 1978). Among the primary beneficiaries of these grants and loans were students at private colleges and universities. In addition to student entitlement programs, states such as New York and New Jersey established programs of direct grants to private institutions, based on enrollment or degree production. This mounting infusion of tax dollars brought with it a more active interest in how colleges made use of the state's investment.

A corresponding, though not so universal, concern began to make itself felt about the question of college closings. Of the forty-seven states, for example, that responded to a questionnaire on the protection of student academic records at closed colleges, twenty-five had established a procedure to safeguard those records (O'Neill and Barnett, 1981). Of the states that have adopted such procedures, at least twelve have done so in the past five years and three other states have the matter under active study.

The federal government and several states have developed financial guidelines or indicators that are used to identify colleges in distress. The U.S. Department of Education characterizes an institution as not financially responsible if it has had a history of operating losses or if, for its most recent fiscal year, it had a deficit net worth. The department does not indicate how long the history of operating losses must be in order for a college to lose eligibility for Title IV student financial aid funds. Deficits in nonprofit organizations are not extraordinary. In fact, most independent colleges and universities have experienced one or two deficit years during the past decade. Other criteria cited by the U.S. Department of Education (in 34 *Code of Federal Regulations* 668.15, 668.17, Dec. 31, 1980) are (1) "a GSL [Guaranteed Student Loan] or NDSL [National Direct Student Loan] default rate which exceeds 20 percent of the principal of all those loans that have reached the repayment period" and (2) a withdrawal rate in which "more than 33 percent of the students regularly enrolled at the beginning of the year withdraw during that academic year."

Some states have established more refined monitoring systems. New York's guidelines, for example, measure the seriousness of a deficit in the operating account in relationship to long-term trends in enrollment, the size of the deficit compared to the size of the endowment, the college's fund-raising capability, and the burden of its debt service (Frances and Coldren, 1979). The problem with most such indicators is that they do not indicate *when* the accumulation of negative signs will cause the college to close. In our study of closed colleges, we identified one clear signal that financial death is imminent: *the inability to borrow,* even short term or for cash management purposes (O'Neill and Barnett, 1981).

Cash-flow management is a perennial problem for institutions that collect tuition and fees only two or three times a year. Inability to borrow in anticipation of tuition receipts will almost inevitably force a slowdown in payments to vendors, and sometimes will even cause missed payrolls. An accrediting association or a state postsecondary agency might examine the effectiveness of requiring a college in distress to notify the agency when the bank with which the college regularly does business refuses either to lend short term or to renegotiate the terms of a loan. Such notification may allow the agency several months' lead time to prevent a mid-term closing. A mid-term closing is the true disaster that a state agency, either through prevention or subvention, should strive to avoid. If a college does not have the financial resources to complete the academic year, it should not be allowed to open in September. If the college does open and is about to collapse in mid-term, the state should examine the possibility of setting aside a disaster reserve in its student financial aid funds to allow the college to teach out the term.

Institutional Size and Corporate Survival

In a study of college mergers and closings, Millett (1976, pp. 83–84) remarked: "Enrollment size as such did not appear to be the controlling factor in the closings. Enrollment decline was the cause of the disaster. No matter how small or how large, when a college begins to lose enrollment, it begins to experience financial and management problems." The qualifiers "size as such" and "controlling factor" are important ones. Millett's argument is that colleges get into trouble because, in a period of declining enrollments, they cannot reduce expenditures as quickly as their income falls. But there is also a very real sense in which the absolute size of a college is a factor in making the decision to close. Consider Fadil and Carter's (1980, p. 1) statement: "In the decade 1970–80, in which 141 private colleges closed, 87 percent of them had an enrollment of less than 500 FTE when the closing actually occurred." A college's ability to fulfill its stated mission is dependent on the size and diversity of its faculty. In many very small colleges, departments are often made up of one or two faculty members. A decline in enrollment means not merely a lower student-faculty ratio; it may mean the elimination of a subject matter area as well.

In the fall of 1980, Colorado Women's College laid off thirty-four full-time faculty members and prepared to replace them with part-time teachers. Students brought suit against the college, alleging that the reduction of the faculty to ten full-time instructors prevented the college from offering the full range of courses required to complete their degrees. Accrediting agencies (especially, professional education accreditation groups) and state higher education agencies may well agree. Their guidelines often prescribe a depth of faculty which the college can no longer afford as absolute size reaches a certain critical stage.

In theory a college could shrink in absolute size until it consists of "Mark Hopkins and a student at the other end of the log." In fact, however, every college must render a core of expected or state-prescribed services to the students whom it recruits. The

maintenance of that core of services requires some absolute
number of tuition-paying students. While no fixed number can
be given to that minimum size, "at some stage cutting back," as
Kershaw (1976, p. 6) remarks, "becomes self-defeating, according
to any criterion, and small colleges must be closer to that point
than larger universities."

The Decision to Close

For a small college in financial distress, the difference between a surplus and a deficit is often determined by a gain or a
decline in enrollment of as few as fifteen to twenty students. To
ensure that its enrollment goals are met, the college keeps pushing
its application and acceptance dates closer and closer to the actual
start of classes. A shortfall in enrollment serious enough to cause
the college to close may not be fully evident until the day that
classes begin. And then it is too late.

In studying the difference between the orderly and the
abrupt (that is, mid-term) closings, we found that the ability to
borrow from a nonbank source was usually crucial to an orderly
closeout. Franconia College in New Hampshire and Windham College in Vermont had no sponsoring organizations to turn to when
their level of debt cut short their ability to borrow from banking
institutions. Newton College in Massachusetts was able to draw on
the resources of Boston College. Annhurst College in Connecticut
had a close call, since it took three months to find a lender who
would provide the college a loan to teach out the year.

How can a postsecondary agency help trustees decide
whether the college has sufficient resources to teach out the year?
There is no easy answer to this question. Colleges in financial distress often become secretive and defensive, especially when dealing
with the agencies that accredit or license them. Colleges are aware
that public knowledge of declining enrollments, operating deficits,
debt moratoria, or withdrawal of program approval is likely to have
severely adverse effects on their recruiting efforts and credit
worthiness. Keeping up a brave front becomes essential to survival.
Agencies with a legal or moral obligation to protect student inter-

ests may find it difficult to get behind that front without further damaging a college's chance for survival.

If a postsecondary agency cannot by law compel an assessment of a college's ability to teach out the year, or does not think it prudent to compel such an assessment, other nonregulatory agencies may be able to perform the task. Funding might be provided to a state association of independent colleges to examine the college's finances and enrollment projections. If the association's team made its report to the school's trustees rather than to the funding agency, the examination would not pose an immediate threat to the college's image. If, however, the association's report rendered a negative judgment, the trustees could ignore it only at their peril—since, if the college then closed before it fulfilled its contractual obligations to students, trustees would find it difficult to avoid the charge of negligence and the potential liability attendant thereto.

The Time to Close

In its efforts to protect the interests of students and staff, a postsecondary agency should concern itself with the timing of a college closing. While there may be no good time to close, some times are worse than others. In an ideal world, the announcement date for the closing would come no later than midway through the first term of the college's final academic year; that is, sometime between Thanksgiving and Christmas. Despite fears that a November-December announcement could result in a high dropout rate for the final semester, this did not prove to be the case at Annhurst College (in Connecticut) or at Immaculate Heart College (in California). In fact, in both these cases, the announcement that the college was closing gave dropouts from previous years an incentive to complete their degree requirements while there was still time and opportunity to do so.

There are four factors that support the choice of a mid-term announcement: (1) A mid-term announcement enables an institution to schedule courses during the subsequent winter, spring, and summer academic terms, to allow the maximum number of students to finish their programs of study without interruption. (2) Students have a greater range of possibilities for transferring to another college. (3) Faculty and staff have time to begin job searches and can be assisted in that process. (4) Arrangements can be made with federal and state officials to ensure continuity of student financial aid (at Immaculate Heart College, for example, the federal regional office allowed summer school students to draw financial aid reserved for the following fall term).

An orderly closing requires both careful planning and sufficient lead time to implement the plan for closing. If, as in the case of Ladycliff College (New York), the closing is announced in late April or early May, students may find it difficult to locate a college nearby which offers the courses they need to graduate; academic and financial aid transcripts may be difficult to complete; and the college may find itself sued by the faculty because the announcement of closing occurred after the contract cancellation date stipulated in their employment contracts.

Postsecondary Agencies and the Closing Process

With the exception of the state of New York, where the board of regents has a statutory role in approving a college closing, the jurisdiction of state postsecondary agencies is limited to ongoing institutions (O'Neill and Barnett, 1981). Once a college board of trustees declares its voluntary intention to dissolve, the approval of its dissolution ordinarily comes under the jurisdiction of the secretary of state (or similar agency responsible for incorporation and dissolution of corporate entities), the attorney general, and the courts. A state postsecondary agency can, of course, force the closing of a college—either directly, through the withdrawal of its license (as the New Jersey Board of Higher Education did in the Shelton College case in 1971), or indirectly, by withdrawing the college's eligibility for student financial aid. But once the college decides to close, jurisdiction over the process of corporate dissolution shifts from a department of higher education to other agencies and branches of state government. Despite this shift in responsibility, informal modes of communication within state government may allow a greater role for the postsecondary education agency to exercise its master-planning function in the dissolution of a college than the statutes expressly give it. The following sections describe existing as well as possible procedures whereby a postsecondary agency might ease the market and debt burdens of private colleges; monitor those in distress; and, when a closing seems inevitable, protect students and staff from unnecessary personal and career distress.

In many states the postsecondary agency's authority to monitor or regulate private colleges and universities is limited by grandfather clauses or is simply not given in the statutes. This lack of statutory authority often gives rise, in times of enrollment decline, to a dichotomy in the master-planning process; that is, retrenchment in the private sector is dictated by market forces, while retrenchment in the public sector becomes a planning exercise. Unequal protection from market forces has had a predictable effect: only one public four-year college has closed in the past twenty years (U.S. Department of Education, 1980). If college recruitment in the northeastern states becomes a zero-sum game in the next few years, postsecondary agencies should recognize their ability to affect the private college through their approval of new programs and facilities in the public sector.

In the process of closing a college, the state postsecondary agency often has direct responsibility for the continuance of the college's degree-granting authority, for the windup of state-sponsored student financial aid accounts, and for the maintenance of student academic records.

Continuance of Degree-Granting Authority. In the desire to minimize damage to students when a closing occurs, several colleges have in the past petitioned state authorities for permission to grant degrees for a specific period of time after the college ceases to offer instruction. If a student can earn the necessary credits at another college within a year's time, then the closed college will award the degree. The advantage to the student is clear: religious study courses or ones in which the student had a *C* grade or below may not be transferable; a new college may require different prerequisites for a major; and graduation requirements differ from college to college. Students can save both time and money if they can graduate from their original college. In Connecticut, for example, the State Board of Higher Education allowed the board of trustees of Annhurst College to award degrees until June 1981, but on two conditions: (1) The board of trustees was required to appoint an academic officer to certify to the Board of Higher Education that degree requirements had been fulfilled. (2) The board of trustees was required to remain in existence until the final degrees were awarded; in effect, the college, although no longer offering instruction, continued to exist as a corporate entity.

Annhurst's effort to deal fairly with students was to a large extent thwarted by federal regulations on student financial aid. Under federal regulations students are eligible for federal student financial aid only if they are enrolled in an eligible program. Once the college ceases its instructional activity, it loses its eligibility as a conduit for federal student financial aid; that is, a college that no longer offers instruction no longer has eligible programs (O'Neill and Barnett, 1981). Thus, after Annhurst closed, students who were matriculated for Annhurst degrees were ineligible for federal student aid even though they were earning the required credit at another eligible institution.

State-Supported Student Financial Aid. The most difficult problems in the area of student financial aid arise when a college closes in the middle of a term. An institution's normal refund policy is unlikely to mention such an eventuality. Students as well as state agencies may well argue that they are entitled to a full refund of tuition and fees for any uncompleted term, since, by virtue of the institution's action, they are not getting what they paid for. A school would have a difficult time arguing that a student should be responsible for 50 percent, or 25 percent, or whatever, of a semester's tuition if a student has not been able to complete any transferable credits during the semester in question. To avoid liability, Goddard College (in Vermont) issued disclosure statements to new students in the fall of 1980, indicating that the college's financial situation was such that it might not be able to deliver all of the services promised.

The state of California took another tack by instituting an insurance program called the Student Tuition Recovery Fund, which covers student tuition losses when a proprietary school closes. The regulations do not apply to nonprofit colleges and universities accredited by a regional (as opposed to a national) accrediting agency. State postsecondary agencies may wish to examine these and other ways to protect the investment of both the student and the state without at the same time hastening a college's demise.

Maintenance of Student Records. One major task that state postsecondary agencies undertake, either informally or by regulation, in a college closing is the preservation and maintenance of student academic records. In a review of the practices of forty-seven states, we found the following regulations (O'Neill and Barnett, 1981, pp. 111–126):

1. *Seizure of Records.* If the college does not comply with state regulations regarding student records or if the records are in danger of being destroyed, four states—Alaska, Nevada, Oregon, and Vermont—explicitly allow their postsecondary agencies to seek a court order to seize the records or compel their delivery to the designated state agency.
2. *Specification of Records and Their Material Form.* Some states are vague in their description of the records to be kept after a college closes. In general, the specification is "academic records," "records required by colleges when considering students for transfer or advanced study," or "records of attendance and academic achievement." Alaska, Washington, Oregon, and Maryland require that colleges file an original copy of the records; New Hampshire requires a certified copy; and Puerto Rico is content with microfilm.
3. *Notification of Students and Transcript Fee.* Florida requires the closing institution to notify, in writing, all current and former students where their records are kept.
4. *State Maintenance and Funding.* Vermont is the only state to specify that state funds may be used to preserve student records when the college is unable to do so. The legislation authorizes the attorney general to seek recovery of the costs involved by placing a lien on the college's property. A number of other states—Connecticut, Alaska, Kansas, Maine, Maryland, New Hampshire, and Oregon—imply that state funding will be used to maintain records by requiring (or allowing) them to be deposited with a state agency.

5. *Penalty for Noncompliance.* Only Nevada specifies that non-compliance is a misdemeanor.

Nonstatutory Assistance in the Process of Closing. Matters dealing with student records, financial aid, and the authority to grant degrees are usually part of the postsecondary agency's statutory responsibility. In other problem areas in a college closing, such responsibility is not as specifically defined. Willingness to help students and staff in distress may depend in these instances more on the attitude of state officials than on their legal obligations. For example, a state postsecondary agency could try to protect both persons and assets in instances where state policies or regulations on student aid or transfer unnecessarily penalize students from a closed college. Students from a closed college in California, for example, experienced difficulty in transferring to four-year state institutions because a fifty-six-credit requirement designed to prevent senior institutions from "poaching"—that is, recruiting—community college students before they graduate also prevented other kinds of transfer. In addition, where a college is bankrupt, a postsecondary agency might provide a grant to protect student records and prepare them for transfer to the repository institution. Finally, when a college closes abruptly and staff support disappears, the state agency might provide funding to another institution to act as a clearinghouse and ombudsman to deal with student problems. In the Windham College closing, for example, foreign students encountered difficulties in maintaining their student status. The bankruptcy trustee withheld academic records because of unpaid bills that students disputed. At another New England college, the sheriff padlocked a dormitory with the students' personal possessions still inside in order to satisfy the college's creditors.

Burden of Federal Debt. From 1951 to 1973, colleges and universities borrowed $3.8 billion from the federal government (under Title IV of the Housing Act of 1950) for dormitories, dining halls, and student unions. Hundreds of millions more were borrowed to build libraries and classroom buildings. As of June 1980, the direct-loan portfolio for academic facilities (Title VII-C of the Higher Education Act) contained 567 loans, with an outstanding principal balance of $411 million. Approximately 70 percent of these loans are to private institutions (unpublished data, Academic Facilities Bureau, U.S. Department of Education). These obligations to the federal government will become increasingly onerous as the decline of the eighteen- to twenty-two-year-old cohort becomes more pronounced. These young unmarried students are the ones most likely to live and eat on campus. Even if a college maintains its full-time-equivalent enrollment by recruiting a larger proportion of women and working adults, that kind of enrollment does little to offset the fixed costs of dormitory debt service. As dorm utilization rates decline, students who choose to live on campus are forced to pay higher room and board rates to make up for the shortfall in income which the college needs to cover its debt obligations. The quality of education may also suffer. Some colleges have been paying federal debt service out of their Educational and General (E&G) budget. Using E&G income to pay to auxiliary services reduces funds available for instruction and counseling.

Colorado Women's College, for example, with dormitory facilities for 1,000 students, had only 200 dorm residents in the fall of 1980. Similar underutilization exists in other colleges, with the result that more than eighty-six small private colleges were delinquent during 1980 in paying the debt service on their federal facilities loans (Magarrell, 1980). This number represents approximately 5 percent of the private colleges in the United States. In a recent survey conducted by the Conference of Small Private Colleges of fifty-five of its member colleges, 30 percent had annual federal debt service payments of $100,000 or more. Five of the fifty-five institutions had a debt moratorium. Clearly, facilities debt constitutes a significant drag on the financial flexibility of private institutions.

It is sometimes argued that the federal government already has a de facto policy to give moratoriums when asked. But if a college seeks a moratorium, not only is it barred from receiving other federal facilities loans and grants but its credit rating suffers with private lenders. Banks and insurance companies are interested in a college's history of repayment of its long-term debt. A major delinquency means a higher interest rate or perhaps a much lower ceiling on the ability to borrow.

A state's interest in the problem of underutilization of dormitory facilities at private colleges grows out of its master-planning function. If a pickup in enrollment is anticipated by 1995, it may be in the state's interest to maintain some portion of that capacity even if it is underutilized. To this end a state might provide direct loans or contracts, or it might encourage Congress to make the schedule of debt service payments more flexible.

Liquidation of Assets. In the actual process of corporate dissolution, the statutory responsibility for the college that is closing shifts, as was mentioned earlier, to the secretary of state, the attorney general, and the courts. Even here, however, the postsecondary agency may have a role to play. For example, once a college has announced that it will close, the state postsecondary agency should examine the possibility of program transfer. Program transfer refers to the process in which an operating (but noncorporate) unit of one college is merged into another college or university. When Franconia College in New Hampshire closed, it transferred an entire operating unit—faculty, students, and funds—to New Hampshire College. In a similar fashion, when Immaculate Heart College in Los Angeles closed, it transferred its bilingual program, including funding, to Loyola Marymount University. Neither transaction was a sale. No cash exchanged hands. Nor was it a gift, since permission of the funding agency was required to effect the transfer. The strategy of program transfer may be an important way to protect faculty and students in a college that cannot survive as a totality but whose several parts may complement the operations of other institutions. By actively assisting and fostering program transfers, a postsecondary agency may be able to further its own master-plan goals. And by transplanting a bilingual or remedial program to another nearby college, the agency can ensure continuity of service for a minority population.

An agency also may play a role in the distribution of a closed college's assets. If, on liquidation, the assets of a closed college exceed its liabilities, the board of trustees must prepare a plan to distribute the remaining assets to another nonprofit institution. If a state has not adopted some form of the Model Non-Profit Corporation Act, the courts are likely to follow the common law doctrine of *cy pres,* in which the assets of a dissolved college are transferred so that they will serve a purpose as close to the donor's original intent as the situation allows. For example, if a Methodist college closes, the courts will likely seek first another Methodist college to receive the assets. Since the court will seek to redirect the assets to similar purposes or agencies, a state postsecondary agency may, through the attorney general, play the role of *amicus curiae* in formulating a disposition plan in accord with the state's master plan for higher education.

Lessons for the Future

In many states, especially in the South and the West, state postsecondary agencies have played only a minor role in monitoring the financial health of private colleges and universities. This task has been left in the capable hands of the regional accrediting associations. And the colleges themselves are often able to draw on the financial resources of a sponsoring church body to bridge the gap when cash flow falters. A state agency might ask why its policy should change. If 141 private colleges closed in the 1970s without significant impact on higher education, why should the prediction that 200 more will close in the 1980s require any greater activity on the state's part? The reason is that the prediction may be too conservative. Of the private college closings reported for the period 1970 to 1979, only fifty-seven were four-year colleges; thirty-nine were specialized institutions (often seminaries or schools of divinity, where the state has little or no regulatory or funding role), and forty-five were two-year colleges (Fadil and Carter, 1980). College closings in the 1980s are much more likely to be concentrated among four-year institutions.

The psychological, competitive, and financial climate of the 1980s will differ markedly from that of the 1970s. It was possible in the 1970s for an administration to look at the year-by-year increases in college enrollment and to say that better management and marketing would maintain the college's share of a growing student population. In the 1980s there is no such light at the end of the tunnel. The desperate plea "If we can only hang on for another year or two, we will have turned the corner" is no longer plausible in a period of enrollment decline.

Even in the 1970s, when college enrollments hit all-time records, small private colleges had to pump ever greater resources into maintaining their enrollment levels. Bowen and Minter's (1978) data on increasing admissions costs at a sample of thirty-four small, less selective liberal arts colleges is instructive. In 1974–75 these colleges employed an average of one admissions staff person for each seventy-one students recruited. In 1977–78 the competition for students had increased so that the yield ratio had declined to sixty-two students for each admissions staff person employed. If the staff salary and support were calculated at $15,000 per year, it cost an average of $240 to recruit each student at each of those colleges.

In a time of declining enrollments, public colleges and universities will begin to use the same marketing techniques that private institutions have long used to maintain their enrollments. The competitive pressure on small private colleges in the 1980s and 1990s will be much more intense than that experienced in the 1970s. And this competition will not be limited to enrollment. Public college faculty members and their unions have already begun to question the allocation of state funds to private institutions. The Professional Staff Congress of the American Federation of Teachers, for example, charged in January 1979 that direct state institutional aid to private institutions in New York has come at the expense of state aid to public institutions (Professional Staff Congress, 1979). As enrollments decline in the Northeast and Midwest, such reactions are unlikely to be confined to the state of New York.

In addition to enrollment decline, religiously affiliated colleges will be affected by the inability or unwillingness of sponsoring church bodies to sustain their traditional level of support. Many religious orders have had their own enrollment declines in the past decade. With fewer incoming recruits, they can no longer maintain the usual supply of contributed services. And, as the average age of their members increases, religious superiors are beginning to give greater priority to financing retirement and hospitalization programs than to the support of their colleges. The unwillingness of a religious order to provide new loans or act as a guarantor of debt was a factor in at least three recent college closings.

Supreme Court decisions such as *Tilton* v. *Richardson,* 403 U.S. 672 (1971); *Hunt* v. *McNair,* 413 U.S. 734 (1973); and *Roemer* v. *Board of Public Works,* 426 U.S. 736 (1976), which allowed public monies to flow to church-related colleges, also weakened the ties between the colleges and their sponsoring bodies. One of the historic ironies of the *Tilton* decision was that one of the parties to that case, Annhurst College, borrowed $2 million for construction purposes the year after the decision was rendered. The college then closed in 1980, partly because of its inability to meet its debt service obligations.

Trustees' fear of legal and financial liability will also be a factor in future college closings. Higher education has become a highly regulated industry, where blatant failure to protect student interests or clear negligence in the management of federal financial aid, of endowment, or of pension funds can result in personal as well as institutional liability. As college closings become more common, the stigma and embarrassment attached to a closing are likely to be less acute, since the market rather than management can be blamed for the school's failure.

Finally, the funding climate for the 1980s will be far more harsh than that of the 1970s. It is unlikely that this decade will see massive new initiatives such as the Basic Educational Opportunity Grant Program or the College Housing Program of the 1950s and 1960s. The private market for long-term loans or bonds is already closed to all but the most credit-worthy corporations. Even when funds are available for capital renewal, recent rates of interest have been prohibitively high for nonprofit corporations. If there is retrenchment in the federal guaranteed student loan programs, independent colleges and universities will find it more difficult to pass on the effects of inflation in the form of higher tuition.

The declining financial flexibility of independent colleges and universities, especially those in small, less selective liberal arts institutions, presents public policy problems to state postsecondary agencies. Should the state provide financial support to prevent a mid-term closing and allow the college to teach out the academic year? What steps should it take to monitor the financial stability of

colleges that exhibit signs of distress? How will it provide for protection and maintenance of student records?

The interest of a state postsecondary agency in ensuring the
orderly closing of a college is not limited to the protection of students and staff. When a college closes in mid-term, when students
are defrauded or left stranded without the records required for
transfer, all of higher education suffers. The Windham College
closing, for example, was aired before a national audience on
ABC's nightly news. And when Grahm Junior College closed in
midyear, the Massachusetts attorney general promulgated new financial reporting requirements for the other junior colleges in the
state. State funding to ensure an orderly closing may be considerably less expensive than a midyear closing.

Reputation has a dollar value. The credit worthiness of
other colleges and universities is affected by the public perception
of stability and responsibility. The bankruptcy of one college raises
the cost of borrowing for others in the region. Even the flow of
public monies into higher education is to some extent dependent
on the legislature's confidence that tax dollars are being used in an
effective and responsible way. The investment that a state postsecondary agency makes in ensuring that a college can teach out
the year or in the maintenance of student records is not merely a
benefit to the individuals involved but to all of higher education.

For Further Reading

In 1980 the Conference of Small Private Colleges conducted
a study of private college closings, directed at administrators and
trustees. The complete report can be found in O'Neill and Barnett
(1981). See also West (1980). For a detailed case study of the decision to close Wilson College and of the subsequent involvement of
the courts, readers are referred to the Lilly Endowment Seminar
publication *Wilson College: A Case Study* (Beeman, 1979). In *Mergers
in Higher Education,* Millett (1976) discusses college closings in the
1960s and 1970s, outlining their general characteristics and noting
the precipitating events.

❧ 19 ❧

Choices Facing
Higher Education
in the 1980s

James R. Mingle

Retrenchment is—to risk understatement—an unsettling issue for higher education. It also resists generalization. Tolstoy said, in *Anna Karenina,* that "happy families are all alike; every unhappy family is unhappy in its own way." Financial cutbacks and enrollment declines have exposed differences in higher education that were masked by growth—differences between administrators and faculty, between systems and campuses, between public and private colleges, between state officials and institutional leaders. These differences are reflected in this volume, but so too are points of agreement. There is, for example, in the variety of recommendations offered, a commitment to a planned approach to contraction. Rejecting the idea that such contingency planning will undermine efforts to gain additional public support for growth, our authors have concluded that an ad hoc mode of operation in colleges which *reacts* to events will, in the long term, lessen the public support on which higher education depends. Administrators and faculty sometimes mistakenly perceive the impact of retrenchment facing colleges and universities as cataclysmic. Although the impact on individual employees may be great, the aggregate adjustments required of the higher education enterprise are small in comparison with the periodic adjustments that the private sector of the economy must make to changes in demand. Fortunately, there exist in higher education both substantial moral commitment to, and legal protection of, the rights of individuals. Careful planning can also reduce the number of individuals harmed by sudden and unexpected cutbacks or financial collapses of colleges. Furthermore, planned approaches to contraction have the best chance of preserving the quality and integrity of higher education, which constitutes the best possible protection of students during a period of retrenchment.

Our authors obviously believe in the benefits of planning, but they also recognize its limitations. They do not suggest, for example, that institutions or states adopt a pure manpower planning approach to retrenchment decisions. (In contrast, Australia, with no private institutions and with a federally dominated system of public colleges, has closed colleges in recent years, because of projections of declining demand for teachers.) In Chapter Fifteen Donald Smith notes that the University of Wisconsin System was confident that it could adjust to projected declines in enrollment, but he is skeptical about its ability to plan for and adjust to the wide fluctuations in state support brought about by changing economic and political conditions. Planned approaches to decision making require a level of consensus on basic educational goals and priorities, which is increasingly hard to find in some institutions. Planners also require that a wider frame of reference be applied to problem solving. They have tended to view events in terms of systems, and with that view has come increased centralization of decision making.

Retrenchment Needs a Constituency

Faculty and administrators accept the necessity for retrenchment with extraordinary difficulty. If the trauma of personnel layoffs can be avoided, an institution can at least maintain a semblance of "business as usual," even if there are significant declines in services to students. In the public sector, the decision to cut back is clouded by political considerations. Public college presidents may tolerate inefficiencies longer than presidents in private institutions will, in order to avoid the public furor caused by retrenchment and in the hope that additional public support can be obtained. It is difficult to argue for greater support from the legislature while cutting programs and staff. Since these savings usually revert to the state, there is little incentive for retrenchment. Understandably, faculty groups also have a hard time dealing with contraction: they are, after all, the targets of cutback—a fact obscured by discussions of "program discontinuance."

The position of faculty groups on the question of dismissal of tenured faculty is often in opposition to the views of administrators and of board members—and, increasingly, of the courts. At the root of the contrasting positions are different views of the rights associated with tenure. As John Gray notes in Chapter Ten, "tenure status is a legal entitlement to continuous employment terminable for cause or by reason of disability, mandatory retirement, or financial exigency." Historically, tenure has served two purposes: to protect academic freedom by providing legal entitlements to due process and, in the words of the AAUP's 1940 Statement of Principles on Academic Freedom and Tenure, to provide "a sufficient degree of economic security to make the profession attractive to men and women of ability" (American Association of University Professors, 1977c, p. 2). Today, many faculty view tenure as guaranteeing permanent job security on the basis of seniority rights.

With this interpretation of tenure in mind, faculty unions have opposed narrow definitions of the retrenchment unit. For example, a strong union contract would use the institution as a whole as the unit of retrenchment and would require that the last hired be the first fired, regardless of program considerations. In contrast, a strong management contract would define the retrenchment unit as narrowly as possible; it might still use seniority to determine the order of layoffs, but would apply that criterion to units of smaller size—subspecialties within academic departments, for instance. In the union-oriented contract, protection of the group as a whole is the objective; in the management-oriented contract, maximum flexibility to pinpoint cutbacks is sought. Faculty have worked for stringent definitions of the conditions under which tenured faculty can be dismissed. This is reflected in the American Association of University Professors' support of the "survival standard" for declarations of financial exigency, which requires that an institution must be on the verge of closing before tenure contracts can be broken. But, as the court in *Scheuer* v. *Creighton University* (260 N.W. 2d 595, 1977) noted, such a requirement flunks the test of common sense. If dismissal of tenured faculty must wait until the survival of an institution as a whole is threatened and the institution has exhausted all its assets—including capital assets—there is little chance for a university or college to take remedial action to avoid closure when its tenure rate is 70, 80, or even above 90 percent, as is the case in some institutions.

There is legitimacy nevertheless in the fears expressed so ably by Paul Strohm in Chapter Eight, that administrators have used the term *exigency* with far too much casualness. His remarks reflect the growing exclusion of faculty from important academic and budget decisions in colleges. (Some presidents would rightly observe that this is self-exclusion.) Strohm's discussion also highlights the deep and growing divisions between faculty and administrators. On the one hand, administrators view faculty as increasingly unable to take action, complacent with the security of their tenure, and generally uninformed about the reality of the hard times facing higher education. On the other hand, faculty view administrators as slaves to consumerism, pursuing students and new occupational programs wherever they lead. Many faculty believe that administrators' motives are purely financial, not philosophical. In times of uncertainty, managers seek flexibility. They want to respond rapidly to the changed circumstances—whether those be in the form of a new student market or a new political environment. They cut costs, avoid long-term commitments, and abandon marginally productive programs. As Strohm notes, such actions in colleges and universities have created an itinerant class of part-time and nontenured faculty without the requisite security to produce either quality teaching or quality research. And as the noose around the neck of tenure grows ever tighter, so does hostility among colleagues, with the old guard resting on its laurels and the new guard struggling to gain permanent positions. As the numbers of tenured faculty are reduced, so too is the power of faculty organizations.

The solution is neither to protect tenured faculty at all costs, as some faculty groups and unions would propose, nor to replace tenure totally with a system of short-term contracts, as many administrators and legislators might wish. Rather, institutions and systems must find ways to increase management's flexibility and create new full-time faculty positions without damaging quality. In the short run, a tightening of standards may cause some resentment among junior faculty denied tenure while less qualified senior faculty continue employment, but this is a necessary step toward correcting the mistakes of the past. Limited use of fixed-term contracts of some duration is another solution.

Increasing Voluntary Faculty Turnover. For a number of years, colleges and universities have been searching for a way to increase voluntary turnover among faculty. The inability of colleges to inject vitality through new hires is the one aspect of organizational decline with few effective solutions yet devised. One approach, first advanced by Richard Atkinson and then proposed by the National Research Council in 1979, calls for the National Science Foundation to establish a program of "Research Excellence Awards." Five-year nonrenewable awards would be made to support the salaries of senior faculty, thus allowing the employing university to use the freed funds to hire young scholars and teachers in the recipient's department (National Research Council, 1979). This program and similar ones have not generated much support, partly because of the opposition from the scientific community to the diversion of research funds for this purpose.

Early-retirement programs have been developed but few takers found. Outdated by inflation and changes in retirement laws, such programs have little or no chance of creating many new positions in higher education, especially in the next five to ten years, when relatively few faculty will be approaching retirement. Faculty retraining programs—at least those seeking to move faculty from one academic discipline to another—have not yet been successful in affecting many problems of maldistribution. Few departments are willing to accept a "retooled product" when a surplus of highly specialized candidates exists. Some programs aimed at retraining faculty for jobs outside higher education have been developed; but thus far the risks have been too great, and the financial incentives too meager, for faculty to pursue this option. Yet more than one of every four faculty members in American universities and colleges considered resignation during the two years preceding a 1977 national survey of the professoriate. Palmer and Patton (1981, p. 391) concluded from this fact that "there is indeed a substantial number of academics who might be willing to participate in some career-change program."

As John Gray notes in Chapter Ten, the courts—in the absence of explicit contract language—have increasingly allowed managerial freedom in defining *financial exigency,* thus permitting termination of tenured faculty. But institutions need more than the power of law on their side for the professoriate to view such actions as necessary and equitable. The traditions of tenure, the expense of possible litigation, and the general disruption caused to a college will remain powerful constraints on the action of administrators. One solution is to provide enough incentive for faculty to relinquish their tenure rights voluntarily. When budget cutbacks at Michigan State University in 1981 required faculty layoffs, the institution offered various financial incentives in exchange for voluntary resignations ("Michigan State U. Offers Options to Professors Who Are to Lose Their Jobs," 1981, p. 2). Institutions not yet in a state of exigency may wish to consider offering retraining fellowships to tenured faculty in return for resignation. The package of benefits attached to the fellowships would need to be generous enough to attract candidates and restrictive enough so that only those faculty viewed as surplus would be eligible. A year's leave with pay and a second year's severance pay—combined with professional employment services, tuition waivers, and internships in business and government—might be enough to attract faculty and make the program successful. Such fellowships could be restricted to tenured faculty in highly tenured departments with declining enrollment. The most likely candidate might be a social science or humanities faculty member in mid-career who is ambitious but frustrated in his or her own academic pursuits by a lack of mobility and scarce institutional resources. Institutions could view such "buyouts" of tenured faculty as investments that would bring returns in salary savings, which, in turn, could be used to provide tenure-track positions in new programs or qualitative improvements in existing programs. (If the savings were to be used for productivity improvements and retrenchment, public institutions would need some incentive for participation; for example, 50 percent of the cost of the program could be absorbed by the institution through productivity improvements, and 50 percent could be funded by the state.)

In addition to funding this type of faculty retraining program, institutions and state governments need to recognize the psychological and physiological trauma that can result from job loss. In his 1969 study of the closing of a manufacturing plant, Alfred Slote noted the great number of health-related problems associated with termination, especially among professional employees. Institutions should consider providing both counseling services and an extension of health care benefits during the period of unemployment. If state provisions prohibit the funding of such programs, the institutions should seek discretionary funds for this purpose.

Convincing Faculty of the Need for Retrenchment. Faced with apathy and often open hostility from faculty, college presidents must sometimes feel as Casey Stengel did: that the biggest job of a manager is to keep the guys who want you fired away from those who don't care what happens to you! It has become axiomatic in higher education that strong executive leadership is needed to cope with retrenchment, but many presidents have forgotten the necessary and valuable role that faculty can and must play. The central problem for administration in a cutback climate is one of finding support for retrenchment actions from among the faculty—not just acquiescence, but willing support. Across-the-board cuts may not engender great opposition, but they leave everyone in an institution with a sense of diminishment and violation. Retrenchment needs a faculty constituency. The majority of the faculty—or at least faculty leaders—must be convinced that retrenchment is a necessary way of meeting the immediate problem and provides some hope for the future. This can be done by (1) including administration in the cutbacks and (2) making retrenchment an instrument for overcoming decline. The most successful examples of institutional response to retrenchment will cut deeply enough to meet immediate shortfalls and to raise money to mount new programs or enhance existing ones. Enhancement usually means salary raises for existing faculty or funds for attracting prestigious scholars. Reductions in the scope of institutional offerings and the resulting savings in personnel costs would be used to provide adequate compensation to faculty in the remaining programs. In reality, retrenchment and reallocation are the only solutions available for many institutions, which must use increases in external support to pay rising costs for materials, equipment, and energy.

Without the involvement of faculty leaders in these decisions, however, and without widespread knowledge among all faculty of the circumstances facing the institution, retrenchment actions will be viewed as illegitimate and unnecessary. Faculty involvement is easier in small colleges with a less complex array of programs than that found in large institutions. But the experience of institutions such as the State University of New York at Albany, Vanderbilt University, and Southern Methodist University, described in this volume, demonstrates that even large universities with highly autonomous units can use faculty reassessment committees to establish institution-wide priorities.

But there are limits to faculty involvement. In April 1981 the American Association of University Professors published a draft statement entitled "On Institutional Mergers and Absorption." Its primary recommendation is that the faculty of both institutions involved in a merger "should be involved before decisions or commitments to affiliate have been made or before any decisions on curtailment of programs . . . become final" (American Association of University Professors, 1981a, p. 84). Unfortunately, such a policy would likely preclude the successful consummation of most mergers, especially those which occur under conditions of financial exigency for one of the two partners. As Gail Chambers notes in Chapter Six, the degree of distress an institution faces is often a carefully guarded secret, in order to avoid panic and because preliminary merger negotiations are best conducted in secrecy. Furthermore, only trustees, not faculty or administrators, are in a position to take a disinterested view of such a major change. Involvement of faculty in the merger negotiations could cause delays, which would greatly add to the costs of merger. In fact, involvement of faculty likely would greatly diminish the number of stronger institutions willing to undertake merger negotiations. The result would be fewer mergers and more closings.

Proposals for State Intervention

At the outset of this study, we asked contributors to consider what actions state government and statewide coordinating bodies should take in response to enrollment decline and financial stringency. In Chapter Two David Breneman speculates that the decade or more of retrenchment which lies ahead for higher education will "expose the limitations of the market as a mechanism for organization, control, and resource allocation." However, he does not believe that state governments will adopt a fully managed approach to contraction; rather, he predicts a reliance on a mixed strategy of market factors and state-level planning. Several of our authors make specific recommendations for changes in state policy—some aimed at enhancing the market mechanisms operating in higher education, others seeking to manage through intervention the nature and timing of contraction.

Enrollment Caps. One possibility being considered by state legislatures and governing boards in response to decline—the imposition of enrollment quotas on popular public institutions—will undoubtedly be a politically unpopular action in many states. A strong relationship persists between enrollment and funding levels in the public sector, and colleges continue to pursue enrollment growth, even when financial conditions prevent less than full funding of additional students. In spite of no funding for growth, colleges may continue to enroll additional students in the hope that they will be in a stronger position to argue for additional funds when state funding returns to a "normal" level. In their review of the use of enrollment and funding caps in four states, Frank Bowen and Lyman Glenny (Chapter Eleven) note the diverse motivations for such actions. The most common use of enrollment ceilings in a time of funding cutbacks will be to protect the quality of offerings by limiting access. (Public college presidents themselves may impose enrollment ceilings in response to legislative proposals to reduce budgets, as a way of marshaling public support for exemptions from the cuts.) In addition, states will consider enrollment ceilings on popular campuses as a method of redirecting students to institutions with excess capacity. If past experience is any indication, such efforts will meet with only limited success. While aiding second-choice campuses, enrollment ceilings on popular campuses are not likely to help campuses that are poorly situated or suffering from declining reputations. Students have too many options for states to be able to fine-tune the system that carefully.

Given the primary mission of public colleges to provide the widest possible access to higher education, the imposition of enrollment ceilings should be approached with caution. However, in many states and locales, the public sector has developed to such an extent that placing enrollment caps on popular public institutions will have little or no effect on the ability of students to find an appropriate program elsewhere. Public systems should consider enrollment ceilings if some combination of the following conditions exists:

1. Declines in state funding are seriously threatening the quality of academic offerings at large popular campuses.
2. Competition for the same students is creating demands for expansion at popular campuses, which can come only at the expense of the other institutions in the system.
3. There is little differentiation in admissions standards among the state's public institutions.
4. There is significant excess capacity in some public institutions in the system. If students denied access in public institutions are provided with financial support through tuition subsidies to attend private colleges, states should also consider the excess capacity in the private sector.

Campus administrators should also consider capping popular programs within their institutions, especially if resources cannot be shifted fast enough to meet growing demand. Enrollment caps enable colleges to curtail the dominance of occupational programs, which can distort and subsume the institution's general education goals. As a result of a tighter employment market for college graduates and increased competition, colleges are rushing to start new programs in business and other professional areas. These programs, with the support of their professional accrediting associations, press the institutions for greater and greater shares of the students' time, neglecting their general education needs.

State Budgeting Reform. The way in which the fifty states fund public higher education is in some flux. However, state funding remains and will continue to be an enrollment-driven system, Frank Bowen and Lyman Glenny believe, if only because such a rationale can easily be justified to legislatures. While many of our authors suggest a variety of adjustments to state funding and budgeting schemes, none have proposed complete abandonment of direct state appropriations to institutions, based in large part on instructional work load. But the changes that they *have* suggested could significantly affect both individual institutions and students.

States with rigid funding formulas that are closely related to student enrollment are faced with considerable problems whenever growth and decline occur simultaneously in the public sector. These formulas fail to recognize the reality of the fixed nature of many costs in higher education and the inability of colleges to adjust rapidly to enrollment decline. A more careful analysis of fixed and variable costs in higher education can have a number of benefits. Such an analysis can determine the resources required to maintain minimally acceptable levels of quality in different types of institutions. It can be used to establish funding floors—points at which, as David Spence and George Weathersby note in Chapter Thirteen, all costs are fixed and cannot be further reduced without affecting the quality of offerings. If operations approaching this minimal size are judged as too expensive to maintain, they can then be closed. A policy of establishing funding floors for institutions might avoid situations like the Athens College case, discussed in Chapter Sixteen, in which state funding was not adequate enough to maintain quality, but the legislature would not act to close the institution. Critics of marginal funding argue that such a policy protects weaker institutions, since the built-in quality subsidy implicit in average-cost funding is diverted from growing institutions to declining ones. Properly designed, though, such a system will allow time for cutbacks to be implemented and will protect students from precipitous reductions in services. Large popular institutions will find the incentives for enrollment growth disappearing and, it is hoped, will choose to limit enrollment rather than see quality deteriorate. The results will be similar to the effects of enrollment and funding caps: redistribution of enrollment from overutilized to underutilized facilities in both public and private colleges.

Funding formulas cannot deal, however, with the problem of establishing a set of funding priorities in a period of retrenchment. For this a state needs a process of determining program priorities. Such a function is the responsibility of a governor and the executive agencies. Most important among these, says James Furman (Chapter Fourteen), is the statewide coordinating or consolidated governing board, which, once the magnitude of the cuts has been established by the governor, must distribute these cuts among the various segments of higher education. The confidence of the governor and the legislature is obviously a prerequisite for such a task. Furman's advice is worth repeating: "As it develops its cutback strategies, the coordinating agency must establish and recognize priorities among the various sectors of higher education as well as among the objects of expenditure within the various colleges and universities. The coordinating board has the obligation to weigh the relative needs of private higher education, the student assistance program, and public higher education, with distinctions being made between types of institutions."

Higher education has little control over some budgeting and financing practices in the states. Both the tax structure and its economic base mean that state revenues are susceptible to radical and sometimes unpredictable fluctuations in the economy. State budgeting practices exacerbate the impact of these business-cycle changes as well. Expenditures of state government increase in good times—sometimes in no relationship to need—and are cut in bad times—often abruptly and beyond the ability of agencies to maintain continuity of service. Such conditions cause special difficulty for higher education, which is labor intensive and based on long-term contractual commitments. The solution, some have asserted, is to bring an end to the constitutional provisions of states for annually balanced budgets. Adams (1977, p. 88) recommends that such provisions "be replaced by a requirement that budgets be balanced over the period of the business cycle," thus allowing for a smoother and more stable funding of public services. The prospects for such changes in state law are extremely unlikely, though, and unwise, given the unpredictability of the economy and the tendency of legislatures to postpone cutback decisions. While state revenue projections—especially those based, for example, on volatile sales tax collections—will always contain an element of uncertainty, some states have deliberately used optimistic revenue projections as a way of avoiding political conflicts. More damaging, many have abandoned all requirements for cash reserves. James Furman believes that the impact of retrenchment can be significantly diminished if governors control substantial contingency funds and if reasonable cash reserves are carried from year to year.

Some public systems of higher education have done little to prepare for enrollment decline. Others, as evidenced by the case studies presented in this book, are far ahead of their own state governments in developing contingency planning. In these cases the higher education system can justifiably ask that state government put its own house in order and provide a more stable environment for contraction to take place.

Program and Institutional Review

As the case studies in this volume illustrate, the most effective responses to decline have included some form of systematic evaluation of an institution's academic programs, in order to reach decisions about reallocation of dollars or termination of programs. Despite a proliferation of review activity in the 1970s—by institutions, by state agencies, by legislatures, and by accrediting agencies—many institutions are still without a workable mechanism for establishing priorities, which can then be used as a guide in making cutbacks. The key to making program cutbacks is to use a review process that can determine both the quality of current programs (and their capacity for improvement) and the relative importance of those programs to institutional goals. As both Edward

Dougherty (Chapter Five) and Robert Barak (Chapter Twelve) note, such program review mechanisms must be in place and operating well in advance of a retrenchment crisis.

What is the appropriate role of statewide program review? The powers and practices of the coordinating agencies in the fifty states vary so greatly that the answer to this question must be shaped by the traditions and structure of each state. My own view is that, despite the dangers to institutional autonomy, in a period of retrenchment it is desirable to have a state higher education agency with the power to terminate academic programs in public institutions. State agencies should exercise this power sparingly, however, using program review as a mechanism for establishing clear divisions of labor among the state's institutions in light of a specific state master plan. That is, state agencies should concentrate their review on the most obvious examples of duplication, low productivity, and incongruence with preestablished mission statements; they should also use the powers of program termination to close down programs that are in violation of minimal standards. At the same time, since this type of state review is not likely to produce substantial cost savings, state agencies must encourage institutions to establish their own review procedures for use in reallocation and retrenchment. Institutions are clearly in a better position to make judgments about specific programs and personnel to be eliminated than are state agencies. If carefully defined divisions of labor have been established in the state between institutions, the program cuts made by institutions are likely to be viewed as appropriate by those at the state level. States can encourage institutions in this process by promising a reduction in state regulations and oversight. If institutions fail to evaluate programs and establish priorities, choosing instead to allow a general deterioration in the quality of institutional programs and services, they should not be surprised if state agencies and legislatures intervene and attempt, through budget bills, to make these decisions for them.

Evaluating the need for major changes in mission or for merging or closing an institution is more difficult for a public institution to accomplish and clearly requires some external intervention. For multicampus systems the process developed for the University of Wisconsin System and described by Donald Smith in Chapter Fifteen is a workable solution. Indicators of distress are used to signal the need for a task force, drawn from the system as a whole, to make judgments for the troubled campus. In states with coordinating boards, the problem is more complex and is likely to have greater political ramifications. If coordinating boards believe that major changes in institutional mission, including merger or closure, are called for, they are faced with three choices: (1) convincing institutional governing boards to take such action on their own initiative, (2) proposing to the legislature that it act directly through the budget bill, and (3) proposing to the legislature that new consolidated boards be created with mandates to carry out the changes. This last alternative may likely be viewed as a prerequisite for carrying out institutional and program consolidations.

State legislatures will find it difficult to independently evaluate the need for public college mergers or closures or to find the political consensus to take such action if necessary. They will need strong gubernatorial support and the judgments of independent boards and professional educators to make these decisions. The coordinating boards have been established in the states to provide such expertise and judgment. But, as the cases discussed in Chapter Sixteen illustrate, coordinating boards are sometimes unable to persuade institutional governing boards or the legislature to take such actions as merging or closing colleges. In the long term, the best policy is for states to strengthen the coordinating boards by upgrading the quality of both the gubernatorial board appointments and the professional staffs. In the short term, however, if the state wants to avoid statewide reorganization, special task forces could be created to consider major institutional reorganizations, mergers, or closures in the public sector. Coordinating boards and their staffs would serve as the monitoring agencies of the financial and academic health of public institutions. When preestablished trip wires similar to those used in Wisconsin are surpassed, the special task force would be appointed by the governor. It might consist of members of the coordinating board, distinguished citizens, and retired educational leaders respected in political circles. Staff assistance would be provided by the coordinating board with the help of outside consultants. Recommendations for action would then be made to the institution's own governing board and/or to the legislature.

The circumstances requiring public sector mergers or closures will often be unique. Although each state will evaluate the need for such actions according to its own criteria, the experiences described in this book suggest that the following situations should alert state boards to the possibility of merger or closure:

1. A period of significant enrollment decline (declines of 25 to 50 percent over a five-year period, for example).
2. Per student costs significantly above the average (for instance, 130 to 150 percent of the state average in comparable institutions).
3. Declining per student support, indicating a deterioration of quality in academic offerings, services, and physical plant.
4. Extremely small campus size (below 400 to 500 students in branch campuses or community colleges, or below 2,000 students in four-year campuses, for example).
5. The existence of duplicative public college programs in close geographical proximity.

Public Policy and Independent Colleges

State governments are increasingly recognizing the financial plight of independent colleges and universities. This is most apparent in the state grant and loan programs aimed at reducing, or at least not increasing, the tuition gap between public and private colleges. Another way of reducing the tuition gap is to increase public college tuition dramatically and at the same time increase the size and scope of student-carried financial aid programs. Such a system of financing would enhance the operation of market mechanisms and put decisions about institutional survival in the hands of consumers. As David Breneman observed in Chapter Two, one result of reliance on the imperfect market that now exists will be the closing of many small private colleges in the 1980s. It is unlikely, though, that state legislators will abandon the low-tuition concept, given the strong public support for such a policy. Despite financial cutbacks in some states, legislators continue to view support of public higher education as a political asset, and public confidence in the quality of most state institutions remains high. A prolonged period of declining state support, however, could change this perception, especially if traditional state budgeting practices result in a diminishment of quality (see McPherson, 1981). If quality indeed diminishes, the independent sector will be in a better competitive position, and there will also be stronger political support for a system of high public tuition and student-carried vouchers.

A substantial level of mistrust and political conflict exists between public and independent colleges in many states. Public college supporters believe strongly that a large and thriving public sector is necessary in order to achieve the goals of access and equal opportunity. Furthermore, they argue, private colleges want only the benefits of state support without the regulatory oversight. At the same time, independent college leaders and their supporters view the public sector as overextended and arrogant—protected from reductions in size and scope by the power of its lobbyists, unions, and the close political ties between trustees and legislators. Some of the independent college associations have become a potent political force in their own right, but they are constrained by self-imposed limits, to prevent loss of their independence in the process of salvation. Knowing that the degree of state oversight is directly related to the degree of state support, many independent college leaders have opposed direct state aid programs. Some of the strongest opponents of state "bailouts" of faltering private colleges can be found among private college presidents.

Independent of questions of financial support of private colleges, state policy must increasingly recognize the contributions made by the private colleges in achieving statewide goals. In practical terms, this means that when decisions are made about expansion of public institutions, their impact on private colleges should be assessed. Given the advocacy role and protective attitude that governing boards usually take toward their institutions, this may be easier to accomplish when there is a coordinating board structure. The procedures and criteria adopted in Tennessee and described by Grady Bogue in Chapter Seventeen should be carefully noted.

Tennessee's process of reviewing new program requests from public colleges does a good job of accounting for the availability of private college programs and considering contract options. At the same time, the state has established a conservative policy on requests for merger with the public sector. State policies should also be developed to protect students when private colleges close. Joseph O'Neill recommends, in Chapter Eighteen, that states develop procedures for maintaining student records and consider intervention to affect the timing of closings.

Should state higher education agencies review the qualitative aspects of academic programs in the private sector? Such reviews might threaten autonomy, but, in reality, the increasing price to be paid for state financial support sought by the private sector will be regulatory oversight. While most states will not initiate mandatory periodic reviews of well-established private college programs, there is likely to be increased regulation for the purpose of establishing minimal standards, especially when the forces of competition produce highly questionable educational practices. State officials have become increasingly skeptical, and sometimes cynical, about the self-accreditation process. The result has been a strengthening of the licensing requirements in many states, aimed primarily at new nontraditional institutions and those operating across state lines. Whatever the form of oversight, whether through licensing or periodic review, states should use executive branch agencies or independent boards to conduct their reviews, rather than public college governing boards, so that there is no question of conflict of interest. Although state regulation might put the most fraudulent operations out of business, a greater impact on the quality of private college offerings will come from a strengthening of the voluntary accreditation process. Both institutions and state officials should continue to work toward that goal.

*   *   *

"Retrenchment," to paraphrase a pundit, "is what happens to you while you are planning other things." The agenda described by the authors of this book seems a strange one indeed for an enterprise which so recently was awash in growth and optimism.

Higher education appropriately expanded in the 1960s to meet demands for what Martin Trow (1970) called its *popular functions;* namely, the transformation of what was formerly a *privilege* to a *right* for all. The acceptance of this obligation has meant a larger but more unstable enterprise, which by necessity will have to adjust its size downward as demand and resources shrink. It is a mistake, however, to exaggerate the gravity of the retrenchment problem in American higher education. There are serious problems, but at the same time there are solutions—which will mean continued vitality for the overwhelming majority of colleges and universities in the United States.

There also remains an agenda for growth: expansion of basic research, meeting new manpower needs, service to business and government, assistance to the public schools in overcoming their formidable problems, development of new educational delivery systems, and revitalization of liberal arts and international education in undergraduate colleges, to mention just a few. It is the time for choices, however. The agenda of the states and of the institutions in the next twenty years should begin with a sorting out of tasks, with each of the nation's diverse institutions choosing to do only what it can do best.

❧ References ❧

Academy for Educational Development. *A Strategic Approach to the Maintenance of Institutional Financial Stability and Flexibility in the Face of Enrollment Instability or Decline.* Columbus: Ohio Board of Regents, 1979.

Adams, W. "Financing Public Higher Education." *American Economic Review,* 1977, *67* (1), 86–89.

Alabama Commission on Higher Education. *Issues for the 1980's: A Plan for the System of Higher Education in Alabama, 1980–85.* Montgomery: Alabama Commission on Higher Education, 1980.

Alfred, R. L. (Ed.). *New Directions for Community Colleges: Coping with Reduced Resources,* no. 22. San Francisco: Jossey-Bass, 1978.

Allison, G. *The Essence of Decision: Explaining the Cuban Missile Crisis.* Boston: Little, Brown, 1971.

Allshouse, M. F. "The New Academic Slalom: Mission, Personnel Planning, Financial Exigency, Due Process." *Liberal Education,* 1975, *61* (3), 349–368.

Alm, K. F., Ehrle, E. B., and Webster, B. R. "Managing Faculty Reductions." *Journal of Higher Education,* 1977, *48* (2), 153–163.

Alm, K. F., Miko, M. B., and Smith, K. *Program Evaluation.* Washington, D.C.: Resource Center for Planned Changes, American Association of State Colleges and Universities, 1976.

American Association for Higher Education, Task Force on Faculty Representation and Academic Negotiations. *Faculty Participation in Academic Governance.* Washington, D.C.: American Association for Higher Education, 1967.

American Association of University Professors. *Statement on Financial Exigency.* Washington, D.C.: American Association of University Professors, 1976.

American Association of University Professors. "Academic Freedom and Tenure: City University of New York: Mass Dismissals

Under Financial Exigency." *AAUP Bulletin,* 1977a, *63,* 60–81.

American Association of University Professors. "Academic Freedom and Tenure: The State University of New York." *AAUP Bulletin,* 1977b, *63,* 237–260.

American Association of University Professors. *AAUP Policy Documents and Reports.* Washington, D.C.: American Association of University Professors, 1977c.

American Association of University Professors. "Draft Statement on Institutional Mergers and Absorption." *Academe,* 1981a, *67* (2), 83–85.

American Association of University Professors. "The Status of Part-Time Faculty." *Academe,* 1981b, *67* (1), 29–39.

Andrew, L. D., and Friedman, B. D. *A Study of the Causes for the Demise of Certain Small, Private, Liberal Arts Colleges in the United States.* Blacksburg: Virginia Polytechnic Institute and State University, 1976.

Arce, C. H. "Historical, Institutional, and Contextual Determinants of Black Enrollment in Predominantly White Colleges and Universities, 1946 to 1976." Unpublished doctoral dissertation, University of Michigan, 1976.

Arns, R. G., and Poland, W. "Changing the University Through Program Review." *Journal of Higher Education,* 1980, *51* (3), 268–284.

Ashworth, K. H. *American Higher Education in Decline.* College Station: Texas A & M University Press, 1979.

Association of American Colleges. *Statement on Financial Exigency and Staff Reduction.* Washington, D.C.: Association of American Colleges, 1971.

Astin, A. W. *Preventing Students from Dropping Out.* San Francisco: Jossey-Bass, 1975.

Bailey, S. K. "Human Resource Development in a World of Decremental Budgets." *Planning for Higher Education,* 1974, *3* (3), 1–5.

Bailey, S. K. "The Peculiar Mixture: Public Norms and Private Space." In W. C. Hobbs (Ed.), *Government Regulation of Higher Education.* Cambridge, Mass.: Ballinger, 1978.

Baker, L. "Kirkland and Hamilton: Does Father Know Best?" *Change,* 1978, *10* (5), 32–35.

Baldridge, J. V., and Tierney, M. L. *New Approaches to Management:*

Creating Practical Systems of Management Information and Management by Objectives. San Francisco: Jossey-Bass, 1979.

Barak, R. J. "Program Reviews by Statewide Higher Education Agencies." In J. K. Folger (Ed.), *New Directions for Institutional Research: Increasing the Public Accountability of Higher Education,* no. 16. San Francisco: Jossey-Bass, 1977.

Barak, R. J. "Study of Program Review." In B. Krauth (Ed.), *Postsecondary Education Program Review.* Boulder, Colo.: Western Interstate Commission for Higher Education, 1980.

Barak, R. J. "Academic Program Review and Approval" (working title). Paper prepared for the National Center for Higher Education Management Systems, Boulder, Colo., 1981.

Barak, R. J., and Berdahl, R. O. *State-Level Academic Program Review in Higher Education.* Denver: Education Commission of the States, 1978.

Beeman, A. L. *Wilson College: A Case Study.* Indianapolis: Lilly Endowment, 1979.

Behn, R. D. "Closing a Government Facility." *Public Administration Review,* 1978a, *38* (4), 332–337.

Behn, R. D. "How to Terminate a Public Policy: A Dozen Hints for the Would Be Terminator." *Policy Analysis,* Summer 1978b, *4,* 393–413.

Behn, R. D. "The End of the Growth Era in Higher Education." Statement presented to the Committee on Labor and Human Resources of the United States Senate, Raleigh, N.C., 1979.

Behn, R. D. "Can Public Policy Termination Be Increased by Making Government More Businesslike?" In C. H. Levine and I. Rubin (Eds.), *Fiscal Stress and Public Policy.* Beverly Hills, Calif.: Sage, 1980.

Bennis, W. G. "Who Sank the Yellow Submarine?" In G. L. Riley and J. V. Baldridge (Eds.), *Governing Academic Organizations: New Problems, New Perspectives.* Berkeley, Calif.: McCutchan, 1977.

Berdahl, R. O. *Statewide Coordination of Higher Education.* Washington, D.C.: American Council on Education, 1971.

Berdahl, R. O. "Criteria and Strategies for Program Discontinuance and Institutional Closure." Paper presented at annual conference of State Higher Education Executive Officers, New Orleans, July 30, 1975a.

Berdahl, R. O. (Ed.). *New Directions for Institutional Research: Evaluating Statewide Boards,* no. 5. San Francisco: Jossey-Bass, 1975b.

Berdahl, R. O. "Legislative Program Evaluation." In J. K. Folger (Ed.), *New Directions for Institutional Research: Increasing the Public Accountability of Higher Education,* no. 16. San Francisco: Jossey-Bass, 1977.

Bergquist, W. H., and Phillips, S. R. *A Handbook for Faculty Development.* Washington, D.C.: Council for the Advancement of Small Colleges, 1975.

Berman, P., and McLaughlin, M. W. *The Management of Decline: Problems, Opportunities, and Research Questions.* Rand Paper Series P-5984. Santa Monica, Calif.: Rand Corporation, 1977.

Bess, J. L. "New Life for Faculty and Their Institutions." *Journal of Higher Education,* 1975, *46* (1), 313–325.

Boberg, A. "Mergers in Higher Education: A Comparative Analysis with Business." Unpublished preliminary qualifying examination available from the Center for the Study of Higher Education, University of Michigan, July 1979.

Bogue, E. G. "State Policy and Private Higher Education in Tennessee." Case study prepared for the Southern Regional Education Board's symposium on Public Policy Strategies for Higher Education, Atlanta, Oct. 1980.

Bouchard, D. R. "Experience with Proposition 13 and Other Retrenchment Conditions." *Journal of the College and University Personnel Association,* 1980, *31* (1), 61–65.

Boulding, K. E. "The Management of Decline." *Change,* 1975, *7* (5), 8, 9, 64.

Boutwell, W. K. "Formula Budgeting on the Down Side." In G. Kaludis (Ed.), *New Directions for Higher Education: Strategies for Budgeting,* no. 2. San Francisco: Jossey-Bass, 1973.

Bowen, F. M. "Dollar, Dollar, Who Gets the Dollar? Making Decisions in a Time of Fiscal Stringency." In M. J. Lavin (Ed.), *On Target: Key Issues of Region, State, and Campus.* Boulder, Colo.: Western Interstate Commission for Higher Education, 1976a.

Bowen, F. M. "State Fiscal Stringency and Public Higher Education." *Research Reporter,* 1976b, *10* (1), 1–4.

Bowen, F. M., and Glenny, L. A. *State Budgeting for Higher Education: State Fiscal Stringency and Public Higher Education.* Berkeley:

Center for Research and Development in Higher Education, University of California, 1976.

Bowen, F. M., and Glenny, L. A. *Uncertainty in Public Higher Education: Responses to Stress at Ten California Colleges and Universities.* Sacramento: California Postsecondary Education Commission, 1980.

Bowen, H. R. *Investment in Learning: The Individual and Social Value of American Higher Education.* San Francisco: Jossey-Bass, 1977.

Bowen, H. R. *The Costs of Higher Education: How Much Do Colleges and Universities Spend per Student and How Much Should They Spend?* San Francisco: Jossey-Bass, 1981.

Bowen, H. R., and Douglass, G. K. "Cutting Instructional Costs." *Liberal Education,* 1971, *57* (2), 181–195.

Brazziel, W. F. "Planning for Enrollment Shifts in Colleges and Universities." *Research in Higher Education,* 1978, *9* (1), 1–13.

Brazziel, W. F., and Brazziel, M. "Recent College and University Enrollment Patterns of Black Students in States Affected by Adams-Califano Litigation." Paper prepared for the Southern Education Foundation, Atlanta, 1980.

Breneman, D. W. "Education." In J. A. Pechman (Ed.), *Setting National Priorities: The 1979 Budget.* Washington, D.C.: Brookings Institution, 1978.

Breneman, D. W. "Economic Trends: What Do They Imply for Higher Education?" *AAHE (American Association for Higher Education) Bulletin,* 1979, *32* (1), 3–5.

Breneman, D. W., and Finn, C. E., Jr. (Eds.). *Public Policy and Private Higher Education.* Washington, D.C.: Brookings Institution, 1978.

Breneman, D. W., and Nelson, S. C. "Education and Training." In J. A. Pechman (Ed.), *Setting National Priorities: Agenda for the 1980s.* Washington, D.C.: Brookings Institution, 1981.

Breneman, D. W., and Nelson, S. C. *Financing Community Colleges: An Economic Perspective.* Washington, D.C.: Brookings Institution, 1981.

Brown, D. G., and Hanger, W. S. "Pragmatics of Faculty Self-Development." *Educational Record,* 1975, *56* (3), 201–206.

Brown, R. S., Jr. "Financial Exigency." *AAUP Bulletin,* 1976, *62* (1), 5–16.

Brown, R. S., Jr., and Finkin, M. W. "The Usefulness of AAUP Policy Statements." *Educational Record,* 1978, *59* (1), 30–44.

Bugliarello, G., and Urrows, H. *Planning and Evaluating an Academic Merger, and Making It Work: Final Report to the Carnegie Corporation of New York.* New York: Polytechnic Institute of New York, 1976.

Bullard, G. S. *Dormitory Authority of the State of New York: A Municipal Research Report.* Albany, N.Y.: First Albany Corporation, 1979.

Burke, J. *Trying to Do Better with Less: The Experience of the SUNY College of Arts and Science at Plattsburgh, New York.* Atlanta: Southern Regional Education Board, 1980.

Cameron, J. M. "Ideology and Policy Termination: Reconstructing California's Mental Health System." In J. V. May and A. B. Wildavsky (Eds.), *The Policy Cycle in Politics and Public Policy.* Beverly Hills, Calif.: Sage, 1978.

Carnegie Commission on Higher Education. *Less Time, More Options: Education Beyond the High School.* New York: McGraw-Hill, 1971a.

Carnegie Commission on Higher Education. *New Students and New Places: Policies for the Future Growth and Development of American Higher Education.* New York: McGraw-Hill, 1971b.

Carnegie Commission on Higher Education. *The More Effective Use of Resources: An Imperative for Higher Education.* New York: McGraw-Hill, 1972.

Carnegie Commission on Higher Education. *Toward a Learning Society: Alternative Channels to Life, Work, and Service.* New York: McGraw-Hill, 1973.

Carnegie Council on Policy Studies in Higher Education. *Selective Admissions in Higher Education: Comment and Recommendations and Two Reports.* San Francisco: Jossey-Bass, 1977a.

Carnegie Council on Policy Studies in Higher Education. *The States and Private Higher Education: Problems and Policies in a New Era.* San Francisco: Jossey-Bass, 1977b.

Carnegie Council on Policy Studies in Higher Education. *Fair Practices in Higher Education: Rights and Responsibilities of Students and*

Their Colleges in a Period of Intensified Competition for Enrollments. San Francisco: Jossey-Bass, 1979.

Carnegie Council on Policy Studies in Higher Education. *Three Thousand Futures: The Next Twenty Years for Higher Education.* San Francisco: Jossey-Bass, 1980.

Carnegie Foundation for the Advancement of Teaching. *More Than Survival: Prospects for Higher Education in a Period of Uncertainty.* San Francisco: Jossey-Bass, 1975.

Carnegie Foundation for the Advancement of Teaching. *The States and Higher Education: A Proud Past and a Vital Future.* San Francisco: Jossey-Bass, 1976.

Carter, V. L., and Garigan, C. S. (Eds.). *A Marketing Approach to Student Recruitment.* Washington, D.C.: Council for Advancement and Support of Education, 1979.

Cartter, A. M. "A New Look at the Supply and Demand for College Teachers." *Educational Record,* 1965, *46* (2), 119–128.

Cartter, A. M. (Ed.). *New Directions for Institutional Research: Assuring Academic Progress Without Growth,* no. 6. San Francisco: Jossey-Bass, 1975.

Cartter, A. M. *Ph.D.'s and the Academic Labor Market.* New York: McGraw-Hill, 1976.

Centra, J. A. *Faculty Development Practices in U.S. Colleges and Universities.* Princeton, N.J.: Educational Testing Service, 1976.

Centra, J. A. *College Enrollment in the 1980s: Projections and Possibilities.* New York: College Entrance Examination Board, 1978a.

Centra, J. A. "Types of Faculty Development Programs." *Journal of Higher Education,* 1978b, *49* (2), 151–162.

Chambers, G. S. "Private College Mergers and State Policy: A Case Study of New York." Case study prepared for the Southern Regional Education Board's symposium on Public Policy Strategies for Higher Education, Atlanta, Oct. 1980.

Cheit, E. F. *The New Depression in Higher Education: A Study of Financial Conditions at 41 Colleges and Universities.* New York: McGraw-Hill, 1971.

Cherry, C. L. "Scalpels and Swords: The Surgery of Contingency Planning." *Educational Record,* 1978, *59* (4), 367–376.

Chronister, J. L., and others. *Independent College and University Participation in Statewide Planning for Postsecondary Education.* Washington, D.C.: National Institute of Independent Colleges and Universities, 1978.

Clark, B. R. *Academic Coordination*. New Haven, Conn.: Institution for Social and Policy Studies, Higher Education Research Group, Yale University, 1978.

Clark, M. J. "A Practical Guide to Graduate Program Review." *Findings,* 1979, *5,* 1–4.

Clark, M. J., Hartnett, R. T., and Baird, L. L. *Assessing Dimensions of Quality in Doctoral Education: A Technical Report of a National Study in Three Fields*. Princeton, N.J.: Educational Testing Service, 1976.

College Entrance Examination Board. *A Role for Marketing in College Admissions*. New York: College Entrance Examination Board, 1976.

College Entrance Examination Board. *Undergraduate Admissions: The Realities of Institutional Policies, Practices, and Procedures*. New York: College Entrance Examination Board, 1980.

Collier, D. *The Strategic Planning Concept*. Boulder, Colo.: National Center for Higher Education Management Systems, 1981.

Colorado Commission on Higher Education. *A Special Place*. Denver: Colorado Commission on Higher Education, 1979.

Colorado State Joint Budget Committee Staff. *Enrollment Caps*. Denver: Colorado State Legislature, 1980.

Colorado State Legislative Council Staff. Memorandum to Representative Tom Tancredo. Denver: Colorado State Legislative Council Staff, Jan. 16, 1980.

Colorado State University. *Survey of Applicants Not Admitted to CSU Due to Enrollment Limitations, Fall 1975*. Fort Collins, Colo.: Office of Admissions and Records, Colorado State University, Jan. 1976.

Connecticut Board of Higher Education. *Anticipating the 1980s: Report and Recommendations to the General Assembly on Higher Education in Connecticut*. Hartford: Connecticut Board of Higher Education, 1979.

Cooper, H. *State Service Contracts with Private Institutions*. Atlanta: Southern Regional Education Board, 1980.

"Coordinating Higher Education: A Changing Role for the States in the 1980's?" *Change,* 1980, *12* (7), entire issue.

Cope, R. G. *Strategic Policy Planning: A Guide for College and University Administrators.* Littleton, Colo.: Ireland Educational Corp., 1978.

Corson, J. J. *The Governance of Colleges and Universities: Modernizing Structure and Processes.* Carnegie Series in American Education. New York: McGraw-Hill, 1975.

Council for Interinstitutional Leadership. *Costing Collegiate Cooperation: A Report on the Costs and Benefits of Interinstitutional Programs with Consortium Case Studies and Guidelines.* University, Ala.: Council for Interinstitutional Leadership, 1979.

Council of Economic Advisers. *America's New Beginning: A Program for Economic Recovery.* Report to the President of the United States. Washington, D.C.: U.S. Government Printing Office, 1981.

Council of Graduate Schools in the United States. *The Assessment of Quality in Graduate Education: Summary of a Multidimensional Approach.* Washington, D.C.: Council of Graduate Schools in the United States, n.d.

Craven, E. C. "Information Decision Systems in Higher Education. A Conceptual Framework." *Journal of Higher Education,* 1975, *46* (2), 125–140.

Craven, E. C. (Ed.). *New Directions for Institutional Research: Academic Program Evaluation,* no. 27. San Francisco: Jossey-Bass, 1980.

Craven, E. C., and Becklin, K. M. "Student Access and the Quality of Instruction." *Educational Record,* 1978, *59* (1), 105–115.

Crossland, F. E. "Learning to Cope with a Downward Slope." *Change,* 1980, *12* (5), 18, 20–25.

Crosson, P. H. *Pennsylvania Postsecondary Education Policy Systems: Coping with Enrollment and Resource Declines.* Pittsburgh: Institute for Higher Education, University of Pittsburgh, 1981.

Cyert, R. M. "The Management of Universities of Constant or Decreasing Size." *Public Administration Review,* 1978, *38* (4), 344–349.

Davis, C. K., and Dougherty, E. A. "Program Discontinuance: Its Role in Strategies of Resource Allocation and Planning for Colleges and Universities." Unpublished manuscript, March 1978.

Deitch, K. "A Price War for Higher Education?" *Change,* 1981, *13* (3), 24–26.

Deleon, P. "A Theory of Policy Termination." In J. V. May and

A. B. Wildavsky (Eds.), *The Policy Cycle in Politics and Public Policy.* Beverly Hills, Calif.: Sage, 1978.

Dickmeyer, N., and Hughes, K. S. *Financial Self-Assessment: A Workbook for Colleges.* Washington, D.C.: National Association of College and University Business Officers, 1980.

Dill, D. D. "Tenure Quotas: Their Impact and an Alternative." *Liberal Education,* 1974, *60* (4), 467–477.

Doby, W. C. (Chairman, Task Group). *Application/Redirection/Enrollment Processes.* Berkeley: Office of the Academic Vice President, University of California, May 1980.

Dougherty, E. A. "What Is the Most Effective Way to Handle Program Discontinuance?" Paper presented at national conference of the American Association of Higher Education, Washington, D.C., April 1979.

Dresch, S. P. "Demography, Technology, and Higher Education: Toward a Formal Model of Educational Adaptation." *Journal of Political Economy,* 1975, *83,* 535–569.

Dressel, P. L. *Handbook of Academic Evaluation: Assessing Institutional Effectiveness, Student Progress, and Professional Performance for Decision Making in Higher Education.* San Francisco: Jossey-Bass, 1976.

Dressel, P. L. (Ed.). *New Directions for Institutional Research: The Autonomy of Public Colleges,* no. 26. San Francisco: Jossey-Bass, 1980.

Economic Report of the President. Washington, D.C.: U.S. Government Printing Office, 1981.

Education Commission of the States. *Final Report and Recommendations: Task Force on State Policy and Independent Higher Education.* Denver: Education Commission of the States, 1977.

Edwards, H. T., and Nordin, V. D. *Higher Education and the Law.* Cambridge, Mass.: Institute for Educational Management, Harvard University, 1979.

Edwards, H. T., and Nordin, V. D. *Higher Education and the Law: 1980 Cumulative Supplement.* Cambridge, Mass.: Institute for Educational Management, Harvard University, 1980.

Evaluation Studies Review Annual. Beverly Hills, California: Sage Publications, 1976–1980.

Fadil, V. A., and Carter, N. A. *Openings, Closings, Mergers and Accreditation Status of Independent Colleges and Universities: Winter*

1970 Through Summer 1979. Washington, D.C.: National Institute of Independent Colleges and Universities, 1980.

Fadil, V. A., and Thrift, J. S. *Openings, Closings, Mergers and Accreditation Status of Independent Colleges and Universities: Winter 1970 Through Summer 1978.* Washington, D.C.: National Institute of Independent Colleges and Universities, 1978.

Feasley, C. E. *Program Evaluation.* AAHE-ERIC/Higher Education Research Report, No. 2. Washington, D.C.: American Association for Higher Education, 1980.

Ferris, N. "Academic Mergers: A Precedent." Unpublished report by an ad hoc committee of the Tennessee Conference of the American Association of University Professors, n.d.

Fields, E. B. "Program Evaluation." In Southern Regional Education Board, *Proceedings of the 25th Legislative Work Conference.* Atlanta: Southern Regional Education Board, 1976.

Finkin, M. W. "Toward a Law of Academic Status." *Buffalo Law Review,* Winter 1973, *22,* 575–602.

Folger, J. K. (Ed.). *New Directions for Institutional Research: Increasing the Public Accountability of Higher Education,* no. 16. San Francisco: Jossey-Bass, 1977.

Ford, L. C. "The Battle over Mandatory Retirement." *Educational Record,* 1978, *59* (3), 204–228.

Frances, C. "Apocalyptic vs. Strategic Planning." *Change,* 1980a, *12* (5), 19, 39–44.

Frances, C. *College Enrollment Trends: Testing the Conventional Wisdom Against the Facts.* Washington, D.C.: American Council on Education, 1980b.

Frances, C., and Coldren, S. L. (Eds.). *New Directions for Higher Education: Assessing Financial Health,* no. 26. San Francisco: Jossey-Bass, 1979.

Freeman, R. B. *The Overeducated American.* New York: Academic Press, 1976.

Furniss, W. T. *Steady-State Staffing in Tenure-Granting Institutions, and Related Papers.* Washington, D.C.: American Council on Education, 1973.

Furniss, W. T. "Retrenchment, Layoff, and Termination." *Educational Record,* 1974a, *55* (3), 159–170.

Furniss, W. T. "Steady-State Staffing: Issues for 1974." *Educational Record*, 1974b, *55* (2), 87–95.

Furniss, W. T. "The 1976 AAUP Retrenchment Policy." *Educational Record*, 1977, *57* (3), 133–139.

Furniss, W. T. "The Status of 'AAUP Policy.'" *Educational Record*, 1978, *59* (1), 7–29.

Furniss, W. T. "New Opportunities for Faculty Members." *Educational Record*, 1981a, *62* (1), 8–15.

Furniss, W. T. *Reshaping Faculty Careers*. Washington, D.C.: American Council on Education, 1981b.

Gaff, J. G. *Toward Faculty Renewal: Advances in Faculty, Instructional, and Organizational Development*. San Francisco: Jossey-Bass, 1975.

Gaff, J. G. "Current Issues in Faculty Development." *Liberal Education*, 1977, *63* (4), 511–519.

Gamson, Z. E., and Arce, C. H. "Implications of the Social Context for Higher Education." In M. W. Peterson and others, *Black Students on White Campuses: The Impacts of Increased Black Enrollments*. Ann Arbor: Institute for Social Research, University of Michigan, 1978.

Gardner, D. E. "Five Evaluation Frameworks: Implications for Decision Making in Higher Education." *Journal of Higher Education*, 1977, *48* (5), 571–593.

Garvin, D. A. *The Economics of University Behavior*. New York: Academic Press, 1980.

Gentile, A. C. "A Model for Internal Review." *Council of Graduate Schools in the U.S. Newsletter*, Feb. 1980, *12* (6), 4–7.

Gillis, J. W. "Academic Staff Reductions in Response to Financial Exigency." *Liberal Education*, 1971, *57* (3), 364–377.

Gladieux, L. E. "What Has Congress Wrought?" *Change*, 1980, *12* (7), 25–31.

Glassberg, A. "Organizational Responses to Municipal Budget Decreases." *Public Administration Review*, 1978, *38* (4), 325–332.

Glenny, L. A. *Autonomy of Public Colleges: The Challenge of Coordination*. New York: McGraw-Hill, 1959.

Glenny, L. A. "Demography and Related Issues for Higher Education in the 1980s." Paper presented at the Center for the Study of Democratic Institutions, Santa Barbara, Calif., Nov. 1978.

Glenny, L. A. "Demographic and Related Issues for Higher Education in the 1980's." *Journal of Higher Education,* 1980, *51* (4), 363–380.

Glenny, L. A., and Bowen, F. M. *Signals for Change: Stress Indicators for Colleges and Universities.* Sacramento: California Postsecondary Education Commission, 1980.

Glenny, L. A., and others. *Coordinating Higher Education for the 70's.* Berkeley: Center for Research and Development in Higher Education, University of California, 1971.

Glenny, L. A., and others. *Presidents Confront Reality: From Edifice Complex to University Without Walls.* San Francisco: Jossey-Bass, 1976.

Godard, J. M. (Ed.). *Black and White Campuses in Urban Areas: Merger or Joint Planning?* Atlanta: Southern Regional Education Board, 1980a.

Godard, J. M. *Educational Factors Related to Federal Criteria for the Desegregation of Public Postsecondary Education.* Atlanta: Southern Regional Education Board, 1980b.

Gomberg, I. L., and Atelsek, F. J. *Trends in Financial Indicators of Colleges and Universities.* Washington, D.C.: American Council on Education, 1981.

Group for Human Development in Higher Education. *Faculty Development in a Time of Retrenchment.* New Rochelle, N.Y.: Change Magazine Press, 1974.

Habbe, D. "Future Faculty Employment Levels, Projected Problems and Possible Solutions: A Commentary." *Journal of the College and University Personnel Association,* 1980, *31* (1), 31–37.

Haines, J. R. *Merger Procedures for Colleges and Universities.* Albany, N.Y.: John R. Haines Associates, 1980.

Halstead, D. K. *Statewide Planning in Higher Education.* Washington, D.C.: U.S. Office of Education, 1974.

Halstead, D. K. *Higher Education Prices and Price Indexes, 1975 Supplement.* Washington, D.C.: U.S. Office of Education, 1975.

Halstead, D. K. *Higher Education Prices and Price Indexes, 1979 Supplement.* Washington, D.C.: U.S. Office of Education, 1979.

Hample, S. R. "Future Faculty Employment: Projected Problems and Possible Solutions: Conclusions and Summary." *Journal of the College and University Personnel Association,* 1980, *31* (1), 105–109.

Hample, S. R. (Ed.). *New Directions for Institutional Research: Coping with Faculty Reduction,* no. 30. San Francisco: Jossey-Bass, 1981.

Hansen, W. L. "Regressing into the Eighties: Annual Report on the Economic Status of the Profession, 1979–80." *Academe,* 1980, *66* (5), 260–274.

Harcleroad, F. F. "The Context of Academic Program Evaluation." In E. C. Craven (Ed.), *New Directions for Institutional Research: Academic Program Evaluation,* no. 27. San Francisco: Jossey-Bass, 1980.

Hartman, R. W. "Federal Options for Student Aid." In D. W. Breneman and C. E. Finn, Jr. (Eds.), *Public Policy and Private Higher Education.* Washington, D.C.: Brookings Institution, 1978.

Hays, G. D. "Perspectives from a Statewide System." *Journal of the College and University Personnel Association,* 1980, *31* (1), 14–21.

Heydinger, R. B. "Does Our Institution Need Program Review?" Paper presented at annual forum of the Association for Institutional Research, Houston, May 1978.

Hill, J. A., Lutterbie, P. H., and Stafford, J. "Systemwide Academic Program Review: The Florida Plan." Paper presented at national conference of the American Association for Higher Education, Washington, D.C., April 1979.

Hobbs, W. C. (Ed.). *Government Regulation of Higher Education.* Cambridge, Mass.: Ballinger, 1978.

Hodgkinson, H. L. *Institutions in Transition: A Profile of Change in Higher Education.* New York: McGraw-Hill, 1971.

Hollander, T. E. Memorandum to Chief Executive Officers of Postsecondary Educational Institutions in New York State. Albany, N.Y.: State Education Department, Feb. 4, 1977.

Holloway, J. P. "Termination of Faculty Due to Financial Exigency." *Journal of the College and University Personnel Association,* 1980, *31* (1), 84–93.

Hollowood, J. R. *College and University Strategic Planning: A Methodological Approach.* Cambridge, Mass.: Arthur D. Little, Dec. 1979.

Honey, J. C. "Will the Faculty Survive?" *Change,* 1972, *4* (5), 24–29.

Hook, S., Kurtz, P., and Todorovich, M. (Eds.). *The University and the State: What Role for Government in Higher Education?* Buffalo, N.Y.: Prometheus Books, 1978.

Hopkins, D. *Analysis of Faculty Appointment, Promotion, and Retirement Policies.* Stanford, Calif.: Academic Planning Office, Stanford University, 1973.

Howe, H., II. "What Future for the Private College?" *Change,* 1979, *11* (4), 28–31, 70.

Ihlanfeldt, W. *Achieving Optimal Enrollments and Tuition Revenues: A Guide to Modern Methods of Market Research, Student Recruitment, and Institutional Pricing.* San Francisco: Jossey-Bass, 1980.

Illinois Board of Higher Education. *Compensation in Illinois Institutions of Higher Education.* Springfield: Illinois Board of Higher Education, Nov. 1980.

Illinois Board of Higher Education. *Fiscal Year 1982 Higher Education Budget Recommendations.* Springfield: Illinois Board of Higher Education, Jan. 1981.

Jacobson, R. L. "Colleges Urged to 'Rethink' Patterns of Faculty Careers." *Chronicle of Higher Education,* 1980, *21* (9), 12.

Johnson, M. D., and Mortimer, K. P. *Faculty Bargaining and the Politics of Retrenchment in the Pennsylvania State Colleges, 1971–1976.* University Park: Center for the Study of Higher Education, Pennsylvania State University, 1977.

"Junior College Issue." *The Birmingham News,* Jan. 14, 1980, p. 8.

Kaplin, W. A. *The Law of Higher Education: Legal Implications of Administrative Decision Making.* San Francisco: Jossey-Bass, 1978.

Kaplin, W. A. *The Law of Higher Education 1980.* San Francisco: Jossey-Bass, 1980.

Karman, J., Mims, R. S., and Poulton, N. L. "Approaches to Ongoing Resource Reallocation and Planning." Paper presented at meeting of the Association for Institutional Research, Atlanta, May 23, 1980.

Kaufman, H. *The Limits of Organizational Change.* University, Ala.: University of Alabama Press, 1971.

Keough, W. F., Jr. "Enrollment Decline: The Dilemma from the Superintendent's Chair." In S. Abramowitz and S. Rosenfeld (Eds.), *Declining Enrollment: The Challenge of the Coming Decade.* Washington, D.C.: National Institute of Education, 1975.

Kerr, C., and others. *12 Systems of Higher Education: 6 Decisive Issues.* New York: International Council for Educational Development, 1978.

Kershaw, J. A. *The Very Small College: A Report to the Ford Foundation.* New York: Ford Foundation, 1976.

Kidner, F. L. *Memorandum.* Berkeley: Office of Vice President–Educational Relations, University of California, May 1971.

Kotler, P. *Marketing for Nonprofit Organizations.* Englewood Cliffs, N.J.: Prentice-Hall, 1975.

Kurland, J. E. "Reducing Faculty Positions: Considerations of Sound Academic Practice." *Liberal Education,* 1972, *58* (2), 304–309.

Ladd, E. C., Jr., and Lipset, S. M. "The Ladd-Lipset Survey: When Colleges Retrench, Where Should Cutbacks Come?" *Chronicle of Higher Education,* 1976, *12* (7), 7.

LaSalle, J. P. "Appointment, Promotion, and Tenure Under Steady-State Staffing." *Notices of the American Mathematical Society,* 1972, *19,* 69–73.

Lawless, R. W., Levi, M., and Wright, D. J. "Linking Academic Priorities to Resource Decisions." Paper presented at annual forum of the Association for Institutional Research, Houston, May 1978.

Leder, C. P. "Economically Necessitated Faculty Dismissals as a Limitation on Academic Freedom." *Denver Law Journal,* 1975, *52,* 911–937.

Lee, E. C., and Bowen, F. M. *Managing Multicampus Systems: Effective Administration in an Unsteady State.* San Francisco: Jossey-Bass, 1975.

Lee, J. *Case Studies of Institutional Decline.* Washington, D.C.: ABT Associates, 1981.

Leibenstein, H. "X-Efficiency vs. Allocative Efficiency." *American Economic Review,* 1966, *56,* 392–415.

Lenning, O. T., Beal, P. E., and Sauer, K. *Retention and Attrition: Evidence for Action and Research.* Boulder, Colo.: National Center for Higher Education Management Systems, 1980.

Leslie, D. W. (Ed.). *New Directions for Institutional Research: Employing Part-Time Faculty,* no. 18. San Francisco: Jossey-Bass, 1978.

Leslie, D. W., and Head, R. B. "Part-Time Faculty Rights." *Educational Record,* 1979, *60* (1), 46–67.

Levine, C. H. "Organizational Decline and Cutback Management." *Public Administration Review,* 1978, *38* (4), 316–325.

Levine, C. H., and Rubin, I. (Eds.). *Fiscal Stress and Public Policy.* Beverly Hills, Calif.: Sage, 1980.

Liaison Committee of the Regents of the University of California and the State Board of Education. *A Master Plan for Higher Education in California, 1960–1975.* Sacramento: California State Department of Education, 1960.

Lozier, G. G. "Negotiating Retrenchment Provisions." In G. W. Angell, E. P. Kelley, Jr., and associates, *Handbook of Faculty Bargaining: Asserting Administrative Leadership for Institutional Progress by Preparing for Bargaining, Negotiating and Administering Contracts, and Improving the Bargaining Process.* San Francisco: Jossey-Bass, 1977.

Lyman, R. W. "Federal Regulation and Institutional Autonomy: A University President's View." In P. Seabury (Ed.), *Bureaucrats and Brainpower: Government Regulation of Universities.* San Francisco: Institute for Contemporary Studies, 1979.

McConnell, T. R. *A General Pattern for American Public Higher Education.* New York: McGraw-Hill, 1962.

McCorkle, C. O., Jr. Letter to Assemblyman John Vasconcellos. Berkeley: Office of the Vice President of the University, University of California, Dec. 4, 1974.

McGuire, J. W. Memorandum to Vice President McCorkle. Berkeley: Office of the Vice President–Planning, University of California, March 13, 1974.

McPherson, M. "Quality and Competition in Public and Private Higher Education." *Change,* 1981, *13* (3), 18–23.

Magarrell, J. "Hidden Decay Seen Afflicting Private Colleges." *Chronicle of Higher Education,* 1980, *20* (22), 1, 4.

Maryland State Board for Higher Education. *Maryland Statewide Plan for Postsecondary Education.* Annapolis: Maryland State Board for Higher Education, July 1978.

Maryland State Board for Higher Education. *Maryland Statewide Plan for Postsecondary Education: Annual Review.* Annapolis: Maryland State Board for Higher Education, 1979.

Maryland State Board for Higher Education. "Terms of Grant to the Peabody Institute Approved." *Record,* 1980, *5* (11).

Mason, H. L. *College and University Government: A Handbook of Principle and Practice.* Tulane Studies in Political Science, Vol. 14. New Orleans: Tulane University Press, 1972.

Mayhew, L. B. *Surviving the Eighties: Strategies and Procedures for Solving Fiscal and Enrollment Problems.* San Francisco: Jossey-Bass, 1979.

Meeth, L. R. *Quality Education for Less Money: A Sourcebook for Improving Cost Effectiveness.* San Francisco: Jossey-Bass, 1974.

Meisinger, R. J., Jr. *State Budgeting for Higher Education: The Use of Formulas.* Berkeley: Center for Research and Development in Higher Education, University of California, 1976.

Meisinger, R. J., Jr. "Evaluating a Private College Request for State Affiliation: A Case Study of Sullins College in Virginia." Paper prepared for the Southern Regional Education Board's symposium on Public Policy Strategies for Higher Education, Atlanta, Oct. 1980.

Melchiori, G. S. "Patterns of Program Discontinuance: A Comparative Analysis of State Agency Procedures for Initiating and Implementing the Discontinuance of Academic Programs." Unpublished doctoral dissertation, University of Michigan, 1980.

"The Memorandum of Understanding." *Vanderbilt Gazette,* May 16, 1979, pp. 2–11.

Meyer, A. R. "Legal Aspects of Merger." In A. S. Knowles (Ed.), *Handbook of College and University Administration.* New York: McGraw-Hill, 1970.

Micek, S. S. (Ed.). *Integrating Academic Planning and Budgeting in a Rapidly Changing Environment: Process and Technical Issues.* Boulder, Colo.: National Center for Higher Education Management Systems, 1980.

Michael, D. N. *The Unprepared Society: Planning for a Precarious Future.* New York: Basic Books, 1968.

"Michigan State U. Offers Options to Professors Who Are to Lose Their Jobs." *Chronicle of Higher Education,* 1981, 22 (18), 2.

Millard, R. M. *State Boards of Higher Education.* ERIC/Higher Education Research Report No. 4. Washington, D.C.: American Association for Higher Education, 1976.

Millett, J. D. *The Academic Community: An Essay on Organization.* New York: McGraw-Hill, 1962.

Millett, J. D. "State Administration of Higher Education." In C. J. Wingfield (Ed.), *The American University: A Public Administration Perspective.* Dallas: Southern Methodist University Press, 1970.

Millett, J. D. *Politics and Higher Education.* University, Ala.: University of Alabama Press, 1974.

Millett, J. D. *Mergers in Higher Education: An Analysis of Ten Case Studies.* Washington, D.C.: American Council on Education, 1976.

Millett, J. D. *New Structures of Campus Power: Success and Failures of Emerging Forms of Institutional Governance.* San Francisco: Jossey-Bass, 1978.

Mims, R. S. "Program Review and Evaluation: Designing and Implementing the Review Process." Paper presented at the annual forum of the Association for Institutional Research, Houston, May 1978.

Mingle, J. R. "Influencing Academic Outcomes: The Power and Impact of Statewide Program Review." In *The Closing System of Academic Employment.* Atlanta: Southern Regional Education Board, 1978.

Mingle, J. R. "Consolidation and Reorganization of Public Higher Education: A Case Study of Alabama." Paper prepared for the Southern Regional Education Board's symposium on Public Policy Strategies for Higher Education, Atlanta, Oct. 1980.

Mingle, J. R., and Berdahl, R. O. *Consolidation and Reorganization in Public Higher Education: A Case Study of Connecticut.* Atlanta: Southern Regional Education Board, 1981.

Mingle, J. R., and Peterson, M. W. *Consolidation and Reorganization in Public Higher Education: A Case Study of Massachusetts.* Atlanta: Southern Regional Education Board, 1981.

Minnesota State Planning Agency. *Planning for Declining Enrollments: Planning Assistance Manual and Case Studies* (ED 128 918). St. Paul: Minnesota State Planning Agency, 1976.

Minter, W. J. "Current Economic Trends in American Higher Education." *Change,* 1979, *11* (1), 19–25.

Minter, W. J., and Bowen, H. R. *Independent Higher Education: Fourth Annual Report on Financial and Educational Trends in the Independent Sector of American Higher Education.* Washington, D.C.: National Institute of Independent Colleges and Universities, 1978.

Minter, W. J., and Bowen, H. R. *Independent Higher Education: Fifth Annual Report on Financial and Educational Trends in the Independent Sector of American Higher Education.* Washington, D.C.: National Institute of Independent Colleges and Universities, 1980.

Missouri Department of Higher Education. *Program Review, Policies, and Procedures.* Jefferson City: Missouri Department of Higher Education, Sept. 1978.

Mitnick, B. M. "Deregulation as a Process of Organizational Reduction." *Public Administration Review,* 1978, *38* (4), 350–357.

Mix, M. C. *Tenure and Termination in Financial Exigency.* Washington, D.C.: American Association for Higher Education, 1978.

Moore, M. A. "On Launching into Exigency Planning." *Journal of Higher Education,* 1978, *49* (6), 620–638.

Moos, M., and Rourke, F. E. *The Campus and the State.* Baltimore: Johns Hopkins University Press, 1959.

Mortimer, K. P., and Tierney, M. L. *The Three "R's" of the Eighties: Reduction, Reallocation, and Retrenchment.* AAHE-ERIC/Higher Education Report No. 4. Washington, D.C.: American Association for Higher Education, 1979.

Mosher, E. K., and Wagoner, J. L., Jr. (Eds.). *The Changing Politics of Education.* Berkeley, Calif.: McCutchan, 1978.

National Association of College and University Business Officers. "Higher Education Prices and Price Indexes: 1980 Update." *NACUBO Business Officer,* Oct. 1980.

National Center for Education Statistics. *Projections of Education Statistics to 1986–87.* Washington, D.C.: U.S. Government Printing Office, 1978.

National Center for Education Statistics. *Digest of Education Statistics, 1979.* Washington, D.C.: U.S. Government Printing Office, 1979.

National Center for Education Statistics. *Digest of Education Statistics, 1980.* Washington, D.C.: U.S. Government Printing Office, 1980a.

National Center for Education Statistics. *Financial Statistics of Institutions of Higher Education: Fiscal Year 1978.* Washington, D.C.: U.S. Office of Education, 1980b.

National Enquiry into Scholarly Communication. *Scholarly Communication.* Baltimore: Johns Hopkins University Press, 1979.

National Research Council. *Research Excellence Through the Year 2000: The Importance of Maintaining a Flow of New Faculty into Academic Research.* Washington, D.C.: National Academy of Sciences, 1979.

National Science Foundation and Department of Education. *Science and Engineering Education for the 1980's and Beyond.* Washington, D.C.: National Science Foundation, 1980.

Nelsen, W. C. (Ed.). "Faculty Development: Key Issues for Effectiveness." *Forum for Liberal Education,* 1979, *2* (1), 1–4.

Nelson, S. C. "Financial Trends and Issues." In D. W. Breneman and C. E. Finn, Jr. (Eds.), *Public Policy and Private Higher Education.* Washington, D.C.: Brookings Institution, 1978.

Nevison, C. H. "Effects of Tenure and Retirement Policies on the College Faculty: A Case Study Using Computer Simulation." *Journal of Higher Education,* 1980, *51* (2), 150–166.

Oklahoma State Board of Regents. *Policy Regarding Review of Requests for Changes in Educational Programs and Course Offerings.* (Rev. ed.) Oklahoma City: Oklahoma State Board of Regents, 1977.

Oliver, R. M. *An Equilibrium Model of Faculty Appointments, Promotions, and Quota Restrictions.* Research report No. 69-10. Berkeley: Office of the Vice President for Planning and Analysis, University of California, 1969.

"On Institutional Mergers and Absorption." *Academe,* 1981. *67* (2), 83–85.

O'Neill, J. P., and Barnett, S. *Colleges and Corporate Change: Merger, Bankruptcy, and Closure.* Princeton, N.J.: Conference-University Press, 1981.

O'Toole, J., Van Alstyne, W. W., and Chait, R. *Three Views: Tenure.* New Rochelle, N.Y.: Change Magazine Press, 1979.

Palmer, D. D., and Patton, C. V. "Mid-Career Change Options in Academe: Experience and Possibilities." *Journal of Higher Education,* 1981, *52* (4), 378–398.

Palola, E. G., Lehmann, T., and Blischke, W. R. *Higher Education by Design: The Sociology of Planning.* Berkeley: Center for Research and Development in Higher Education, University of California, 1970.

Patton, C. V., Kell, D., and Zelan, J. *A Survey of Institutional Practices and an Assessment of Possible Options Relating to Voluntary Mid- and Late-Career Changes and Early Retirement for University and College Faculty.* Cambridge, Mass.: ABT Publications, 1977.

Peat, Marwick, Mitchell & Co. *Ratio Analysis in Higher Education: A Guide to Assessing the Institution's Financial Condition.* (2 vols.) New York: Peat, Marwick, Mitchell & Co., 1980.

Pechman, J. A. (Ed.). *Setting National Priorities: The 1982 Budget.* Washington, D.C.: Brookings Institution, 1981.

Pennsylvania State College and University System. "Guidelines for Use in Planning Retrenchment in the State Colleges and University of Pennsylvania." Unpublished paper. April 16, 1975.

Peters, M. H. "Mergers of Institutions of Higher Education." *College and University,* 1977, *52* (2), 202–210.

Peterson, J. L. "The Dismissal of Tenured Faculty for Reasons of Financial Exigency." *Indiana Law Journal,* 1976, *51* (2), 417–432.

Peterson, M. W. *The State Level Performance Assessment Process: Concepts, Perspectives and Issues.* Ann Arbor: Center for Higher Education, University of Michigan, 1977.

Peterson, M. W. "Faculty and Academic Responsiveness in a Period of Decline: An Organizational Perspective." *Journal of the College and University Personnel Association,* 1980, *31* (1), 95–104.

Peterson, M. W., and others. *Black Students on White Campuses: The Impacts of Increased Black Enrollments.* Ann Arbor: Institute for Social Research, University of Michigan, 1978.

Pondrom, C. "Faculty Retrenchment: Problems and Possible Solutions. The Experience of the University of Wisconsin System." *Journal of the College and University Personnel Association,* 1980, *31* (1), 47–55.

Pondrom, C. "Faculty Retrenchment: The Experience of the University of Wisconsin System." In S. Hample (Ed.), *New Directions for Institutional Research: Coping with Faculty Reduction,* no. 30. San Francisco: Jossey-Bass, 1981.

Poulton, N. L. "Comparing Perceived Outcomes of Different Planning Processes." Paper presented at annual forum of the Association for Institutional Research, Houston, May 1978.

"Private-College Openings, Closings, and Mergers, 1970–79." *Chronicle of Higher Education,* 1980, *20* (18), 7–8.

Professional Staff Congress. *The State Investment in Private Higher Education in New York: A Report.* New York: Professional Staff Congress, Jan. 1979.

Purves, R. A., and Glenny, L. A. *State Budgeting for Higher Education: Information Systems and Technical Analyses.* Berkeley: Center for Research and Development in Higher Education, University of California, 1976.

Radner, R., and Kuh, C. V. *Preserving a Lost Generation: Policies to Assure a Steady Flow of Young Scholars Until the Year 2000.* Berkeley, Calif.: Carnegie Council on Policy Studies in Higher Education, 1978.

Rideout, E. B., and others. *Educational, Social, and Financial Implications to School Boards of Declining Enrollments.* Toronto: Ontario Department of Education, 1977.

Riesman, D. *On Higher Education: The Academic Enterprise in an Era of Rising Student Consumerism.* San Francisco: Jossey-Bass, 1980.

Rivlin, A. M. Statement before Subcommittee on Postsecondary Education, Committee on Education and Labor, U.S. House of Representatives, Feb. 24, 1981.

Rood, H. J. "Legal Issues in Faculty Termination: An Analysis Based on Recent Court Cases." *Journal of Higher Education,* 1977, *48* (2), 123–152.

Rubin, I. "Universities in Stress: Decision Making Under Conditions of Reduced Resources." *Social Science Quarterly,* 1977, *58* (2), 242–254.

Ruyle, J., and Glenny, L. A. *State Appropriations for Higher Education.* Berkeley: Center for Research and Development in Higher Education, University of California, 1980.

Ryland, J. N. *Indicators of Institutional Financial and Academic Viability: State Studies.* Boulder, Colo.: SHEEO/NCES (State Higher Education Executive Officers sponsored by the National Center for Education Statistics) Communication Network, Feb. 1981.

Schurr, G. M. "Freeing the 'Stuck' and Aiding the Terminated: Expanding the Career Horizons of Tenured College Professors." Unpublished report to the Ford Foundation, Jan. 22, 1980.

Scott, J. E., and Taylor, R. H. "A Model for Investigating the Effects of Growth Limitations and Alternative Appointment, Promotion, and Retirement Policies on Faculty Flows and Distributions." Paper presented at fifth national conference of the American Institute for Decision Sciences, Boston, Nov. 1973.

Scriven, M. "The Methodology of Evaluation." In R. W. Tyler, R. M. Gagné, and M. Scriven, *Perspectives of Curriculum Evaluation.* Chicago: Rand McNally, 1967.

Scriven, M. "Pros and Cons About Goal Free Evaluation." *Evaluation Comment,* Dec. 1972, *3,* 1–4.

Seldin, P. "Fostering Faculty Talent." *Change,* 1976, *8* (8), 10–13.

Shirley, R. C., and Volkwein, J. F. "Establishing Academic Program Priorities." *Journal of Higher Education,* 1978, *49* (5), 472–488.

Shulman, C. H. *University Admissions: Dilemmas and Potential.* ERIC/Higher Education Research Report No. 5. Washington, D.C.: American Association for Higher Education, 1977.

Simon, H. A., Smithburg, D. W., and Thompson, V. A. *Public Administration.* New York: Knopf, 1950.

Simpson, W. A. "Tenure: A Perspective View of Past, Present, and Future." *Educational Record,* 1975, *56* (1), 48–54.

Sloan Commission on Government and Higher Education. *A Program for Renewed Partnership.* Cambridge, Mass.: Ballinger, 1980.

Slote, A. *Termination: The Closing at Baker Plant.* Indianapolis: Bobbs-Merrill, 1969.

Small, M. "Impact of Retrenchment in Idaho." Paper presented at annual conference of the State Higher Education Executive Officers, Jackson Hole, Wyo., 1978.

Smartt, S. H. *Fact Book on Higher Education in the South: 1979 and 1980.* Atlanta: Southern Regional Education Board, 1980.

Smith, D. K. "Coping, Improvising, and Planning for the Future During Fiscal Decline: A Case Study for the University of Wisconsin." In M. Kaplan (Ed.), *The Monday Morning Imagination: Report from the Boyer Workshop on State University Systems.* Aspen, Colo.: Aspen Institute for Humanistic Studies, 1977.

Smith, D. K. "Faculty Vitality and the Management of University Personnel Policies." In W. C. Kirschling (Ed.), *New Directions for Institutional Research: Evaluating Faculty Performance and Vitality,* no. 20. San Francisco: Jossey-Bass, 1978.

Smith, D. K. "Multi-Campus System Approaches to Academic Program Evaluation." In E. C. Craven (Ed.), *New Directions for Institutional Research: Academic Program Evaluation,* no. 27. San Francisco: Jossey-Bass, 1980a.

Smith, D. K. "Preparing for a Decade of Enrollment Decline." Paper prepared for the Southern Regional Education Board's Legislative Work Conference, Hilton Head, S.C., July 1980b.

Southern Regional Education Board. *Priorities for Postsecondary Education in the South: A Position Statement.* Atlanta: Southern Regional Education Board, 1976.

Southern Regional Education Board. *Budgeting of Postsecondary Education in the Eighties.* Financing Higher Education, No. 28. Atlanta: Southern Regional Education Board, 1978.

Southern Regional Education Board. *Proceedings: 1980 Annual Meeting, Southern Regional Education Board.* Atlanta: Southern Regional Education Board, 1980.

Spitzberg, I. J. "Professors and State Policy." *Academe,* 1980, *66* (8), 425–426.

Stadtman, V. A. *Academic Adaptations: Higher Education Prepares for the 1980s and 1990s.* San Francisco: Jossey-Bass, 1980.

Stampen, J. *The Financing of Public Higher Education: Low Tuition, Student Aid, and the Federal Government.* AAHE-ERIC/Higher Education Research Report No. 9. Washington, D.C.: American Association for Higher Education, 1980.

Stauffer, T. M. (Ed.). *Competition and Cooperation in American Higher Education.* Washington, D.C.: American Council on Education, 1981.

Steiner, P. O. *Mergers: Motives, Effects, Policies.* Ann Arbor: University of Michigan Press, 1975.

Stevenson, M., and Walleri, R. D. "Budget Unit Analysis in an Era of Retrenchment: The Interface Between Financial Planning and Program Evaluation." Paper presented at annual forum of the Association for Institutional Research, Atlanta, April 27–May 1, 1980.

Stoltz, R. *Emerging Patterns for Teacher Education and Certification in the South.* Atlanta: Southern Regional Education Board, 1981.

Stufflebeam, D. L., and others. *Educational Evaluation and Decision Making.* Itasca, Ill.: Peacock, 1971.

Suchar, E. W. *Financial Aid Guide for College.* New York: Monarch Press, 1978.

Tennessee Higher Education Commission. *Higher Education in Tennessee: A Statewide Master Plan.* (2 vols.) Nashville: Tennessee Higher Education Commission, 1979.

Terenzini, P. T., and Pascarella, E. T. "Toward the Validation of Tinto's Model of College Student Attrition: A Review of Recent Studies." *Research in Higher Education,* 1980, *12* (3), 271–282.

Thomas, G. (Ed.). *Black Students in Higher Education: Conditions and Experiences in the 1970's.* Westport, Conn.: Greenwood Press, 1981.

Tinto, V. "Dropout from Higher Education: A Theoretical Synthesis of Recent Research." *Review of Educational Research,* 1975, *45* (1), 89–125.

Toombs, W. "A Three-Dimensional View of Faculty Development." *Journal of Higher Education,* 1975, *46* (6), 701–717.

Trow, M. "Reflections on the Transition from Mass to Universal Higher Education." *Daedalus,* 1970, *99,* 1–42.

Tyler, R. W., Gagné, R. M., and Scriven, M. *Perspectives of Curriculum Evaluation.* Chicago: Rand McNally, 1967.

U.S. Bureau of the Census. "Projections of the Population of the United States: 1977 to 2050." *Current Population Reports.* Series P-25, No. 704. Washington, D.C.: U.S. Government Printing Office, 1977.

U.S. Bureau of the Census. "School Enrollment—Social and Economic Characteristics of Students: October 1978." *Current Population Reports.* Series P-20, No. 346. Washington, D.C.: U.S. Government Printing Office, 1979.

U.S. Congressional Budget Office. *Reducing the Federal Budget: Strategies and Examples, Fiscal Years 1982–1986.* Washington, D.C.: U.S. Government Printing Office, 1981.

U.S. Department of Education. *The Condition of Education: 1980.* Washington, D.C.: U.S. Government Printing Office, 1980.

U.S. Department of Health, Education and Welfare. *Toward a Social Report.* Washington, D.C.: U.S. Government Printing Office, 1969.

U.S. Office of Management and Budget. *Budget of the United States Government, Fiscal Year 1982.* Washington, D.C.: U.S. Government Printing Office, 1981.

University of California Academic Senate. *Record of the Assembly.* Berkeley: University of California Academic Senate, May 29, 1964.

University of California, Berkeley. *Redirection Review.* Berkeley: Office of Admissions and Records, University of California, Sept. 1979.

University of California. *The University of California: A Multi-Campus System in the 1980s.* Berkeley: University of California, Sept. 1979.

University of Cincinnati and AAUP, University of Cincinnati Chapter. *Agreement, September 1, 1979 to August 31, 1981.* Cincinnati: AAUP, University of Cincinnati Chapter, 1979.

University of Connecticut Board of Trustees. Unpublished statement adopted Nov. 9, 1979.

University of Wisconsin System. *President's Report in Response to the Governor's Request on Reducing the Scope of the UWS* (SCOPE Report). Madison: University of Wisconsin System, April 1975.

University of Wisconsin System. *Student Access and Instructional Quality in a Time of Fiscal Constraint.* Madison: University of Wisconsin System, May 1977.

University of Wisconsin System. *Preparing for a Decade of Enrollment Decline.* Report from the Board of Regents. Madison: University of Wisconsin System, Nov. 30, 1979.

University System of Georgia. "Report of the Committee to Define Retrenchment Policies." Unpublished paper. 1980.

Vanderbilt University. "General Procedures for the Reassessment of Vanderbilt University, 1978–79." Unpublished report, n.d.

Vogel, E. F. *Japan as Number One: Lessons for America.* Cambridge, Mass.: Harvard University Press, 1979.

Volpe, E. L. "Retrenchment: The Case at CUNY." In R. W. Heyns (Ed.), *Leadership for Higher Education: The Campus View.* Washington, D.C.: American Council on Education, 1977.

Weaver, W. T. "In Search of Quality: The Need for Talent in Teaching." *Phi Delta Kappan,* 1979, *61* (1), 29–32, 46.

West, R. R. "Tenure Quotas and Financial Flexibility in Colleges and Universities." *Educational Record,* 1974, *55* (2), 96–100.

West, T. W. "The Right Way to Close." *AGB* (Association of Governing Boards of Universities and Colleges) *Reports,* 1980, *22* (5), 36–40.

Western Interstate Commission for Higher Education. *High School Graduates: Projections for the Fifty States.* Boulder, Colo.: Western Interstate Commission for Higher Education, 1979.

Wilson, L. *American Academics: Then and Now.* New York: Oxford University Press, 1979.

Wing, P. "Monitoring the Financial Status of Nonpublic Institutions in New York State." In C. Frances and S. L. Coldren (Eds.), *New Directions for Higher Education: Assessing Financial Health,* no. 26. San Francisco: Jossey-Bass, 1979.

Wood, H. H. "Death of a College." *AGB* (Association of Governing Boards of Universities and Colleges) *Reports,* 1975, *17* (5), 2–6.

❧ Index ❧

381

DATE DUE